Home-School Connectior Multicultural Society

Educators everywhere confront critical issues related to families, schooling, and teaching in diverse settings. Directly addressing this reality, *Home-School Connections in a Multicultural Society* shows pre-service and practicing teachers how to recognize and build on the rich resources for enhancing school learning that exist within culturally and linguistically diverse families.

Combining engaging cases and relevant key concepts with thought-provoking pedagogical features, this valuable resource for educators at all levels:

- Provides detailed portraits of diverse families that highlight their unique cultural practices related to schooling and the challenges that their children face in school settings
- Introduces key sociocultural and ethnographic concepts, in ways that are both accessible and challenging, and applies these concepts as lenses through which to examine the portraits
- Shows how teachers and researchers have worked with diverse families to build positive relationships and develop learning activities that incorporate children's unique experiences and resources
- Engages readers in grappling deeply and personally with the chapters' meanings and implications, and in envisioning their own practical ways to learn from and with families and children

Disrupting deficit assumptions about the experiences and knowledge that culturally and linguistically diverse children acquire in their homes and communities, this book will help educators to extend their notions of learning resources, to rethink the conventional practices used to evaluate and foster students' "readiness" for school learning, and to reconsider the types of knowledge and dispositions that teachers in a multicultural society need in order to foster student engagement and home-school connections.

Maria Luiza Dantas is Educational Consultant and Visiting Scholar at the University of California, Santa Barbara.

Patrick C. Manyak is Associate Professor of Literacy Education, Department of Elementary and Early Childhood Education, University of Wyoming.

Language, Culture, and Teaching
Sonia Nieto, Series Editor

Visit www.routledge.com/education for additional information on titles in the Language, Culture, and Teaching series.

Home-School Connections in a Multicultural Society

Learning from and with Culturally and Linguistically Diverse Families

Edited by

Maria Luiza Dantas

Educational Consultant and Visiting Scholar at the University of California, Santa Barbara

Patrick C. Manyak

University of Wyoming

NEW YORK AND LONDON

First published 2010
by Routledge
270 Madison Avenue, New York, NY 10016

Simultaneously published in the UK
by Routledge
2 Park Square, Milton Park, Abingdon, Oxon OX14 4RN

Routledge is an imprint of the Taylor & Francis Group, an informa business

© 2010 Taylor & Francis

Typeset in Minion by
RefineCatch Limited, Bungay, Suffolk
Printed and bound in the United States of America on acid-free paper by
Edwards Brothers, Inc.

Library of Congress Cataloging-in-Publication Data
Home-school connections in a multicultural society : learning from and with
culturally and linguistically diverse families / edited by Maria Luiza Dantas,
Patrick Manyak.
p. cm.—(Language, culture, and teaching)
Includes bibliographical references and index.
1. Home schooling—Social aspects—United States.   2. Multicultural
education—United States.   3. Bilingual education—United States.   I. Dantas,
Maria Luiza.   II. Manyak, Patrick.
LC40.H6384 2010
371.19′20973—dc22

2009018390

ISBN 10: 0–415–99756–9 (hbk)
ISBN 10: 0–415–99757–7 (pbk)
ISBN 10: 0–203–86843–9 (ebk)

ISBN 13: 978–0–415–99756–0 (hbk)
ISBN 13: 978–0–415–99757–7 (pbk)
ISBN 13: 978–0–203–86843–0 (ebk)

Dedicated to our families and the many families who continually teach us about diversity, resilience and ways of knowing and acting as change agents. Patrick also dedicates this book to the Latina/o families that embraced and fed him and enriched his life immeasurably during his years as a bilingual teacher in Pasadena, California, in particular, the Mora family, Maria Quiroz, and the Colorado family.

Contents

PART III
Conclusion 263

Foreword

Sonia Nieto

The Language, Culture, and Teaching Series reframes the conventional idea of the textbook by envisioning classroom practice in multicultural settings as critical, creative, and liberatory. The series also challenges traditional and limiting biases about diversity and about students of diverse languages and cultures. As such, *Home-School Connections in a Multicultural Society* is a perfect fit for the series as well as a valuable contribution to the field of family engagement.

When I became a teacher many years ago, I received no guidance about how to connect with the families of my students: I didn't have a clue about how to conduct a parent–teacher conference, nor did I know any strategies for welcoming parents into the school and classroom. Neither in my teacher preparation program nor in the inservice workshops that I attended as a new teacher had I been prepared to think creatively about how to tap into the cultural and linguistic resources of my students and their families. My own Puerto Rican background and upbringing, of course, gave me insights into working with this community, and the fact that I was raised in neighborhoods that were primarily Puerto Rican and African American also helped. But rather than being encouraged to promote parent engagement, at my first school, a junior high school in Brooklyn, I was warned not to pay home visits because it was too dangerous, and I was also discouraged in other subtle ways from interacting too closely with families. A basic distrust of the Latino and Black families whose children we taught permeated the teacher's room.

Years later, as a doctoral student, the major focus of my research interest was parent involvement and I found that very little had changed. My dissertation centered on parent involvement in curriculum development, but in the schools I studied, there was little more than lip service given to parent involvement, especially when the parents in question were immigrants or lived in poverty. Several years later, as a teacher educator and researcher, I conducted a study to determine if and how parent involvement was promoted within teacher education programs that received federal monies from Chapter 7, the Bilingual Education Law (where parent involvement was mandated). I found that although 100 percent of the programs that completed the survey agreed that parent involvement was important and necessary, only 8 percent of them actually provided courses—or even workshops of any kind—on this topic (Nieto, 1985).

I wish I could say that the situation has changed, that nowadays teachers are well prepared and eager to work with families. Unfortunately, my experience tells me this is not the case. In my travels to schools and colleges around the country, I have found that few teacher preparation programs and even fewer textbooks adequately prepare teachers for one of the most significant relationships they need to develop and sustain, that is, their relationships with families. As a consequence, I have met many teachers—most of them well-intentioned and caring—who are wary of parent involvement in schools because they have little experience with, or information on, how to engage with families, especially when those families are different from them in experience, social class, race, ethnicity, and in other ways. How, then, can teachers learn these things?

Fortunately, *Home-School Connections in a Multicultural Society* fills that gap beautifully. In this text, editors Maria Luiza Dantas and Patrick Manyak have gathered an impressive group of researchers to provide insights into working with families in productive and empowering ways. In this highly readable and engaging text, the authors offer fascinating portraits of families of linguistically and culturally diverse backgrounds in both the United States and Canada. In the process, they take us on a journey that not only challenges how teachers and schools think about family engagement, but also helps them rethink how to connect with families in their own classrooms and schools. In these absorbing and informative stories, the authors and editors describe the fertile resources of students and families—from Sudanese to Latino, from Appalachian to African American—by focusing on what these families *know* and *can do* rather than on what they *do not know* and *cannot do*. The result is a rich mosaic of the kinds of families that define U.S. and Canadian life at the beginning of the twenty-first century. It will be a guide for all preservice and practicing teachers whether they teach at the preschool, elementary, or secondary school level, and whether they are ESL, bilingual, or science teachers. It will especially be a treasured resource for teachers who want to go beyond simplistic and static understandings of culture and truly connect with the families of their students in respectful and empowering ways.

Reference

Nieto, S. (1985). Who's afraid of bilingual parents? *The Bilingual Review, 12*(3), 179–189.

Preface

Monica's mom informs Monica's fifth grade teacher, Mr. Davis, that the family will leave Los Angeles on Wednesday evening, traveling by bus to Ciudad Juarez, Mexico to take care of some business matters. Consequently, Monica will miss two days of school. How will Mr. Davis respond to this news? Will he complain bitterly to colleagues that Monica, like other of his Latina/o students, will miss school and criticize her parents for their lack of concern for her education? Will he simply acknowledge the necessity of the family's trip and put together a homework packet for Monica that he hopes will compensate for her absence from class? Or, in addition to providing a work packet, will he also envision the trip itself as a fascinating learning opportunity for Monica and create a plan to help maximize the potential of her upcoming international experience, perhaps involving taking snapshots of distinctive Mexican cultural scenes or artifacts with a disposable camera or interviewing her relatives about their views on her developing bilingualism and the importance of maintaining her Spanish?

This book addresses the perspectives that teachers take and the decisions that they make when, like Mr. Davis, they interact with students and parents whose family structures, customs, knowledge base, everyday activities, and language practices are unlike their own. The rapid growth and spread of ethnically, culturally, and linguistically diverse populations in the United States and other countries around the world guarantee that nearly all teachers today will work with many such students. Unfortunately, when teachers are unprepared to understand and appreciate the unique experiences that make up diverse children's out-of-school lives and the unique resources that these children bring to school learning, they often turn to prevalent folk theories that view difference as deficit (Compton-Lilly, 2003; Lareau, 1989; Valdés, 1996). We have often heard from well-meaning educators that many diverse families deprive their children of the experiences that form a foundation for school success or fail to value schooling and support their children's academic achievement. However, the researchers who have contributed to this book have gone beyond negative stereotypes and well-intentioned generalities and carefully documented the multifaceted nature of diverse families' lives, the families' perceptions of schooling, and the challenges that the children confront as they move between home and school. In addition, the authors frequently call attention to the rich cultural knowledge, linguistic abilities, and social and problem solving skills that children from diverse families possess and, in some cases, describe the work of sensitive teachers who have utilized these resources to enhance students' engagement and learning. We hope that the richly detailed portraits of families, communities, and classrooms and the discussions of related theoretical concepts provided in this book will enable readers to appreciate the complex experiences and distinctive resources of diverse children and families, think creatively about how to build on these experiences and resources in classrooms, and develop the knowledge, understanding, and desire necessary to foster productive home-school connections in a multicultural society.

Overview of the Book

The chapters in Part I provide detailed portraits of diverse families that highlight their unique cultural practices related to schooling and the challenges that their children face in school settings. We believe that these portraits provide an important view into the complex lives of diverse families that will help teachers and researchers see such families from a sensitive, ethnographic perspective.

The chapters in Part II focus on the ways that teachers and researchers have worked with diverse families to build positive relationships and develop learning activities that incorporate children's unique experiences and resources. We hope that these rich examples will help educators at all levels to envision their own practical ways to learn from and with families and children.

Parts I and II each conclude with a Teacher Commentary—a short response written by classroom teachers. In these responses, the teachers reflect on how the chapters connect to their teaching experience and cause them to rethink past decisions and future directions.

Finally, Francisco Rios concludes the book by highlighting important themes that run throughout it and reflecting on their meanings for teachers and researchers within the current educational climate in the United States.

We have utilized several textual strategies to help readers grapple deeply and personally with the chapters' meanings and implications. First, in a feature called "Theoretical Applications" we identify key theoretical concepts in each chapter and prompt readers to connect these concepts to their own teaching or research. Second, we have asked each author or authors to conclude their chapter by making practical suggestions to teachers and researchers. Third, at the end of each chapter, a feature called "Ideas for Discussion, Extension, and Application" provides activities for students to engage in while reading the volume in education courses.

References

Compton-Lilly, C. (2003). *Reading families: The literate lives of urban children*. New York: Teachers' College Press.

Lareau, A. (1989). *Home advantage: Social class and parental intervention in elementary education*. New York: Falmer Press.

Valdés, G. (1996). *Con respeto: Bridging the distances between culturally diverse families and schools: An ethnographic portrait*. New York: Teachers' College Press.

Acknowledgments

From its conception to the writing and editing of the final manuscript, this book was possible only through the encouragement and support of many people. We appreciate the support of colleagues and friends who believed in this project and encouraged its development including Judith Green and Adrian and Emily Rodgers. Special thanks to all contributors, who continually re-energized us with their enthusiasm for the book. We are indebted to Naomi Silverman and Sonia Nieto for their suggestions and continued support through the development of the book. We are also appreciative of the support of our spouses, Joel and Ann-Margaret. Both of them spent extra hours caring for our children—Benjamin, Danya, and Sierra—as we worked on this project. Our own difficulties in managing our complicated family lives were an important point of reference as we reflected on the experiences of other families.

1 Introduction

Patrick C. Manyak and
Maria Luiza Dantas

In this introductory chapter we introduce major themes and key concepts related to diversity, families, and schooling. To begin, we survey important previous research on families and schooling, focusing the reader's attention on a set of overarching themes that provide a historical background for understanding the studies presented in this book. Next, we carefully define a core set of theoretical concepts, stressing that these concepts represent lenses that can help readers to see families, schooling, learning, and teaching in new ways.

Diversity, Families, and Schooling: Overarching Themes

Educators have perhaps always recognized the fact that families play a critical role in children's schooling. However, for some 40 years, researchers have delved into the complex relationships between diverse families and schools, producing a revealing array of studies that offer insight into the ways that families differ; how families perceive school, relate to teachers, and support their children's education; and how educators think about and relate to families (Delgado-Gaitan, 1990; Guerra, 1998; Heath, 1983; Li, 2002; Taylor & Dorsey-Gaines, 1988; Valdés, 1996). In this section, we discuss four broad themes that we have distilled from this research. These themes provide a context for understanding the studies presented in this book, enabling readers to make connections between the individual chapters and important previous findings and perspectives on diverse families and schooling.

The Depth of Difference

Several seminal research studies have underscored the deep differences between families across cultures and the significant discontinuity that children from diverse cultural groups often experience as they enter school. In her highly acclaimed study of language socialization in distinct cultural communities in the Piedmont Carolinas, Heath (1983) described the vast differences in the ways that working-class African American, working-class White, and middle-class White families used language and literacy. Her rich portrait of the language experience of the African American children highlighted the fact that very young children, while constantly held and thus exposed to an ongoing stream of speech, were not talked to directly and were expected to find their own ways into adult conversation. As the children grew, adults encouraged performance-oriented modes of speech, with which the children earned their place on the public stage, but rarely asked them questions, since "children [were] not seen as information-givers or question-answers" (p. 103). These behaviors contrasted dramatically from those of the White families, who cooed over, talked to, questioned, and generally bathed young children in encouragement to speak and later "[taught] them to label items and events, to describe their features, to read books, and to play with educational toys" (p. 350). Significantly, Heath pointed out that these patterns of language use were not casual ones but rather issued from contrasting, deeply held beliefs on the nature of childhood, childrearing, and community life. Further, she demonstrated that, for the African American children, school brought a "sudden flood of discontinuities in the ways people talk, the values they hold, and the consistency with which the rewards go to some and not others" (p. 348).

In another important study of families and schooling, Valdés (1996) documented the lives of 10 Mexican immigrant families. Her research emphasized the central importance of extended family relationships, household- rather than child-centeredness, and the parents' orientation toward raising respectful, responsible children who understood their role within the family and were prepared to contribute to its welfare. Against this backdrop, Valdés described a number of specific family practices related to children: children learned by observing and doing rather than by explicit teaching, spent nearly all of their time with siblings and cousins, and were expected to demonstrate deep respect for and obedience to their parents. In summary, Valdés concluded that the families held profoundly "familistic values" and that meant that, despite parents' expressed belief in the importance of school, "Family activities did not center around children's school lives, and parents' views about their success or failure as parents were not closely tied to their children's academic success" (p. 188).

These two studies underscore the fact that family differences across cultures are not superficial: They reflect deeply held beliefs and values and have tremendous consequences for families' views of and children's experience in school.

Variations in Family–School Relations

Diverse families' cultural assumptions and personal histories powerfully shape the ways that they understand and relate to schools. Nevertheless, research has consistently discovered that diverse families place great value on schooling, particularly as a stepping-stone to economic mobility. For example, the African American parents in Heath's (1983) study, the Mexican-American parents researched by Delgado-Gaitan (1992), and the Chinese immigrant families described by Li (2002) all expressed a deep value of schooling and clearly communicated that value to their children. However, it is also evident that families vary widely in their assumptions about schooling and the roles that they play in supporting children's school learning.

Detailed studies of home and school settings have revealed that teachers generally want parents to actively support their children's school learning by adopting a kind of "teacher's helper" role (Lareau, 1989; Valdés, 1996). After examining the relationships between working- and upper-middle-class families and their children's teachers, Lareau (1989) summarized this desire succinctly:

> [T]eachers view education as a round-the-clock experience in which parents can, and should, play a role in supplementing the classroom experience by preparing children for school, reinforcing the curriculum, and showing support . . . by attending school events. Teachers saw an interdependency between home and school, not a separation.
>
> (p. 35)

In contrast, Lareau found that the working-class parents viewed the school and family domains as largely separate and the teachers as having the requisite expertise, and thus as bearing the responsibility, for teaching academic skills to their children. Furthermore, in comparison to the middle-class parents in the study, Lareau stressed the working-class parents' lack of confidence in their ability to support their children's academic learning and their lack of information about the ways that school worked.

Valdés (1996) documented a similar separation between school and family spheres and responsibilities in her study. The Mexican immigrant families she observed understood *educación*, in the Mexican sense, as raising children to be respectful, obedient, and moral, a task to which they were deeply committed. However, like Lareau's working-class parents, they viewed academic development as the responsibility of the teachers. Raising the issue of whether it was appropriate for the school to help these families change this view of their children's schooling, Valdés poignantly argued:

> The point is that if Rosario Castro, for example, were made to believe that she should read to her children every evening . . . or practice multiplication tables, she would do just that. She is indeed committed to her children's schooling, and she would hope to do her best for them in spite of her many other obligations. On the other hand, she would be replacing *educación* in the Mexican sense with an American middle-class focus on schooling and school learning. Given the demands on her life, she perhaps would not have time to do the real teaching that Mexican mothers do . . . In essence, Rosario would be helping the teachers to do their jobs, but she herself would fail to do her own.
>
> (pp. 202–203)

In her study of Mexican immigrant families in California, Delgado-Gaitan (1992) encountered a similar cultural perspective on the meaning of education. However, she also stressed the many ways that the parents provided social, motivational, and emotional support aimed at enhancing children's success in school.

These brief portraits of working-class and Mexican immigrant families' understanding of schooling highlight the gulf that may exist between the assumptions of culturally diverse parents and those of teachers. Research with other ethnic groups, such as Chinese immigrants (Li, 2002), has demonstrated other conflicting beliefs, understandings, and goals that can result when parents' cultural beliefs and histories differ greatly from those of school personnel. Unfortunately, as we discuss next, these conflicts can lead teachers to view diverse families in a negative light.

Diverse Families and the Deficit Perspective

A number of research studies focused on families and schooling have demonstrated that educators may find themselves confused by families whose values and practices differ greatly from their own, and, at times, develop negative views about such families' interest in and support of their children's schooling (Compton-Lilly, 2003; Heath, 1983; Moll, Amanti, & González, 2005; Valdés, 1996). Valdés (1996) summarized how conflicting cultural views on the part of parents and teachers led teachers to make deficit assumptions about the Latina/o families in her study: "When children came to school without certain skills that their families, in good faith, believed the teachers should teach (e.g., the alphabet, the colors, the numbers), school personnel assumed parental indifference, troubled homes, and little interest in education" (p. 167). We refer to this tendency to make negative assumptions, judge, or criticize poor or diverse families as the deficit perspective, and like Compton-Lilly (2003), find it to be powerfully prevalent within schools that serve poor, non-White children.

To illustrate this deficit perspective in greater detail, we draw on data that Patrick Manyak collected while researching the school experience of a class of Latina/o primary grade students (Manyak, 1999). The children's bilingual classroom teacher, Ms. Page, maintained a close relationship with many of the children's families, valuing their unique histories and cultural practices, provided a rich instructional environment, and supported the children's developing bilingualism. However, since the children also visited Ms. Jones' English-only first grade classroom for integration time, Patrick observed these visits and talked with Ms. Jones regularly for a period of three months. Several times Ms. Jones, a White, middle-class, monolingual-English-speaking young teacher, acknowledged that while teachers wanted to have high expectations for the Latina/o children, "you can't expect [them to master] the same things at the same rate." She explained this need for lower expectations by referring to the children's lack of stimulating experiences outside of school and the fact that they spoke only Spanish at home. Addressing the resources that children bring to school tasks, Ms. Jones stated: "I think that we rely too much on children having experiences, and sometimes not a whole lot happens in their family, nothing too great anyway. You have to give them experiences." Thus, Ms. Jones, despite having little knowledge of the children's families and communities, assumed that many of the Latina/o students experienced little of value outside of school. In addition to this failure to provide meaningful life experiences, Ms. Jones also suggested that the children's families did not consider school success important. This appeared particularly true for "old world" families that only spoke Spanish to the children:

If everything is in Spanish, the family is saying that English is not the important language. How well do you want your child to do in an English-
dominated society? The more they hear it—if the family uses it—the better
off they will be.

This statement included several deficit-oriented assumptions. First, Ms. Jones
equated the families' use of Spanish to their devaluing of English and implied that
it would have been easy for the families to switch to using English at home if they
desired. In addition, she failed to recognize any redeeming value in the children's
emerging bilingualism or the important role of the parents in helping the children to develop their Spanish skills. Through informal conversations, Patrick
found that many teachers at the school shared Ms. Jones' attitude and assumptions. Fortunately, as we discuss next, researchers and teachers in many settings
have worked together in ways that discredit the assumptions of the deficit
perspective.

Recognizing and Building on Cultural Resources

Over the last several decades, a number of researchers have worked alongside
teachers to incorporate diverse children's home experiences and resources into
meaningful classroom instruction. These projects have demonstrated that diverse
children possess a broad range of cultural knowledge, linguistic abilities, and
problem-solving skills that represent important resources for school learning
(McIntyre, Rosebery, & González, 2001; Moll, L., Amanti, & González, 2005).
In one renowned project, Moll and his colleagues (Moll et al., 2005) conducted a
long-term investigation among Mexican immigrant families in Tucson, Arizona.
Together with teachers, they visited families and documented the vast funds of
knowledge, "socially distributed cultural resources," that these families possessed.
The researchers and teachers then worked together to create instructional units
that utilized these funds of knowledge. These units produced rich contexts for
students' literacy and content learning. In one example, teachers drew on the
families' knowledge of construction to develop a unit on construction, structures,
and community development (Moll & Greenberg, 1990). In the course of the
unit, students read and wrote in sophisticated ways as they researched comparative structures. Furthermore, parents involved in construction frequently visited
and shared with the class, making "an intellectual contribution to the content and
process of classroom learning" (p. 339).

In a somewhat different vein, Patrick (Manyak, 2004) described how Ms. Page,
a primary grade teacher, encouraged and extended her Latina/o children's unique
ability to communicate across languages and cultural communities. Aware that
research had documented that Latina/o adults and children engage in numerous
"intercultural transactions" that prompt the children to develop as "language
and cultural brokers" (Vásquez, Pease-Alvarez, & Shannon, 1994, p. 13), Ms. Page
frequently tapped into this important resource during classroom literacy activities. For instance, on a daily basis, children told short narratives about events
from their home lives and these narratives were written down to form the

class's daily newspaper. Ms. Page allowed students to share in Spanish but she encouraged the children to translate their peers' Spanish narratives into English. Similarly, when monolingual students from another first-grade class integrated with Ms. Page's students during a period of literature study, Ms. Page's students often facilitated rich discussions or role-plays by translating comments across languages or answering questions in both Spanish and English. These classroom activities, organized to encourage children's translation of oral and written texts, affirmed and extended the bilingual children's broad linguistic repertoires and positioned bilingualism as a special emblem of academic competence.

In conclusion, these studies reveal how knowledge of and appreciation for diverse children's unique cultural resources led teachers to develop creative ways to incorporate and build on these resources in the classroom. The resulting instruction demonstrated that connecting instruction to the children's out-of-school lives could produce meaningful, engaging, and sophisticated learning activities.

This necessarily brief discussion of important themes in studies focused on diverse families and school provides a backdrop for this book. We encourage readers to keep these themes in mind as they move through the book and to reflect on how the research presented in each chapter relates to and extends them.

Orienting Concepts

Educators often draw a sharp line between theory and practice. We hear frequently that theory captivates idealistic scholars who discuss abstractions in books and university classrooms but proves impractical or useless in the real world of schools. However, we believe that there is much truth to the familiar axiom, "There is nothing as practical as a good theory." In particular, we find that powerful theoretical concepts can function as lenses that enable us to see our everyday experiences in new ways and thus lead to very practical changes in our behavior. We define theoretical concepts as terms or phrases that concisely encapsulate the meanings of a broad set of related ideas. As our understanding of theoretical concepts becomes clearer and deeper, they become more useful to us. Like a new pair of prescription glasses, they sharpen our vision and allow us to see things that we did not see before. For example, we both experienced this sharpening of vision after encountering the theoretical concept of "funds of knowledge" in the work of Moll, González and their colleagues (Moll, Amanti, & González, 2005). For us, as for many educators familiar with this research, the concept of funds of knowledge transformed our view of diverse families. Instead of focusing on the knowledge, experiences, or material resources that such families lacked in comparison to the prototypical "mainstream" family, we began to recognize the unique resources that diverse families possessed and passed on to their children. In a recent book on the funds of knowledge project, a number of teachers describe how this new perspective on their students' families pushed them to plan more relevant, meaningful, and challenging instruction (Moll, González, & Amanti, 2005).

In this section we introduce a set of core theoretical concepts that equip readers with the conceptual tools necessary to see, understand, and respond to diverse students and their families in sensitive and productive ways. These seven concepts—ethnographic perspective, deficit perspective, sociocultural perspective on learning, cultural practices, learning resources, literacy practices, and permeability—represent our own collection of thinking tools, developed and refined over many years of working with diverse children, families, and classrooms. These concepts provide an important theoretical orientation that prepares the reader to engage deeply with the meanings and implications of the following chapters.

Ethnographic Perspective

We base the concept of ethnographic perspective on the broader notion of ethnography, an approach to research and writing central to the discipline of anthropology. Ethnography generally refers to the study and interpretation of cultural patterns of behavior and involves extensive fieldwork within a cultural community. Through observation of and participation in the daily activities of a group and ongoing interviews conducted to elicit members' interpretations of those activities, ethnographic research seeks to arrive at "the set of understandings and specific knowledge shared among participants that guide their behavior in that specific context" (Hornberger, 1994, p. 667). We use the concept ethnographic perspective to refer to a way of looking at the world that shares the assumptions, dispositions, and goals of those who engage in ethnographic research. This concept helps us to envision and to enact this particular way of seeing and relating to others. However, it is important to recognize that the ethnographic perspective does not represent a point of view that can be adopted once-for-all but rather a mindset that develops slowly as we reflect on, embrace, and begin to act in accordance with its qualities.

Six key qualities constitute our understanding of the ethnographic perspective. First and foremost, it involves the recognition of the significance of culture in all human activity. It assumes that all behavior, no matter how strange it appears to us, makes sense within the cultural world of the actors. Second, the ethnographic perspective implies a recognition that one's own way of being in the world is just one of many ways of being and is not inherently superior to others. Consequently, taking on the ethnographic perspective means withholding judgment on others' actions and constantly striving to understand the deeper meanings of those actions. Next, the ethnographic perspective entails seeking to understand behavior from the point of view of the actors themselves. In order to move toward this "insider perspective," we attempt to connect specific actions to the actors' beliefs, values, histories, and goals. At the same time, when operating from an ethnographic perspective, we also recognize the deep nature of cultural frames of reference and are highly conscious of the ways in which our own frames shape the way that we see the world, limit our ability to fully understand those from different cultures, and can cause us to judge or criticize differences. Fifth, an ethnographic perspective leads to the recognition of the complexity of others' lives and of the heterogeneity inherent within any cultural group. This recognition challenges us to resist the urge to simplify, categorize, and generalize as we think about and describe others. Finally, the adoption of an ethnographic perspective brings a sincere interest in others' ways of life and a willingness to cross cultural borders to build relationships.

For teachers, the concept of the ethnographic perspective has many practical implications. It prompts a conscious effort to see students holistically, as having complex, multifaceted lives both inside and outside of school. Furthermore, it leads to a healthy interest in students' outside-of-school experiences and family practices. Finally, the ethnographic perspective challenges teachers to replace the impulse to make quick negative judgments about students' home lives with a willingness to recognize, appreciate, and build on their diverse experiences and resources.

Deficit Perspective

The concept of the *deficit perspective* refers a way of looking at students and families that is characterized by narrowness, presumption, and judgment. We use the deficit perspective as conceptual shorthand to represent a mindset that constantly compares diverse students' experiences to those of the prototypical middle-class child, judges or criticizes students and families whose experiences differ from "mainstream" standards, fails to recognize and appreciate the complexity of diverse students' and families' lives or the unique resources they possess, makes quick assumptions about families' values, particularly as they relate to schooling, ascribes to narrow views of school-readiness and parent involvement and blames families for not sharing or living up to these views, and blames children and families for the children's lack engagement in classroom activities rather than questioning the adequacy of the classroom climate or instruction. By listing these characteristics, we do not mean to imply that any individual exhibits all (or none) of them all the time. Furthermore, as with the ethnographic perspective, we do not believe that anyone, consciously or unconsciously, accepts or rejects the deficit perspective and the attitudes and behaviors that embody it once-for-all. Instead, we see the concept of deficit perspective as a thinking tool that helps us to examine the ways that we look at, talk about, and relate to diverse students and families, illuminates those moments when we slip into narrow or judgmental modes, and challenges us to move toward greater openness, sensitivity, and appreciation of difference.

Cultural Practices

As should be clear already, culture is at the heart of this book. Influenced by the work of Moll, Amanti and González (2005) and Gutiérrez and Rogoff (2003), we believe that this broad, complex notion becomes most meaningful when used in reference to how people "live culturally" in their everyday lives. The concept of cultural practices emphasizes this everyday, lived dimension of culture. Specifically, we employ it to refer to the repeated patterns of activity that people engage in and the ways of believing, valuing, thinking, feeling, behaving, interacting, and speaking that make up these activities. The concept of cultural practices sheds light on the existence of both commonalities and variations within cultural groups. To the extent that members of cultural groups repeatedly participate in a set of similar activities, they develop, to a greater or lesser degree, shared forms of thinking, behaving, and interacting. However, people inevitably and idiosyncratically modify their everyday activities in response to countless changing needs, influences, settings, and circumstances; cultural groups are heterogeneous, cultural practices are dynamic, and the experiences and attributes of those who participate in them vary widely. Furthermore, as researchers in the funds of knowledge project observed, "households draw from multiple cultural systems and use these systems as strategic resources" (Moll et al., 2005, p. 10). This finding stresses that individuals and groups actively shape their cultural practices and that, in this era of globalization, they frequently do so by blending elements from multiple cultural communities to create novel, hybrid forms of everyday activity. Finally, the concept of cultural practices emphasizes that children participate in and even help to create a dynamic set of everyday activities within their families and communities and thus acquire a broad repertoire of resources—ways of thinking, relating to others, speaking, problem solving, etc.—that they draw on as they move through the diverse settings and accomplish the varied purposes that constitute their lives.

We believe that the concept of cultural practices can help teachers avoid viewing all children of the same ethnic group as possessing a stereotypical set of traits and prompt the teachers to learn more about the particularities of children's unique home and community activities. In addition, we appreciate how a focus on cultural practices often reveals children and families to be active, resourceful, and creative participants in various overlapping cultural systems.

Sociocultural Perspectives on Learning

While we introduce the term "sociocultural perspective" on learning here as a single theoretical concept, it is more appropriately understood as a complex approach to understanding human development as it occurs in and is shaped by social and cultural contexts. Within education, learning is frequently pictured as a largely cognitive process that takes place within the heads of individual learners. However, sociocultural theorists have stressed the ways that people acquire knowledge, skills, and identities through participation in historically, culturally, and socially constituted practices. Our concept of sociocultural perspectives on learning distills this general orientation toward learning into three key principles.

First, learning occurs as individuals fulfill various roles and responsibilities alongside others in a range of cultural practices. This principle reflects the essence of Lave and Wenger's (1991) theory of legitimate peripheral participation. Lave and Wenger suggest that individuals belong to multiple communities of practice that result from mutual engagement in joint enterprises. Within these enterprises, diverse participatory roles, social interactions, and learning experiences offer newcomers opportunities to acquire new knowledge and skills. Further, as learners participate in everyday practices, complex webs of interaction result in dynamic, overlapping, and multidirectional zones of proximal development

(ZPD). Vygotsky (1978) conceived of the ZPD as the space between what an individual can do alone and what she can do in collaboration with a more competent other and suggested that social interaction within the ZPD produced cognitive development. Based on their research in an elementary classroom, Moll and Whitmore (1993) proposed that a " 'collective' zone of proximal development" resulting from "the interdependence of adults and children, and how they use social and cultural resources" (p. 20) captured the dynamic spirit of Vygotsky's concept. Informed by this expansive understanding of the ZPD, we view participation in community practice as producing multiple and multidirectional ZPDs in which powerful learning occurs.

Second, learning must be seen from a holistic perspective that takes into account identities, purposes and motivation. Lave and Wenger (1991) accentuated the intrinsic relationship between social relations, learning, and identity, stating, "Learning implies becoming a different person with respect to the possibilities enabled by systems of relations. To ignore this aspect of learning is to overlook the fact that learning involves the construction of identities" (p. 53). This perspective emphasizes that individuals often acquire new knowledge and skills as they develop a sense of belonging to a community and increasingly identify with its members. In simple terms, as people come to see themselves as members of a particular group, they strive to acquire the ways of thinking, talking, and interacting that reflect that group.

Finally, no single theoretical perspective is sufficiently powerful to explain the complex process of human learning. Thus, we stress that cognitive and sociocultural theories complement one other, each offering powerful explanations for certain dimensions of learning and, importantly, serving to illuminate and mitigate the limitations of the other. For example, when pursued narrowly, cognitive theories of learning and the practices that they produce may prove perilous for diverse learners. Lave (1996) explicitly addressed the danger inherent within psychological conceptions of learning:

> Theories that reduce learning to individual mental capacity/activity in the last instance blame marginalized people for being marginal . . . Such theories are deeply concerned with individual differences, with notions of better and worse, more and less learning, and with comparison of these things across groups-of-individuals. Psychological theories of learning prescribe ideals and paths to excellence and identify the kinds of individuals (by no means all) who should arrive; the absence of movement away from some putatively common starting point becomes grounds for labeling others sub-normal.
>
> (p. 149)

The sociocultural perspective on learning immediately casts doubt on this tendency to evaluate and label diverse learners according to supposedly universal mental processes, highlighting instead the plurality of developmental pathways, the diversity of learning resources, and the centrality of aspects such as social contexts, engagement, purpose, and identity in understanding, assessing, and facilitating learning.

Learning Resources

The concept of learning resources sits at the nexus of the concepts of ethnographic perspective, cultural practices, and sociocultural perspectives on learning and represents a useful way for teachers to remain cognizant of these concepts and to apply them in practice. We use the concept of learning resources to represent the wide range of experiences, relationships, knowledge, and artifacts that children encounter or acquire as a result of their participation in family and community practices. These resources include families' shared histories; the unique knowledge possessed by family members; the special tools and problem-solving processes utilized within families and communities; social relations that provide for diverse forms of collaboration, support, and encouragement; and diverse linguistic experiences and repertoires. All children bring a variety of such learning resources to school, and, when recognized, these resources can serve to enhance their classroom learning. Consequently, the concept of learning resources helps educators to see beyond narrowly conceived definitions of school readiness. For instance, while it is indeed important to consider children's knowledge of letters and numbers or ability to rhyme as they enter kindergarten, teachers attuned to the notion of learning resources also take stock of other resources such as emergent bilingualism, experience with storytelling, close relationships with older siblings and relatives, knowledge of popular culture, or Internet skills.

The concept of learning resources also focuses attention on how particular communities define learning and resources for learning. Wertsch (1998) emphasized the constant presence of "mediational means"—learning resources—in human activity and points out that often many such resources may serve to accomplish a given task. However, he suggests that one of these resources is frequently privileged above others. The notion of privileging raises questions about the learning resources considered appropriate for participation in schools. Is the teacher defined as the sole source of knowledge in an activity or is peer input or family knowledge also considered a valued learning resource? Is so-called "standard English" defined as the only appropriate code for a practice or are children's broad linguistic repertoires also considered viable resources for participation and learning? These questions address the issue of how learning resources are defined in classroom activities and, subsequently, the relative legitimacy and value ascribed to children's out-of-school experiences.

We find that consciously asking ourselves about the nature of students' learning resources constitutes a practical way to look at children from an ethnographic rather than deficit perspective. An interest in children's learning resources prompts us to view them as active and resourceful, to inquire into their unique family and community practices, and to consider ways to organize classroom instruction that enable all students to draw on, display, and extend their unique resources.

Literacy Practices

References to literacy appear frequently throughout the chapters in this book and nearly all of these references draw on the concept of literacy practices. In contrast to an "individual skills paradigm" (Reder, 1994) of literacy that focuses attention on the individual internalization of knowledge and skills related to print, the concept of literacy practices recognizes that instances of reading and writing are always embedded in and shaped by social and cultural contexts. Barton and Hamilton (2000) have defined literacy practices as the observable, recurring ways that people interact with text along with the assumptions, values, feelings, and social processes that underpin these interactions. From the literacy practices perspective, literacy acquisition involves not just learning to recognize words and construct meanings from print but also socialization into various, highly situated forms and functions of print and the "ways of acting, interacting, feeling, valuing, thinking, and believing" (Gee, 1999, p. 356) that they incorporate.

Much research oriented by the concept of literacy practices has targeted non-school settings in which people use widely divergent forms of reading and writing to accomplish a myriad of everyday purposes. This research makes clear that given today's print-saturated world, virtually all children have numerous experiences with literacy in their homes and communities (Hull & Schultz, 2002; Taylor & Dorsey-Gaines, 1988). However, it also stresses that the literacy practices in ethnically diverse families often differ from those of the prototypically "mainstream" families and conflict with or are neglected by schools as potential resources for literacy development (Compton-Lilly, 2003; Guerra, 1998; Hull & Schultz, 2002; Li, 2002; Vásquez et al., 1994).

Permeability

We use the concept of permeability to capture the quality of classrooms, curricula, and instruction that allow children's out-of-school experiences and resources to flow into and enrich official school learning. Permeable classrooms do not abandon the teaching of traditional school subjects and the skills that they incorporate. However, when constructing permeable curricula and instructional activities, teachers find ways to incorporate, build on, and extend children's diverse experiences and learning resources. For instance, Manyak (2008) has described "Daily News," a classroom literacy activity that he observed in several primary grade classrooms of Latina/o children, as an event that recognized and extended the children's budding bilingualism, created space in the classroom for their out-of-school experiences, and created a context for the teachers to provide explicit instruction and meaningful practice in various writing skills. Daily News involved the students sharing stories about events from their out-of-school lives and collaborating with the teacher to scribe, edit, and read these stories. Elaborating on the permeability of the activity, Manyak (2008) concluded:

> By sanctioning such subject matter as appropriate for classroom literacy tasks, daily news repositioned the children's sociocultural experience as a legitimate source of knowledge and demonstrated to them that literacy was an effective tool for recording and reflecting on their lived experience.
>
> (p. 454)

Significantly, this example of permeable instruction does not simply involve "warm and fuzzy" connections to children's lives but rather represents a complex and challenging activity characterized by careful instruction in and practice of key literacy skills within a meaningful, engaging, and collaborative context. Consequently, we stress that the concept of permeability does not include any and every effort to bring students' experiences into the classroom but rather implies the careful, strategic, and rigorous use of such experiences to extend children's repertoire of skills, build meaningful connections to new knowledge, and enhance students' engagement in school learning. We find that permeability functions as an ideal conclusion to our set of core theoretical constructs, as it represents one of the major goals behind and perhaps the most practical classroom outcome of learning from and with diverse families.

This concludes our discussion of the seven core concepts that form the basis of our understanding of the relationships between families, diversity, learning, and teaching:

- Ethnographic perspective
- Deficit perspective
- Sociocultural perspectives on learning
- Cultural practices
- Learning resources
- Literacy practices
- Permeability

While this chapter provides an introduction to the particular meanings that we give to these critical concepts, we believe that the portraits of families, classrooms, teachers, and researchers in the subsequent chapters will greatly enhance these meanings. Therefore, we ask readers to keep these concepts in mind as they move through the book and to consider how each chapter imbues them with deeper, richer shades of meanings.

Ideas for Discussion, Extension, and Application

1. Discuss how you would respond to Monica's family trip (described in the Preface to this book) if you were Mr. Davis. What factors shape your thinking on this matter?
2. Discuss specific findings in the Diversity, Families, and Schooling: Overarching Themes section that surprised you or are particular crucial for understanding diverse families and children's perception and experience of schooling.
3. Select two or three of the seven concepts discussed in the chapter—ethnographic perspective, deficit perspective, cultural practices, sociocultural perspective on learning, learning resources, literacy practices, permeability—and write quickly for a few minutes about what they mean to you and how they have or will apply to your teaching or research. Discuss your responses in a group.

References

Barton, D., & Hamilton, M. (2000). Literacy practices. In D. Barton, M. Hamilton & R. Ivanič (Eds.), *Situated literacies: Reading and writing in context* (pp. 7–15). New York: Routledge.

Compton-Lilly, C. (2003). *Reading families: The literate lives of urban children.* New York: Teachers College Press.

Delgado-Gaitan, C. (1990). *Literacy for empowerment: The role of parents in children's education.* New York: Falmer Press.

Delgado-Gaitan, C. (1992). School matters in the Mexican-American home: Socializing children to education. *American Educational Research Journal, 29*(3), 495–513.

Gee, J. (1999). Reading and the new literacy studies: Reframing the National Academy of Sciences report on reading. *Journal of Literacy Research, 31,* 355–374.

Guerra, J. (1998). *Close to home: Oral and literate practices in a transnational Mexicano community.* New York: Teachers College Press.

Gutiérrez, K. D., & Rogoff, B. (2003). Cultural ways of learning: Individual traits or repertoires of practice. *Educational Researcher, 32*(5), 19–25.

Heath, S. B. (1983). *Ways with words.* Cambridge: Cambridge University Press.

Hornberger, N. (1994). Ethnography. In A. Cumming (Ed.), Alternatives in TESOL research: Descriptive, interpretive, and ideological orientations (pp. 687–689). *TESOL Quarterly, 28*(4), 673–703.

Hull, G., & Schultz, K. (2002). *School's out: Bridging out-of-school literacies with classroom practice.* New York: Teachers College Press.

Lareau, A. (1989). *Home advantage: Social class and parental intervention in elementary education.* New York: Falmer Press.

Lave, J. (1996). Teaching, as learning, in practice. *Mind, Culture, and Activity, 3,* 149–164.

Lave, J., & Wenger, E. (1991). *Situated learning: Legitimate peripheral participation.* New York: Cambridge University Press.

Li, G. (2002). *"East is East, West is West"? Home literacy, culture, and schooling.* New York: Peter Lang.

Manyak, P. (1999). "Integration time:" Contrasting perspectives on and practices with primary grade Latina/o children. Unpublished manuscript.

Manyak, P. (2004). "What did she say?": Translation in a primary-grade English immersion class. *Multicultural Perspectives, 6*(1), 12–18.

Manyak, P. (2008). "What's your news?": Portraits of a dynamic literacy activity for English language learners. *The Reading Teacher, 61*(6), 450–458.

McIntyre, E., Rosebery, & González, N. (2001). *Classroom diversity: Connecting curriculum to students' lives* (pp. 100–114). Portsmouth, NH: Heinemann.

Moll, L., Amanti, C., & González, N. (2005). *Funds of knowledge: Theorizing practices in households and classrooms.* Mahwah, NJ: LEA Publishing.

Moll, L. C., & Greenberg, J. B. (1990). Creating zones of possibilities: Combining social contexts for instruction. In L. Moll (Ed.), *Vygotsky and education: Instructional implications and applications of sociohistorical psychology,* (pp. 319–348). Cambridge: Cambridge University Press.

Moll, L., & Whitmore, K. (1993). Vygotsky in classroom practice: Moving from individual transmission to social transaction. In E. Forman, N. Minick, & C. A. Stone (Eds.), *Contexts for learning: Sociocultural dynamics in children's development* (pp. 230–253). New York: Oxford University Press.

Reder, S. (1994). Practice engagement theory: A sociocultural approach to literacy across languages and cultures. In B. Ferdman, R. M. Weber, & A. Ramirez (Eds.), *Literacy across languages and cultures.* Albany, NY: SUNY Press.

Taylor, D., & Dorsey-Gaines, C. (1988). *Growing up literate: Learning from inner-city families.* Portsmouth, NH: Heinemann.

Valdés, G. (1996). *Con respeto: Bridging the distances between culturally diverse families and schools: An ethnographic portrait.* New York: Teachers College Press.

Vásquez, O., Pease-Alvarez, L., & Shannon, S. (1994). *Pushing boundaries: Language and culture in a Mexicano community.* New York: Cambridge University Press.

Vygotsky, L. (1978). *Mind in society.* Cambridge, MA: Harvard University Press.

Wertsch, J. V. (1998). *Mind as action.* New York: Oxford University Press.

Part I

Home–School (Dis)connections

2 "Lost Boys," Cousins and Aunties

Using Sudanese Refugee Relationships to Complicate Definitions of "Family"

Kristen H. Perry

In June of 2005, I sat in the living room of a Sudanese refugee family that I had recently begun tutoring. The family consisted of a mother and father, both in their late twenties, a 5-year-old girl, and a nearly-3-year-old boy. Akhlas, the mother of the family, was working diligently on her ESL homework, which dealt that day with the concept of *family*. Akhlas stared at the workbook page, momentarily stumped. She was supposed to fill in the blank in the statement "There are _____ people in my family." Akhlas confirmed that she understood what she was supposed to do, but she could not count up all the people in her family because there were "a *LOT!*" I told Akhlas that in America, this sort of question usually refers to the people who live in one household, and I suggested that she just count the people in her home.

When Akhlas wrote "8" in the blank, it was my turn to be perplexed. I knew that only four people lived in the apartment. Akhlas' English abilities were advanced enough that I also knew she had not misunderstood the instructions or the context of the statement. I quickly realized that Akhlas and I were operating on very different concepts of *family*. Akhlas' reaction to the statement about the size of her family indicated that she included a great number of people in her definition of family, a far greater number than I, a White middle-class American, might include. Perhaps she had been thinking of her family of origin rather than her family of marriage. Perhaps she defined *family* differently. As I came to better know the Sudanese refugees who participated in my research, it became increasingly clear that *family* held a very different connotation among the Sudanese than it did for me. This realization led me to ask many questions: What does this different conceptualization of family suggest about the diverse nature of families living in the US? How might this different notion of family impact refugee children's learning in schools? What would happen if teachers and schools used a broader definition of family? How might teachers' understandings of the resources children bring to the classroom change by broadening this definition of family? How might schools change their relationships with the families of their students by embracing this broader concept?

Examining the Concept of "Family"

Teachers know that families come in all shapes and sizes. Officially, however, we tend to define *family* as all of the related individuals who live in a single household. Typically, we mean nuclear families—parents and their children—when we say "family." This meaning is certainly reflected in official documents, such as census or food stamps forms, and in the research literature. My response to Akhlas' dilemma illustrates this cultural understanding; I automatically assumed that Akhlas' ESL homework referred to a nuclear family, all living in one household. In reality, however, families in the US, just like families around the world, come in all sorts of interesting configurations. The nuclear model of the family leaves out many common family types—single-parent households, children who are being raised by grandparents, step-families, and families where several generations live together in the same home, to name a few. However, this model also fails to recognize that even traditional nuclear families may have extended family networks in the same area—cousins who live down the street, grandparents across town, etc.

Family Literacy: A Lens for Thinking about Families

My own area of expertise is literacy, specifically family and community literacy, and the field of family literacy provides a useful lens for examining the ways in which the broader educational community treats the concept of family. Within the field of literacy, *family* has been defined using the nuclear model—members living in the same immediate household that is headed by biological parents. For example, language and literacy research conducted in this area tends to focus on the immediate home environment only, looking at such factors as socio-economic status, language spoken in the home, and available print in the home (Auerbach, 1989; Gadsden, 2000; Purcell-Gates, 2000). This research also focuses almost entirely on a child's parents; in fact, the majority of this research has focused exclusively on mothers, although there have been calls to look more closely at paternal literacy skills (Gadsden, 2000). In addition, research into parent–child interactions in the home tends to focus on storybook reading (Anderson, Smythe, & Shapiro, 2005; Auerbach, 1989; Edwards, 1995; Gadsden, 2000; Purcell-Gates, 2000) and not on other types of literacy and learning practices. Finally, these models also typically operate under the assumption that language and literacy development is unidirectional—that is, that children are influenced by parents. For these reasons, educational programs tend to focus on developing parents' skills (Auerbach, 1989; Edwards, 1995; Gadsden, 1998; Purcell-Gates, 2000).

Although the majority of family literacy research has focused on nuclear families, Gadsden (1998, 2000) prefers to define families using an intergenerational model. An intergenerational model of family, according to Gadsden, acknowledges that literacy development is impacted by more than just the individuals living in a particular household. It also challenges the one-way transmission model by arguing that literacy development is multi-directional; that is, children also influence their parents' (and other generations') literacy practices. Much of the ethnographic research investigating literacy in home and community settings supports this model. For example, Gregory (2005; Gregory & Williams, 2000) noted that siblings often play an important role as literacy teachers, or "guiding lights," in Bengali populations in East London. Similarly, Long and Volk's Chapter 10 in this book illustrates the ways in which children participate in extended networks of support for learning and teaching. In my own work with Sudanese refugee families, I have often seen young children specifically teaching their parents about English or computer technologies. Examples such as these challenge traditional conceptualizations of family and one-way transmission models of teaching and learning.

I hope to show that an expanded conceptualization of family has much to offer educators. An expanded definition of family may help us understand that children have many resources at their disposal. In my work with Sudanese families, I have seen both parents and children draw upon broad support networks of extended family and community mentors. In my work with orphaned Sudanese youth, I have seen the youth create a new definition of *family*. In both cases, non-nuclear families have provided important resources and support for students' educational achievement. By recognizing and valuing these extended networks and by learning how to tap into them, teachers will be better able to support literacy achievement for all students, but especially for marginalized students such as refugees.

THEORETICAL APPLICATION: BROADENING THE "FAMILY" IN FAMILY LITERACY

Research on family literacy helps educators recognize that children experience a wide variety of literacy experiences in their homes before and during their school years and to understand the ways that these experiences interact with school literacy learning. However, this research often focuses narrowly on the ways in which parents engage children in literacy practices. This may leave out many important relationships, events, settings, and resources that strongly influence children's literate activity and school learning. Think about your own schooling and literacy development and use. What individuals other than your parents influenced your learning or engaged with you in reading and writing? Picture in your mind a non-nuclear family with one or more children that you have known well. Who are the members of that family that shared responsibility for the children? How were or could they have been engaged in the children's schooling and literacy development?

My Research with Southern Sudanese Refugees: Context and Ideas

My work with Southern Sudanese refugees began shortly after I returned from serving as a U.S. Peace Corps Volunteer in Lesotho, Southern Africa. I learned about a local community of the so-called "Lost Boys of Sudan" who were seeking academic tutors, and I began working closely with three orphaned youth. After a year and a half, I joined the board of the Southern Sudan Rescue and Relief Association, a local organization comprised of both Sudanese refugee youth and Americans. My relationship with these youth ultimately led to a study of how they practiced literacy in their everyday lives. This work, and my deepening relationship with the local Sudanese community, led to a second research project, which involved: (1) examining the role of culture in the development of literacy practices of young children in intact Sudanese refugee families; and (2) the ways in which these families used literacy brokering to make sense of texts they encountered in the US.

My research with Sudanese refugees has been shaped by a sociocultural perspective on language and literacy. Within this framework, literacy is a social practice shaped by social, cultural, economic, political, and ideological forces (Barton & Hamilton, 1998; Barton, Hamilton, & Ivanič, 2000; Street, 2001). Researchers who study real-world, everyday literacy practices shed light on the multiple ways in which people use literacy, and they offer implications for the ways in which literacy instruction may be made more relevant to learners' lives. In my study with the orphaned youth (Perry, 2008; Perry, 2007a; Perry, 2005), I wanted to understand the refugees' beliefs about literacy, the different ways they used literacy in their lives, the ways in which different languages (e.g., English, Arabic, KiSwahili, and Dinka) related to literacy for the youth, and how well school literacy practices aligned with the everyday literacy practices of these refugees. In my study of refugee families with young children (see Perry, 2007b), I explored the ways that the refugee experience shaped parents' literacy practices, as well as the ways in which young children made sense of their literacy worlds across the contexts of home, community, and formal schooling.

For both studies, I used an ethnographic research methodology. Both studies relied on participant-observation, various types of interviews, and the collection of different literacy artifacts. Participant-observation in both studies involved spending a great deal of time in participants' homes. In the Lost Boys study, I collected data for seven months, from April to October, 2003. In the family study, data collection occurred over a period of 18 months, from February 2005 to July 2006. The research also involved spending time at community events such as church services and cultural celebrations. In the study of refugee families, I observed the focal children in their kindergarten or first grade classrooms. I interviewed participants about the types of texts and literacy practices that participants engaged with, both in their previous lives in Africa and in the US. I also collected life histories and other important cultural information. I gathered a variety of literacy artifacts, including texts that were read and written by focal participants and other community members, audio recordings of events such as church services, and photographs of literacy events and the literacy environments. I offered academic tutoring and community mentoring or cultural brokering services to the participants in both studies, which helped me gain access and build trust with the community and also was a way in which I could give back to participants.

Sudanese Refugees

Historical and Cultural Context

Issues facing Sudan are increasingly prominent in both international news media and global politics. Although much of the world is now aware of the plight of Darfur, many people are not aware that Southern Sudan has faced similar conflicts for over two decades. The Southern Sudanese are members of various tribes located in southern Sudan. These southerners, typically black African Christians (unlike the people of Darfur, who are Muslim), have been engaged in a civil war against the northern-dominated Arab Muslim government for over twenty years. This war was the result of centuries of deep ethnic and religious divisions (Bok, 2003; Deng, 1995), and it completely devastated Southern Sudan. At least two and a half million people were killed, and five million people were displaced as refugees—far more than have been affected in Darfur. The conflict in Southern Sudan caused a mass exodus of southerners, many of whom ended up as refugees in Egypt or the Kakuma Refugee Camp in Kenya, where they typically spent many years before being granted asylum in countries such as the United States, Canada, Great Britain, and Australia. The so-called "Lost Boys"[1] are a special case among the Southern Sudanese refugees. These orphaned youth began an arduous and dangerous journey of over 1,000 miles—entirely on foot. Only 7,000 of the original group survived to reach the Kakuma Refugee Camp in Kenya in 1992 (Yang, 2002).

The U.S. government has made a particular effort to resettle these youth (U.S. Department of State, 2001), who ranged in age from early teens to late twenties. In 2001, the US settled 3,800 youth, of which 85 were girls. According to a 2005 Office of Refugee Resettlement report, these youth

> have settled in eighteen states including Arizona, California, Colorado, Florida, Illinois, Kentucky, Massachusetts, Maine, Michigan, Minnesota, Missouri, North Carolina, New York, Pennsylvania, Texas, Utah, Virginia, Washington. The largest number of Lost Boys initially resettled in Texas (106), followed by Massachusetts (65), California (53), Pennsylvania (49), Washington (45), Utah (37), Arizona (33), New York (20), and Virginia (20).

At the time of my study, Michigan had resettled well over 200 orphaned youth, most of whom lived in Lansing and Grand Rapids.

The orphaned Sudanese youth, however, are not the only refugees who have resettled in Michigan. Like many states, Michigan has experienced unprecedented growth in immigrant and refugee populations: Michigan currently ranks 11th among states for total number of refugees in the US (GCIR, 2006). By 2007, nearly 10,000 refugees from Sudan, Cuba, Bosnia, Sierra Leone, Vietnam, Somalia, and many other countries lived in Lansing (Refugee Development Center, 2007).

---

1 These orphans were first called "Lost Boys" by a Western journalist who compared them to characters in *Peter Pan*. I prefer to call these refugees "orphaned youth," although some of the youth in Michigan refer to themselves as "Lost Boys" and others as "New Sudan Youth."

A Sudanese Definition of Family

The Sudanese refugees that I worked with think of family in a very broad sense; as Akhlas noted, there can be too many members to count. In fact, I often found myself perplexed by the relationships described by the families. The same individual might be referred to as an "aunt" on one occasion and as a "cousin" on another. The children often referred to their cousins as sisters and brothers. When some relatives were coming from Omaha, Nebraska, to visit Viola's family, for example, Viola told her son, Boni, that the family would be bringing their baby daughter. She told him, "Your sister is coming," and she let him know that he would be responsible for helping to watch over her. Extended family is so valued in this community that they even play an important role in wedding ceremonies. I attended a Sudanese wedding in which five members each of the bride's and the groom's extended families sat in places of honor and were served wedding cake by the bride and groom. The best man explained that in this culture, the bride and groom were not just marrying each other, they were also marrying each other's families.

Even those refugees who have been separated from their families by war manage to create new family-like networks. Yang (2002) documented the lives of the orphaned youth while they were still in Africa and the close bonds that the youth developed. He noted, "In the weeks and months of their journeys, traveling mostly at night to avoid being bombed from the air or captured by ground troops, lions were a constant threat. The boys began to form close-knit groups, a new sense of family following the loss of their own" (2002). The youth brought this new sense of family with them to the US, where several youth often lived together in an apartment or house. In fact, one tactic that the youth used in order to stay together when they were applying to come to the US was to claim kinship with other orphaned youth, because the refugee resettlement agencies tried to keep relatives together.

The Sudanese community in Lansing is relatively large, consisting of several hundred people, some of whom are related and some of whom are not. However, even unrelated refugees sometimes refer to each other as family. Viola, for example, introduced me to Falabia and told me, "We are like one family." She also told me that Falabia's elderly mother lived in Lansing, and that she was "like a mother" to the whole community. In many ways, there does not seem to be a clear boundary between the Sudanese definitions of *family* and *community* as they are enacted in the US; they are fluid and interconnecting concepts. Some of the refugees that I worked with even referred to Americans in familial terms. Akhlas' daughter, Remaz, not only referred to a White friend from church as her "auntie," but Remaz and her mother also called me "Auntie Kristen" as well! Clearly, close friends and other caregivers can be "family" as well as relatives by blood and by marriage.[2]

---

2 Of course, this occurs in the US, too; Dyson (2003), for example, describes a group of unrelated first graders who referred to themselves as "the brothers and the sisters."

Language and Literacy Practices of Sudanese Refugees: An Overview

The results of my research show that Southern Sudanese refugees use literacy in a variety of meaningful ways, and in many languages (see Table 2.1 for an overview). The orphaned youth, for example, attended school in English in Kakuma. They also learned KiSwahili, the national language of Kenya, and some became literate in Dinka or other local languages. Most also spoke Arabic to some degree. The refugee families were similarly multilingual and multi-literate. All of the parents were literate in both Arabic and English, although their comfort

Table 2.1 Overview of language and literacy practices among Sudanese refugees in Lansing

Participants	Languages spoken	Languages read and written	Sample literacy practices in key life domains

Orphaned youth	• Sudanese local languages (Dinka, Madi, etc.)
	• English
	• KiSwahili
	• Some Arabic
		• English
		• KiSwahili
		• Some Arabic
			School
			  • Reading textbooks and the Internet
			  • Writing essays, reports and other assignments
			Religion
			  • Reading the Bible
			  • Writing sermons
			Community participation
			  • Writing for community newsletters
			  • Reading Sudanese news websites
			  • Posting on Sudanese online bulletin boards
			  • Writing letters to the editor
			  • Taking notes at meetings
			Interpersonal communication
			  • Writing and reading emails and letters
			  • Jotting phone messages

Sudanese Parents	• Arabic
	• Sudanese local languages (Nuba, Baria, Zande, Latuka, etc.)
	• English
		• Arabic
		• English
		• Some local Sudanese languages
			Family life/parenting
			  • Reading letters, newsletters, forms and other texts from school
			  • Helping children with homework
			  • Filling in forms
			  • Reading to children
			  • Making grocery lists
			  • Reading prescription instructions
			    (*Continued overleaf*)

Table 2.1 Continued

Participants	Languages spoken	Languages read and written	Sample literacy practices in key life domains
			Religion • Reading the Bible • Writing to request prayers • Participating in spiritual book clubs • Reading church newsletters • Singing from the hymnal School • Reading textbooks • Searching the Internet • Writing essays, reports and other assignments • Completing ESL workbook exercises • Using the dictionary • Taking notes from lectures • Completing exams Work • Filling in job applications • Checking schedules • Completing paperwork News/Information • Reading newspapers • Searching the Internet
Young Sudanese children	• Arabic • English	• English (emerging)	School • Participating in reading groups • Writing in journals • Filling in worksheets • Completing homework Family life • Explaining documents to parents • Helping parents with English • Going to the library Play • Pretend reading • Writing notes/letters to friends • Labeling drawings • Playing online computer games • Exploring the Internet

levels with English varied. The families spoke both English and Arabic at home, and the parents also spoke a variety of other local Sudanese languages. The children in these families, therefore, drew upon a rich variety of linguistic resources.

Many of the meaningful literacy practices in this community of refugees focused around key areas of their lives. Religion, for example, played an important role in shaping literacy practices for most of these refugees. Church life and reading the Bible, in both English and Arabic, provided important motivations for these refugees to read and write. In addition, staying in touch with friends and family who had either been left behind in Africa or resettled in other parts of the world guided many of the literacy practices of this community. The Sudanese refugees also actively sought information about the political situation and the peace process in Sudan. Although most had had little, if any, access to computer technology in Africa, many refugees had become very skilled in the US at navigating the Internet to access information about their homeland. Significantly, education and formal schooling played a very large role in the literacy lives of these refugees. The Sudanese community highly valued education—they saw it as not only a way to better their own individual lives, but more importantly as a way to improve the situation in Sudan. Many of the refugees felt that it was their duty to obtain a good education so that they could go back to Africa and help to build a New Sudan. The orphaned youth, in particular, strongly believed in the power of education. Ezra explained his hunger for education this way:

> I saw it necessary for me to be able to read and write, because—maybe partly because I was there by myself, alone, and I have seen many professionals, and I admired what they do and their positions, and the kind of life that they were living. I was so desperate, living by myself without any parents, without any relatives, without any older person to give me advice and guidance—so, I felt that as long as I live and as long as God keeps me alive and lets me breathe, I would do anything I could to become one day a professional like some of the people that I saw there.

In fact, there is even a proverb among the youth: "Education is my mother and my father" (Lost Boys of Sudan, n.d.).

Individual Snapshots

The Sudanese refugees drew upon extended family resources in many ways as they adjusted to life in America and as they pursued education. In this section, I will provide snapshots of two refugees—one orphaned young man, and a little girl from an intact family—to show how family networks supported these students' educational and literacy achievement. Table 2.2 provides an overview of available family networks and community resources.

Table 2.2 Two snapshots of the intertwined issues of family and community for young refugees

Individual snapshots	Extended family networks	Community resources
Chol	• Dinka tribal elders in Kakuma Refugee Camp • Sudanese foster parents in Kakuma • American foster families • Sudanese refugee youth in the U.S. • Brothers' Union Investment Club	• Social worker at Lutheran Social Services • Academic tutor • Community mentors • Southern Sudan Rescue and Relief Association members • Church network
Remaz	• Biological parents • Aunts, uncles and cousins • Other Sudanese community members • Sponsoring family from U.S. church	• American "Aunties" • Social worker at Refugee Services • Academic tutor • Community mentors • Church network

Chol[3]

Chol was the first Sudanese refugee that I began tutoring, shortly after I returned from living in Africa myself. When I met him, Chol was about 18 years old, although he was not exactly sure of his age. He was still a senior in high school, and he had recently moved out of a foster home and into an apartment with other Sudanese refugee youth. Lutheran Social Services hired me to tutor Chol and two other youth still living in foster homes. Chol graduated from high school a few months after I began working with him, and I continued to tutor him as he began a degree program at a local private university.

Chol's story is typical of most of the orphaned Sudanese youth. Chol, a member of the Dinka tribe, became separated from his family when he was about four years old. He has since regained contact with a brother and some other relatives who live in Khartoum. In an autobiography assignment for school, Chol wrote,

> The war separated me from [my] parents in 1986, and I have learned and experienced problems and many other consequences from it. I have seen many people dying, drowning and starving. I am a survivor of that war. In 1986 I escaped to Ethiopia, where I learned the life of being a child refugee in that country. I was lonely without my parents.

The Lost Boys were forced out of Ethiopia and went to Kenya. Chol explained that in Kakuma he formed new family units with other refugees. Many of the

---

3 A pseudonym. The Institutional Review Board approval for this project required me to use pseudonyms. The families in my second study, however, all chose to use their real names as they participated in my research.

orphaned children, including Chol, lived with foster mothers there. Chol and the other youth that I interviewed for my first study explained that few community elders lived in the camp, but those who were available were very important to the youth. These elders used storytelling to pass on Dinka culture, history, beliefs and values to the youth, and they also offered important guidance. For example, Chol told me that when the youth were first offered the opportunity to come and live in America, they consulted with the community elders. These elders at first advised them not to go, worried that the youth might be sold into slavery. Chol explained, "The community said, 'No, maybe you are going to be given to the Arab people.' " In fact, the American representative made several visits over two years before she convinced the community that bringing orphaned youth to the US was a good idea. Southern Sudanese cultures tend to view orphanhood as an exceptionally deprived condition (Deng, 1995), so it is not surprising that the community came together to provide family-like structures and guidance to the orphaned youth.

These new family structures carried over into the youths' lives in the US. Many chose to live together. Those who had access to academic tutors or helpful American foster families frequently called upon these people to help mentor those who had less access. Chol, for example, often asked if I could come over and fix his roommate's computer. The youth with better jobs and steadier sources of income often supported those who did not. In fact, Chol organized several of his friends into the Brothers' Union Investment Club (see Figure 2.1). The members of the Brothers' Union each deposited a small sum of money in the club's account each month, and this money was used to support members in need. For example, a member who needed to pay for car repairs could use the pooled money. This is a common support system in many African communities; indeed, the women in my village in Lesotho had a similar investment club. What I think is particularly interesting here is the name of the group: the Brothers' Union. This name clearly reflects the ways in which these unrelated young men created a new sense of family—not only in name, but also as a source of real, practical support.

The wider American community also embraced these orphaned youth and provided them with many family-like resources. Social services agencies not only provided caseworkers for the refugees, but they also received grant money to support the youths' education and cultural adjustment. For two years or so after the youths' arrival in Lansing, social service agencies offered a weekly evening program that provided academic tutoring, sessions in cultural adjustment, drivers' education, and recreation time. Each refugee youth who came over as a minor also had funding available to him (and to the handful of "Lost Girls" who also came to this area) specifically for educational uses. This money could be used for tutoring, to buy textbooks once the youth reached college-level education, or for other educational resources. Chol, for example, used some of the money to buy himself a computer to use for schoolwork.

Like many refugee youth, Chol developed relationships with Americans who could help him in different ways. Because Chol knew me as a tutor and as a teacher, he often called upon me to help him (and his friends) with academic tasks. Once, Chol's friend wanted to send a letter to a church asking if they could

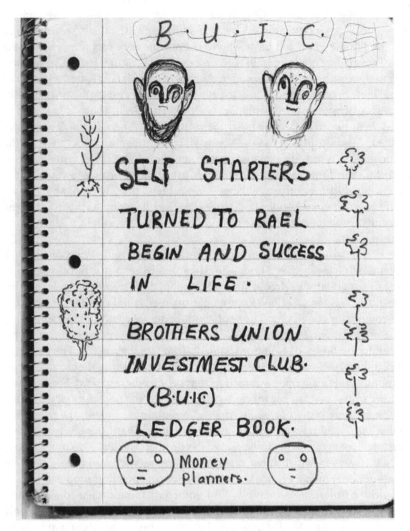

Figure 2.1 A page from the Brother's Union Investment Club ledger.

provide support for his family back in Africa. Chol asked me to come over and help edit the letter. Chol also developed a relationship with a middle-aged couple who helped him get his apartment set up, taught him how to drive, and helped him with car-related problems. As he delved more deeply into his business studies, he found a retired businessman who mentored him. In fact, these other Americans and I developed a family-like relationship with Chol. At times when Chol needed help—after an auto accident, for example—we often called or emailed each other to check on Chol, much like anxious parents.

Chol was also a community leader among the other orphaned youth in the area, and Lutheran Social Services tapped into his leadership abilities. He helped them organize Sudanese community events, and he regularly contributed a column to the refugee newsletter. Chol also helped found the Southern Sudan Rescue and Relief Association, a community organization comprised of both Sudanese refugees and Americans that worked on improving the lives of the Sudanese. All of the Americans on the board worked closely with Sudanese orphaned youth, serving as foster parents and community mentors. Chol's participation in this group shows how intertwined issues of family and community are for this group of refugees.

Remaz

Remaz is a much younger refugee child, just beginning her education in a US kindergarten. She is the daughter of Akhlas, the mother I described at the beginning of this chapter. Akhlas and her husband Amin come from the Nuba Mountains region of Sudan. The Nuba live farther to the north than most Southern Sudanese, but they have been similarly marginalized and are allied with the Southerners. When I first met Remaz, she was a precocious five-year-old who was equally comfortable conversing in English and in her family's dialect of Arabic. Unlike Chol, Remaz lived with both of her parents and her younger brother, Remon. Remaz's parents both attended school in Sudan; her mother completed primary school, and her father attended a year or two of high school. In Michigan, Remaz's mother worked as a seamstress at a uniform factory, and her father washed dishes in a local hotel, until he became very ill and had to have surgery as a result of complications from a gunshot wound he had received in the conflict in Sudan.

Lansing has a large Sudanese refugee community, and Remaz's family was part of a network of many refugee families with children. Akhlas was close friends with Falabia, another mother whose family participated in my research, and Remaz often played with Falabia's children. Remaz was close with Juana, the focal child from Falabia's family, and she adored Juana's live-in teenage cousin Golda, who often braided Remaz's hair into intricate hairstyles. It was common for various Sudanese community members to visit Remaz's home while I was there. Other Sudanese families also lived in the same apartment complex, and they often stopped by for tea, to have their hair done, or to watch DVDs of African television programs and music videos. Remaz referred to many of these community members as relatives. One day, she waved to someone who was pulling out of the parking lot and said, "That's my auntie!"

Remaz had several extended family members who lived in the area, as well. Akhlas' cousin (whom she sometimes referred to as "sister") lived nearby, and Akhlas and the children often stayed there if Amin was out of town. Amin was hospitalized for several weeks, and Akhlas' cousin cared for Remaz and her brother for much of that time. Another time, Akhlas showed me a picture of a large group of Sudanese women that was taken when the family was still living in Egypt. Akhlas lovingly named the women, carefully explaining their relationship to her (e.g., her uncle's wife) and telling me where these women now lived, scattered across Africa, Europe, North America, and Australia. Although Remaz's nuclear family was intact, her extended family was spread across the globe, and they keenly felt the separation. A much larger community of people from the

Nuba Mountains lived in Ohio, and Akhlas and her family often traveled there to visit extended family members. Indeed, they seriously contemplated a move to that region to be closer to their family and ethnic group.

Like Chol, Remaz had access to an extended American support group as well. Remaz's family had been sponsored by a local church, which they continued to attend, despite the fact that most Sudanese refugees in the area attended two other churches with large African congregations. Church members actively supported Remaz's family. For example, when Amin was out of work due to his surgery, the church provided gift cards to local stores to help with living expenses. When it became apparent that the family's apartment was not a healthy living environment, someone at the church offered one of her rental properties to the family at a discounted rate. Carrie,[4] a middle-class White member of the church, frequently acted as a cultural broker and community mentor for the family. She took the children on outings, invited them over to swim in her pool, and handed down used children's books and educational videos. Carrie also dropped Remaz off at school every morning and picked her up each afternoon, and she kept in touch with Remaz's teacher. I often heard Akhlas and Remaz refer to Carrie as "auntie." "Auntie" Carrie clearly played an important role in Remaz's family; Remaz even insisted, "She's my auntie for real."

Like Carrie, I also became Remaz's "auntie." After I had been working with Akhlas' family for several months, she and the children began referring to me as "Auntie Kristen." When I once discussed with Remaz the issue of Carrie being her auntie, Remaz told me, "You're my auntie, too." In fact, becoming an "auntie" in this family was what first caused me to think about family in a broader way. I was clearly not part of Remaz's actual family, nor was I a true member of the Sudanese community, but I did play an important role in the family's literacy practices and educational development. I helped Remaz with her homework each week and also tutored her mother in English literacy. Because my research also took me into Remaz's classroom, I sometimes acted as a liaison between the family and Remaz's teacher. In addition, I also acted as a literacy broker for the family—Akhlas regularly called me to help her understand a letter from the school or fill in a necessary form, such as food stamps paperwork. Carrie and I are both good examples of how refugee families draw upon family-like resources outside of their cultural communities as they adjust to life in this country and as they support their children's educational experiences.

Remaz's family also challenges the traditional one-way transmission model of literacy development that suggests that literacy skills are only passed from parents to children. Like many bilingual children, Remaz often acted as a language and literacy broker for her parents. In conversations with me, Akhlas often called upon Remaz to supply her with an English word. Akhlas frequently described Remaz as her teacher, and I often observed this little girl (who had just turned six) not only supplying her mother with English vocabulary, but also actively explaining English grammar and spelling rules! "Yeah, she teach me," Akhlas explained, "My best

4 A pseudonym.

teacher—Remaz!" Clearly, Remaz played an important role in shaping her parents' English literacy development, just as they supported her by seeking out tutors and providing her with the time, space, and materials to complete her schoolwork.

What Can Teachers Do?

As these cases illustrate, refugee students have a wide variety of supportive familial resources available to them, although they do not necessarily fit neatly within traditional conceptualizations of family. Clearly, Chol was without family in the traditional American sense. He had no parents, and the "brothers" with whom he was close in the US are biologically unrelated to him. Yet, without traditional family supports, Chol succeeded very well in the American educational system; not only did he earn a high school diploma but also recently finished his bachelor's degree. A traditional concept of *family* is largely irrelevant for a student like Chol. A broadened concept of family—one that includes both an extended definition of family and community resources—would fit him well. This broadened concept shows that Chol's family—community mentors, tutors, social workers, and Sudanese "brothers"—supports his learning in a variety of ways. Similarly, according to traditional family models, most schools would likely consider Remaz's family as "deficient" because they were still developing their English language and literacy skills, and because they had no experience with the American educational system. Yet, Remaz had access to an extensive network of both Sudanese and American community resources; her Sudanese cousins and her American "aunties" provided a great deal of familial and educational support.

Chol and Remaz illustrate why traditional definitions of family may shortchange refugee students. Family literacy programs that only target parents and students' immediate households ignore the fact that children's lives draw upon extended family resources and community connections. Programs that assume that literacy development is a one-way street from parents to children also ignore the realities of many immigrant and refugee families where the children's English literacy skills may be more developed than the parents, and where children may be important partners in developing other family members' literacy skills. Other adults in the Sudanese community also take important roles in educating children and providing them with important developmental experiences. For example, Viola explained to me that one woman in the Sudanese community often gathered together the young children and took them on important outings to such things as the movies and the zoo: "Some kids, they don't know what is the—what is a movie. They don't know people go out to watch movies, because parents cannot take them, never take them there."

THEORETICAL APPLICATION: CULTURALLY RESPONSIVE PEDAGOGY

Often teachers have limited understanding of immigrant families' communities and available resources. Most teachers live in outside communities and their interactions with students tend to be limited to the school environment. Research on *culturally responsive pedagogy* argues for educational practices that build upon and are responsive to the linguistic, interactional, cognitive and learning patterns of diverse families. A culturally sensitive curriculum encompasses the social, cultural and intellectual resources and expertise of diverse students, families and communities. Central to this view is using students' prior knowledge and experiences as entry points into school curricula. Students' realities are seen as resources rather than tagged as "deficient" or "at risk." Thus, the concept of "family" literacy programs go beyond mainstream practices and training minority families on how to emulate them. They are designed based on partnership principles in which families, like the educators involved, are viewed as experts. Consider family literacy programs in your local area. What are their definitions of family literacy? What types of knowledge are valued and who possesses them? What types of role are families expected to take on?

Investigating Family Networks

The revised conceptualization of family that I am proposing would take into account these extended family and community networks. How can teachers and schools use such a model to their advantage? Most importantly, teachers and other school officials should find out what sorts of familial and community networks support their students. Home visits and parent interviews or surveys are, of course, useful tools for finding out about students' home lives. These tools are less useful, however, if parents' English language skills are limited. Home visits also may simply reinforce traditional conceptualizations of family, because as the name implies, home visits focus on a student's immediate household and may not account for extended family or community resources. Table 2.3 summarizes ways in which teachers can investigate family and community networks.

Teachers may want to interview their students individually. Most teachers spend a great deal of time assessing students' literacy development in the classroom through running records, reading and writing conferences, and other regularly-scheduled assessments. Teachers can substitute student interviews in place of one round of running records or other similar assessments. The teacher would use this interview to gather information about the student's family and other support networks, about literacy and learning practices in the home, and other information relevant to schooling. Table 2.3 offers questions that may guide such interviews.

If students have older siblings or cousins who attend the same school or who are known to the teacher, these relatives also can be important sources of family information, particularly in immigrant and refugee families where adults may have limited English abilities or who may work job shifts that make it difficult to connect with the teacher. Teachers also may find it useful to have a concrete object, such as a family photograph, that can help facilitate these interviews. Gadsden (1998) found similar family portraits to be particularly useful ways to

Table 2.3 Learning about family and community networks: What can teachers do?

Investigating family and community networks	Guiding questions	Examples of types of information that can support school learning
• Individual interviews	• Who lives in your house? • Do you have other family members who live near here? • In your family, who goes to school? • Who helps you with homework? • What languages do people speak and/or read in your family? • What kinds of things do people in the family read? • What kinds of things do people in the family write? • Does the family have a computer? A connection to the Internet? • Do family members have library cards? If so, how often do they visit the library? Does the library offer computer access? • What does your family do in the evenings and on weekends?	• Who counts as "family" for a child? • Languages spoken, read and/or written in the home and community • Valued family practices • Family schedules, including parents'/guardians' work
• Using concrete objects (like a photograph, drawing or family tree) to facilitate conversation	• Who lives in your house? • Who is part of your family? • Do you have other family members who live near here? • Tell me what you remember about life in your country. • What was school like in your country?	• Definitions of family • Extended family and community resources • Knowledge about past experiences, including education • Familial beliefs, values, and attitudes about education
• Interviewing siblings and cousins	• [See questions for individual interviews, above] • Are there other significant adults who live outside of the home also involved in the child's life (e.g., aunts/uncles, cousins, grandparents, community mentors, tutors, social workers, etc.)? • How are these significant adults involved? What do they do with/for the child and family?	• Who helps with homework or provides other learning opportunities (trips to the library, access to the Internet, etc.) • Valued family practices • Access to learning resources • Access to community services, such as tutoring or mentoring • Access to other support networks, such as faith communities *(Continued overleaf)*

36 Kristen H. Perry

Investigating family and community networks	Guiding questions	Examples of types of information that can support school learning
	• What kinds of activities does the family take part in with this community? • Do family members participate in any community clubs or organizations (YMCA, Scouting, Boys and Girls Clubs, etc)?	
• Accessing community resources	• Does the family belong to a church, mosque, synagogue, or other faith community? • Does the family have a social worker, community mentor, or sponsor? • What tutoring/mentoring services are available for immigrant or refugee families in this area? • Is there funding to support academic tutoring and educational materials?	• Access to community resources • Access to social services, tutoring, and mentoring • Access to funding that may support education
• Examining school-based programs	• Does our program include family members beyond parents? • How can our program draw upon siblings or other community youth as resources? • How can our program include non-family members, such as tutors, mentors, or "big brothers/ sisters"? • How can we learn about the families and communities we serve, and use that information to improve our programs?	• Awareness of extended familial support networks • Knowledge about individual families and communities • Familiarity with family or community beliefs, values, attitudes and expectations about education • Possibilities for collaboration with families and communities

find out about family relationships and family cultures. Asking students to bring in photos of family members and other significant individuals in the child's life could be supplemented by children's own drawings of family portraits or their creation of family trees. Students could create these artifacts in class or as a homework project with their families.

Accessing Community Resources

Most children—immigrants, refugees, and those born in the US—have access to some community resources. Many children who are affiliated with churches or other faith communities have access to educational and other support services through their churches, as Remaz's case illustrates. Through faith communities, children may be involved in religious education classes or youth groups that can serve as a support for literacy development. In a literacy interview, teachers may want to ask their students about religious affiliation. Although discussing religion in school can be uncomfortable, teachers may be able to use this information to contact the child's church, mosque, or synagogue to find out about available resources. Other children may be involved in programs such as Boy or Girl Scouts, Big Brothers/Big Sisters, or the Boys and Girls Club of America. These programs often serve as an important source of mentoring and tutoring for children, and again, teachers may be able to work with their child's tutor or mentor.

Refugee children often have a variety of community resources available to them that other immigrant children do not. Unlike other immigrants, refugee families typically are assigned a caseworker within the social services agency that resettled them in the area. Asking about and contacting the family's caseworker may prove useful to both the teacher and the student; the teacher may be able to learn important information about the family and the broader ethnic community of refugees, and she may also discover that there are resources available to the family—such as tutoring or funding for educational supplies—that the family is currently unaware of. Some refugee communities have access to specific grant funding for educational support, as Chol did, and social service agencies often have networks of tutors who have experience working with refugee families. Many refugee families are sponsored by local churches, even if the families are not members of that faith community. These churches sometimes have specific funds available to support sponsored families, and they also may be able to connect families with tutors or community mentors. In addition, contacting a family's sponsoring church could alert the church to the fact that the family may be in need of certain resources, such as school supplies or children's books in English.

School-Based Family Programs

Many schools or districts offer family programs in literacy, math, science and other academic content areas, and some individual teachers offer parent workshops or send home support materials if their schools or districts do not offer such programs. These programs would do well to consider broader conceptions of family as they design their programs and their materials. These programs must recognize that parents may not be the only significant caregivers or resources that children draw upon. In many African cultures, for example, older children play an important role in the care and education of younger siblings (Rogoff, 2003). This was certainly the case among the Sudanese community in Lansing. In Remaz's friend Juana's family, for example, older children played a significant role in helping younger children with homework or in engaging them in storybook reading; again, a relationship that most traditional family programs neglect. Extended family and community mentors may also spend significant amounts of time with children and work to support their educational development in different ways.

School-based programs can build upon the knowledge that teachers gain through student interviews to develop family and community educational programs that reflect the actual networks that support children's learning. These programs should offer activities not only for parents and children, for example, but they should also include older siblings and cousins, grandparents, aunts and uncles and other extended family, and tutors or other mentors. Based upon what teachers and school administrators know about their students, these programs could put together packets of materials that direct families to the relevant available community resources. For example, schools with large refugee populations could compile a list of the resources available through the social service and other resettlement agencies.

Conclusion: Implications for Teaching and Research

Why should we expand our notion of what constitutes family? Too often, children from marginalized communities, such as the Sudanese refugees that I worked with, are characterized as "deficient" or "at-risk." Educators often believe that these students have few resources available to them. Using a broader conception of family, one based upon how non-mainstream communities such as the Sudanese refugees define family, shows that children actually have a wide variety of supportive resources available to them. It is true that many children may not be getting the support from parents that educators might like them to get, but it is equally true that this important support could be coming from extended family members or the wider community. A broader notion of family also better reflects the realities of many cultural communities, where family is not limited to the nuclear family/household model. It also helps to counteract traditional deficit models that suggest that refugee and other immigrant children necessarily are at risk in terms of language and literacy development or general academic achievement. This expanded model can help teachers to understand the rich resources that refugee children bring to the classroom, as well as help teachers understand how to tap into extended family and community support for the child.

Ideas for Discussion, Extension, and Application

1. Quickly make a list of individuals other than your parents who supported your school learning. Share your list with a group of classmates, briefly describing some of the specific ways that those individuals assisted or encouraged you.
2. Discuss what stands out or surprises you about Chol's and Remaz's cases. Imagine having one of them as a student. As a teacher, how

might you benefit from the detailed knowledge about their extended families and community resources that Perry provides?
3. Discuss how teachers and schools can avoid falling into using the traditional conception of the nuclear family as they think about, communicate with, assign work to, and plan events and develop materials for students' families.
4. Discuss the specific strategies that you have or will use to learn about and utilize your students' extended family networks in ways that might support and extend their school learning.

References

Anderson, J., Smythe, S., & Shapiro, J. (2005). Working and learning with families, communities, and schools: A critical case study. In Anderson, J., Kendrick, M., Rogers, T., & Smythe, S. (Eds.), *Portraits of literacy across families, communities, and schools* (pp. 63–86). Mahwah, NJ: Lawrence Erlbaum Associates.

Auerbach, E. R. (1989). Toward a socio-contextual approach to family literacy. *Harvard Educational Review, 59*, 165–181.

Barton, D., & Hamilton, M. (1998). *Local literacies: Reading and writing in one community.* London: Routledge.

Barton, D., Hamilton, M., & Ivanič, R. (Eds.). (2000). *Situated literacies: Reading and writing in context.* London: Routledge.

Bok, F. (2003). *Escape from slavery.* New York: St. Martin's Press.

Camarota, S. A. (2005). *Immigrants at mid-decade: A snapshot of America's foreign-born in 2005.* Retrieved March 30, 2007 from: http://www.cis.org/articles/2005/back1405.html.

Deng, F. M. (1995). *War of visions: Conflict of identities in the Sudan.* Washington, DC: The Brookings Institution.

Dyson, A. H. (2003). *The Brothers and the Sisters learn to write: Popular literacies in childhood and school cultures.* New York: Teachers College Press.

Edwards, P. A. (1995). Empowering low-income mothers and fathers to share books with young children. *The Reading Teacher, 48*, 558–565.

Gadsden, V. L. (1998). Family cultures and literacy learning. In J. Osborn, & F. Lehr (Eds.), *Literacy for all: Issues in teaching and learning* (pp. 32–50). New York: Guilford Press.

Gadsden, V. L. (2000). Intergenerational literacy within families. In M. L. Kamil, P. B. Mosenthal, P. D. Pearson, & R. Barr (Eds.), *Handbook of reading research* (pp. 871–887). Mahwah, NJ: Lawrence Erlbaum Associates.

Grantmakers Concerned with Immigrants and Refugees (GCIR) (2006). *U.S. immigration statistics by state.* Retrieved March 29, 2006, from: http://www.gcir.org/about_immigration/usmap/michigan.htm.

Gregory, E. (2005). Guiding lights: Siblings as literacy teachers in a multilingual community. In J. Anderson, M. Kendrick, T. Rogers, & S. Smythe, (Eds.), *Portraits of literacy across families, communities, and schools,* (pp. 21–40). Mahwah, NJ: Lawrence Erlbaum Associates.

Gregory, E., & Williams, A. (2000). *City literacies: Learning to read across generations and cultures.* London: Routledge.

Lost Boys of Sudan (n.d.). *Lost Boys of Sudan.* Retrieved March 20, 2005, from http://www.lostboysofsudan.com.

Migration Policy Institute (2007). *Fact sheet on the foreign born: Demographic & social characteristics (Michigan).* Retrieved March 29, 2007, from http://www.migration information.org/DataHub/state.cfm?ID=MI.

Office of Refugee Resettlement (2005). *Annual ORR Reports to Congress—2005.* Retrieved June 10, 2008, from http://www.acf.hhs.gov/programs/orr/data/05arc9.htm#1.

Perry, K. (2005). "Helping our people": The role of literacies in mediating community among Sudanese refugees. Paper presented at the meeting of the American Educational Research Association, Montreal, Canada, April.

Perry, K. (2007a). Sharing stories, linking lives: Literacy practices among Sudanese refugees. In V. Purcell-Gates (Ed.), *Cultural practices of literacy: Case studies of language, literacy, social practice, and power.* Mahwah, NJ: Lawrence Erlbaum.

Perry, K. (2007b). "Look, you have to sign": Literacy practices among Sudanese refugee families. Unpublished doctoral dissertation, Michigan State University, East Lansing.

Perry, K. (2008). From storytelling to writing: Transforming literacy practices among Sudanese refugees. *Journal of Literacy Research, 40,* 317–358.

Purcell-Gates, V. (2000). Family literacy. In M. L. Kamil, P. B. Mosenthal, P. D. Pearson, & R. Barr (Eds), *Handbook of reading research* (pp. 853–870). Mahwah, NJ: Lawrence Erlbaum Associates.

Refugee Development Center (2007). *Who are the refugees?* Retrieved June 26, 2007, from http://www.refugeedevelopmmentcenter.com/refugees/refugees.htm

Rogoff, B. (2003). *The cultural nature of human development.* Oxford: Oxford University Press.

Street, B. (2001). The new literacy studies. In E. Cushman, G.R. Kintgen, B.M. Kroll, & M. Rose (Eds.), *Literacy: A critical sourcebook* (pp. 430–442). Boston: St. Martin's Press.

U.S. Dept of State (2001). Fact sheet: Sudanese (Kakuma) youth, June 11. Retrieved February 28, 2004, from: http://www.state.gov/g/prm/rls/fs/2001/3398.htm.

Yang, D. C. (2002). *Kakuma Turkana.* St. Paul, MN: Pangaea.

3 The Impact of Social Dynamics on Immigrant Children's Language and Literacy Practices

Learning from Asian Families

Guofang Li

> It's 9:30 a.m. on a Monday morning. Mrs. Haines, the teacher of a grade one and two combined class, finished her routine morning messages and started to check her students' reading logs that were returned from home. The reading logs required the parents to record the titles of the books that their children read at home in the past two weeks. She found that Ling-ling's reading log was left blank again. Ling-ling was a student who came from China and her parents could not speak English. Mrs. Haines wondered whether Ling-ling read any books even in Chinese at home; otherwise her parents would have recorded the titles in Chinese as they should know how to write Chinese. Frustrated, Mrs. Haines did not know how to find out what Ling-ling did after school or whether her parents valued reading, especially parent–child shared reading at home.

The above vignette demonstrates the challenges many classroom teachers face when they try to understand children from diverse cultural and linguistic backgrounds in order to better facilitate learning in the classroom. These children bring with them diversity in language, culture, religion, and even academic preparation (Moll & González, 1994). The changing demographics in today's schools pose unprecedented urgency for educators to understand children's outside school social and academic experiences. According to the U.S. Census Bureau's 2001 population projection, in 2050, one of the greatest increases in the U.S. population will be Asian Pacific American (Asian-American) (from 3.7% in 2000 to 8.9% in 2050), an increase second only to that of the Hispanic population. In Canada, Asia and Pacific countries have become the leading source of immigrants since the 1990s (53.01% in 2001), with China (including Hong Kong) being the No. 1 source country (Citizenship and Immigration Canada, 2002). With the increase of the Asian population in North America, the number of school age Asian Pacific children has also increased tremendously, with a six-fold increase between 1960 and 1990. The growth is expected to continue at a high rate in the U.S. and Canada.

Although Asian-American children have become one of the fastest growing populations in North American schools, we know very little about the ways in which their learning is supported at home, the factors that influence their home experiences, and how their home learning (e.g., in language and literacy) differs from school experiences. Previous research on Asian families have predominantly focused on cultural aspects (e.g., parenting styles and acculturation and identity issues) and few studies have explored how the social dynamics within the families influence Asian children's home literacy and learning experiences. In order to better understand Asian children's home experiences, in this chapter, I draw on several ethnographic studies conducted in the home milieu of Asian families to examine divergent social dynamics that affect Asian immigrant children and their families' home literacy experiences. These social dynamics include intergenerational issues, differential experiences among siblings of different gender, and issues of school and home relations and connections.

Theoretical Framework

This analysis is situated within a socio-constructivist and socio-cultural framework. From a socio-constructivist perspective, literacy learning is seen as a dynamic process that involves complex social relationships between the learners and members of their particular socio-cultural contexts, such as the mainstream school and the Chinese family's home milieu. Gee (1989, 1996) refers to these different socio-cultural contexts as different Discourses. By Discourses with a capital "D," he means a plural set of cultural practices or culturally appropriate ways of thinking, believing, valuing, acting, interacting, speaking, reading, writing, and listening). In Gee's terms, the home milieu is the place where students are socialized into the primary Discourses that are often associated with their first languages and cultures or one's first identity. The socializations outside of home such as school, church, and businesses are considered secondary Discourses. These Discourses are not equal, however. As Gee (1989, 1996) points out, there is also a distinction between the dominant or non-dominant Discourses. Dominant Discourses are those Discourses (often secondary Discourses) that add social status and privilege, and are thus accompanied by the associated benefits and social goods. Non-dominant Discourses allow membership and belonging within a particular social network but are not often accompanied by any wider benefits or social goods. Therefore, primary and secondary Discourses can sometimes become competing forces that affect students' identity development and social networks. In this chapter, I focus on the competing forces and factors across the two Discourses that affect Asian students' learning and socialization in and out of their home contexts. In this chapter, the Asian home literacy experiences are seen as different from the mainstream literacy beliefs and cultural traditions in the school Discourse.

THEORETICAL APPLICATION: BIG "D" DISCOURSE

It is easy to see that children inherit different ways of speaking in different families and cultural communities. The concept of big "D" Discourse extends this basic point, stressing that families socialize children into not just a way of speaking but also into a broader Discourse, a way of looking at one's self and the world, understanding and interacting with others, and valuing and engaging in many types of everyday activities. Further, the idea of secondary Discourses allows us to see that schools produce and reward a particular pattern of beliefs, values, and ways of behaving, interacting, speaking, reading, writing, etc. While all children will inevitably experience some degree of conflict as they move from home Discourses to school Discourses, this transition will be far easier for those children whose primary or family Discourse more closely parallels school Discourse. Teachers of children whose primary Discourses differ greatly from school Discourse should understand and value the students' primary Discourses and also help them acquire crucial dispositions and behaviors associated with school Discourse. Think about school Discourse. What specific kinds of beliefs, values, and ways of behaving, interacting, speaking, and using literacy are rewarded in schools? Have you known children whose primary Discourse differed greatly from school Discourse? What was their school experience like? What specific actions can you take to be a sensitive and effective teacher of such children?

From a socio-cultural perspective, literacy is part of culture. People of a given culture practice literacy in ways that reflect what they value and what they do; beliefs of what literacy is and what it means vary from culture to culture. Thus, shaped by different social and cultural norms, literacy practices—their functions, meanings, and methods of transmission and instruction—vary from one cultural group to another (Street, 1993). In cross-cultural contexts, the meaning of literacy practices arises in ongoing interaction and negotiation between individuals or groups from different cultural backgrounds (Spradley & McCurdy, 1990). For the families included in this study, the meaning of literacy is often negotiated among different family members, including siblings, their parents and grandparents, and between family members and members of the school community, such as peers and teachers. Therefore, different interactions and social dynamics among various members and groups may influence how the meaning of literacy is negotiated.

Methods: Multi-sited, Cross-Case Analyses

In order to further illustrate the ways literacy is supported in different Asian families and the social dynamics that influence their home practices, I conducted a multi-sited, cross-case analysis of qualitative data from three ethnographic studies previously completed in three different cities, namely, Saskatoon and Vancouver, Canada, and Buffalo, New York. The multi-site cross-case analyses allowed me to address the same research question in different settings with studies that have used similar data collection and analysis procedures. The similarities in the settings permitted me to conduct cross-site comparison without necessarily sacrificing within-site understanding (Heaton, 1998; Merriam, 1998). Such an analytical approach will help facilitate a better understanding of the complexity of home literacy practices embedded in different socio-cultural contexts.

Three studies in the three sites were selected because they each represent a different socio-cultural location and/or a different ethnic group. As indicated earlier, all studies were ethnographic in nature and data for each study were collected through interviews (formal and informal), participant observations, fieldnotes, and document collections. Specifically, one Filipino family from the Saskatoon site, one Chinese family from the Vancouver site and one Vietnamese family from the Buffalo site were selected. Data for the Filipino family were collected during 1998–1999; data for the Chinese family were collected during 2000–2001; and data for the Vietnamese family were collected during 2004–2006.

Following Merriam's (1998) suggestion for cross-case analysis, a within-case analysis is first carried out to determine whether the separate studies have both the uniqueness and the commonality of participants' experiences to be pooled together for a fresh analysis. This entails sifting through all the data, discarding whatever is irrelevant and bringing together what seems most important (Heriott & Firestone, 1983). The process allowed the most significant observations to emerge from all the data gathered in the setting. The second step of the analysis consists of a cross-site search for patterns and themes that are related to Asian children's home literacy experiences. This analysis allows me to develop more sophisticated descriptions and more powerful explanations of the varied social and interactional factors that affect Asian children's learning at home and in school (Miles & Huberman, 1994). Three major themes emerged from the analysis: (1) intergenerational dissonance; (2) differential distribution of literacy practices among siblings; and (3) school and home (dis)connection.

Facets of Social Dynamics in Asian Families: An Analysis of Home Literacy Practices

In the following, I provide an account of the three families' home literacy practices, highlighting one social factor that was prominent in each family's social dynamics. In the Filipino family, I highlight the intergenerational issues that are central to their home language and literacy experiences. In the Vietnamese family, I highlight the differential literacy engagement among siblings of different gender that may result in dissimilar learning outcomes. Finally, in the Chinese family, I highlight the issue of school-home disconnection that has significant consequences on the children's learning experiences.

Intergenerational Gaps: Learning from a Filipino Family

One notable issue among immigrant families is the growing generation gap between the parents and the children, which can result in generational consonance and dissonance (Gadsden, 2000; Portes & Rumbaut, 2001). Generational consonance occurs when both parents and children remain unacculturated, or both acculturate at roughly the same rate, or when the immigrant community encourages selective second-generation acculturation. However, for immigrant families with multiple generations, it is more common for them to experience generational dissonance. Since the first generation parents or grandparents often lack sufficient education or integration into the mainstream culture, their children, who often acquire the new language and culture more quickly than their parents, increasingly become more acculturated (Suárez-Orozco & Suárez-Orozco, 2001). These children progressively adopt more parental roles, while parents gradually lose control and the ability to exercise guidance—developments that often lead to intensified parent–child conflicts, role reversal, rupture of family ties, children's abandonment of ethnic language and culture, and ultimately the loss of parental authority (Portes & Rumbaut, 2001).

Many Asian families live with extended families, especially grandparents who often do not speak English. For many families, intergenerational dissonance occurs not only between children and grandparents but also between children and parents. The Holman family from the Philippines illustrates the changing intergenerational relationships between children, parents, and grandparent. The family had three generations living in the same house. Mr. and Mrs. Holman were first generation immigrants, who learned English through employment in Canada. They were fluent in their first language, Tagalog. Their three daughters, Salsha, Jasmine, and Jessie (age 6, 13, and 15) were born in Canada and were not fluent in Tagalog, and they all preferred to use English at home and in school. They lived with their grandma Anna who was in her seventies, and only spoke Tagalog.

Mr. and Mrs. Holman considered themselves to "be Filipino by blood" even though they were both Canadian citizens. Mr. Holman was an electrician and Mrs. Holman worked as a kitchen aide in a nursing home. They spoke English with a heavy accent and they both were "learning to become Canadian" by reading the newspapers and watching TV. However, they believed that it was hard for them to "go all the way Canadian" as they did not share many of the Canadian values. For example, they thought that Canadians were too liberal and Canadian children were given too much freedom and were less respectful to their parents or elders compared to the children in the Philippines. Mrs. Holman explained, "They are so liberated in Canada. And in the Philippines it was not like that. I was raised as a modest girl and we have to listen to the parents all the time. You can't break the rules or they'll 'kill' you!" They tried to raise the children similarly to the ways in which they were raised in the Philippines, attempting to instill similar values and beliefs, but it was very difficult, as the children had already grown up with Canadian values.

Jessie, Jasmine, and Salsha identified themselves as Canadians. They did what all the other European-Canadian classmates did—they read, studied, and played in English, hung out with English-speaking friends, and watched English movies and TV. Although they mostly followed their parents' rules at home, the children acknowledged that they held very different values from those of their parents. Jessie stated, "They want to keep the Filipino culture in us, because it is part of them and of us, but they know and understand that we've grown up with Canadian values. They tried to mix the two together."

The girls' values were even more different from that of their grandmother, Anna, whom they rarely communicated with at home. Anna usually watched the girls play or watch TV from a distance and hoped that they could communicate more. However, Anna understood that the children were "very Canadian" compared to her other grandchildren in the Philippines. She felt the girls had less respect for her. She believed that if the girls spoke Tagalog more at home they would be able to understand each other better and have closer relationships. She told me via her son's translation that she did not blame them when the girls always spoke English to her, "So communication just stopped. I don't blame them when they speak English [to me] because what they learn in school is English."

The Holman family's experiences mirror many immigrant families' experiences in their adjustment to the mainstream culture. Though generational dissonance did not directly affect the children's academic achievement as the Holman parents were able to communicate with them in English, for many other families, intergenerational dissonance in language and literacy can have a significant impact on the children's learning in school and at home. In Li's (2003) study, for example, the Liu parents' inability to speak, read or write English prevented them from being able to communicate with teachers or get involved in their young son's school work. Since their son was not fluent in Chinese or English, he was struggling in school and had to repeat the first grade. Their experience illustrates the serious consequences intergenerational dissonance can have on children's learning.

Differential Home Experiences among Siblings of Different Gender: Learning from a Vietnamese Family

Research on home literacy has focused on the availability of print materials, the nature of parent–child interaction (Morrow, 1989; Teale & Sulzby, 1986) and the reciprocal role siblings play in each other's literacy development (Gregory, 2001). Though we know that the interplay between siblings is important to their literacy development, we know very little about how differential experiences among siblings may contribute to children's differential achievement in literacy. Research on adolescent immigrant students' home experiences has suggested that many immigrant youth, especially older female youth, make many more contributions to their households and often assume much more responsibilities than their male and/or American peers (Orellana, 2001, 2003). This means that these youths, especially the older female youths, may engage in more literacy-related activities at home than other siblings. The question is then, how or whether the siblings' different experiences at home shape their differential learning outcomes.

Among Asian immigrant families, older siblings, especially girls, are found to take on more household responsibilities for their parents and some even assume many tasks of parenting at home (Li, 2008a; Zhou & Bankston, 1998). In Asian families, traditional gender roles are also reported to be observed very closely, especially for girls (Kibria, 1993; Lam, 2003). Therefore, in many Asian families, girls, especially older girls, may be socialized into different literacy practices than their younger and/or male siblings. In the Phan family, a Vietnamese refugee family in the US, the older daughter Hanh, 16, and her brother Chinh, 11, had very different learning experiences as well as literacy outcomes. Mr. and Mrs. Phan, who could not speak fluent English, "follow[ed] a Vietnamese culture a lot" in raising their two children. They wanted Hanh to become a virtuous and obedient woman following the traditions in Vietnam, and enforced stricter discipline and social control for her than for her brother. Hanh described, "[My mother] let my brother go outside with little friends whatever, but I can't do that because I am a girl. . . . I stay home 24 hours a day unless I'm going to grocery shopping with my mother." The parents also held very high academic expectations: they wanted Hanh to become a medical doctor and Chinh to become a tennis star like Michael Chang.

Chinh liked to play video games and play outside with his friends. He did not enjoy reading, studying or going to the library. He read simple picture books such as those with cars and helicopters; and at age 11, he did not want to read them any longer. He preferred to read the instructions on the TV screen when he played video games than reading something in print. Chinh had not developed fluency in English even though he considered English as his first language because he was born in the United States and grew up here. He had difficulty not only with English pronunciation and vocabulary but also with reading comprehension. His parents could not help him much with his studies as they were very busy working and could not afford to take time off, and they spoke broken English with a heavy accent, which they were afraid Chinh would acquire. Chinh was often left at home alone with his sister. He was exempt from doing any household chores as "he was just a baby boy." The only household activity which he enjoyed doing was baking a chocolate cake from a baking mix, yet his sister usually helped him read the instructions when he baked.

Hanh, however, assumed multiple responsibilities and roles at home. She was often a language broker for her parents, helper with various house chores, and teacher and supervisor to her brother who struggled with English learning and received little help from school. Her mother told her when she started school, "Whatever you are doing, you have to learn yourself because if you bring it home I can't help you. So if you don't understand, you ask your teachers." As a result, Hanh had been very independent since she was little. Hanh assisted her parents with language in every single way possible. She read and interpreted school letters and documents for her parents, especially those concerning her little brother. When they bought items that required assembly, she either translated the instructions for them or simply completed the assembly herself. When they bought expensive items with mail-in rebates, such as a computer or a calculator for school, Hanh filled out the forms, barcodes, and addresses for her parents. She also took care of tax forms for the family and helped her mother pay bills. If her mother needed to call a bank or a credit card company or to order something from a restaurant, Hanh would make the call. In addition to helping with language, Hanh also helped with some household chores such as grocery shopping, preparing food, and cleaning. During shopping, Hanh helped her mother when she could not read the product names or did not know what the products were. Sometimes when their heating or cooling systems broke down, Hanh checked the yellow pages for her parents in order to obtain repair information.

Besides helping her parents with language and house chores, Hanh's biggest responsibility was to help her brother with his schoolwork. She explained,

I'm the only one in the house that can speak English fluently or other stuff you know. So, in reading and stuff, I'm the person in the house to be teaching him. And math, I mean my father is good at math, but he is limited in his vocabulary, so he can't communicate as clearly as I could communicate with him. So I do have a big hand in teaching him.

Hanh checked her brother's homework and made sure that he completed it every day, "If there are notes from the teacher, I will read them, and I'll do for him what he needs to be done." Though she was willing to help, she felt overwhelmed by her responsibility to teach her brother reading and math, "If he is going to school, where he needs to learn from teachers; the teachers should be the one who teach him. They shouldn't assign work for us to come to teach him. That's what he goes school for." She felt angry that her brother was left behind by the school, "Teachers, whether or not if he'll fail, they'll still make same amount of money, so if one child is left behind, they just don't really care." When she and her mother told the teachers that Chinh needed help, the teachers always asked them, "Is there anyone home that can help him? Doesn't he have older sister or something?" Hanh felt very frustrated with the school:

And he usually doesn't understand the materials that he learns in school. So whenever he comes home, I basically have to teach him the material and it does irritate me because he's going to school for 6 hours but he is not learning anything . . . So he comes home and expects me to sit there to teach him. It irritates me because I have my own work and I don't mind teaching him if he doesn't understand, but he goes to school for 6 hours and he is not learning anything and he is coming home and asking me for help. Why don't I get paid to teach him, you know?

Hanh's responsibilities at home had affected her school experiences. Unlike her peers, she had to give up the opportunities to join clubs or attend after school activities in school in order to come home to help. She explained, "I have to be home to take care of my brother and stuff. I just can't stay after school whenever I feel like it, whenever [the teachers] need me to stay in school. I have more responsibility for home." She struggled to understand why her life was different from other children: "When I was a little . . . like I said, 7th or 8th grade, I started to hate my parents, but I [ask my parents], Why can't I go outside? What the hell are the problems with me going outside? Why can't I go to the movies or something?"

The Phan family's experiences suggest that the family members, especially the two children, seem to differ greatly in what and how they are engaged in literacy activities. For Hanh, she learned to become literate by engaging in pleasure reading and reading informational textbooks and by participating in a variety of "hands-on" or "real-life" literacy activities at home, including reading documents, letters, instructions, flyers, yellow pages and labels for her parents, teachers' notes, textbooks and storybooks for her brother, and filling out forms and applications. These varied literacy activities, without a doubt, have improved

Hanh's reading and writing as well as her confidence as an English language learner at home and in school.

In contrast, Chinh's exposure to and use of literacy in both Vietnamese and English were limited. In order for him to learn English, Chinh's parents did not try to teach him how to speak Vietnamese, and therefore, he did not develop the kind of oral language skills and comprehension in Vietnamese that his sister did. In addition to the lack of development in his first language, Chinh's home literacy practices were also characterized by a lack of interaction with the English literacy materials in the home environment. Except for his school work and his game playing and TV watching, Chinh did not engage in much reading and writing at home nor did he have the opportunities to spend much time with his parents. Unlike his sister, who was responsible for a variety of tasks like reading and writing for her parents, Chinh was well taken care of at home, and therefore, did not have the need to be involved in different reading and writing activities. In sum, Chinh was not socialized into "doing" literacy like his sister, despite the availability of print resources at home. Since meaningful engagement in reading and writing activities is crucial for children's emergent literacy development (Puchner, 1997; Teale & Sulzby, 1986), Chinh's lack of interaction with literacy materials and involvement in different kinds of literacy events at home may have contributed to his slow progress in acquiring English literacy skills.

School and Home Dis(connections): Learning from a Chinese Family

Research on minority students' failure suggests that it can be the result of a mismatch between learners' home and school discourses including differences in language, literacy beliefs, and interactional patterns (Ogbu, 1982). As familiarity with schooled literacy discourses is a mark of school success, students from non-mainstream cultural backgrounds have to learn a different set of literacy conventions and often experience difficulties with schooling (Lopez, 1999). Cultural differences between immigrant Chinese home practices and mainstream practices have been well documented. Several comparative studies have found Chinese immigrant parents' cultural beliefs to be different from their mainstream counterparts. For example, these parents are reportedly more likely than Anglo-American parents to engage their children in varying literacy activities every day or at least provide a nurturing literacy environment; they also may provide more structured and formal educational experiences for their children after school and on weekends than do Anglo-American parents (Xu, 1999; Zhang & Carrasquillo, 1995). Chinese immigrant parents also hold beliefs about specific literacy instructional practices that may be different from the beliefs of mainstream parents. Chinese immigrant parents are reported to favor traditional, skill-based approaches over holistic principles of literacy learning (Li, 2006a). Further, affluent Chinese immigrant families more often provide after-school tutoring/learning opportunities to their children than low SES Chinese parents (Li, 2002, 2006b).

The Chinese parents' cultural beliefs on literacy education were well reflected in the Lou household. Mrs. Lou, a former accountant at a large firm who left her job in order to care for her two children, came from Hong Kong and was a believer of traditional, skill-based approaches to language and literacy instruction. Both of her two children, daughter Courtney, 16, and son, Andy, 10, were struggling in school, with not only reading and writing but also core academic areas such as science and math. The school followed a literature-based approach to literacy instruction. It was an integrated process of learning that included experiential/interactive literacy activities such as silent reading, teacher read-aloud, literature circles, reading and writing in content areas, and writers' workshops. This integrated approach was very different from Mr. and Mrs. Lou's beliefs in subject-specific instruction in which core areas are taught as separate skills. Mr. and Mrs. Lou realized that their children, who were born in Canada, were far behind their peers who had schooling experiences in Hong Kong, where academic subjects were taught separately. Mrs. Lou described her daughter's English ability: "Her English is backward—because she was born here, speaking fluent English; but by the time she write, she is lousy. She write like she talk." In her opinion, it was the Canadian educational system to blame. She explained, "I cannot blame her because this is the educational system too. They didn't really do anything until recently from last . . . two years. And they realize how come high school children, when they go into college, they have so much problem." According to Mrs. Lou, Courtney's reading and writing ability in both English and Chinese had affected her academic skills in math and science. She reasoned:

> [The teachers] ask kids to write, but they didn't teach how to write. [For example,] this is subject, this is object, how to produce things, how to express things, how to use [words], how to put more adjectives in, to put more verbs in, to make sentences more fluent, no . . . [the teachers] thought from reading the books themselves, I emphasize *themselves*, [the students] should know!

Similarly, Andy, who was in fourth grade in a combined grade 4–5 class, also performed below his age/peer group level in English reading, writing, listening, and speaking, and all other core curriculum subjects such as Science and Social Studies. He was a low-level ESL student when he finished the third grade and was also diagnosed as having attention-deficit disorder by the school. Andy's English learning was Mrs. Lou's top concern. One thing Mrs. Lou decided to do was to stop speaking Chinese to Andy at home even though she discovered that Andy had problems with Chinese as well: "But if you talk to him in Cantonese, he didn't really understand completely . . . He is in-between the gap." While the school believed that speaking too much Chinese was the reason that Andy was not yet proficient in English, Mrs. Lou believed that it was insufficient English instruction that put him at a disadvantage. In order for him to receive more exposure to English in school, Mrs. Lou asked the school to take him off the official ESL student list so that he wouldn't be pulled out of regular classes. Mrs. Lou thought that the school was putting him in a level lower than his ability and the placement may have blocked his learning because he was not challenged. She explained,

Because if they [teachers] put him in the much much lower grade, that means he won't improve himself. They pull him out from the regular class and he lose the exposure, the regular learning. This is why I pull him out. And, his lack of concentration makes problems more seriously. They thought maybe because he is ESL, he cannot understand English. But they didn't realize he doesn't really understand Cantonese too.

The teachers, however, believed that Andy needed more language support and withdrawing from the ESL program would further put him at a disadvantage. Andy's teacher explained,

> As far as his language development, I mean he hasn't been out for any small group or anything. So if I am in there, or there is an educational assistant, he might get a little bit of help or something. But otherwise, he is pretty much on his own, but his mom requested that.

In terms of Andy's diagnosis as having attention-deficit disorder, Mrs. Lou regarded it as his "lack of concentration." She believed that it was "the class, the environment" (e.g., the group seating arrangement and the combined grade 4–5 class) that was distracting for younger children. She preferred the traditional seating by rows. She explained, "Because the way that [the teacher] put the kids together, the kids talking to each other ... Of course, each other facing each other, they just chat, chat, chat. Who want to concentrate?" She also preferred a single-grade class where "Everybody in a class reading the same book, and then the teacher can read the book to the kids. Then they can learn at the same level, the same pace, the same pronunciation." She argued,

> I don't think this system [combined class] work well ... Because the teacher have only half the time to teach the class, that's why they need so much so-called assistants—"Oh, I don't have time because there are so many kids. I can only helping one at a time." That means the kids going to the school wasting their time. They don't learn anything. One thing is if you put him in the higher level, it is hard for them to concentrate and it is hard to them to understand. Next year if you put him into the lower class, that means he heard them [the materials] already, nothing new to him, no initiatives, no incentives for him to concentrate in the class.

For these reasons, Mrs. Lou disagreed with (and refused to comply with) the school's recommendation to use medication to solve Andy's problem. She commented, "I ask them how can you improve him? They say only medication. I say, no, medication only worsens the case." Instead, she sent Andy to take piano and swimming lessons every week to train Andy's concentration skills. She believed that lessons such as playing the piano would coordinate his body and mind as he had to read, think, and play at the same time.

In order to improve his math skills, Mrs. Lou sent him to a private tutoring school twice a week. The school followed a traditional approach and used a lot of math worksheets. It also offered feedback when a student had a problem or question. Andy had a folder in the school. Every time he went there, he would pick up his folder that contained his worksheets for the day. He finished them by himself and returned them to the teacher. Mrs. Lou believed that it was this kind of training, not the public school's efforts, that had contributed to Andy's good performance in math.

Mrs. Lou required Andy to read aloud in English every day and encouraged him to write on the computer. Sometimes Andy's parents would read with him. Sometimes they asked Andy to record his reading aloud on a tape-recorder so that they could check his reading later. Mrs. Lou believed that this method was very effective for checking Andy's pronunciation, but she admitted that Andy often lost interest in recording his reading because she often pointed out his pronunciation mistakes.

According to Mrs. Lou, Andy liked to play games on the computer and watch his favorite cartoon shows *Pokemon* and *Digimon*. But he would always do his homework or practice the piano after half an hour's break. In addition, Andy had a variety of literacy experiences outside of school, given his homework, reading, games, TV shows, and swimming and piano lessons. He commented that he learned more at home than at school, and described his home as a school, "Sometimes when you are at home, you can learn. My mom actually thinks my house is a school. So she taught me everything—15 minutes' recess, and then an hour of studying, then recess, then another 45 minutes, and then recess."

Although Mrs. Lou was doing her best to help Andy learn, she felt she was under tremendous pressure to "get it right." She felt that the school was not doing the job; instead much of the responsibility of educating children was "dumped on the parents" who were not proficient in English. She expressed her frustration, "Most of the time, 90% or 80% depend on your parents. Every time, [the teachers] keep emphasizing that parents are supposed to read with the kids every day . . . We rely on you guys teaching English but instead you rely on me to teach my son English?" She believed overreliance on parents further put children whose parents did not have a good command of English at a disadvantage,

> [The teacher] asks us parents to proofread for them instead of her doing the work. The other thing is, a lot of parents don't speak fluent English. This is why the multicultural kids had difficulty in language, because they didn't receive quality education from school. [The teachers] rely on parents instead of rely on them. This is the big problem. They [teachers] force the parents go out for tutors, because they [parents] cannot help the kids.

Conclusions and Implications

In this chapter, I have presented three case studies to illustrate the influence of different dimensions of family social and cultural dynamics on Asian children's learning experiences outside of school. With respect to intergenerational issues, conflicts exist not only between children and their grandparents but also between children and their parents. The conflicts were linked not only to degrees of

English language proficiency and heritage language maintenance among the different generations but also to degrees of enculturation into the mainstream societies—that is, their respective identity formations in the host society.

In terms of children's disparate learning opportunities and literacy experiences, the Phan children's experiences of growing up in the same household with differential success suggest that cultural values, gender roles, and parental expectations play a significant role in shaping immigrant children's home learning experiences. Some children may engage in a variety of household activities that help them improve their literacy development. Other children may be sheltered from these activities and thus not engaged in the opportunities to use language. The differences in roles and responsibilities also raise the issue of the potential harm to immigrant youth's psychosocial well-being as a result of over-engagement in household responsibilities and a lack of socio-emotional support.

Finally, the Lou family's stories suggest that home-school cultural mismatch can be a hindrance to immigrant children's learning in school and at home. Home-school mismatch can be found not only in cultural differences in literacy instruction (e.g., skill-based vs. literature-based) but also in labeling children (e.g., the label of attention-deficit disorder). The parents' beliefs also differed from the school's practices with regard to classroom environment (e.g., row or group seating arrangement), school organization (e.g., single-grade or combined classes), and the parent's and teacher's roles in the children's education.

Analyses across the studies also suggest that the issue of first language and cultural identity has a profound influence on the children's learning experiences at home and in school. First language and culture become an identity marker. The family members' individual (dis)association with their first language and culture influences their language choices and their literacy activities at home, which in turn embodies their different cultural identification with their native culture. The Holman children, for example, chose to disassociate with their first language and culture. To them, to adhere to their first language and culture was a symbolic refusal to be assimilated into the mainstream culture (Suárez-Orozco & Suárez-Orozco, 2001). Furthermore, first language and literacy in all three families (and their schools) were seen as a "barrier" to the children's English development, rather than a resource or asset that they could use to facilitate their first and second language learning. Even though all families wanted their children to know their first language, none of the parents encouraged the children to use their first language at home. On the contrary, all families stopped speaking their first language to their children for fear of its negative interference with English learning. The lack of first language development and the bilingual continuum, however, may have put some immigrant children at a further disadvantage. Research has concluded that the use of the child's first language does not impede the acquisition of English. Instead, it benefits learners' cognitive and second language development and should be used as a resource for children to learn English (August & Hakuta, 1997; August & Shanahan, 2006; Cummins, 1989; Li, 2002, 2006a).

The studies also suggest that immigrant parents' own English language proficiency and their social class backgrounds (occupation and education) also play a significant role in shaping the children's home (and school) experiences (Li, 2002,

2006b). In the Holman family, the parents were proficient in English and were able to communicate with the children (and/or school if they needed to). Their double income had afforded them a house in a predominantly white middle-class neighborhood where the children were socialized into mainstream culture. Similarly, in the Lou household, Mr. and Mrs. Lou were proficient in English and were upper middle-class in terms of their income. Their middle-class status afforded their children the opportunity to attend costly after-school tutoring programs and also the ability and power to challenge the school practices such as the ESL programs and seating arrangements—agency that is rarely seen in low SES families (Fine, 1993; Li, 2008b). Further, their class status also allowed Mrs. Lou to take time off work to care for the children because she saw the need. In contrast, the Phan parents were not proficient in English and were unable to take time off work to be with the children, especially their son who needed more support at home. As a result, they relied mainly on their older daughter to be the "surrogate parent."

These findings have important implications for both teachers and immigrant parents. The divergent factors that influence the children's home literacy learning suggest that teachers need to learn not only about students' cultures and backgrounds but also need to recognize how students' learning is differentially situated and represented in their respective socio-cultural contexts such as the home milieu (Li, 2006a). With the knowledge of students, who they are and what their learning experiences are like outside of school, teachers will be able to make culturally sensitive decisions on how to adapt instruction to the social, academic, and linguistic differences of the minority students and address the divergent needs of the minority children who have very different learning experiences outside of school (Nieto, 2002). Teachers must ask themselves these questions:

- Who are my Asian students? Where do they come from and what languages do they speak at home?
- How much do I know about my Asian students outside school? What do they do after they leave my classroom?
- What are the social and cultural factors that might influence their learning? How do I learn about them? And how can I help address them?
- How can I open up my classroom so that Asian parents feel comfortable and welcome to share their thoughts on their children' education with me?
- What can I do to help build a school culture that respects Asian families' culture and their different views about education?

The answers to the above questions will allow teachers to understand who the students are and what they need in order to succeed in school. Teachers can then design innovative instructional practices that can open up spaces in their class-rooms to address the dissonance in students' lives that may impede their learning. These instructional activities must recognize the multiple and diverse learning resources in children's lives and create ample opportunities for parents' and grandparents' direct or indirect participation in and out of school. These activities do not have to be overly complicated. For example, teachers can look around

their classrooms and identify whether there are any material
environment that reflect the diversity of the class. If not, th
some print materials such as signs and posters in differen
the classroom so that students feel that their first langua
respected. Teachers can involve their Asian students, parents
in decorating their classrooms (e.g., ask them to help pr
culturally relevant materials for the classroom), and this sir
ity can become a family-school literacy activity that involves students, parents and
grandparents and uses their funds of knowledge. Another example might be a
literature unit where the teacher selects a story or novel about Asia or Asian
students or uses multi-media materials such as films, music, or poetry in English
or students' native languages that are related to the themes and symbols of the
book/story. Instead of doing the traditional "literature circle" activity with students in class, teachers can construct activities that require the participation of
siblings, parents or grandparents in the reading and writing process. These activities can be bilingual, with parents and grandparents using their native languages.

In addition to facilitating students' English learning through effective pedagogical approaches, teachers can help foster positive attitudes toward learners'
heritage languages by valuing its use in both school and home. Since parents and/
or grandparents play a vital role in shaping children's learning experiences,
teachers need to work closely with parents to help develop a school-home continuum that benefits both students' first and second language learning. Teachers
can use individuals from the student culture as guides to learn from parents about
their literacy practices. As Li (2006a) suggests, approaching the parents with a
desire to learn, rather than with an intention to change them, would significantly
empower the parents and may result in parents becoming more willing to participate in dialogue with school. Moreover, teachers could involve the parents by
incorporating some of the parents' opinions (e.g., classroom seating arrangement,
and explicit instruction) in the classroom to show their sincerity and respect for
the parents' concerns.

Finally, the findings from my research also have significant implications for
parents. It is necessary for parents to examine their own beliefs and practices and
become aware of the importance of their role in supporting biliteracy development (August & Shanahan, 2006; Li, 2007). Like the teachers, they need to be
informed that first language learning benefits rather than hinders second
language development. For parents, such an understanding will help them form
more positive attitudes toward their first language and make better decisions
about the ways they promote first language learning. For example, parents can
reinforce their children's continuing effort to learn and use their first languages at
home by constantly speaking to the children in their first language or engaging
them in a variety of authentic reading and writing activities in that language.
Parents can also adopt a first-language-only policy at home and make use of
community resources such as heritage language schools to develop their children's literacy skills in first language.

In conclusion, I want to point out that though the divergent social dynamics
were illustrated using cases from Asian families, they are not unique to Asian

nities. Rather, similar issues can be found in other immigrant and ethnic ority groups. By highlighting the issues within these Asian families, I hope to raw attention to the complexity of social and interactional issues that can have a significant impact on all immigrant and minority children's home literacy and learning experiences.

Ideas for Discussion, Extension, and Application

1. How would your life and sense of identity be impacted if now you were to move to another country in which your native language took on a minority language status?

2. The three cases presented here offer glimpses into the inner workings of three Asian-immigrant families. What aspects of the lives of these families surprised you? What dynamics within the families might most strongly influence the children's schooling?

3. Li documents the variety of conflictive issues—differential acculturation across generations, language choice, gender roles, home beliefs, values, and practices that conflict with those of school—that children (and parents) in immigrant families must negotiate. Discuss how the recognition of the complex experience of these families and children might affect the way that you, as a teacher, understand and work with such families and children.

4. Discuss which specific strategies might be used to help immigrant children feel comfortable at school and maximize their academic learning despite the complexity of their cross-cultural lives. Which types of strategies could support their development as bilingual and bi-literate learners?

References

August, D., & Hakuta, K. (1997). *Improving schooling for language minority children: A research agenda.* Washington, DC: National Academy Press.

August, D., & Shanahan, T. (2006). *Developing literacy in second-language learners: Report of the National Literacy Panel on language-minority children and youth.* Mahwah, NJ: LEA.

Citizenship and Immigration Canada (2002). *Demographics.* On-line. Available at: http://www.cic.gc.ca/.

Cummins, J. (1989). *Empowering minority students.* Sacramento, CA: CA Association for Bilingual Education.

Fine, M. (1993). [Ap]parent involvement: Reflections on parents, power, and urban public schools. *Teachers College Record, 94*(4), 682–710.

Gadsden, V. L. (2000). Intergenerational literacy within families. In M. Kamil, P. B. Mosenthal, P. D. Pearson, and R. Barr (Eds.), *Handbook of reading research* (pp. 871–888). Mahwah, NJ: LEA.

Gee, J. P. (1996). *Social linguistics and literacies: Ideology in discourses.* London: Taylor & Francis.

Gee, J. P. (1989). Literacy, discourse, and linguistics: Introduction. *Journal of Education*, *171*(1), 5–17.

Gregory, E. (2001). Sisters and brothers as language and literacy teachers: Synergy between siblings playing and working together. *Journal of Early Childhood Literacy*, *1*(3), 301–322

Heaton, J. (1998). Secondary analysis of qualitative data. *Social Research Update*, *22*, 1–6.

Heriott, R. E. & Firestone, W. A. (1983). Multisite qualitative policy research: Optimizing description and generalizability. *Educational Researcher*, *12*(2), 14–19.

Kibria, Z. (1993). *Family tightrope: The changing lives of Vietnamese Americans*. Princeton, NJ: Princeton University Press.

Lam, B. T. (2003). The psychological distress among Vietnamese American adolescents: Toward an ecological model. Unpublished doctoral dissertation, Columbia University, New York.

Li, G. (2002). *"East is East, West is West"? Home literacy, culture, and schooling*. New York: Peter Lang.

Li, G. (2003). Literacy, culture, and politics of schooling: Counter narratives of a Chinese Canadian family. *Anthropology & Education Quarterly*, *34*(2), 184–206.

Li, G. (2006a). *Culturally contested pedagogy: Battles of literacy and schooling between mainstream teachers and Asian immigrant parents*. Albany, NY: SUNY Press.

Li, G. (2006b). Biliteracy and trilingual practices in the home context: Case studies of Chinese-Canadian children. *Journal of Early Childhood Literacy*, *6*(3), 359–385.

Li, G. (2007). The role of parents in heritage language maintenance and development: Case studies of Chinese immigrant children's home practices. In K. Kondo-Brown (Ed.), *Multiple factors and contexts promoting heritage language: Focus on East Asian immigrants*. Amsterdam: John Benjamin Publishing.

Li, G. (2008a). *Culturally contested literacies: America's "rainbow underclass" and urban schools*. New York: Routledge.

Li, G. (2008b). Parenting practices and schooling: The way class works for new immigrant groups. In L. Weis (Ed.), *The way class works*. New York: Routledge.

Lopez, M. E. (1999). *When discourses collide: An ethnography of migrant children at home and in school*. New York: Peter Lang Publishing, Inc.

Merriam, S. B. (1998). *Qualitative research and case study applications in education*. San Francisco: Jossey-Bass Publishers.

Miles, M. B., & Huberman, A. M. (1994). *Qualitative data analysis: A sourcebook*. Thousand Oaks, CA: Sage Publishing.

Moll, L., & González, N. (1994). Lessons from research with language minority children. *Journal of Reading Behavior*, *26*(4), 439–456.

Morrow, L. M. (1989). Developing reading through concepts about print. In *Literacy development in the early years: Helping children read and write* (pp. 120–140). Englewood Cliffs, NJ: Prentice Hall.

Nieto, S. (2002). *Language, culture, and teaching: Critical perspectives for a new century*. Mahwah, NJ: Lawrence Erlbaum.

Ogbu, J. U. (1982). Cultural discontinuities and schooling. *Anthropology & Education Quarterly*, *XIII*(4), 290–307.

Orellana, M. F. (2001). The work kids do: Mexican and Central American immigrant children's contribution to households and schools in California. *Harvard Educational Review*, *71*(3), 366–389.

Orellana, M. F. (2003). Responsibilities of children in Latino immigrant homes. *New Directions for Youth Development*, *100*, 25–39.

Portes, A., & Rumbaut, R. (2001). *Legacies: The story of the immigrant second generation*. Berkeley, CA: University of California Press.

Puchner, L. D. (1997). *Family literacy in cultural context: Lessons from two case Studies* (NCAL Technical Rep. TR97-01). Retrieved May 21, 2007, from http://www.literacy.org/products/ncal/pdf/TR9701.pdf

Spradley, J. P., & McCurdy, D. W. (1990). *Culture and conflict: Readings in social anthropology*. New York: HarperCollins.

Street, B. (1993). Introduction: The new literacy studies. In B. Street (Ed.), *Cross-cultural approaches to literacy* (pp. 1–22). New York: Cambridge University Press.

Suárez-Orozco, C., & Suárez-Orozco, M. M. (2001). *Children of immigrants*. Cambridge, MA: Harvard University Press.

Teale, W., & Sulzby, E. (1986). *Emergent literacy: Reading and writing*. Norwood, NJ: Ablex.

Xu, H. (1999). Young Chinese ESL children's home literacy experiences. *Reading Horizons, 40*(1), 47–64.

Yin, R. K. (1994). *Case study research: design and methods* (2nd ed.). Thousand Oaks, CA: Sage.

Zhang, S. Y., & Carrasquillo, A. (1995). Chinese parents' influence on academic performance. *New York State Association for Bilingual Education Journal, 10*, 46–53.

Zhou, M., & Bankston, C. L. III. (1998). *Growing up American: How Vietnamese children adapt to life in the United States*. New York: Russell Sage.

4 A Mother and Daughter Go to School

A Story of Strengths and Challenges

Catherine Compton-Lilly

When I first met Marisa, I asked her why she had decided to enter the GED [General Education Diploma] program and the Certified Nursing Assistant [CNA] program at a local adult learning center.

> My reasons? Um, to succeed, to have a future not just for me, for my kids. I want them to follow in my footsteps and I want to get better in reading, math, things I want to know. [Things] that I don't know. And my GED, you know a lot of places require [a] GED for you to get a good job and [I] need that. And I want to get into college . . . I want to go for RN [Registered Nursing]. I want to go for doctor, I know I'll be a little old for that but no matter I know it's going to be [rough]; you know, I might not enjoy the money, but my kids will.

At the age of 22, Marisa thinks that she is getting too old to realize her dreams; yet she has not lost faith in her ability. Life has not been easy for her. Her GED teacher, Ms. Horeb, tells me that Marisa has had a "horrible life." Her daughter's second grade teacher references Anna's background and the difficulties she has faced, but emphasizes repeatedly that Anna has "come a long way" and is doing well in school. Clearly Marisa and Anna bring rich resources to their respective classrooms. Marisa has strong convictions about her life and her future; during the time I knew Marisa she never lost faith in her ability, although her goals did change. Likewise, Anna worked hard in school and kept me updated on her accomplishments when I came to visit.

In this chapter, I explore the many resources that Marisa and Anna bring to school. Yet their story is complicated and I worry at the fragility of their situation. On the pages that follow, I tell the story of a remarkable family that brings powerful resources, strengths, and dedication to difficult situations. In the year I knew Marisa and Anna, changes occurred, bad advice was followed, and in the end little had changed economically for this family despite their strength and determination. This portrait of literacy and schooling for a mother and daughter raises many questions about the lives of students and the possibilities that literacy and schooling offer alongside the challenges imposed by the institutions they encounter.

THEORETICAL APPLICATION: REFUTING THE MYTH OF POVERTY

Poverty involves a set of complicated institutional relations and negative stereo-types about low-income families' engagement in their children's education. Often, educators have low expectations for students from poor single parent homes. Research shows that low-income families (including single parent families) strongly value education. However, parents in these families frequently had negative experiences in school and lack knowledge of how to navigate the educational system. These families also often experience hardships and exhibit resilience in ways unknown to teachers. It is also difficult for middle-class teachers to be aware of the negative assumptions that might exist alongside their genuine good intentions. Think of your assumptions when interacting and working with low-income families. What would be your first response to a student's ability to participate in the classroom if his/her clothes were not clean? How would you react if their families did not respond to survey questions or phone calls? How would you react to your students' constant school absences? What would you imagine as reasons for their situation and actions?

Theoretical Framework

To explore the resources that Marisa and Anna bring to literacy and learning, I draw upon a theoretical framework that builds on Gee's (1992) notion of discourse alongside discussions of resilience and power. Like all of us, Marisa and Anna operate within school, home and community settings that involve particular ways of acting and being. Marisa is actively involved in trying to rethink and recreate her life while various discourses, familiar and new, swirl around her. These discourses are embodied by individuals and representatives of institutions.

As James Paul Gee explains, we all function within worlds that feature multiple discourse communities that act and interact in complex ways. Gee uses "Discourse" in the upper case to describe the ways of being that are assumed and accepted within a given community or organization:

> A Discourse is a socially accepted association among ways of using language, of thinking, feeling, believing, valuing, and of acting that can be used to identify oneself as a member of a socially meaningful group or social network or to signal (that one is playing) a socially meaningful role.

(Gee, 1990, p. 143)

We all engage in various discourses as we act and interact with people in different communities and situations.

People learn to participate in some discourse communities as they grow up within a particular family and community. The ways of talking, acting, dressing, and being we initially assume are acquired within our families and homes. As we interact with people outside our homes we expand our range of discourse communities.

However, it is critical to understand that all discourse communities are not equal. Some discourse communities are populated by people with relative social, economic, and political power. These mainstream Discourses (Compton-Lilly, 2003) or dominant Discourses (Compton-Lilly, 2007) support existing power structures and the institutions that sustain those power structures while promoting "pervasive social theories" (Gee, 1990, p. 139) about the distribution of material goods and beliefs. Pervasive social theories suggest that the ways in which the world is structured are natural and unquestionable. Generally accepted pervasive theories include the belief that having a job, owning a home, being financially independent of social services, and having a high school diploma are desirable and evidence of personal accomplishments. People who do not fulfill those norms are often considered unsuccessful and perhaps unworthy. As Gee (1999) maintains, our understandings about the world are not just ideas in our heads. Our knowledge of the world operates on our abilities to "coordinate and be coordinated by constellations of expressions, actions, objects, and people" (Gee, 1999, p. 19).

Norman Fairclough (1989) reminds us that power acts on us through language, particularly when language is voiced in contexts that entail unequal social positionings; power is manifested when dominant discourses serve some people well and fail to fulfill their promises to others and is evident in the values and acts of people within historically constructed institutions. Fairclough argues that the everyday worlds of people are riddled with assumptions and expectations that are "implicit, backgrounded, taken for granted" (Fairclough, 1989, p. 77). He argues that these ways of understanding the world are passed down over time through schools, businesses, media, and other institutions. Generally accepted and rarely questioned ways of understanding the world are deeply ingrained in our collective knowledge and are only revealed when they fail to reflect our lived experiences.

Dominant discourses operate in Marisa and Anna's lives as they encounter expectations related to school attendance, past histories, school norms, and housing commitments that require adherence to ways of being that were not easy, and sometimes impossible, to fulfill. While Marisa has always experienced these mainstream discourses, these discourses have not reflected her experiences. Through her commitment to education and obtaining a new life for her children, Marisa is now ascribing to these discourses for herself and her children. Marisa is learning to function within and through dominant discourses that in the past were often antithetical to her own experiences and alternative ways of making sense of the world.

Thankfully, Marisa and Anna have found supportive people within both school and home contexts. However, despite their hard work at school and the support of caring others, they find themselves confronting challenges and obstacles that threaten to vanquish the gains they have made and may have led Marisa to compromise the goals that she expressed in the opening anecdote.

Methodology

Several years ago, I interviewed ten of my first grade students and their parents about their conceptions of reading. During those interviews, I was surprised to learn, with the exception of one parent, they had all participated in various educational programs including business/secretarial training, GED preparation, food service training, and childcare training programs after leaving high school. I am a monolingual English-speaking, currently middle-class, woman of European heritage. My surprise led to intrigue as I wondered about parents as readers and their educational experiences beyond high school. In the yearlong project described in this chapter, my goal was to focus on the literacy experiences of adult students who were pursuing their GEDs and the literacy learning experiences of their children.

The Researcher and the Study

As a teacher who had taught in this neighborhood for over a decade prior to beginning this research, I brought a wealth of knowledge alongside a set of assumptions to this research project. While my earlier research endeavors had alerted me to the probability that much of what I thought I knew about people in this community was flawed, incomplete, and/or wrong, I continue to be amazed at how much I need to learn. Years of good intentions, thorough assessments of students, careful classroom observations, and thoughtful lesson plans were not enough; I still have much to learn.

My first lesson occurred when I started the tutoring of the ten adult students. While my intention, inspired by the work of Freire (1986), was to design lessons that focused on students' lives and interests, my students resisted. They were interested in passing the GED test and wanted my help in achieving that goal. I soon found myself revisiting mathematical concepts that I had not encountered since high school and sharing test-taking strategies. I also learned that in most cases students' personal literacy lives were intact. I learned that among my students were young adults who competently read the bible, the newspaper, texts from the internet, books from Oprah's book club, their children's school books, nursing textbooks, magazines, and even a student who had recently read Dante's Inferno and another who read easily and with good comprehension from the books I brought him on engineering from the college library. In most cases, the students' officially tested reading levels seemed to have little correspondence with their personal literacy practices.

Of the ten students, Marisa stood out because of her remarkable strengths and the significant challenges she faced. Marisa was one of two adult students who remained in the GED program throughout the school year. She was also the only student who, to my knowledge, had spent time in prison. My first interview with Marisa was serendipitous. A couple of weeks after I had met all of the adult students at the center and commenced our tutoring sessions, I went to one of the students' homes on a Saturday morning for our first interview. I knocked on the door of the upstairs apartment a couple times and was disappointed to get no response. Just then a voice came up behind me, "Hi, Miss, I know you from the GED center." It was Marisa. Apparently Marisa lived in the bottom floor of the same house. I explained that I had come to interview Karin but that she was not home. Without hesitating, Marisa suggested that I interview her instead. Marisa's openness and enthusiasm made working with Marisa and Anna easy and enjoyable. Throughout the year, we shared a close friendship and a strong working relationship.

Overall, this not a study that easily and simply translates into revised classroom practices. Its findings do not point to particular materials or pedagogical practices. This study reminds us of the many resources our students, both adults and children, bring and the challenges that they face in schools and classrooms. It also reminds us that both the resources families possess and the challenges they face can be invisible to teachers even as we try to help. Talking, asking questions, seeking common ground, listening, caring, and supporting are part of the answer. In Marisa's and Anna's story, teachers play an important role and this reveals opportunities for educators to support others in achieving their goals.

Data Collection and Analysis

For this chapter I revisited data from the larger study including: spoken data, observational data, and documents. Spoken data included four audiotaped interviews that were transcribed in full for each adult and child. The interviews with adults lasted approximately one hour whereas interviews with children were shorter, lasting approximately 30 minutes. Interviews with staff at the GED center and with the children's teachers provided further information about parents and children as readers and learners. In the Fall, I interviewed teachers and staff at the GED center. These interviews provided most of the information presented in this chapter.

Observations of parents and children in learning situations contextualized interview data, often challenging, confirming, or extending the descriptions offered by parents, children, and teachers. Adults participated in weekly half-hour tutoring sessions at the GED center with the researcher; these sessions focused the specific challenges that each student faced in his/her GED classroom. Children were visited at their schools for one morning during the Spring of the school year. Finally, I videotaped interactions of parents and myself participating in literacy events with the children to provide an additional lens on literacy.

Documents included reading assessments that were administered to both children and adults (Beaver, 1997; Ekwall & Shanker, 1993). In addition, writing samples focused on reading or school-related topics were collected from adults and children three times during the year (Winter, Spring, and early Summer).

The research incorporated two broad contexts that affect literacy learning: home and school. Home-based data contributed to a detailed account of specific literacy experiences and perspectives for each of the ten focus families and led to a preliminary list of codes according to salient topics in the data. A constant comparative approach was used in which home incidents, events and activities from the data were identified, compared with each other, and sorted according to similarities and differences. Relationships between codes were then identified through categorical analysis (Rose & Sullivan, 1996) as various codes were grouped into larger categories and/or juxtaposed with each other. Next, coding methods were applied to the school-based data and the codebook was expanded and revised. These data provided an official school-sanctioned perspective.

Although adult tutoring sessions ended when participants stopped attending GED classes, all ten participating families completed the full series of four interviews and the teachers of all parents and children were observed and interviewed.

Marisa and Anna: Strengths and Accomplishments

Marisa is a 22-year-old mother of Puerto Rican descent. She is the mother of Anna, who is in second grade, and a 4-year-old son. Marisa attends both the GED/CNA Program. She explains that she chose to attend this GED center because it is right around the corner from her house and it is free. Marisa currently receives social service benefits. One month prior to the start of this study, Marisa was released from prison. She explains that she had been selling drugs since she was 12 years old and that it was a "family thing." Marisa grew up in the Bronx and was relocated to a smaller Northeast city after she was released from prison. She says that it helps to be away from her old neighborhood. Although Marisa did not use drugs, she is enrolled in a drug rehabilitation program; her trial lawyer counseled her to admit to drug use in order to get a lighter sentence. Now that she has been released from prison, drug rehabilitation is part of her release program. She attends the drug rehabilitation program every evening, Monday through Friday, after being at the GED center all day.

Marisa's living room table is covered with magazines. At one point in the interviews, I had promised to give her an old copy of *Oprah Magazine* that we had used in her tutoring sessions. When I repeatedly forgot to bring her the issue, she repeatedly reminded me. Every few weeks, Anna receives a mail-order *Winnie the Pooh* book. Both Anna and her mother share a love for the little bear. As Anna explained, "Winnie the Pooh is my favorite character. He's a very nice person. He sings and shows manners."

Marisa's mother and stepfather have moved away from the Bronx to be close to Marisa and her children. Marisa's parents took care of both children while Marisa was incarcerated and continue to play an active role in the children's lives. Anna's grandparents pay Anna's tuition at a private Catholic school; although they pay a subsidized rate, they anticipate not being able to afford payments next year and Marisa is making plans to send Anna to a public school. Both Anna and her mother describe the large children's book collection that the grandparents have collected for the children. Anna proudly announces that she had more books than the library.

When asked about her own schooling, Marisa explains that she did very well in elementary school but that she sometimes experienced reading in school as "annoying" and "boring." She explains that she did not understand the purpose of reading until she was much older. She talks about "just sitting there reading" in school; now she tells me how important reading is, "Cause there's a lot of things you need to know about in life . . . you know, your kids need help. You won't be able to help them enough, so they feel left out 'cause you don't know how to read." She spoke passionately about her fourth grade teacher whom she describes as a caring person who made school learning fun and took her students to church on Sundays.

Things changed for Marisa as she grew older. She explained that it is a "tradition" for many Puerto Rican girls to have babies while they are very young and that she became a mother to Anna when she was 14 years old. She explains that she was not a good student in high school and that she often skipped classes. Marisa described her home life as being very controlled and sheltered and that she enjoyed the freedoms that going to school offered, however, these freedoms led to problems,

> [T]o be honest, I never even went to class when I was in high school. I was hanging out with my friends, and other things and I never really concentrated on school. And when I used to go, I used to be playing in the hallway and now at the Adult Learning Center it's like I go to my class.

She complains that her teachers did not care about the "Spanish" students and says that if her teachers had talked to her more she might have stayed in school.

During the year of the study while Marisa was attending the GED program, her reading level as tested by the TABE improved from grade six to grade nine. Marisa and her teachers were very pleased with this improvement. Despite her improving scores, Marisa worries that she cannot remember everything she reads and worries about reading hard words. Marisa is bilingual, speaking both English and Spanish. She tells me that she prefers English; however, when she encounters tough materials in class she often writes her notes in Spanish, "I sometimes start the note in Spanish if I don't understand too much the English part. I just write it in Spanish and I can remember it." When Marisa talks about her own reading and learning, she talks about memorizing; she worries about the words she needs to know for her nursing class and remembering the texts that she reads in the GED program. Marisa has also earned certificates in various computer programs such as Excel and Word. She tells me that she helps Anna to memorize poems and prayers that are assigned in class. Anna's reading levels in the Accelerated Reading program rose steadily over the school year.

Marisa tells me that the way she talks sounds "ghetto" saying, "I want to sound professional." She explains that sometimes she pronounces English words as if they were Spanish words and that sometimes people don't understand her "when it comes to, like, professional words."

Both Marisa and Anna agree that Anna loves books. Anna reads every night before bed and enthusiastically names her favorite books from home, her grandparent's house, and school. Her mother reports that Anna had been reading one of Marisa's self-help books that was left sitting on the coffee table. When I videotaped Anna reading with her mother, Marisa was very involved. She helped Anna by supplying problematic words, voicing initial letter sounds, and encouraging

Anna to "sound out" tricky words. Anna reports that her teacher also helps her by supplying problematic words and telling her to sound out words.

Anna's teacher considers Anna to be an average or slightly above average reader. She says that Anna is a hard worker who completes her work carefully. However, when tested, she qualified for Title I services because her reading scores fell below the 40th percentile. Despite these scores, her teacher is not worried and considers this extra help as a "back-up" in case she starts to fall behind. In school, Anna has a writing journal that she enjoys and reads with her friends and in front of her class. Anna explains that when they read in front of the class, they get a treat from the teacher. She loves earning treats and privileges at school. The students in her class earn tickets for good behavior that they enter in a contest for prizes; they also get to play outside when they are well behaved. She takes great pride in her progress with the Accelerated Reader Program. In this program, children read leveled books and take multiple-choice, comprehension tests on the computer. Anna keeps me updated on her test scores and her rising reading levels throughout the school year and Marisa shows me the certificates Anna has earned.

Marisa and Anna have both developed strong relationships with their teachers and their teachers recognize their strengths and talents. Ms. Mackel, Marisa's nursing teacher, reported having a great respect for Marisa. She explains that Marisa "was really changing her life and really working hard." She tells me that "there is something about her [that is very special]." Marisa's GED teacher, Ms. Horeb, also describes Marisa passionately. "She sees education as more than just you know, I gotta go [to school]. She really does. I mean I have that sense about her and I've had it almost from the very beginning with her." Ms. Horeb tells me that Marisa is bright and has made great progress; "when she's shown what's missing, she can learn it and retain it." Ms. Horeb believes that Marisa views "school as a safe, encouraging place." I suspect that her strong relationship with Ms. Horeb contributes to this sense of security. Anna's teacher describes her as a good student who has made significant improvements over the school year.

The resources Marisa and Anna possess are notable (see Table 4.1). Marisa has survived many challenges that led to her present situation, and she has managed to provide for her children, attend school, and is working to create a new life for the family. Marisa tells me that she wants Anna and her son to finish school and someday be able to own a house.

While Marisa's and Anna's story is clearly full of hope and resilience, difficulties have occurred as well. The complex context in which Marisa and Anna live complicates their lives as issues related to relationships, money, and resources complicate their accomplishments. The volatility and fragility of their current situation remind us of the very real struggles they face as they attempt to enter a new discourse community and create a new life for themselves. Having summarized their many strengths and accomplishments, I now explore some of the challenges that have haunted Marisa and Anna despite their efforts and dedication.

Table 4.1 Resources brought and accessed by Marisa and Anna

Resource	Aims and Source
Literacy/Learning Goals	"get better in reading, math, things I want to know"
Academic Goals	Getting a GED/and CAN "I want to get into college"
Employment goals	"a lot of places require [a] GED for you to get a good job" "I want to go for doctor"
Programs	GED/CNA program Drug rehabilitation Employment program at the GED center
Literacy resources	Marisa's living room table is covered with magazines. Mail-order *Winnie the Pooh* books Anna's school books and Accelerated Reader books that she brings home. Grandma's and grandpa's library of children's books Anna's love for books
Family	Marisa's mom and dad
Teachers	Marisa's fourth grade teacher Marisa's close relationship with her GED teacher Anna's supportive relationship with her second grade teacher
Academic progress	Marisa's reading level from grade six to grade nine.
Language resources	Marisa's competence with English and Spanish
Academic support	Marisa helping Anna with her reading and memorizing words Title I support for Anna
Friends	Marisa's roommate and daughter who are in a similar situation Marisa's friend at the health center who helps her deal with her landlord

Formidable Challenges

Despite their strengths, a pattern of obstacles and challenges exists for this family. The volatility of urban life, the continual existence of distractions that might lead back to her former life, policies that are ostensibly established to serve the general good, and the susceptibility of educational programs to funding cuts and administrative preferences all threaten to disrupt Marisa's and Anna's dreams.

It is important to recognize that Marisa is entering a new discourse community. Selling drugs, becoming a mother at age 14, and dropping out of school contributed to Marisa's participation in what Flores-González (2002) and others calls "street culture" which involves particular ways of talking, acting, dressing and valuing. Eventually, selling drugs led to her arrest and two-year incarceration; during this time she did not see her children. Upon release, she was relocated to a city almost 400 miles away from where she grew up. Her parents also moved to this city and Marisa was reunited with her children. During and after relocation,

Marisa was involved with several agencies including the drug rehabilitation program, GED program, social services, employment programs, and the CNA program. Marisa reports that she misses her friends but believes that being away from them is necessary; she reports, "I don't have no friends out here . . . I like it that way cause I just stay home and nobody bothers me."

In the GED program and in her interactions with various social services agencies, Marisa has begun to participate in different set of discourses that require different ways of talking, acting, dressing and valuing. Marisa describes her desire to "go legit":

> I feel different about, you know, being in the street. I used to be, um, selling drugs on the corners and now I'm trying to go legit . . . so it's a different lifestyle. But I like it, cause I'm more calm . . . it's good for me and my kids.

Maneuvering this transition is challenging and the support provided by various agencies was not always helpful, timely, or consistent.

When I spoke with Marisa at our second interview, she recounted how she had been "kicked out" of the CNA program. Unlike most programs at the Adult Learning Center, the CNA program had very strict attendance requirements. As Marisa explained, she had used up most of her allotted absences and had only a half day more that she could be absent from the program when her daughter's school called to report that Anna had been involved in fight. Apparently Marisa left the Adult Learning center to check on her daughter at 11:00 rather than waiting until 11:30 as she was required. Ms. Mackel felt bad because she wasn't there that day: "Marisa made that snap decision to leave to go check on her daughter. Her daughter had gotten in a fight and they called her [and she left] but she only had 30 minutes before the end of the class."

Not only did this result in her being expelled from the CNA program but it also resulted in a review of her case. During this review it became apparent that because of her felony record she was ineligible for the CNA program and should never have been accepted into the program. Marisa would have been ineligible for a job in the medical field. This was a devastating blow for Marisa and her dreams of becoming a doctor. Marisa transferred into the computer technology program where there was no attendance policy and where her past record would not disqualify her from getting a job.

Transferring out of the CNA program created additional tension because it changed her status with the Department of Social Services which required her to meet with her "worker" to revisit her case; she was then required to find a part-time job which she was able to secure at the Adult Learning Center by working in the computer lab for an hour each day.

At this time, Marisa's relationship with Anna was becoming difficult. After two years apart, mother and daughter went through a difficult time when Anna began challenging her mother's authority and misbehaving in class. Now that Marisa was back with her children she was trying hard to fulfill her role as mother but the strain of her mother being gone and then returning was challenging for

Anna. While at times she seemed to be pleased to be back with her mother, the transition was difficult. Marisa describes the situation:

> She tried to hit me and I was getting loose [upset], um, I caught her smoking a cigarette. She's only 7 years old. I can't even believe that. And I been like really stressful, cause sometimes I've been ready to hurt her real bad.

Marisa mentioned to her mother that she planned to work with her social worker to find a program that might help Marisa deal with Anna. Marisa's mother was not comfortable with social services getting involved and took Anna to stay with her for a few days. Marisa acquiesced, "[My mom] know I have an open case [with social services] . . . she'll call the cops or whatever [if I don't let her take Anna]." Fearing that would complicate her legal case and her custody situation, Marisa let her mother take Anna temporarily. In consultation with staff at the drug rehabilitation program and with support from Marisa's teacher, and the school social worker, Marisa and Anna worked through their difficulties; by the end of the year Anna's teacher referred only briefly to this difficult transitional period emphasizing that Anna had come "a long way" during the school year.

Entering the computer training program created another obstacle. It meant that Marisa would need to move to a new GED class because the class she had been in was reserved for students in the CNA Program. Marisa and her original GED teacher, Ms. Horeb, shared a very close relationship. Even after Marisa left the CNA Program, she remained in close contact with Ms. Horeb. Marisa proudly showed me packets of papers that Ms. Horeb had set aside for her knowing that Marisa would stop by for the extra work, "So I would just stay catching up with the class even though I got kicked down."

Ms. Horeb told me that she tried to convince the administrators to allow her to keep Marisa in her class, but school policies prevailed. She was very "sad" to see Marisa leave the program and missed having Marisa in her class. By the end of the year, budget cuts had resulted in Ms. Horeb being relocated for part of her schedule to a different adult education facility where she started teaching evening classes. Marisa followed her there. She explains, "You know, I expect no matter where she's going I'm right behind."

After Marisa left the CNA program, her attendance dropped off significantly. Without the attendance requirement, the support of her favorite teacher, and the possibility of working in the medical field, Marisa's attendance became sporadic and she was rarely there when I came to get her for our tutoring sessions. Meanwhile, by January, most of the students who had completed the CNA program had dropped out of the GED program entirely when they found jobs as nursing assistants in local nursing homes. Despite her inconsistent attendance, Marisa continued in the GED program until the end of the school year, long after most other students in the study had left.

Marisa often noted that she liked nursing better than computers; she complained that the computer class hurt her wrists and fingers and that she got frustrated when she pushed the wrong keys. In addition, her employment in the computer lab made her an hour late each day for her new GED class. This caused tension between her and the new GED teacher. She recounted her first day in the Ms. Grip's GED class telling me how she was yelled at for being late and not bringing a pen; she reported that "she [Ms. Grip] got a nasty attitude." As Marisa explained, "I was like ready to just get up and walk out, like this is not working for me today." Luckily, things calmed down between Marisa and Ms. Grip, although Ms. Grip never replaced Ms. Horeb as Marisa's favorite teacher and Marisa ended up following Ms. Horeb to the evening program at another adult learning center.

Marisa was attending school all day, spending the late afternoons with her children and attending the drug rehabilitation program in the evenings. The stress of going to school all day, attending the evening program, re-establishing her family, dealing with changes in her academic program, maneuvering personnel changes at the adult center, and dealing with social services was immense. In addition, Marisa was having difficulties with her landlord and she was planning to move. Marisa reported that in addition to her landlord cheating social services out of extra rent, the house has no smoke detectors, was infested with roaches, and the furnace did not work well. She shows me a plastic bag full of dead mice that she has caught and was saving as evidence in case she needed it to break her lease. Apparently, her landlord has threatened to evict her without returning her deposit if she reported him to the city for the housing code violations. With the help of a friend at the local health center, Marisa was photographing the bags of dead mice and then taking the photographs to be notarized so that she could use them as evidence to get her deposit back from the landlord and get another apartment

In addition, to these challenges, Marisa lives with the fear that the custody of her children, which is contingent on her fulfilling the requirements of her probation, might be revoked. In February, I wrote a letter to the judge who was ruling on her case in support of Marisa. At that time the judge's decision was delayed due to a lack of paperwork and the case floundered in court through the end of the study. Despite the challenges Marisa has faced, by summer Marisa remained intent on getting her GED; however, her responsibilities at the adult learning center had shifted. Rather than being demoted to sweeping floors she opted to find a new job as required by social services. She was looking for a job saying, "I'll probably go to Wal-Mart." This would be temporary as she was enrolled in a job placement program that would help her once she had her GED.

Despite these challenges, Anna was doing well in school. The struggles she encountered earlier in the school year were resolved as Marisa kept in daily contact with Anna's teacher and monitored her schoolwork. Marisa and Anna enjoyed the time they spent together. I heard stories of visiting the park, spending time with Anna's grandparents, and making gingerbread cookies. At the end of the school year, Marisa was planning to send Anna to a public school the following year. She explained that her parents were no longer able to afford the private school and she now felt that Anna could handle the change.

Marisa was still attending Ms. Horeb's evening classes and hoping to go to college. With her reading at high school level, Marisa would be able to take and pass her GED test in a couple months. Regardless, Ms. Mackel tells me she worries about Marisa.

Now I wonder where she is. I just hope she's not lost. She comes periodically [to the GED center]. But when I see her, she's not dressed the same way. She's not, you know, so I hope we haven't lost her. You know what I mean? So I keep telling her, I said, "Now just keep reading and keep yourself going." I try to give her words of encouragement but . . . I hope I can.

While Marisa's hopes have been compromised, she has not given up. She continues to pursue her GED and with the help of the job employment program she is hoping to make enough money to care for her family without help from social services. The resources and abilities she brings are admirable, but so far they have not protected her and her family from setbacks.

Conclusion

Marisa and Anna are clearly remarkable people. Challenging stereotypes that depict urban families, Puerto Rican families, the families of released prisoners, poor families, and GED families as deficit, dysfunctional, and undereducated, Marisa and Anna are smart, capable, engaging young women who expertly maneuver difficult situations with the help of a rich set of resources that include purposeful goals for education and employment, a rich set of literacy practices, family support, the support of teachers, and a set of institutions (i.e., GED classes, drug rehabilitation, the public school system, job employment programs).

However, Marisa and Anna are operating in power-laden contexts that do not always recognize the resources they bring. As Gee's (1990) discussion of Discourses reveals, some ways of being, acting, knowing, and valuing are rewarded over others. To function within the mainstream discourse community, Marisa is expected to attend school regularly, delay her visit to Anna's school until the designated time, refrain from a lively social life, and not engage in behaviors that are viewed as detrimental to herself or her children. The ways of being that allow one to participate in mainstream discourses promote "pervasive social theories" (Gee, 1990, p. 139) about success and worth while supporting existing power structures and the institutions that sustain those power structures.

The adult learning center, the CNA program, the Catholic school, the computer training program, and the job placement program are all resources that Marisa utilizes yet they are also part of the existing power structure. The attendance policies associated with the CNA program, policies on employment for released felons, budget cuts, and staff changes at the adult learning center have created challenges. Marisa is trying to work within a system that does not always support her and her family to create a new life. Nancy Fraser (1989) explains that agencies often feel entitled to define the needs of the people they serve and to prescribe solutions. However, generic answers to complicated and personal issues have created ongoing struggles for Marisa and these agencies fail to provide consistent and flexible support. For example, Marisa experiences the actions of social services as surveillance of her as a parent. Marisa views the attendance policies as unfair when she is forced to choose between her daughter and the nursing program. Helpful programs exist but they often bring with them distrust for the people they serve.

Marisa is doing what she has been asked to do. She is attending school and doing well, participating in drug rehabilitation despite the fact that she was not a drug user, and is active with her child's education. She has also given up much of her former life including her friends, her community, and the money she earned selling drugs. Likewise Anna has made an investment in school. She celebrates her success in the Accelerated Reader program and when asked proudly provided me with an extensive grand tour of the items in her schoolbag. Despite early challenges, Anna has adjusted well to second grade and both her mother and her teacher are pleased. However, challenges continue. Regardless of Marisa and Anna's commitment to education and to a "calmer" lifestyle, Marisa continues to face challenges. Much of what has happened to Marisa over the year I knew her was outside of her control. Certainly Marisa was a change agent for her family; yet, despite her strong will and initiative, difficulties persisted.

What is remarkable about Marisa and Anna is the faith they maintain in institutions (i.e., the GED Center, the Catholic School, the job placement program) despite the disappointments they have experienced. Mainstream discourses are extremely powerful and persuasive to the point that Marisa continues to ascribe to them despite the setbacks and challenges she faces. Mainstream discourses can play a positive role for all of us. They give us something to believe in; for some it is a chance at the American Dream that equates success with hard work. Yet mainstream discourses are also dangerous because the American Dream does not hold equally true for all of us. The rewards promised by pervasive social theories (Gee, 1990) are not always realized. Marisa's story helps us to recognize the vast sets of contingencies that interfere with simple solutions and easy formulas.

THEORETICAL APPLICATION: PERSUASIVE SOCIAL THEORIES

Persuasive social theories represent taken-for-granted assumptions about how various aspects of society work. The assumption that contemporary societies are largely meritocratic, that individuals can improve their status and material conditions in life simply as a result of desire, effort, or persistence constitutes a central persuasive social theory. Marisa's case helps us to see that people can indeed aspire to and acquire new sets of beliefs, values, and behaviors. At the same time, her case reveals the real obstacles—often having little to do with personal will and effort—that individuals may encounter as they navigate a variety of social institutions in attempt to improve their lives. Seeing beyond the simple meritocratic formula of desire + effort = success (and its inverse, lack of success = lack of desire + lack of effort) may be critical to creating more caring and responsive schools. How can educators resist the seductively simplistic assumptions about success and failure so prevalent in our societies? How might recognizing the complexity of the lives of your students and their families affect your work as a teacher?

The hope arising from Marisa's and Anna's story lies in the people who populate the institutions they encounter: Anna's teacher, Ms. Horeb, Ms. Mackel, and Marisa's friend at the health center. These are some of the people who make a difference. The most powerful person in Marisa's story is Ms. Horeb who supported Marisa in several ways. First, she conveyed to Marisa the faith she had in her and encouraged her efforts to achieve. Second, she attempted to get permission to allow Marisa to remain in her class after she was removed from the CNA program. When Marisa was forced to leave the CNA program and Ms. Horeb's class, Ms. Horeb continued to provide Marisa with assignments that she could do independently. When Ms. Horeb's schedule was changed due to budget cuts, she began teaching evening classes at a neighboring community center and invited Marisa to join her class. Ms. Horeb provided emotional support conveying her confidence in Marisa, institutional support by attempting to bypass program policies and keep Marisa in her class, and academic support by providing instruction even when Marisa was not her student.

Learning a new discourse requires effort and commitment and Marisa brings these qualities to her learning experiences, but as her story illustrates, effort and commitment might not be enough. Staying out of trouble, making good progress in school, attending the drug rehabilitation program, and focusing on her children were not enough to protect her from the challenges that she encountered as she attempts "to go legit." The emotional, academic and institutional support provided by Ms. Horeb, along with the support from Anna's teacher, Ms. Mackel, and Marisa's friend at the local health center was critical. This is the message that educators must hear. Despite everything, educators can make a difference, and when we don't, it matters to the people we serve. The volatility of being poor, inhabiting urban communities, attending under-funded schools, relying on public services, dealing with social services, and not being White matter in people's lives. They have real effects and create real challenges.

There was one other person who supported Marisa during her year at the GED center. While my primary goal was to understand literacy learning for children and adults, my work had benefits for Marisa and Anna. I tutored Marisa one day a week, brought books and gifts for her daughter, wrote a letter of support to the judge who was ruling in her custody case, awarded her a small stipend at the end of the project, and listened to her as she talked about her life. While I cannot claim to have had the influence that Ms. Horeb had in Marisa's life, I did strive to be supportive and helpful. Researchers can play an important role in the lives of the people we encounter.

Ms. Horeb, myself, and the others, have something in common. We are all working as border crossers, people who routinely participate in more than one world. While we are all primarily situated in the institutional world, there were opportunities for each of us to cross over. I assume that in attempting to cross over we all have made errors and encountered difficulties. But I do believe that in Marisa's case we each managed to make a positive difference. The question is whether these differences are enough.

Of the ten adults students in the larger study, I wish I could say that Marisa and

Anna's case is unique. It is not. The adult students in this study were all committed to the GED program. They all found teachers who supported them. They all supported their children with literacy and learning. But they all faced serious challenges and difficult decisions that too often cast a shadow on their efforts and commitment to create a new life and participate in new discourse communities.

Based on Maria's and Anna's stories, I propose the following bold suggestions for teachers and others who interact with struggling families:

- Institutions need to work together, coordinating their support so that families experience continuity and do not have to struggle to meet their various needs.
- As educators we must recognize that reading and education are not enough; literacy is not a silver bullet to solve social ills. People can be successful readers and writers yet remain vulnerable in their daily lives.
- We need to consistently work with students like Marisa to listen, to understand what they need, and have access to flexible resources to provide those services and opportunities.
- Teachers must recognize the complexities and difficulties that many students face. It is essential that educators develop caring relationships and supportive classroom communities to support their students.
- Teachers need better understandings of the struggles faced by students at all levels; this story provides examples of helpful supportive teachers that we can all learn from.
- Finally, teachers need to risk crossing borders. This entails listening and finding our own stores of agency and our own means of reaching out.

The lessons I have learned from Marisa and Anna include being willing to listen, maintaining flexibility so that policies are not allowed to dictate practice, and having faith and trust in the people we serve. It is my hope that their story helps us all to recognize our own potential to help others realize theirs.

Ideas for Discussion, Extension, and Application

1. Discuss what surprised you or not about Marisa and Anna's story. What would you do if you were in Marisa's situation? How would you cope with her challenges and enter new discourse communities?
2. Imagine yourself as Anna's second grade teacher. Discuss how the knowledge of her home life might influence the way that you perceive and work with her and with her mother during the year.
3. Poor families often experience hardships and exhibit resilience in ways unknown to middle class teachers. Discuss practical strategies that teachers can use to learn about students' stories and their families' challenges, difficult decisions, efforts, and resilience.

References

Beaver, J. (1997). *Developmental reading assessment.* Parsippany, NJ: Celebration Press.

Compton-Lilly, C. (2003). *Reading families: The literate lives of urban children.* New York: Teachers College Press.

Compton-Lilly, C. (2007). *Rereading families: The literate lives of urban children, four years later.* New York: Teachers College Press.

Ekwall, E., & Shanker, J. L. (1993). *Ekwall/Shanker reading inventory.* Needham Heights, MA: Allyn & Bacon.

Fairclough, N. (1989). *Language and power.* London: Longman.

Fairclough, N. (1995). *Critical discourse analysis: The critical study of language.* London and New York: Longman.

Flores-González, N. (2002). *School kids/street kids: Identity development in Latino students.* New York: Teachers College Press.

Fraser, N. (1989). *Unruly practices: Power, discourse, and gender in contemporary social theory.* Minneapolis: University of Minnesota Press.

Freire, P. (1986). *Pedagogy of the oppressed.* New York: Continuum.

Gee, J. P. (1990). *Social linguistics and literacies: Ideology in discourses.* London: Falmer Press.

Gee, J. P. (1992). *The social mind: Language, ideology and social practice.* New York: Bergin and Garvey.

Gee, J. P. (1999). *An introduction to discourse analysis: Theory and method.* New York, New York: Routledge.

Rose, D., & Sullivan, O. (1996). *Introducing data analysis for social scientists,* 2nd ed. Buckingham, UK: Open University Press.

5 Discontinuities and Differences among Muslim Arab-Americans

Making It at Home and School

Loukia K. Sarroub

After long days with our teachers who were all, as I recall, ethnically European Christian people, the same kind of people who belonged to the culture that we watched on TV, we went back home. As soon as we walked over the threshold into our house, we walked into Yemen. In this Yemeni world, I had a certain role to play based on my gender. I was very protected and worried about. Every day before I went off to school, my mother would remind me not to play with boys because they were very bad and had nothing better to do than take advantage of girls and ruin their reputations. I believed her and stayed away from boys ... My mother often told me that if I did not learn how to cook and keep house, my husband would divorce me. Because she was sincerely worried that I would be of no use as a wife without these skills, she began training me when I was ten years old, so that by the time I became a teenager, and was old enough to marry, I would be able to cook for my husband.

(Alwujude, 2000)

Introduction

Cohen and Neufeld (1981) have remarked that schools are a great theater in which conflicts of culture get played out. The same can be said about homes and families in relation to schools. In fact, scholars and educators have attempted to understand, define, and refine the parameters and connections that bind schools and homes together. In this chapter, I explore the ways in which students' success at home and school has been conceptualized in scholarly literature, and then connect this literature to the lives of Arab-American youth and their families. The underlying premise undergirding the ideas in this chapter is that identity development as it is enacted in home and school discourses is related to socialization, learning, and achievement. I discuss cultural capital theory (Bourdieu, 1987; Lareau, 2000; Bowles & Gintis, 1976) and a cultural-ecological perspective (Ogbu, 1982a) to examine models of congruence and difference and to explain students' achievement in two worlds. Then, I proceed to describe and analyze the two theories in relation to data collected in Arab-American neighborhoods by situating each within the context of research conducted in education. Next, I offer an ethnographic case of Yemeni youth and their literacies and a socio-historical case of Palestinian women's lives and situate these within the afore-mentioned theoretical models. Before concluding the chapter, I offer some suggestions for teachers and schools in relation to Muslim Arab populations.

Two Theoretical Perspectives that Continue to Inform Public Schooling

I turn next to an analysis of cultural-ecology as a basis for discerning discontinuities between home and school and cultural capital as a model for explaining differences in achievement based on social class. Bourdieu's cultural capital theory instantiates social class as the key factor of success in school but not necessarily at home. Bourdieu (1977a) argues that social class provides individuals with high status roles and the resources to maintain positions of power in society. The home and family contribute certain resources, such as language (and forms of discourse) and other types of cultural experiences that can be altered by social class (Bourdieu, 1977b, 1987). As Labaree (1997) observes, individuals from low socio-economic backgrounds aim at upward social mobility by using school as a necessary credential for status positions in society. However, cultural capital theory suggests that upward mobility (and the realization of credentials) are controlled by one's social class. In other words, some social class ideologies are better suited to schools than others.

For example, in her work on social class and its relationship to parent involvement in schools, Lareau (2000) maintains that the relationship between working-class families and schools is characterized by separation (parents and students think of school and education as a job which stops when the children arrive home). The relationship middle-to-upper middle-class families have with schools is characterized by interconnectedness, such that the business of school and education is an ongoing endeavor in everyday home life. Meanwhile, schools are thought to accept, reproduce, and reflect societal hierarchies. This was corroborated by Bowles and Gintis (1976), who suggest that schools are class-based institutions that often reproduce the advantages and deficits of class-based consciousness and knowledge. Deterministic in nature, Bowles and Gintis' argument proposes a one-to-one relationship between schools and other societal structures, such as the home. Fortunately, this may not really be representative of the levels of congruence and discontinuity between home and school environments. In fact, the main thrust of Lareau's argument is that although cultural capital theory improves upon other existing explanations of why middle-class families seem to be more involved in school than working-class families, it needs to be modified if it is to explain that in fact, "possession of high status cultural resources does not automatically yield a social profit [unless] these cultural resources are activated by the individual" (p. 10). The activation of resources by individuals is key to understanding why social class, although a potent and at times an accurate predictor of student success in schools, may not account for the enactment of competencies that can cut across social class barriers.

One example of the enactment of competencies that cuts across social class comes from research conducted within Latino populations where family cultural resources get played out and instantiated in school settings (Moll, 1992; Moll,

Amanti, Neff, & González, 1992; Moll & González, 1994). Moll (1992) defines funds of knowledge as "the historically accumulated and culturally developed bodies of knowledge and skills essential for household or individual functioning and well-being" (p. 133). The "funds of knowledge" perspective acknowledges that social class can be an impediment to or a catalyst of learning and achievement. However, "the essential cultural practices and bodies of knowledge and information that households use to survive, to get ahead, or to thrive" (Moll, 1992, p. 21) are part of wider social networks and are required by diverse labor markets. In other words, Moll suggests that if schools could find a way to explicitly privilege other cultural tools, some students would be successful. Therefore, schools and teachers would do well to become familiar with these funds of knowledge simply because they represent "a *potential* major social and intellectual resource for the schools" (p. 22). Moll's research illustrates that when schools make attempts to understand the underlying social and cultural networks of the populations they service, it is more likely that there will be congruence between what and how content is taught and students' ability to learn, thus broadening the definitions of privileged cultures and tools to include more than just social class distinctions. It is clear that researchers who have studied and analyzed the impact of home cultures and social class on success at home and in school, have concluded that although social class (and cultural capital theory) are a useful tool, they do not always explicate the ways through which individuals learn, produce knowledge, and sustain cultural and/or social identities in multiple worlds.

Having briefly discussed cultural capital theory as a model for explaining differences in achievement based on social class distinctions, I consider next the implications of a cultural-ecological model on success at school and home. Anthropologist John Ogbu first conceptualized a cultural-ecological perspective as a framework for cross-cultural research when he studied competence and child-rearing practices from a non-ethnocentric perspective in a given population (Ogbu, 1982b). Ogbu maintains that child rearing in the family and subsequent adolescent socialization aim at developing instrumental competencies required for adult economic, political, and social roles. Furthermore, cultural imperatives vary from one population to another as do the required competencies. He defines competence as "the ability to perform a culturally specific task, or a set of functional or instrumental skills" (p. 114). Ogbu disagrees with views on human development that assumes that a child's later school success depends on the acquisition of white middle-class competencies (and sources of cultural capital) through White middle-class child-rearing practices. He claims that there are immigrant groups in the US who do not ascribe to middle-class practices and values and whose children have still succeeded in school. This is so because "the origins of human competencies lie in the nature of culturally defined adult tasks" (p. 120). The implications of such a cultural-ecological model of society come into play when one studies populations that are considered to be "minorities" in a society. Ogbu suggests that the reason minority groups (Blacks and Hispanics, specifically) experience a continuing disproportion of school failure is due to the fact that their historical and structural relationship with the dominant groups has produced alternate competencies. For instance, generally both White middle class students and inner-city minorities might value money, power, social credit, and self-esteem, but these two populations might differ in how to go about attaining these goals, i.e., the extent to which they believe that the appropriate school credentials will result in the desired goal and rewards.

Ogbu (1982a) elaborates the cultural-ecological perspective further when he addresses more specifically the connections between home and school. He notes that all children experience an "initial discontinuity between home and school in language use, contextual learning, and style of learning" (p. 293). For example, classroom organization, student–teacher relations, and grading promote attributes of "impersonality, specificity, universal standards, achievement norms, and independence similar to those valued and rewarded in the workplace of the corporate economy" (p. 292), while a child's socialization in the family promotes "intimacy, diffuseness, and particularism in interpersonal relationships, particularistic standards and ascription in achievement and reward, as well as a certain degree of independence" (p. 292). In addition, inherent to the home in contrast to the school is that home is an oral culture, whereas when children first attend school cognitive strategies rely very much on writing and reading (Cook-Gumperz & Gumperz, 1979). It is clear that home life and school life are discontinuous at one level for all students.

Ogbu's cultural-ecological perspective has established that all students experience discontinuity when they make the transition from home to school. Ogbu differentiates among types of discontinuity, primary and secondary, by claiming that primary cultural differences (those experienced by what "voluntary" minorities) "result from cultural developments before members of a given population come in contact with American or Western white middle-class culture or enter American/[Western] public schools" (Ogbu, 1982a). However, the students and parents experiencing primary cultural differences are "willing to learn the culture of the school *because* of the expected material and nonmaterial rewards in [the] emerging Western-type status system" (p. 294). This occurs regardless of social class. Getting ahead requires school credentials, and non-Western and Western voluntary minorities are willing to learn new values, new rules of intercommunication, and new social competence to achieve their goals. Equally important, these minorities, even if they experience discrimination, think that they are better off in the US than in their "home" countries. Ogbu suggests that persevering to overcome discontinuities means that the new language and school culture are not perceived as threatening to individual or group identities. That is the key to success at home and school for these populations.

In contrast to primary cultural differences, which are usually experienced by "voluntary minorities," secondary cultural discontinuities "develop *after* members of two populations have been in contact or after members of a given population have begun to participate in an institution controlled by another group, such as a school system" (p. 298). These differences evolve as a response to a contact situation where stratified domination is the norm. Ogbu refers to these populations as "caste-like" or "involuntary" minorities (Blacks, Native American Indians, and Mexican-Americans). They are distinct from other populations in that they identify themselves from the cultural frame of reference of "opposition." Ogbu (1993) defines "cultural frame of reference" as "the correct or ideal way of behaving within a culture—attitudes, beliefs, preferences, and practices considered appropriate for members of the culture" (p. 490). Unlike voluntary minorities, their cultural frames of reference do not allow them to cross-cultural or language boundaries (Ogbu, 1993). This oppositional cultural frame indicates that involuntary minorities perceive schooling as a "linear acculturation process, an assimilation process, or a displacement process" (p. 501). Voluntary minorities, on the other hand, usually view their lives in the US as an improvement over their "old country" and have a positive frame of reference such that it "enhances symbolic responses conducive to academic striving and success" (p. 499). They can accommodate the system without assimilating.

In many ways, a cultural-ecological perspective goes further in explaining both structural and individual patterns of learning and achievement at home and school than does cultural capital theory. The notion that there are alternative competencies within a culture which are based on future adult tasks within a population rather than on hierarchies rooted in static social class roles, values, and knowledge means that individuals and groups of individuals who might have been deemed "failures" in school can be seen in a different and more progressive light. However, Ogbu (1982a) notes that there has not been much data or explanation about immigrant minority-group children who are successful in school and perform better than involuntary minorities yet differ markedly from their public school teachers in terms of communicative strategies, interpretation of situated meanings, rules of interaction, and literate cultural background (see Sarroub, 2001, 2002, 2005, for such an explanation). Ogbu gives the example of the Buraku outcaste in Japan who underperform in school when compared to the dominant Ippan group. However, in the United States, where the Buraku show primary cultural differences, and where they are treated like any other Japanese immigrants, they do at least as well as other Japanese and American students (see McDermott, 1974). Ogbu suggests that the lack of success in Japan is due to language, communication, and interaction differences. In the United States, these students do what they can to get ahead because their cultural frame of reference is a positive one even if they do represent low socio-economic class values and ways of learning. While Ogbu's theory offers a way to think about home and school expectations for success, it does not account for the role and power of teachers who connect to students through formal and informal curricula.

THEORETICAL APPLICATION: EXPLANATIONS OF MINORITY STUDENT SCHOOL ACHIEVEMENT

Scholars have developed many theories to explain why minority students have, on average, historically suffered from lower school achievement than White students. Often, these theories focus on the ways that schools disadvantage non-White, non-middle-class students by privileging the cultural resources (beliefs, values, knowledge, speech, etc.) of the prototypical White middle-class student and ignoring or denigrating those of minority students. However, this perspective does not explain why some minority students succeed in school. As discussed in this section, Ogbu's ideas provide an important extension of such theories. While Ogbu did not necessarily challenge the idea that schools may be less hospitable for minorities than they are for White students, he shifted the focus from the school to the students' and their families' response to the schooling process, suggesting that families and children respond in one of two general ways. Some families and/or children respond in an oppositional manner to schools that they perceive as biased against them and thus reject the values associated with schooling and school success. Thus, these students may actively participate in their own failure because they view school success as requiring a rejection of their own cultural identity. In contrast, Ogbu's "voluntary minorities" see difficulties in the school process as normal challenges to be overcome. These children do not see schooling as an attack on their traditions and identities and often succeed in maintaining a strong sense of cultural identity at home while simultaneously taking on school-valued dispositions and behaviors when in school. While this book aims to help educators make schooling more hospitable for diverse students and families, Ogbu's theory stresses that families and students must also move toward less oppositional responses to schooling. Have you known minority students who demonstrated resistance to schooling and seemed to reject the idea of school achievement? Why did (or could) this occur? What specific strategies might teachers use to help prevent students from developing an oppositional attitude toward school? How can diverse students learn to acquire dispositions and behaviors that enable school success while also maintaining a healthy sense of cultural identity?

Ethnographic and Historical Perspectives of Arab-American Populations

Having described and analyzed how scholars in education have conceptualized cultural capital theory and cultural-ecology as models for the ways in which students meet the expectations of both school and home, I consider next the implications of these models within a specific population, Muslim Arab-Americans. First, I lay out the historical context within which this population exists and identifies itself. Then, I examine identity and identity development by focusing on a couple of specific segments of this population, Yemeni and Palestinian women because most of the research on Arab Americans has concentrated on these sub-groups. In the US, unlike countries such as France and Britain, research on education and Muslim Arabs has been minimal (see Sarroub, 2005).

Muslim Arab Americans have a long history in the United States and elsewhere in the world (see Raissiguier, 1994). They represent all social classes, and because they are representative of a variety of Arab countries, they do exhibit internal cultural differences even though as a population, they have religion, language, and a vast array of traditions and customs in common. Specifically, one common

characteristic of most Arab societies is that the role women play in this population is key to understanding their cultural frame of reference. A case in point is
the evolution of the Arab identity. In the early twentieth century, hundreds
of Syrian and Lebanese Christians (mostly peddlers who came to realize the
"American Dream") immigrated to the US. By WWII, for these "Arab" communities (they did not identify themselves with this term), integration into US
society was nearly complete and witnessed the near extinction of Arab ethnicity
(Suleiman, 1994). In fact, the Arabic language ceased to be spoken simply because
these traders traveled so much in order to sell their wares that they learned to
speak Standard American English and follow the predominantly Protestant cultural norms faster than any other immigrant population in the US at that time
(Naff, 1994). Arabs who immigrated to the US after WWII and the late 1960s
were comprised of mostly well-educated Muslims. According to Suleiman (1994),
ethnic unity, no matter from which Arab country these immigrants originated,
was of special importance to these immigrants. This was due, in part, to the
creation of the state of Israel and to the displacement of many Palestinians and,
second, to post-independence ruptures in North Africa and the Middle East (p.
46). Furthermore, the strong anti-Arab sentiments that pervaded the US media in
the 1970s and 1980s, 1990s (and recently) also became the subject of study and
analysis by several Arab intellectuals such as Edward Said (1979), thus further
grouping many nationalities within "Arab" and further politicizing cultural
identity.

> On the one hand, as this identification forged it took on a visibility that made
> it more easily the target of prejudice and hatred. On the other hand,
> Arab-Americans found security through belonging to a group and having an
> identity in which they could feel a common sense of pride.
>
> (Haddad, 1994, p. 80)

Arab identity has developed over time through internal and external pressures. It
was not until the 1980s that Arab-Americans became politically active in seeking
to be heard on political matters. This identification with becoming American and
at the same time maintaining ethnic roots has been a painful one, just as it has for
other immigrant populations such as Latinos, Jews, Eastern Europeans, Asians,
and Africans.

The relationship between ethnic identity, whether it be religious and/or cultural such as Islam, is connected to the intellectual and social self-definition for
young Muslim "Arab" women in the US. According to Suleiman (1994), "for
Christians, Muslims, and Jews from the Middle East, one's religious affiliation
determines one's identity. A person is born, grows up, and dies in a specific
religious community" (p. 65). In the United States, identity development is
further complicated because other factors such as social class, educational background, and gender relations among men and women play a role in people's self-
projections. Arabs fear that the fabric of U.S. society and its moral and ethical
underpinnings are undermining and eroding their cultural values, and in differing ways they rely on their own communities to provide the structures in which

to relate socially as individuals and as families, and in which they can feel comfortable raising their children" (Haddad, 1994, p. 78). Whereas these Arab communities may at one time have felt powerless politically, they currently understand that acceptance by the dominant society has moved to a deeper level in which individuals do not have to renounce their own culture but can actually share it (p. 78). This resembles Ogbu's observation of primary cultural differences—one accommodates without assimilation. In other words, identification with the host culture need not obliterate identification with the home culture because *identity* comes to encompass affiliation with both.

Yemeni American Girls' Literacies In and Out of School

Yemeni migration to the United States is part of a larger historical trend of Arab immigration to North America. Many recent immigrants moved to the Detroit area because they could find work in the shipping and auto industries, and since the 1970s, southeastern Michigan has had the highest concentration of Arabic-speaking people outside of the Middle East, an estimated 250,000 residents (Sarroub 2000; Zogby 1984). Unlike earlier Arab immigrants, recent arrivals from northern Yemen have persisted in preserving both their Muslim ways of life and their Arab identities. These immigrants have kept strong ties with their motherland, buying land in Yemen with the intention of going back, visiting for long periods, and sending their children there to marry. Consequently, in the United States, the children of these immigrants straddle two worlds, the literate world of school and the home world of religious and cultural values where the text of the *Qur'an* sanctions behavior and social norms (Sarroub, 2005).

Yemeni American high school girls or *hijabat* (what the girls called themselves—from the Arabic feminine plural for girls who wear the head scarf) live in the Detroit working-class suburb of Dearborn. While their experiences are unique, they are also instructive in understanding the roles of religious oral and print texts among other Muslim women immigrants—and their daughters—in contemporary North America. The Yemeni community of Dearborn, Michigan, lives in a neighborhood called the "Southend" where they have formed their own social and linguistic spaces. Girls leave the Southend only to go to school or during family outings. Living in two worlds can be difficult for all of the residents, but especially for young women who struggle to negotiate their Yemeni and American identities as well as to meet their families' expectations of being good daughters. Their responsibilities are three-fold: uphold the transnational honor of the family; become good mothers (most are engaged or married by the ages of 14 or 15); and succeed in school. In their daily efforts to meet these responsibilities, Yemeni *hijabat* rely not only upon a variety of religious texts but also on the process of discussing these texts with their peers in school, home, and community spaces.

Religiously Motivated Textual Categories

The public high school is a key cultural intersection and where Yemeni American girls adapt to American life by organizing behaviors into three categories which stem from the *Qur'an* and religious teachings: *haram*, meaning forbidden; *halal* meaning lawful; and, *mahkru*, meaning not written as forbidden in the *Qur'an* but condemned by the Prophet Muhammad. The young Yemeni American women said that all things *haram* are written in the *Qur'an*, such as drinking alcohol. Things *halal* are good deeds, which include learning and being learned. Things *mahkru* include wearing make-up before marriage or listening to music. Indeed, many of the *hijabat* wore nail polish or eyeliner and listened to popular music even though the Prophet forbade it. However, because nothing is written in the *Qur'an* about such things, Islamic scholars and ordinary Muslims debate these issues constantly. At school, the *hijabat* used *haram* and *halal* liberally, especially when one's modesty was in question. The students argued about what was *haram* when something was called into question, and advice was often sought from peers who were respected for their knowledge of the *Qur'an* and the *Hadith* (recorded words, actions, sanctions of the Prophet Muhammad). Girls who were pious or wanted to appear pious did not do or say anything that was likely to be considered *mahkru*. In fact, except for some girls who studied and read the *Qur'an*, the category *mahkru* was not known or well understood by most girls and boys. For the *hijabat*, most of life fell under *haram* or *halal*, and when scripture did not provide an answer, there was always what they called the Yemeni "folk Islam," that is, occult beliefs or superstitions that helped explain and remedy problems.

Arranging life into religiously motivated textual categories gave the *hijabat* the opportunity to maintain Yemeni social status and norms within the confines of school. Yet, school also gave the girls the chance to stretch home and community-imposed limits. For example, unlike most teenagers, the *hijabat* were often not allowed to listen to American popular music, which was in the *mahkru* category, and they were also not allowed to read teen magazines, or anything that might be sexually explicit or imply sexuality. At school they created a private space for themselves in their cafeteria cluster of tables, buffered by the non-Arab students against the Yemeni boys, whom they called "boaters," and who would often report back to the Southend on the *hijabat* if they did not maintain a proper social performance of modesty, thus damaging the *hijabat*'s reputations. Here the girls brought forth their contraband: teen magazines, yearbook pictures which could only be seen by them, and fable-like poems and stories, especially about girls who misbehaved. They gossiped around these texts, sharing personal information about their marriages, their families, and the men they would like to marry (often in opposition to the ones to whom they were betrothed). They argued about the difference between culture and religion, an important distinction for these girls because it meant that while their religion and their Holy Book could not be questioned, their culture and cultural acts could. Thus, when the *hijabat* were upset with family decisions about education or marriage, they were very careful to blame it on Yemeni culture and not on Islam.

The significance of the relatively safe crowded cafeteria is that it offered a haven for sharing secret texts, including texts which were American and which represented American values that differed from Yemeni ones. For example, a poem written in English about a girl who secretly goes out on a date with a drunken boy, who inadvertently kills her parents in a car crash, was downloaded from the

Internet and was passed among the girls. The girls reacted to this poem with loud exclamations of "*haram!*" and said that although they admired the girl for taking a risk, that disobeying and hurting their parents through their actions are forbidden.

Religious Instruction and Practices

Daily reading of the *Qur'an* was as symbolically important in the *hijabat's* lives as their modest form of dress. Reading the *Qur'an* led to three distinct results: being more knowledgeable about the contents of the *Qur'an* and therefore more respected by one's family and community, reaching a state of grace by virtue of the fact that reading it endows a spirituality or holiness, and empowering one's self against culturally-biased acts against Muslims. Parents were proud of their sons and daughters, but especially their daughters who read the *Qur'an* and prayed. At a parent/school meeting about school violence, one father praised his son's high grades but chose to describe his daughter's success at being prayerful, noting, "She prays more than I do." Although most of the Yemeni families desired both their male and female children to know the *Qur'an* and to pray, these characteristics were especially valued in girls because they reflected on the family's honor. It was the girls' responsibility to maintain religious values, thus reinforcing a gendered notion of religion. The girls knew this and were genuinely involved in their religious practice, but they were also cognizant of the power one assumed with the thorough knowledge of the *Qur'an*. Consequently, the *hijabat* also attended Arabic school at the mosque, classes that were gender segregated, included grades K-7, and met on the weekends from 8:30am until noon for instruction, after which lectures were scheduled. All of the instruction revolved around reading, writing, and the *Qur'an*. The oral and written texts with which the *hijabat* engaged allowed them to connect their religious practice to their identities as teenagers, but they also positioned them as pious girls for whom reading the *Qur'an* and chanting verses presented an antidote to the influences of the outside world.

Some girls also attended *muhathara* (lectures) and discussions organized by women in the community that took place either at the mosque or in a private home. The ones at the mosque were talks where a woman speaker addressed women's issues in front of an audience with discussion at the end, but the *muhathara* held in someone's home were different, more private and informal. The *hijabat* noted that they could talk to the woman who was hosting it and respected her because, unlike many of the women in the local community, she could read and write in Arabic and recite the entire *Qur'an*. She had achieved the state of grace and power into which the girls wanted to enter. After the evening prayer, each of the women brought something specific to read from the *Qur'an* or from a book on Muslim religious conduct, followed by a lecture on morality. The conversations during *muhathara* were characterized by the girls as more intellectual and religious and they saw the reading of the *Qur'an* and the conversation which ensued around the readings as knowledge to be learned rather than just talk among friends or "stuff you learn at school." These groups of girls grappled with religious and moral issues for a purpose: to stay true and pure to Islam, to show their community that they were good Muslim girls, and to vocalize potentially risky topics that they could not openly discuss in school or elsewhere.

The Yemeni American *hijabat* from the Southend shoulder a great deal of responsibility at a young age. They must excel in all domains of their lives—school, community, home, and housekeeping—in preparation for marriage, their adult roles, and the possibility of more education in university setting. For them, religious texts provide meaningful and relevant maps for navigating their complex personal, social, and cultural realities.

Palestinian Women's Experiences in Historical Perspective

Are Arab women able to participate in their identity formation by actively integrating their ethnicity and the dominant host culture of the United States? Cainkar (1994) points out that studies on "Arab" women immigrants are sorely lacking even though many more women than men have immigrated to the US since 1930. Cainkar argues that Palestinian women bear more of the anti-assimilation burden than men because they must maintain a strong attachment to their native culture in the home. Whereas Palestinian men often immigrated on their own as individuals, Palestinian women always immigrated as sisters, daughters, wives, or mothers. This means, according to Cainkar, that women, similarly to the young Yemeni American women I studied, were not free to determine how they would interact with their new host society and that the roles they held in their families carried over when they immigrated (p. 88). Their identities may have developed from an "oppositional" frame of reference, thus pointing to secondary cultural differences in Ogbu's framework. The excerpt at the beginning of the chapter illustrates this opposition by highlighting the possibility of resentment toward male authority over life and death. In addition, certain social values such as "the primacy of the extended family, collective responsibility for kin, hospitality, respect for status superiors, and control of women's sexuality" (p. 88) are highly respected and are commonly held among other "Third-World" immigrant populations such as Latinos (Carger, 1996).

Although there may be many similarities among Palestinian women, there are also significant differences based on socio-economic class values. Cainkar (1994) explains this phenomenon by referencing Gordon's (1964) *ethclass* concept, that people have two types of identification simultaneously: historical identifica-tion and participation identification, i.e., shared values and behavior patterns (pp. 89–90). To exemplify this dichotomy, Cainkar compares middle-class Pales-tinian women who immigrated to the US prior to 1967 to the "peasant" class Palestinian women who immigrated later. The middle-class women, although somewhat culturally traditional, wear Western clothing and simply exclude short skirts, shorts, and sleeveless tops. Their homes are filled with Palestinian artifacts and are well known for their hospitality, but the women tend to forego making elaborate Palestinian dishes and usually prepare American foods. Mothers usually speak English, so their children do not speak Arabic. These women are not highly educated because university education was not available to them in their home country prior to 1980. However, they expect their daughters to have a college education in order to take better care of themselves and their families after marriage and in case they must work outside the home. In this subgroup of Palestinians, women are generally not allowed to date, and marriage to non-Muslim Arabs is frowned upon. However, within the middle class, exceptions are made to some traditions. For instance, women are often allowed to choose which Arab-Muslim men they wish to marry. Of course, none of these rules apply to the men. Men may date publicly and marry whomever they wish. This often makes it difficult for Palestinian women to find eligible Palestinian men. Cainkar also notes that gatherings such as weddings and parties are not separated by gender as they traditionally once were because it is understood that men and women can interact socially without expressing or inviting sexual interest. This is not the case among Yemeni Americans in the United States (Sarroub 2001; 2002; 2005).

In contrast to the middle-class Palestinian women, women who immigrated to the US after 1967 and especially after 1975 uprooted themselves from traditional peasant life in West Bank villages. For these women and the men who accompanied them to the US, "traditionalism is a badge of honor" (Cainkar, 1994, p. 97). The women spend most of their time at home doing housework and preparing elaborate Palestinian dishes. Guests are often separated by gender and the families speak Arabic at home. Parents usually send their children to the Middle East during the summers so that they will be immersed in Palestinian culture and language. Although these people are voluntary minorities, unlike Ogbu's examples of the Japanese, the home country is perceived as better than the host culture. Going "back home" is often the underlying goal for maintaining strict enactment of cultural and linguistic separation from the host culture. For example, these Palestinian women rarely work outside the home (and therefore have very little contact with the host culture) because it might be interpreted that the husband does not earn enough. They are usually not highly educated, and although they do think that a college education is valuable, because of "concerns over women's sexuality and virginity, members of this subgroup tend to want their daughters married shortly after high school" (p. 99). Cainkar points out that this is not necessarily the case in the Middle East, but Palestinian parents are especially afraid of the freedoms U.S. women have and the preponderance of premarital sex. Consequently, self-control is highly valued in these Palestinian women. "Lack of self-control invites sexual innuendo, [and] a woman repeatedly lacking self-control is seen to be sexually untrustworthy" (p. 99). Lacking self-control is evidenced by aggressiveness in front of one's elders and around men or being too outspoken. Dating, of course, is completely forbidden and attending community gatherings or parties without family supervision and in the presence of men is also a taboo. Marriage is usually offered by a Palestinian Muslim to the family and only after the family approves, does the daughter meet to speak with her suitor. Only after the engagement has taken place, which in Muslim tradition is actually the signing of a binding marriage contract, will the couple go out together alone (p. 99). Consequently, women of Palestinian lower socio-economic background are closely scrutinized for possible violations, and "in a milieu where socializing is confined to family and local women, and women are chosen for marriage based partly on their reputation, social ostracism is a heavy price to pay" (p. 100). Again, men do not have to abide by any of the constraints imposed on women.

In summarizing her interview findings about the middle-class and lower socioeconomic class immigrant Palestinian women in the US, Cainkar makes the following observation.

> While middle-class Palestinian women see the United States for all the opportunities it affords them, lower-middle and lower-class Palestinian women see it merely as a place to live for a while, devoid of the land, family, customs, foods, and community life that gave their lives meaning in Palestine. These women have little in common with each other aside from their ethnic background, continued respect for certain cultural values . . . which requires that they maintain their Palestinian identity and avoid full assimilation.

(p. 101)

The Palestinian women are actively negotiating their roles in American society and doing it in different ways depending on their social class locations. It may very well be that lower-class Palestinian women are not negotiating a role in American society—they are just there living their traditional Palestinian roles. Their identification with the host culture is limited. An example of this is brought out by Zogby (1984) of Arab women actively negotiating their roles in Muslim culture through their involvement in mosque life where they attend Sunday school with their children and plan community gatherings. Recently, however, in the case of Muslim women in the US, the negotiation and shifting of identity and social position within their religious practices have not been easy. Much of these women's participation in formal religious life has been curtailed by a coalition of traditionalist print-illiterate rural men and highly educated young students or immigrants committed to a strict Islamic order with the end result being that the mosques can pattern themselves after those of Arab countries. Women are expected to stay out of the mosques (Zogby, 1984, p. 104). For the middle-class women, identity formation is more flexible and at times more of a struggle than that of the lower-class women because they constantly attempt to maintain a balance between both the United States and their own cultures even when they are told to sustain a more traditional woman's role by the more conservative elements in their communities.

THEORETICAL APPLICATION: NEGOTIATION

While the idea of negotiation is a familiar one in the contexts of business and politics, when applied to diverse students' lives inside and outside of school, it highlights the complexity of the issues that they frequently face. The previous sections on Yemeni and Palestinian girls and women suggest the range and intensity of challenges that culturally diverse adolescents confront as they actively negotiate their identities, relationships to home and school cultures and languages, gender roles, religious faiths, etc. How might this engagement in complicated negotiations of identity, culture, gender, and values affect diverse adolescents' school experience in general and participation in classroom activities in particular? How might an awareness of the kinds of issues that such students face affect your teaching?

I have described some provocative aspects of a population rich with cultural capital that remains relatively unknown in schools in relation to students' education or social advancement in the larger society. The cultural capital preserves the status quo of the home culture by taking advantage of the cultural resources (language, tradition, customs, religion) from the "old country," even to the extent that people travel "back home" to do so. Social class and primary and secondary cultural differences are intertwined such that it is not at all clear whether this rather diverse population of Muslim Arabs can in fact be called either voluntary or involuntary minorities. Unfortunately, so little research has focused on the education of this population and their successes or failure, that it is impossible to suggest one classification or the other (see Haw, 1998, for a rich analysis of Muslim women and schools in Great Britain). Unlike European education scholars, U.S. scholars in education tend, for the most part, not to focus on issues such as religion and its impact on education and schooling, although a notable exception is Peshkin's (1986) work on schools and Christian fundamentalism.

Research conducted in France, where the largest minority population constitutes North African Muslim Arabs, shows that Muslim Arab students, especially female students, spend a lot of time negotiating possibilities for themselves within the existing French cultural boundaries of appropriate behavior, and in the process, they stretch the limits of those boundaries. School socialization in France is regulated and differentiated on the basis of ethnicity and gender, a process that is conducive to the hegemonic goals of the French state.

The research on Arab Muslims in the United States and elsewhere illustrates that there are tensions between Western and non-Western goals for learning and achievement at home and at school, even though, as Ogbu observes, students do succeed in both places. As the world grows smaller and as cultural differentiation and identification increase, more accurate portrayals of these differences and discontinuities need to be documented and resolved so that congruence among previously irreconcilable contrasts can become possibility.

Suggestions for Teachers and Schools

Perhaps the most significant goal of teachers and schools' proactive roles with regard to Muslim Arab populations is a mindfulness of the connections between cultural and religious differences and socio-economic status and an understanding that the two combined make possible a more thoughtful and inclusive academic and social curriculum in schools. Second, a greater knowledge of the transnational experiences of youth and families and an acknowledgment of its global presence in school is key. Third, in addition to scholarly research, there are resources available to teachers that may be helpful for accommodation. Examples include:

- Classroom Windows 06/17 Episode 05: Culturally Responsive Teaching: http://video.google.com/videoplay?docid=6066894268476055581
- Arab Community Center for Economic and Social Services, Dearborn, Michigan: http://www.accesscommunity.org/site/PageServer
- Arab-American Association of New York: http://www.arabamericanny.org;
- *The middle of everywhere: The world's refugees come to our town* by Mary Pipher (2002).

Fourth, garnering a sense of a student's biography or an ethnic group's history in and out of the United States is immensely helpful in enacting transformative learning experiences. I learned that youth such as the young Yemeni American women in Michigan had great respect for their teachers. In their teachers, they saw possibility in education and in life in the United States, no matter how difficult it was to negotiate being Yemeni and American at the same time. As Florio-Ruane (2001) suggests, teachers who dare to imagine culture in relation to their selves are more likely to share common cultural spaces with those they teach.

Conclusion

In the US, media representations of Muslim Arabs have also not been positive. In light of the fact that the US allowed Muslim refugees from Iraq to make new lives in this country (currently between 3,000–5,000 are residing in the state of Nebraska and 12,000 were expected to arrive in the United States in 2008) and that there are over three million Arab-Americans in southeastern Michigan alone, it is imperative that researchers and teachers begin to understand how their cultures and social classes will impact the transition into becoming "Americans." A cultural-ecological model that also accounts for social class practice distinctions is helpful because in laying out the links between education, home, and school, the model allows for a non-ethnocentric basis of differentiation for understanding school achievement without minimizing the impact of historical, political, social, and contextual situations. It also has the further advantage of incorporating a social class lens of cultural capital theory, thus permitting other lenses and factors to emerge as powerful explanatory tools. The two cases I highlight among Muslim Arab Americans shed some light on the rather complex problems Western societies deal with today as many non-Western peoples continue to cross geographic and ideological boundaries and as they attempt to identify with home and host cultures.

By analyzing two historically pervasive perspectives used in education research, cultural capital from sociology and cultural-ecology from anthropology, as models of how to ensure that students succeed to learn in the worlds they travel, I suggest that social class *and* cultural difference have often explained why people fail or succeed, but most scholarship has involved doing research by looking at one or the other of these lenses. In my own research, I have examined how identity development as it is enacted in home and school discourses is related to socialization, learning, and achievement, and have illustrated that it may be necessary to employ interdisciplinary perspectives in order to probe more fully the complex and complicated continuities and discontinuities between home and school. Only then will we understand how to enable both the pragmatic and aesthetic goals families and schools undertake to achieve. We have much to learn from populations of youth and their families who simultaneously live in the United States and elsewhere.

Ideas for Discussion, Extension, and Application

1. Imagine that you have a group of Yemeni girls in your high school class. Make a quick list of the ways that their life experience will likely differ greatly from that of their peers. Discuss these differences and the effect that they might have on the groups' participation in classroom and school activities.

2. Ogbu suggests that some diverse students, particularly those from African American, Latino, and American Indian communities (in his terms, "involuntary minorities"), develop an oppositional attitude toward school and school success. Discuss why this might occur and any specific cases that you have experienced. Brainstorm specific ways that schools, communities, and families might prevent this oppositional development.

3. Examine the notion of accommodation versus assimilation. What are the pros and cons of each process? How does each impact one's sense of identity and ability to successfully negotiate host and home languages and cultures?

References

Adeeb, P., & Smith, G. P. (1995). The Arab Americans. In C. A. Grant (Ed.), *Educating for diversity: An anthology of multicultural voices.* Boston: Simon & Schuster Company.

Alwujude, S. (2000). Daughter of America. In N. Abraham & A. Shyrock (Eds.), *Arab Detroit: From margin to mainstream* (pp. 381–390). Detroit: Wayne State University Press.

Bourdieu, P. (1977a). Cultural reproduction and social reproduction. In J. Karabel, & A. H. Halsey (Eds.), *Power and ideology in education.* New York: Oxford University Press.

Bourdieu, P. (1977b). *Outline of a theory of practice.* London: Cambridge University Press.

Bourdieu, P. (1987). Forms of capital. In J. G. Richardson (Ed.), *Handbook of theory and research for sociology of education.* New York: Greenwood Press.

Bowles, S., & Gintis, H. (1976). *Schooling in capitalist America.* New York: Basic Books.

Cainkar, L. (1994). Palestinian women in American society: The interaction of social class, culture, and politic. In E. McCarus (Ed.), *The development of Arab-American identity*. Michigan: University of Michigan Press.

Carger, C. L. (1996). *Of borders and dreams: A Mexican-American experience of urban education*. New York: Teachers College Press.

Cohen, D., & Neufeld, B. (1981). The failure of high schools and the progress of education. *Daedalus, 110,* 69–89.

Cook-Gumperz, J., & Gumperz, J. (1979). From oral to written culture: The transition to literacy. In M. Farr Whitehead (Ed.), *Variation in writing*. Hillsdale, NJ: Lawrence Erlbaum Associates.

Florio-Ruane, S. (2001). *Teacher education and the cultural imagination: Autobiography, conversation, and narrative*. Mahwah, NJ: Erlbaum.

Gee, J. P. (1989). Literacy, discourse, and linguistics: Introduction. *Journal of Education, 171*(1), 4–25.

Gordon, M. (1964). *Assimilation in American life: The role of race, religion, and national origins*. New York: Oxford University Press.

Haddad, Y. (1994). Maintaining faith of the fathers: Dilemmas of religious identity in the Christian and Muslim Arab-American communities. In E. McCarus (Ed.), *The development of Arab-American identity*. Michigan: University of Michigan Press.

Haw, K. (1998). *Educating Muslim girls: Shifting discourses*. Philadelphia, PA: Open University Press.

Labaree, D. (1997). Public goods, private goods: The American struggle over educational goals. *American Educational Research Journal, 34*(1), 39–81.

Lareau, A. (2000). *Home advantage: Social class and parental intervention in elementary education*. Boston: Rowman & Littlefield.

McDermott, R. P. (1974). Achieving school failure: An anthropological approach to illiteracy and social stratification. In G. D. Spindle (Ed.), *Education and the cultural process*. New York: Holt, Rinehart and Winston.

Moll, L. C. (1992). Bilingual classroom studies and community analysis: Some recent trends. *Educational Researcher, 21*(2), 20–24.

Moll, L. C., Amanti, C., Neff, D., & Gonzáles, N. (1992). Funds of knowledge for teaching: Using a qualitative approach to connect homes to schools. *Theory into Practice, 31*(2), 132–141.

Moll, L. C., & González, N. (1994). Lessons from research with language-minority children. *Journal of Reading Behavior, 26*(4), 439–456.

Naff, A. (1994). The early Arab immigrant experience. In E. McCarus (Ed.), *The development of Arab-American identity*. Michigan: University of Michigan Press.

Ogbu, J. (1982a). Cultural discontinuities and schooling. *Anthropology and education Quarterly, 13*(4), 290–307.

Ogbu, J. U. (1982b). Origins of human competence: A cultural-ecological perspective. In S. Chess, & A. Thomas (Eds.), *Annual progress in child psychiatry and child development* (pp. 113–140). New York: Brunner/Mazel Publishers.

Ogbu, J. U. (1988). Cultural diversity and human development. *New Directions for Child Development, 42,* 11–28.

Ogbu, J. U. (1993). Differences in cultural frame of reference. *International Journal of Behavioral Development, 16*(3), 483–506.

Peshkin, Alan. (1986). *God's choice: The total world of a fundamentalist Christian school*. Chicago: University of Chicago Press.

Pipher, M. (2002). *The middle of everywhere: The world's refugees come to our town*. Boston: Harcourt.

Raissiguier, C. (1994). *Becoming women, becoming workers: Identity formation in a French vocational school.* New York: State University of New York Press.

Said, E. (1979). *Orientalism.* New York: Vintage Books.

Sarroub, L. K. (2000). Education. In A. Ameri, & D. Ramey (Eds.), *Arab American Encyclopedia.* Detroit: UXL/Gale Group.

Sarroub, L. K. (2001). The sojourner experience of Yemeni American high school students: An ethnographic portrait. *Harvard Educational Review, 71*(3), 390–415.

Sarroub, L. K. (2002). "In-betweenness": Religion and conflicting visions of literacy. *Reading Research Quarterly, 37*(2), 130–148.

Sarroub, L. K. (2005). *All American Yemeni girls: Being Muslim in a public school.* Philadelphia: University of Pennsylvania Press.

Suleiman, M. (1994). Arab-Americans and the political process. In E. McCarus (Ed.), *The development of Arab-American identity.* Michigan: University of Michigan Press.

Zogby, J. (1984). *Taking root, bearing fruit: The Arab-American experience.* Washington, DC: Arab American Institute.

6   Building Connections between Homes and Schools

Melissa M. Schulz

Melissa:	Did you participate in school-related activities in kindergarten and first grade such as parent–teacher conferences, curriculum nights, and attend school plays?
Nilesh:	Yes, I attend all parent–teacher conferences and curriculum nights; whatever the teacher asked me to do I did to help Andrew. I did not go into the school for Andrew's musical but I took him to school and waited in the car for him.

Melissa:	Do you participate in school-related activities with your children such as parent–teacher conferences, curriculum nights, and attend school plays?
Mary:	Yes, my husband and I go to all of the school events. I have always had a lot of communication with my kids' teachers. Either the teachers have chosen to email me or since I have been volunteering in the classrooms for the last three years, my children's teachers keep me updated about what is going on. So I probably know more than the typical parent just because of my involvement in the classroom. The teachers choose to tell me things all of the time. Like in Allison's progress note, this year's teacher said because Mrs. Smith comes in on a weekly basis, I will keep her in contact with what is going on with Allison in the classroom and how she is doing. On a *weekly* basis! I never asked for that! I was like WOW! When I go in to volunteer in the classroom, I don't want to ask the teacher about how my kids are doing because I feel that distracts the teacher from why I am there, to help her with her students. So I have never chosen to ask specifically about my kid's academic progress but this specific teacher is just willing to do that.

Leah:	I have test-preparation workbooks galore.
Melissa:	How did you know what kind to get for them?
Leah:	I got some that were just reading and math. But these are good, I have got these every year for them.
Melissa:	So it is test-preparation.
Mary:	Yes, we'll start this summer. They think it is really cool and they sit down and work on these. They are just incredible. I bought this 4th grade proficiency book for her to through the summer before the test and I threw it away. But I even have workbooks for his age. [Seth is working on computer as we talk.]

Melissa: When do they work on these workbooks?

Leah: Weekends and after school if they don't have homework. It is also our summer work.

The parents in these scenarios experienced a vastly different relationship to their children's school community. Mainstream families, who are native English speakers and who have attended school in the United States, are typically effective at seeking information to support their children at home. In contrast, immigrant families, independent of their social status, need additional support to learn how to utilize the public schools and gain valuable curriculum information necessary to support their children at home. Many first generation immigrant parents are unfamiliar with the social, cultural, and academic expectations embedded within the school community because they did not attend public schools in the United States.

I first met Nilesh at a "Meet the Teacher Night" at Highland Elementary School. I was his son Andrew's second grade teacher. At that time, my perception was that we worked together to establish a strong parent–teacher relationship. Thus, I was astonished by Nilesh's comment about the musical. The metaphor of Nilesh waiting in the car for his son Andrew, who is performing in a school musical, illustrates how he was on the "outside" of the schooling process. Nilesh shared that he simply felt like too much of an outsider with the school community to join the other parents in the auditorium. Nilesh and his wife Lee Nguyen were immigrants to the United States from Vietnam. Andrew was born in the United States. Nilesh and Lee encouraged their son to be successful in school. As Nilesh and Lee revealed their personal and educational histories with me, I learned how foreign and dislocating a school can be for some linguistically and culturally diverse families.

In the second vignette, Mary had two children enrolled in the school district and she felt very comfortable communicating with her children's teachers and spending time volunteering in her children's classrooms. Mary, Rick, and all three of their children were born in the United States and are native English speakers. Mary and Rick encouraged their children to be successful in school. As Mary and Rick shared their personal and educational histories with me, I learned how seamless the transition from home to school can be for many Caucasian families. Mary and Rick, as well as the other "mainstream" parents in this study, had insider information about how public schools operate because they once were successful students in public schools in the United States.

Leah, in the third vignette, learned about the school's curricula through volunteering in her children's classroom since kindergarten.

When I began a research study that focused on family literacy practices, I asked Nilesh and Lee Nguyen, Mary and Rick Smith, and Leah and Jay Sanders (all are former students' families) if they were willing to participate in the study. I also worked with one additional family, the Walkers, from the same community. This chapter focuses on the Nguyens, the Smiths, the Walkers and the Sanders, families who lived only miles apart from each other in the same community yet displayed significant differences in language, culture, religion, and understanding of school processes. The demographics in today's schools require teachers and administrators to understand the diverse cultural and linguistic backgrounds of their students in order to better facilitate membership in the school community. My own difficulties as an eight-year veteran elementary teacher led me into a search for new questions and answers. What are the challenges of and opportunities for gaining access to an insider membership as first generation immigrant parent(s)? What were the family's experiences as insiders or outsiders in the school community? What are the traditional ways that teachers connect with families to build understanding? What are the contemporary ways that teachers connect with families to build understanding? What were the lessons for me as a veteran teacher within the school district? This chapter looks closely at four families, one immigrant family and three native English-speaking families. The focus is on home and school connections; that is, the learning resources families used to support their child at home, and how they were connected or disconnected with school instruction.

Theoretical Framework

This analysis is situated within a range of disciplines that document the importance of teachers and administrators understanding children's home-based and school-based literacy practices (Heath, 1983; Ladson-Billings, 1994; Taylor & Dorsey-Gaines, 1988). There is widespread agreement among teachers and researchers that children's literacy learning process is complex and cannot always be understood by looking at their school experiences alone (Edwards, Pleasants, & Franklin, 1999; Gadsden, 1994; Heath, 1982, 1989; Hull & Schultz, 2002; Purcell-Gates, 1993, 1995; Taylor, 1983; Taylor & Dorsey-Gaines, 1988). All children in a literate society have a multitude of experiences with print and other oral literacy practices before coming to school (Hull & Schultz, 2002; Taylor & Dorsey-Gaines, 1988). In fact, a robust literature has examined the highly contextualized and diverse nature of literacy learning across cultures and socioeconomic communities (Compton-Lilly, 2003; Finn, 1999; Hale, 2001; Heath, 1983, 1989; Hicks, 2002; Moll & Gonzáles, 2004; Taylor & Dorsey-Gaines, 1988). This diversity underscores the need for schools to understand how to reach students from cultural, socioeconomic, and linguistic backgrounds that differ from the prototypical mainstream family (Hull & Schultz, 2002). In short, not all families share the same reading, writing, and speaking practices in their homes and communities.

My study was guided by a socio-constructivist framework (Vygotsky & Kozulin 1986). Vygotsky stated:

> What the child can do in cooperation today he can do alone tomorrow. Therefore, the only good kind of instruction is that which marches ahead of development and leads it; it must be aimed not so much at the ripe as at the ripening functions.
>
> (p. 188)

Whether a learner is learning how to ride a bicycle for the first time or how to write their name; parents, teachers, and more knowledgeable "others" provide support and scaffolding so that the learner is successful with the new learning task. Educators who believe in and understand a social-constructivist perspective recognize, learn about, and draw from the many people who are part of the learner's world outside of school (Edwards, Pleasants, & Franklin, 1999; Gadsden, 1994; Heath, 1982, 1989; Hull & Schultz, 2002; Purcell-Gates, 1993, 1995; Taylor, 1983, Taylor & Dorsey-Gaines, 1988). Further, such educators view literacy learning as a sociocultural process that includes literate activities in homes, communities, and work places (Hull & Schultz, 2002). From a sociocultural perspective, literacy learning is situated within historical contexts. According to Barton, Hamilton and Ivanič, "Literacy practices are culturally constructed, and, like, all cultural phenomena, they have their roots in the past" (2000, p. 13). The four of the families included in this study supported and negotiated literacy learning differently based on the unique, historically-shaped practices embedded in each home.

THEORETICAL APPLICATION: WHAT COUNTS AS DIVERSITY

Multicultural research makes a case for teacher education pedagogies that cultivate prospective and in-service teachers' ability to reflect and examine assumptions and beliefs about themselves and others as well as immerse themselves in diverse contexts. However, diversity is an open-ended and complex construct. This book provides snapshots into the lives of families who are linguistically, culturally and/or socioeconomically diverse. Underlying each chapter are key questions about diversity, such as What counts as diversity? To whom and in what situation? What are the opportunities and challenges for school learning within these contexts? These questions complicate what counts as diversity and cause educators to avoid the tendency to make interpretations based on generalizations. This chapter is a good example of one teacher's re-examination of her assumptions and beliefs. Schulz's immersion in a diverse context prompted her to see one family's experiences as outsiders in a new light. Take a moment to write down your current definition of diversity. What does it encompass? Does it help you to see all the possible challenges diverse families face when participating in school communities?

Demographics of Diversity

There are a growing number of diverse learners who enter the public schools. For example, Meyer, Madden and McGrath (2004) indicate that 18% or nearly 47 million people over the age of five in the United States speak a language other than English. This increase in English Language Learners has affected schools significantly. The number of language minority students in U. S. public schools is projected to be 40% of the school age population by the 2030s and, according to Thomas and Collier (2002), most schools are under-educating this group of students.

As the U.S. population is rapidly becoming more diverse, so are the public schools. Students will arrive at the school door with a varied range of academic competence and out-of-school experiences. Teachers need to be prepared to meet the diversity represented in the student population and embrace the richness it offers for the school and the classroom. At the beginning of each school year in preschool through third grade, teachers assess students' literacy skills. Some skills include letter recognition, knowledge of letter and sound relationships, word knowledge, writing vocabulary, concepts of print, and text reading level. Mounting evidence continues to document an achievement gap between students. The variation is obvious as early as kindergarten on measures of letter recognition and letter sound relationships between Caucasian and Latino students (West, Denton, & Reaney, 2000). Another similar gap is found along economic lines (West, Denton, & Germino Hausken, 2000; Zill & West, 2000). Evidence from longitudinal research suggests that while the differences among students' literacy progress is apparent early on, they become even more pronounced after four years. It is unlikely that students will change their classroom ranking from first to fourth grade. In short, students who are struggling in first grade will continue to struggle in fourth grade and students who are making average progress will be average in fourth grade as well (Juel, 1988).

The Homestead Study

As an elementary school teacher in the Homestead City School District for eight years, I wanted to become knowledgeable about how literacy was embedded into the families' lives and I wanted to observe the children's firsthand experiences with literacy outside of my classroom. I engaged in a year-long ethnographic study that included a total of four case studies of families who lived in a Midwestern city I call Homestead, population 24,230 (U.S. Census Bureau, 2001). According to a Citizen Survey conducted by the city of Homestead in December of 2002, the average income for the community was $23,749. According to Homestead City School District historical information, in 1991–1992 there were 7,255 students enrolled in the entire (K-12) school district, while in 2001–2002, there were 13,130 enrolled students. The rapid increase in enrollment has been an impetus for increased diversity.

The purpose of the comparative case studies was to illuminate the interaction of theory, research, and practice for linguistically and culturally diverse learners, family literacy, and culturally responsive teaching. As a former teacher in the Homestead school district, I wanted a more in-depth understanding of the cultural and literacy practices of some of my former students and their families. I wanted to learn how the schools could further support children and families from diverse backgrounds as they tried to engage with and utilize schools. Specifically, I wanted to know: (1) How can teachers gain an understanding of the learning resources that students' bring from the homes and communities? and (2) How can teachers and administrators facilitate communication between the school and homes of children from diverse backgrounds? In addition, since educators know very little about the family literacy (e.g. language and literacy acquisition) practices Asian-American children experience and the learning resources they bring to school, I sought to provide a glimpse into one Asian-American family and its approach to supporting their child's school learning.

Methodology

This year-long ethnographic study was conducted in two contexts that impact literacy learning: home and school. Three kinds of data were collected from both contexts: interview data, observational data, and documents. I visited each home for at least two hours per week. I interviewed the parents, children, and teachers (Bogden & Biklen, 1982). Adult interviews lasted approximately one hour, while interviews with children lasted approximately 30 minutes. I observed conversations between parents, children, and siblings, and parents and children in learning situations. Documents and artifacts were collected from home and school, such as the children's writing journals, children's email correspondence between family and friends, and a home-school communication journal between children's teachers and parents. By using a variety of methods, I was able to establish sound descriptions of literacy behaviors and events and communication among individuals.

Using multiple data sources across two different contexts allowed me to triangulate findings and identify themes. During the data collection phase, I engaged in on-going data analysis of the preliminary data through the review of fieldnotes and the transcription of interview data. The interviews were transcribed in full for each adult and child to capture ways of speaking, being, and valuing. The data from the four different homes contributed to a detailed account of certain family literacy experiences and learning resources.

One major theme emerged from the analysis: school and home connection or disconnection. In the following sections, I provide an account of the four families' home literacy practices. In each family I highlight one example of the school and home connection or disconnection. In the Walker family, I highlight how the emphasis on computer skills and parental support provided a seamless transition with the beginning computer skills that elementary students are expected to use in the Homestead City School District. In the Smith family, I highlight how the increased use of email correspondence among the children with their friends and family provided additional social-based writing practice that was helpful for the type of open-ended writing the children were expected to produce in the Homestead City School District. In the Sanders family, I highlight how Mrs. Sanders focused on test-preparation work with her children in the summer so they were more successful on the state-mandated standardized tests that her children took in school. Finally, in the Nguyen family, I highlight how Mr. and Mrs. Nguyen lacked critical "insider" knowledge of school-based literacy practices.

School and Home Connection

The Walker, Smith and Sanders families shared similar histories in regard to their "insider" knowledge and ability to navigate and gain access to information about the school curriculum and their children's teachers' expectations. They were all native English speakers who successfully went through the schooling process in American public schools.

Learning from the Walker Family

The Walker family consisted of the parents, Scott and Andrea, and their two children, Lucy and Ellie. Lucy was 6 years old and in kindergarten. Ellie was 2 years old and in preschool. Lucy was just beginning to learn how to type on the computer and send email messages. She was proficient with starting the computer and knew how to load and play her favorite computer programs by herself. One morning I observed as Lucy and her mother worked at the computer together:

Andrea:	Let's check your email first then we'll go to PBS. Ok it says to sign in your name so you need to type in Lucy.
Lucy:	L-U-C-Y, now I have to spell Walker.
Andrea:	It is Lucy Walker, you are right, it wasn't just Lucy.
Lucy:	Daddy said that it wasn't just Lucy it was Lucy Walker altogether.
Andrea:	Oh, ok. Now what is your password? Do you know how to spell it?
Lucy:	Yeah!
Andrea:	Now, go to the inbox, it is right there. Double click on the message. Do you know what it says right there?
Lucy:	Yeah! Dear Lucy.

Andrea was patient and supportive of Lucy's emerging writing attempts as they worked together on the computer. Andrea valued computer-generated writing and encouraged Lucy to practice by writing email to friends and family. Andrea, an elementary school teacher, worked on literacy-related tasks such as writing on the computer or storybook reading and informally socialized Lucy and Ellie into school-based literacy learning practices in the context of their home. For example, in the vignette above, Andrea used a school-like questioning strategy to guide Lucy through her learning of how to write an email message. The congruence between home-based and school-based literacy practices was evident in Lucy's successful, seamless transition into kindergarten. Scott and Andrea were supportive and wanted Lucy to be successful in school. They both participated in school activities. At the parent–teacher conference in the fall, Scott learned that Lucy really liked her journal. This prompted Scott to buy Lucy a Barbie notebook as a way to encourage fun writing at home. Andrea provided other examples of their involvement early in the school year:

> They have had two field trips and one of them was on a day when I was working but I did go on a trip to the zoo. I have talked to the teacher a couple

of times about volunteering in the classroom. She hasn't put together a schedule yet. I am hoping and looking forward to going to her classroom. So far, Scott and I have been able to go all of the things they have had at school, you know, curriculum night and meet the teacher night. I am as involved as I can be.

In literacy research, consistently there has been much interest in documenting and analyzing the reading, writing, listening, and speaking activities that occur in out of school activities that are diverse in function, form, and purpose. It is my belief that research on students' literacy practices and out-of-school learning can help researchers, teachers, parents, and community members revisit and reconsider the literacy teaching and learning in the classroom. By understanding and becoming knowledgeable about students' lives outside of the classroom, teachers will be more equipped to embed students' out-of-school learning, literacy values, beliefs, and knowledge into the school curriculum.

Learning from the Smith Family

The Smith family consisted of parents, Mary and Rick, and their three children. Allison was 11 years old, Rachel was 9 years old, and Seth was 6 years old. Mary and Rick used technology on a daily basis and they encouraged their children to use it as a tool to enhance their literacy learning at home. Significantly, Mary purchased travel journals to encourage the children to write about family trips and Mary and Rick encouraged their children to engage in school-like open-ended writing at home and to use the computer for email correspondence and educational and recreational computer games. Table 6.1 provides a summary of the various technology practices the children engaged in at home. All three children engaged in social-based computer writing for approximately thirty minutes a day. At age 3, Seth Smith began using the computer with his Mom and Dad to write letters to friends and grandparents. Their experience is in line with

Table 6.1 Strategies and conditions that supported literacy learning in the Smith family's home

Child's name	Frequency literacy event occurred	Strategies and conditions supporting learning	Learning that occurred
Allison, age 11 Rachel, age 9	Daily	Email correspondence	Writing practice Writing fluency
Allison, age 11 Rachel, age 9 Seth, age 6	2–3 times per week	Educational computer games	Math skill practice Reading skill practice
Allison, age 11 Rachel, age 9 Seth, age 6	Daily	Recreational computer games	Computer typing skills Reading skill practice

Lewis' (2000) research which indicates that "Twenty-five percent of the recently polled AOL parents say their children are coming online as early as age two, with that number climbing to 90% by age six" (p. 25).

Children from the Smith family enter school with reading, writing, listening, and speaking practices that are congruent to the teacher which helps them in terms of academic success. Heath's (1983) seminal study of three different communities in the Piedmont Carolinas, documented each community's "ways with words" and found that only middle-class students whose language use was similar to that of the teachers, were successful. My research with the Smith family validates Heath's (1983) research findings.

The elementary schools in the Homestead City School District implemented a writing workshop approach that encouraged children to create their own writing topics and write for an extended period. Children were expected to write independently daily in their journal, on the computer and within small groups.

Learning from the Sanders Family

The Sanders family consisted of parents, Leah and Jay, and their two children. Nate was 11 years old and Jenny was 8 years old. Leah worked as a nurse before Jenny was born. Her children were highly successful in school and both were my former students in 2nd grade. Leah volunteered once a week for one and half hours in my classroom and we had a strong parent–teacher relationship. Leah often helped in my classroom in the morning when I was working with small reading groups and during writing workshop. Leah would help students in my classroom with revising and editing their writing. Leah became knowledgeable about the reading and writing curriculum in the school district and specifically in my classroom. By spending considerable time working with students firsthand on their writing and by observing me as I taught reading and writing to students, she learned about my specific student expectations for reading, writing, listening, and speaking.

As her children's classroom teacher, I did not realize how much time she spent working with her children on test preparation during the summer months. When I started spending time in their home she described the routines she established to help prepare her children for the school and state mandated testing. Based on her knowledge of the school's curriculum, Leah purchased test-preparation workbooks, maze books, and geography books to further encourage her children to be successful in school. In second grade, Nate and Jenny were highly motivated and successful students. Due to the considerable amount of time each week throughout the school years, Leah knows how much emphasis is placed on standardized tests by the school district. Leah, like many parents, wanted her children to be successful in school so she spent time getting her children academically prepared for the standardized tests that they would take in school.

School and Home Disconnection

Learning from the Nguyen Family

The Nguyen family consists of parents, Nilesh and Lee, and their 8-year-old son, Andrew. Nilesh and Lee worked at the same computer factory. Nilesh started as a janitor and later progressed into computer work. Lee worked on packaging CDs. Unlike the other families, Nilesh, Lee, and Andrew did not use the computer for social-based literacy practices (i.e., email). Nilesh was the only family member who used the computer, primarily to read work-related material online. Although I observed Lee reading Vietnamese recipes for dinner preparation, Lee shared that she hand-wrote letters to her friends and family abroad rather than using the computer.

Andrew was introduced to reading at school, rather than at home, which is unique in comparison to the children in the other families in the study. Andrew read some recreational books at home. He did not engage in any narrative (story) writing at home. Ironically, although Andrew enjoyed playing video games that involved some reading skills, he was not allowed to use the computer at home after an experience in which he damaged it.

When I was Andrew's teacher, I did not realize how foreign and dislocating the school community was for his parents. As I spent time in the Nguyen home I gained more information about the social, cultural, and literacy values embedded in their home. Both parents came to the United States from Vietnam. Nilesh, the father, immigrated to the United States as an adult refugee in his forties. Lee, the mother, immigrated to the United States in her thirties. Nilesh went to grade school and high school in North Vietnam. He was required to join the army at 20. In 1975, the Communist Party took over his country and he was jailed for over six years. Nilesh escaped from North Vietnam to the Philippines in 1971 and after getting his legal documents in order he became a refugee to the United States. Lee did not attend school in Vietnam as a child. Women were considered second-class citizens when Lee was a child in Vietnam. She was not given the opportunity to attend school, but learned some reading and writing skills at home. Nilesh explains:

Melissa: Was Lee encouraged to read and write at home?
Nilesh: Just a little bit, she picked it up real slow.
Melissa: Did her parents read and write at home?
Nilesh: Not English but Vietnamese.
Melissa: Did your parents read and write?
Nilesh: Yes, but mostly my Dad. My mom just a little bit, as I told you before, women in my country are second class, they don't have a chance to go to school if they were born before 1950. But now a girl can go to school equal to a boy but not in my mom and dad's time or in Lee's time.

I also learned Nilesh establishes a daily routine in their home for Andrew. As described by Puchner and Hardman (1996), it is typical for many immigrant families to focus on monitoring homework and offer incentives for good grades as a way to academically support children at home. Andrew has a snack after school and watched television until 5:00pm each day. But, at 5:00pm, Andrew sat at the quiet dining room table to complete all of his homework assigned by his classroom teacher. After Andrew completed his school homework, Nilesh gave him additional work. The daily reading work that Nilesh assigned for Andrew was to read one chapter from a book that Andrew selected independently (e.g, R.L. Stine's *Goosebumps: Horror at Camp Jellyjam,* 1995). After Andrew read a chapter, he was expected to copy the entire chapter verbatim in his writing journal, a composition notebook. Approximately 15 of these composition notebooks filled with transcribed books were stored on a shelf in Andrew's bedroom. When I asked Nilesh about the purpose of this writing journal assignment, Nilesh explained that this was the way he was taught to read and write in Vietnam. Nilesh had limited English proficiency, impeding the assistance he could provide to Andrew. His instructional guidance was limited to a writing routine I called "chapter book summaries." Chapter book summaries were a unique literacy practice in comparison to the other families I studied. It is common for parents and teachers to support and teach children based on the way they learned in school or in their homes. With the "chapter book summary," Nilesh clearly conserved a literacy practice that he personally experienced as a child in school in Vietnam.

THEORETICAL APPLICATION: HISTORICAL INFLUENCE ON LITERACY PRACTICES AND SCHOOL RELATIONS

The "chapter book summary" is a striking example of how parents' past experiences with literacy and schooling powerfully shape their understanding of and vision for supporting their children's schooling—in this case in a way that clearly has negative consequences for the child. As teachers, we need to be aware of this type of historical influence. How does your own personal history with family literacy and home-school relationships shape your values and expectations of family literacy and parental roles in schooling? How might you learn about parents' values and expectations with regard to these issues? Given the deep historical roots of many parenting practices, teachers should be sensitive to the fact that such practices may not be easily changed. How might you help a parent like Nilesh to revise his understanding of literacy and schooling and improve the ways he supports his child's academic development?

I remember that when Andrew was a student in my classroom, he casually told me about how he wrote in a journal at home every night. I *assumed* that that he was reading a chapter from a book similar to the familiar reading books he read at school. I also incorrectly *assumed* that when he wrote in a "writing journal" it was similar to the narrative (story) writing he engaged in at school. It was not until I began my visits to the Nguyen family's home that I realized Andrew was copying books verbatim each night. I also *assumed* that Nilesh helped Andrew select t̶ that were at his independent reading level. I learned that Andrew was frequently reading books at home that he could not read independently. Andrew's teachers (including myself) did not send home lists of books that were at his independent reading level, which would have helped Nilesh. In the other families, the children were reading books at their reading level most of the time. Upon questioning the other parents about how they selected appropriate books for their children, they said they asked the librarian at the public library and one parent said she asked her child's teacher for a book list.

I also gained an in-depth understanding of how Nilesh tried to help Andrew while reading. Since English is a second language for Nilesh, he was occasionally unable to read some of Andrew's words in his books, and therefore, he was unable to help him. If Andrew came to a word that he could not read, Nilesh asked Andrew to attempt to read the word several times to commit it to memory. Nilesh explained that he learned this way in Vietnam. Nilesh wanted Andrew to learn English at school because he knew from his own personal experience as an immigrant that English is essential for work and daily living. Nilesh explained:

Nilesh: I do think it is necessary to teach him [Andrew] reading at home but I am not able to do it well because I don't think my English is good enough.
Melissa: What kinds of things have you done with Andrew at home to help with reading?
Nilesh: We go to the library and I let him read every night. It is all I can do but I don't know if I pronounce good enough or not. I don't know the American sayings only the Vietnamese sayings, so I listen to him read the whole book or half of the book. I want him to read hard books.
Melissa: Who picks out the books when you go to the library?
Nilesh: I take him but he chooses the books.

The vignette above illustrates the challenges Nilesh faced as a first generation immigrant parent when he tried to support his son Andrew. Nilesh was doing everything he could to support Andrew with his school work and he wanted Andrew to be academically successful in school.

Children are socialized differently in their homes and communities, therefore, parents and children have vastly different reading, writing, listening, and speaking values and practices. A major finding of Jacobs and Jordan's (1993) research indicates that when children are socialized in different contexts they come to school differentially prepared to participate in school, which may result in failure—an argument now referred to as continuity-discontinuity theory.

Conclusions and Implications for Teaching and Research

In this chapter, I have presented four case studies to illustrate the connection or disconnection between home and school. Within each family the social and

s are different. Parental expectations, knowledge of the school
*t*eacher's expectations play a significant role in shaping the child-
*l*ing experiences. In three of the families, the children engaged in
*l*eracy activities that were aligned with the literacy practices at
*family, the children were not exposed to literacy activities congru-
*l*eracy practices frequently used at school. Andrew's case suggests
th e-school cultural mismatch, particularly for immigrant families, can
interfere with children's learning in school and at home. The home-school mismatch is apparent in the type of educational support that parents provide at
home (e.g. amount of time to work on narrative writing on a computer or in
a journal). While this issue was illustrated using cases from Vietnamese and
Caucasian families, these issues are not unique to Vietnamese and Caucasian
communities;.

Analyses across the studies forced me to consider four important practical
questions. In this section, I address these questions in light of my findings.

1. What could have made a Difference in how the Nguyen Family Experienced Andrew's Schooling?

Many immigrant parents are unfamiliar with the social, cultural, and academic
expectations embedded within the school community because they did not
attend American schools. Communication between teachers and families ideally
allows parents to become more knowledgeable about the events that take place in
school. However, if parents are not provided with specific information about the
school curriculum (i.e. the narrative writing curriculum and the role of technology in the writing curriculum) and ways parents can support their children at
home, the home-school connection is reduced. Teachers can learn more about
immigrant families and the ways they support their children at home by visiting
families in their homes. Home visits provide teachers with useful and relevant
information about the social and cultural dynamics embedded within their
student's homes.

If I had known as Andrew's classroom teacher that Andrew was selecting books
at the library that were too difficult, I would have provided a list of books to
Andrew and his father so he could have been able to read books independently
that would have enhanced his reading fluency and comprehension. I was unaware
of this issue until I visited the Nguyen family home for research. Home visits
provide teachers with the opportunity to better understand and honor a child's
world outside of school because they gain information about their students'
learning resources and families' cultural background, and their reading, writing,
and speaking practices at home (Moll et al., 1992; Moll & Gonzáles, 2004).

As Andrew's second grade teacher I utilized all of the ways that teachers typically use to communicate with their students' families. I first met Nilesh at the
"Meet the Teacher Open House" that teachers frequently offer at the beginning of
the school year. We met again in November and March for parent–teacher conferences. These "traditional" methods of communication between teacher and parent were not enough to make a profound difference in my understanding and

knowledge of the social, cultural, and literacy practices present in the Nguyen family's home. I learned so much more about Andrew and his life outside of school when I entered the Nguyen's home for research the year after I taught Andrew in my second grade classroom. If I had conducted a home visit when Andrew was my student, I would have learned more about the rich funds of knowledge, networks of support, and strategies that Lee and Nilesh Nguyen used to help support Andrew with his schoolwork.

In Table 6.2, I provide a summary of the traditional and culturally sensitive ways teachers might connect with families to build understanding.

2. What are the Traditional Ways that Teachers Connect with Families to Build Understanding?

One traditional way that teachers connect with families is by offering parent–teacher conferences at least twice per school year. Most parents want to know how their child is settling into a classroom and how he or she is learning the curriculum. Another traditional way for teachers and administrators to build understanding and connect with families is to invite them to the school for "Meet the Teacher Night" to get to know each other before the school year begins. Open houses and parent–teacher conferences are effective but they do not provide enough information to first generation immigrant parents who have not attended school in the United States. Teachers do not have time in an open house or during a parent–teacher conference that lasts for 15–20 minutes, to explain the curriculum to first generation immigrant parents who are learning about the social and cultural dynamics of the school in addition to trying to gain information about how to support their child at home. There are more meaningful methods of building understanding and a relationship with first generation immigrant families.

Table 6.2 Ways to build understanding between teachers and families

Traditional ways that teachers connect with families	Contemporary ways that teachers connect with families
Teachers offer parent–teacher conferences to provide parents with academic information about their children.	Teachers conducts home visits to gain knowledge about their student's families and to build a relationship with their student's families.
Teachers offer an open house at the beginning of the school year to meet families.	Teachers have classroom newsletters and school information translated into languages spoken by families.
Parents or caregivers volunteer for a field trip or to help the teacher in the classroom.	Teachers offer curriculum night so parents can come to school to learn about the curriculum that is being taught in the school. Teachers have translators available for parent–teacher conferences and for curriculum night.

3. What are Socioculturally-Informed Ways that Teachers Connect with Families to Build Understanding?

A socioculturally-informed way for teachers to connect with families and build understanding is to hold an event called "Curriculum Night" to help parents become familiarized with their child's grade level curriculum. All of the teachers at a specific grade level may coordinate the curriculum night together or individual teachers may prepare their own specific agenda for parents and hold the curriculum night within their own classrooms.

For example, as a second grade teacher, my colleagues and I met and prepared a 2nd grade Curriculum Night in the auditorium. We each were responsible for a certain aspect of the presentation to all of the 2nd grade parents. Afterwards, we met with parents in our own classrooms and talked more informally about the curriculum or just engaged in casual conversation. It will be more meaningful for English language learners and their families to have interpreters or liaisons on hand for school sponsored events so parents feel comfortable asking questions about the curriculum in their native language. Parents or caregivers from diverse backgrounds may lack knowledge of English because it is not their native language; this is the most significant barrier for them. If schools provide a resource such as an interpreter or liaison, communication and understanding between the school and student's homes will be enhanced.

One other relatively simple way for teachers to connect with families and build understanding for immigrant families is to have information about school open houses, curriculum night, parent–teacher conferences, book lists, and classroom newsletters translated into the different languages that the students and their families speak at home. If parents are not able to read information sent home from the school, it can be difficult for parents to stay informed or know when to attend school-based events. To truly build rapport and credibility with diverse families, their native languages should be respected and embraced so that their children may optimize new opportunities and not become victims of the cultural gap that frequently exists between schools and homes

4. What were the Lessons for me as a Veteran, Eight-Year Teacher within the School District?

The interviews, observations of conversations between parents and children, field notes, and artifacts collected from home and school reveal that children and parents from linguistically and culturally diverse homes need additional support from teachers or administrators, compared with mainstream families who are native English speakers and who have attended school in the United States. Schools and families can work together to improve methods of communication to enhance student learning. Professional development for teachers and administrators will help educators understand and interface more effectively within its culturally diverse community. In order to create equitable spaces for all students and their families, teachers can make home visits to learn more about the learning resources embedded within the social and cultural context of their homes.

Too often, when parents feel uncomfortable or unwelcome in different cultural settings, these feelings may deter direct participation in school activities (Nieto, 1996). The first step educators can take is to visit their immigrant student's homes to learn more about the social, cultural, and literacy practices embedded in their homes. Home visits will enhance the educator's understanding of the students and parents' current literacy practices, how the parents themselves learned to read and write at home, and the specific literacy practices that they value at home. Teachers can also invite parents to their classrooms to learn firsthand about how they teach the curriculum at school. Teachers can be ambassadors to immigrant children and their families and make a concerted effort to embrace children and parents who are potentially "outsiders" such as the Nguyen family.

Teachers have known for a long time that parental participation is a key factor in children's success in school. As the population in the United States becomes more linguistically and culturally diverse each day, it points to the vital need for educators to reinvent how they are supporting parent participation for *all* students and their families. The resulting home-school connection will provide parents with a better understanding of classroom life (Anderson & Gunderson, 1997), and teachers will gain a more intimate understanding of their students' lives outside of school, creating a more seamless integration of home-based learning and school-based learning.

Ideas for Discussion, Extension, and Application

1. Briefly make a list of methods of communicating with families utilized by your former teachers. Categorize them from the most to the least effective. How did they impact the quality of communication between your family and school community?
2. As a teacher, how would you expand your methods of communication to continually further your understanding and knowledge of the cultural practices, learning resources, social dynamics, and identity issues within your students' homes?
3. Consider the Smiths, Walkers and Sanders' family literacy practices. What stands out or surprises you about the diversity within mainstream English speaking families? As a teacher, how would you address this diversity in your relationships with mainstream families?

References

Anderson, J., & Gunderson, L. (1997). Literacy learning from a multicultural perspective. *The Reading Teacher, 50,* 514–516.

Barton, D., Hamilton, M., & Ivanič, R. (Eds.). (2000). *Situated literacies: Reading and writing in context.* New York: Routledge.

Bogden, R., & Biklen, S. (1982). *Qualitative research for education: An introduction to theory and methods.* Boston: Allyn & Bacon.

Compton-Lilly, C. (2003). *Reading families: The literate lives of urban children.* New York: Teachers College Press.

Edwards, P. A., Pleasants, H. M., & Franklin, S. H. (1999). *A path to follow: Learning to listen to parents.* Portsmouth, NH: Heinemann.

Finn, P. (1999). *Literacy with an attitude: Educating working-class in their own self interest.* New York: University of New York Press.

Gadsden, V. L. (1994). Understanding family literacy: Conceptual issues facing the field. *Teachers College Record, 96*(1), 56–86.

Hale, J. (2001). *Learning while black: Creating educational excellence for African American children.* Baltimore, MD: Johns Hopkins University Press.

Heath, S. B. (1982). Questioning at home and at school: A comparative study. In G. Spindler (Ed.), *Doing the ethnography of schooling: Educational anthropology in action* (pp. 103–131). Prospect Heights, IL: Waveland Press Inc.

Heath, S. B. (1983). *Ways with words: Language, life, and working communities and class-rooms.* New York: Cambridge University Press.

Heath, S. B. (1989). Oral and literate traditions among black Americans living in poverty. *American Psychologist, 44*(2), 367–372.

Hicks, D. (2002). *Reading lives: Working class children and literacy learning.* New York: Cambridge University Press.

Hull, G., & Schultz, K. (2002). Locating literacy theory in out-of-school contexts. In G. Hull., & K. Schultz (Eds.), *School's out: Bridging out-of-school literacies with classroom practice* (pp. 1–31). New York: Teachers College Press.

Jacobs, E., & Jordan, C. (Eds.). (1993). *Minority education: Anthropological perspectives.* Norwood, NJ: Ablex.

Juel, C. (1988). Learning to read and write: A longitudinal study of fifty-four children from first grade through fourth grades. *Journal of Educational Psychology, 80*, 437–447.

Ladson-Billings, G. (1994). *The dreamkeepers: Successful teachers of African American children.* San Francisco: Jossey-Bass.

Lewis, R. (2000). *Wired in a week: How AOL can improve your life in ten minutes a day.* New York: Warner Books.

Meyer, D., Madden, D., & McGrath, D. J. (2004). *English language learners students in the U.S. public schools: 1994 and 2000* (Rep. No. NCES 2004-035). Washington, DC: National Center for Education Statistics.

Moll, L. C., Amanti, C., Neff, D., & Gonzáles, N. (1992). Funds of knowledge for teaching: Using a qualitative approach to connect homes and classrooms. *Theory into Practice, 31*(1), 132–141.

Moll, L. C., & Gonzáles, N. (2004). Engaging life: A funds of knowledge approach to multicultural education. In J. A. Banks, & C. A. M. Banks (Eds.), *Handbook of research on multicultural education* (2nd ed., pp. 699–715). San Francisco: Jossey-Bass.

Nieto, S. (1996). *Affirming diversity.* White Plains, NY: Longman Publishers.

Puchner, L. D., & Hardman, J. (1996). Family literacy in a cultural context: Southeast Asian immigrants in the United States. *NCAL Connections* (pp. 1–3). Philadelphia: National Center on Adult Literacy, University of Pennsylvania.

Purcell-Gates, V. (1993). Focus on research issues for family literacy: Voices from the trenches. *Language Arts, 70*, 670–677.

Purcell-Gates, V. (1995). *Other people's words: The cycle of low literacy.* Cambridge, MA: Harvard University Press.

Stine, R. L. (1995). *Goosebumps: Horror at Camp Jellyjam.* New York: Scholastic.

Taylor, D. (1983). *Family literacy: Young children learning to read and write.* Portsmouth, NH: Heinemann.

Taylor, D., & Dorsey-Gaines, C. (1988). *Growing up literate: Learning from inner-city families.* Portsmouth, NH: Heinemann.

Thomas, W., & Collier, V. (2002). *A national study of school effectiveness for language minority students' long-term academic achievement.* Washington, DC: The Center for Research on Education, Diversity & Excellence (CREDE), Office of Educational Research and Improvement (OERI) of the U.S. Department of Education.

U.S. Census Bureau (2001). The Asian Pacific American population in the United States: Population characteristics. Online: www.census.gov/population/socdemo/hispanic/p. 20-535.pdf.

Vygotsky. L. S., & Kozulin, A. (1986). *Thought and language.* Boston, MA: MIT Press.

West, J., Denton, K., & Reaney, L. M. (2000). The kindergarten year: Findings from the early childhood longitudinal study, kindergarten class of 1998–99. *Education Statistics Quarterly, 2*(4), 25–30.

West, J., Denton, K., & Germino Hausken, E. (2000). Kindergartners' educational progress in reading: A study of language minority and non-language minority children. *Education Statistics Quarterly, 2*(1), 7–13.

Zill, N., & West, J. (2000). *Entering kindergarten: A portrait of American children when they begin school.* Washington, DC: U.S. Government Printing Office.

7 Fostering Academic Identities among Latino Immigrant Students

Contextualizing Parents' Roles

Lilia D. Monzó

At 6:15pm, Sra. Gomez knocks on the door to her apartment. Her three daughters scramble to open the door to the small one room apartment. The TV is quickly shut off as if to pretend it had not been on at all. When the door is opened Sra. Gomez walks in greeting her children and myself. She seems out of breath as she places two large grocery bags on one of the beds that doubles as a couch during the day. The children quickly rummage through their contents. The bags are filled with thick chapter books, all in English. Sra. Gomez addresses me, "Son libros que me dió la señora donde trabajo. Ella a cada rato me da los libros que sus hijas ya no quieren." (They are books that the woman I work for gave me. She often gives me the books that her daughters no longer want.) "¿Tuvo que traerlos caminando desde el camión?" (You had to bring them walking from the bus?) I asked. "Oh sí. Pesan un poco pero ya estoy acostumbrada. Me gusta que tengan libros aquí para leer." (Oh yes. They're a bit heavy but I'm used to it. I like them to have books here to read.) She motions to the shelf against the wall that holds a collection of over 100 books. "Casi todos me los ha dado esta señora." (This woman has given me almost all of them.) The children have already left the books and moved on to other things.

Above we see the value that this mother holds for academic reading and we sense the difficulty that providing opportunities for academic literacy practices present for this immigrant Latino family. Ethnographic work with Latino families has consistently shown that Latino parents have a strong value for education and want their children to reach a level of financial and social success beyond that which they themselves have known, often having aspirations for higher education (Auerbach, 2006; Delgado-Gaitan, 2001). However, their efforts toward orienting their children toward academic ends are often misunderstood or dismissed because they do not resemble the types of white middle-class practices that have come to characterize parent involvement (Crozier, 2001; Lopez, 2001). Indeed my work in California public schools shows that Latino parents are often poorly informed and sometimes deceived about their children's educational trajectories (Monzó, 2005). This suggests that there may be a perception that because families lack sufficient knowledge about our educational system their input on academic matters is of little consequence. However, Latino parents support their children's education in a variety of non-mainstream ways, including offering *consejos*

(Delgado-Gaitan, 1994) and showing them what hard work really is to encourage educational persistence (Lopez, 2001).

Nonetheless, the cultural deficit model continues to shape many school practices and policies in urban schools (Flores, Cousin, & Díaz, 1991; Volk & Long, 2005). This model suggests that there is something inherently inferior in the cultural practices of Latino communities that prevent them from achieving academically. The remedy is to quickly assimilate to the dominant society and acquire English and "American norms" as quickly as possible, or so the argument goes (Gibson, 1998). This nativist argument is the result of both outright prejudice and what Villenas (2001) has termed "benevolent racisms," or deficiency perspectives cloaked under the guise of "helping" students and families develop the white, middle-class practices that are rewarded in schools.

This argument, however, is flawed in that it is based on simplistic, unidirectional notions of socialization and acculturation, the idea that children automatically pick up the practices and associated values and beliefs that they are taught. Indeed, English immersion policies are embedded with the idea that English language development is best supported through maximum exposure and negatively impacted by primary language use in schools. This replacement model of acculturation denies the complex process of negotiation that occurs in cultural production (Monzó & Rueda, 2006). Indeed, research has found that primary language maintenance supports English learning (Cummins, 1996) and that cultural practices and associated values and beliefs are highly impacted by numerous sociocultural factors (Fillmore, 2000; Ogbu & Simmons, 1998; Olsen, 1997).

This chapter deals with students' cultural productions and identity development regarding literacy. Specifically, I examine the literacy practices of eight Latino immigrant students at home and at school and parents' attempts to foster academic identities. Drawing on Vygotsky (1987) and Bakhtin (1981), I show that the process of cultural production and identity development for these students involved an agentic struggle between multiple languages (in Bakhtin's terms) that often resulted in varied "responses" and multiple identities.

Identity as Sociocultural Production

Identity can be thought of as a sense of self, how one perceives oneself in a given context. A sociocultural perspective on identity draws on Vygotsky (1978; 1987) and Bakhtin (1981) and others who have advanced their work (Holland, Lachicotte, Skinner, & Cain, 1998; Wertsch, 1991, 1998). According to Vygotsky (1987), cognition is a result of mediated action, influenced by social, political, and economic factors. From this perspective, cognitive development occurs in the *zone of proximal development*, as a novice takes on greater responsibility in cultural activity while working with a more competent other. This change in participation (Rogoff, 1995) occurs through the mediation of cultural tools and leads to a qualitative transformation of cognitive functions, cultural activity, and the cultural tools (Wertch, 1998). This qualitative transformation occurs as the mediational tool is mastered and used internally (for example, social speech becomes inner speech). However, internalized mediation, although invisible, is still social in that it reflects the historical development of tools and their use (Wertsch, 1991).

From this theoretical perspective it follows that culture, including identity formation, is continually being produced through the moment by moment negotiation of individual factors and social context. That is, neither is identity an innate, individual characteristic that people are born with nor is it a purely social phenomena. Rather, identity is produced through participation in cultural activity and mediated by cultural tools. It is produced through the interaction of individual and the social phenomena. It involves the development of values, attitudes, and beliefs. Holland and her colleagues (Holland, Lachicotte, Skinner, & Cain, 1998) have posited that identity is not evidenced out of context but enacted in practice. The developmental aspect of Vygotsky's work on cognition leads us to understand identity as "history in person" (Holland et al., 1998).

Bakhtin (1981) dealt explicitly with identity, what he called "authoring the self." Like Vygotsky, Bakhtin saw the interconnection between social and individual aspects of cognition. Bakhtin discussed making meaning of the world through the appropriation of others' words. Words, he argued, are always "half someone else's" because they come embedded with someone else's perspectives and functions. Bakhtin noted that words are taken from particular languages or perspectives on the world and thus carry particular discourses that are historically conceived and continually changing. One's voice, Bakhtin argued, is developed through a process of appropriation wherein one takes the words of others and fills them with one's own intentions and purposes.

Holland and her colleagues (Holland et al., 1998) argue that Bakhtin's contribution to this theory of identity is his emphasis on the relational aspects of social languages. For him, languages were not each equivalent but rather carried different amounts of power and status. Languages were learned in communities of practice (Lave & Wenger, 1991), what Holland and colleagues (1998) have called "figured worlds" as a way of highlighting the relations of power which parallel the social relations of power in the broader society. Within these figured worlds in which we participate, we are exposed to multiple and often conflicting languages, each with its own values and perspectives. To understand the world, to develop one's voice, is to see through the perspective of others, to reach "outsidedness" (Bakhtin, 1981). Identity, then, involves seeing ourselves through the eyes of others or in Bakhtinian terms, through multiple languages, and choosing words that we then fill with our own intentions, "authoring the self" (Bakhtin, 1981). The development of an authentic voice, a more or less stable identity, involves a struggle between the multiple languages to which one is exposed.

Following the above theoretical perspective, I define an academic identity as seeing oneself as academically oriented by enacting the cultural practices (and the related beliefs, values, and attitudes) that are generally associated in our society with academic activities. I presume these to include the types of activities and behaviors that are often expected and rewarded in schools, such as completing homework in a timely fashion, studying for exams, participating in class activities, reading, using the library, and seeking good grades. In my definition, it also involves aspirations and expectations of pursuing a college education. However, aspirations and expectations for college education require a sense of self as successful in academic activities and capable of achieving a college education.

THEORETICAL APPLICATION: ACADEMIC IDENTITY

Taking on or performing an academic identity involves adopting a range of attitudes and behaviors typically associated with being a good student. Can you picture a student—perhaps even yourself—who demonstrated a strong academic identity? What specific attitudes and behaviors did that student exhibit? The theoretical perspective developed here suggests that many forces and factors influence a child's development of an academic identity. In that light, think about how academic identities are constructed. Do academic identities always look the same or might they differ across cultural communities? What role do you as a teacher play in enabling diverse students to develop positive academic identities? What specific actions could you take to do so?

Methodology

This chapter draws from a two-year ethnography of eight Latino families. The study focused on the negotiation of the diverse cultural practices that children brought home from school. The study began at the neighborhood public school where eight fifth grade children from the same fifth grade class and their families were sought for participation.

Home and Community Contexts

The study took place in a low-income, predominantly Latino immigrant community in the Los Angeles area that I call La Fuente. All parents were immigrants of Mexico, El Salvador, and Guatemala. Spanish was the primary language of the homes among both parents and children.

School Context

La Fuente elementary school was the neighborhood public school. It was 99% Latino, with a 100% of students receiving free or reduced lunch. All children but one were classified as English language learners. Post Proposition 227, the school offered few appropriately implemented bilingual waivered classes (see Monzó (2005) to learn how bilingual waivers were mishandled). The ethnography extended to the school culture but one fifth-grade class was targeted.

Sources of Data and Collection

Home Visits. I visited each of the eight families, with a varying degree of frequency. While one family was visited over 50 times, another was visited only ten times due to the family's busy schedule. In total, over 200 home visits were conducted, each approximately two hours long. Interactions during home visits took place with all members of the family, but especially with mothers and children.

During home visits, I participated in routine family tasks, including homework, dinner, play, and community outings, such as going to the park, the library, the supermarket, and other nearby shops. I often asked children if they wanted to read books or read to younger siblings. I initiated outings to various locations, including the library, the university, and the mall. A number of families sought my assistance for translation purposes in reading documents and accompanying them to various service agencies. Fieldnotes from home visits were written up after leaving the site.

Participant Observation. The bulk of my school observations and interactions took place in one fifth-grade class, I observed the class an average of three days per week. I engaged almost exclusively with students, sitting next to them, talking to them informally, helping them with work, I often ate with them at lunch and played and hung out with them at recess.

Interviews. At least one formal interview was conducted with each of the eight children, their parents, and their older siblings, separately. Interviews were also conducted with the classroom teacher, additional community members, and other teachers at the school. All interviews were tape-recorded and transcribed.

Fostering Academic Identities

I observed numerous social practices among families that likely supported the development of academic identities. Even though each family seemed to organize their lives in very diverse ways—challenging old notions of culture as homogeneous and static, three themes stood out as particularly salient because the practices they represent were common to all of the families in the study.

Possibility

Among the families, children were key players in family functioning, particularly as they gained English language and literacy skills. Previous research has documented the important task of translating that is often relegated to even very young children in immigrant families (Orellana, 2001). In my observations, families demanded their children with English skills translate important documents, magazines, TV programs, commercials, restaurant menus, street signs, and numerous other artifacts for parents. Although some of these items were easy to translate, others were much more difficult. In addition, children were often asked to serve as translators for face-to-face interactions such as at the doctor's office and/or to completely take over the activity, such as ordering at a restaurant or inquiring into an apartment vacancy.

In addition, children were also often expected to take over activities that parents had little knowledge of, activities that were not necessarily language-based but that parents felt they knew little about. For example, during the two years I spent in this study, two of the families decided to purchase a computer. The eldest children in these families were completely in charge of making selections, completing purchasing transaction, setting up the computer, and securing Internet services. Other tasks that children often managed on their own were their school activities. This was especially true for children as they entered junior high and high school. Parents had very little instrumental knowledge about the ways schools worked at these levels and they were completely at a loss to assist their children in making course selections, completing homework assignments, signing up for extracurricular activities, or making up credits.

The children's active and influential participation in family functioning provided them with a sense of confidence in their abilities to overcome obstacles and to persist in unfamiliar contexts. I would argue that for Latino immigrant youth, these are attitudes that are highly associated with academic identities. However, an important note of caution is that not all children were successful in managing translation activities or the tasks they were asked to complete on their own. How children and parents dealt with the difficulties children faced may have an important impact on children's notions of possibility. For example, some parents knew a little English and were able to tell if the translation had been accurate. When it was not, children were sometimes reprimanded for not learning English fast enough or for lacking the knowledge that parents expected them to have. Unsuccessful attempts at managing family functioning may cause children to lose confidence in their abilities to achieve in unfamiliar terrains such as college.

Responsibility

The many conversations I had with parents during home visits revealed a strong value for education. Over and over they claimed that they had come to this country in search of a better life and indicated that education was the key to success. They said that they wanted their children to have better than they had and they felt that learning English and doing well in school were essential to finding a good job. All of the families indicated that they wanted their children to go to college and some of them spoke of college attendance as a *fait accompli*. That is, they had the expectation that their children would attend college after high school. These discussions, held in the presence of children, likely had an impact on children as they listened silently but intently. In many cases, parents turned to speak directly to their children, offering *consejos*, about the importance of getting an education, as in the following examples:

Sr. Perez: (to Lucía) ¡Tienes que estudiar, mi amor! ¿Si no, qué? Vas a estar igual que uno, trabajando en una factoría o hasta sin trabajo a veces. [You have to study *mi amor*! If not, what? You will be just like us, working in a factory or even without work sometimes.]

Sra Gomez: Yo quisiera que ellas salgan adelante en el estudio y, si Díos nos presta vida, pues ayudarles hasta que ellas estudien lo mejor posible para que no vayan a pasar la vida que yo he vivido. Porque yo no tuve la dicha y la suerte de estudiar como ellas la tienen ahorita. [I would like them to succeed in school and, if God gives us life, then to help them until they study the best possible way so that they do not have to live the life I have lived. Because I did not have the joy and luck to study like they have it now.]

In essence, parents were saying that it was up to them to fulfill the goals that had brought their families to this country. They had immigrated for the sake of their children and had left behind family and friends, and in some cases better living conditions and better jobs. Clearly these were conversation meant to encourage children, perhaps guilt them, into feeling a sense of responsibility toward achieving educational and economic success.

Making Schooling and Literacy a Priority

Parents actively sought to organize their lives in ways that supported their children's educational achievement, particularly with respect to language and literacy. All of the parents held a strong commitment to bilingualism, wanting their children to maintain their Spanish but also to develop their English language and literacy skills. In all homes, parents attempted to stay informed of their children's schooling activities by asking them on a daily basis about their homework and making sure the children had time after school that was devoted specifically for homework activities. With very young children, parents were always seen helping the children complete their homework. Fifth graders in the study and their older siblings, however, were asked about their homework but it was primarily up to them to complete it. Most of the parents were unable to assist them at these levels because books and materials were in English.

Although none of the parents volunteered at schools, they did attend every back to school, open house, and parent–teacher conference to which they were invited in the elementary school. This type of support was difficult to maintain with children in middle school and high school because, at this level, children sometimes opted to keep notices and information about school back from parents (see Monzó, 2009).

In addition, parents attempted in multiple ways to get their children to read books at home in addition to their daily homework. Young children (2nd grade and below) seemed to enjoy reading books and in the families that had young children, parents were often viewed reading books in Spanish with them. However, their efforts to socialize their fifth-grade children and older siblings to reading books at home were almost always met with complaints and sometimes hostility. When parents commented to me that their children would not read at home even when they reminded them, children typically rolled their eyes or commented that it was "boring."

Parents explained that teachers told them that their children should be reading at home on a daily basis to help them develop greater literacy skills. The Open Court reading program (for a description, see section below entitled "The literacy contexts of an urban school") that some of the fifth grade students were placed in consisted of unit fluency tests in which fluency was tested by counting the number of words read correctly per minute in a given passage. Parents of children who were reading less words per minute than expected according to the program were told and asked to have their children read on a daily basis at home as a means of increasing their fluency scores. This became an important cause for concern among parents and the practice of reading became a forced activity, which only fueled the children's resistance to reading.

In the Perez family, the two older children, Lucia (age 16) and Julie (age 10) declared that they "hate(d) reading." Julie added "You are the only person I know who likes to read." As a means of resisting the forced reading activity, Julie, who was aware of having strict confidentiality with respect to any of our interactions, bragged to me about the sneaky way she was getting away with not reading at home. Her mother who was cooking in the kitchen reminded her it was time to read. She and I were sitting on the bed in their living room. She went to her backpack and got her book out. It was a chapter book that had a piece of paper in it that served as a bookmarker. She explained that when her mother came in to check on how much she had read, she would move the piece of paper forward some pages so that her mother would think she had been reading. Given that Sra. Perez typically arrived home from work about 6:00 pm and at that time had to start dinner, sometimes run errands, help her younger daughter who was in pre-school with homework, she certainly could not sit and watch her daughter read.

Interestingly, although most children resisted reading books at home when asked to do so and claimed they disliked or, according to two students, "hated" reading, I observed children engage in numerous literacy activities that differed from school-like reading but involved reading nonetheless. However, children did not consider these literacy practices such. Table 7.1 shows these various home literacy practices I observed.

In addition, when I came to do my home visits, children were eager to read with me in Spanish and in English and even books that seemed school-like. The difference was that our reading together was never forced nor was there any evaluation tied to it. I never checked for understanding but merely stopped to talk about the text as I went along as a way of both contextualizing the material and making ties to our (theirs' and mine) funds of knowledge (Moll & Greenberg, 1990). This was a way of facilitating content comprehension without asking questions that often serve to put students' language needs on display. Sometimes they read aloud to me and I listened. Sometimes I read a page and they read a page. Sometimes we stopped in the middle when they wanted to stop. It was always their choice.

Table 7.1 Home literacy practices

Literacy practices	Language(s)
Mail (bills, notices, fliers)	Spanish and English
Reading clothing catalogs	English
Completing mail order forms	English
Billboards	Spanish and English
Restaurant menus	Spanish and English
School notices	English
Report cards	English
Grocery store signs and food labels	English
Teen magazines at doctor's offices and bookstores	English
Poetry books at the bookstore (and copying poems to share with friends)	English
Internet sites	English
Email	English

Cultural Productions of Literacy: Becoming (Non)academic

The Literacy Contexts of an Urban School

The study took place post Proposition 227, which passed into law an English immersion program in which the primary language was to be used only minimally and all instruction, materials, and assignments had to be in English. However, waivers signed by parents to place their children in a transitional bilingual program were available. The ambiguity of the law as well as the beliefs both regarding bilingual education and district demands created tremendous variability in the ways in which the law regarding language of instruction became implemented at a district, school, and even classroom level (Stritikus, & García, 2000). The fifth grade class under study included English immersion students as well as students whose parents had signed waivers to keep them in the bilingual program. In addition, Open Court (at the time available only in English) had been adopted as the schoolwide literacy program and Breaking the Code, an intervention program, was adopted for children who were reading below a fifth-grade level.

The Open Court program was highly structured, with strict pacing guidelines and activities outlined for each day. There was virtually no opportunity for teachers to develop additional activities to further support children's learning or to better tie readings to children's interests and/or prior knowledge. The program included weekly spelling tests, unit fluency exams that tested the number of words read per minute, and unit comprehension tests. Reading was typically whole group, Round Robin or Popcorn style. Given this format, discussions of text were minimal. Comprehension was supported through individually written responses to questions and activity sheets. A majority of questions posed to students were descriptive as opposed to analytical or evaluative.

Breaking the Code was a six-week intervention reading program mandated for fifth graders who were two or more years behind grade level. Materials consisted of a workbook with short paragraphs followed by primarily on-the-page comprehension questions, grammar worksheets, and word lists. The program focused on memorizing letter sounds and letter combination sounds. Word lists were read aloud Round Robin style daily. Little discussion of paragraphs read ensued and activities tended to be worksheet oriented with specific answers.

Placement decisions were highly confounded as the mandate required beginning on a particular date, thus causing a "last minute scrambling" to place children. Classes were required to mix so that one teacher could teach Open Court and the other Breaking the Code. As the year progressed, we noted and the teachers recognized many misplacements but could not rectify the problem as program guidelines indicated students must begin with the group at the very beginning. Thus many students who were reading at grade level in English and in Spanish continued in a reading program that focused on letter sounds and decoding skills. Examining language program placements revealed that students whose parents had signed waivers to proposition 227 and been placed in the transitional bilingual program had been placed in Breaking the Code under the assumption that they would be performing below fifth-grade level in reading in English and that this program (which specifically states in the guidelines is not intended for bilingual students) would teach them English word attack skills that would improve their standardized test scores.

Children's Conceptions of Literacy

Students described the process of reading as sounding out and breaking the words into syllables as they had been taught to do in their respective programs. They explained that "good reading" meant "sounding the words out right," "reading fast," reading "sin acento" (without an accent) and "not making mistakes." Students did not refer to comprehension as an important aspect of reading until we specifically asked about it.

Most of the children seemed disinterested during the literacy block and reading aloud practices were often cut short because students would become disruptive, calling out for readers to speak up. In one example during Round Robin reading, a girl sat with her anthology on her desk open to the appropriate page but with a different book on her lap that she read silently to herself. All of the students indicated that they much preferred to read silently to themselves than aloud in front of the class and many expressed a desire to have small group reading instruction. Students who had been misplaced in the Breaking the Code were particularly antagonistic toward it saying they were not learning anything and that they did not "really read any stories."

When asked why they thought it might be important to read, their responses were primarily academically based, indicating that it helped them "to learn" and "to do well in school." None of the students indicated that they enjoyed reading. It was only when I pointed out that they sometimes enjoyed reading magazines or reading with me at their homes that they would say, "Oh, that's different." Indeed, I had to make a specific reference to books in Spanish or other types of reading materials in order for them to think of literacy in reference to contexts other than schooling.

On visits to nearby libraries I noted that none of the children had a clear idea of what types of books they enjoyed reading and would consider checking out. When asked what topics might be of interest in order to help them navigate the large library, they were at a loss and could articulate neither authors nor topics of interest. As a result, library visits were often frustrating and many of the children simply gave up trying to find books they might enjoy.

Developing Notions of Failure

Most of the students thought of themselves as "not very good" readers. One basis of their self-evaluations were the weekly fluency tests that indicated they were reading less words per minute than expected of fifth graders. These tests, which were given to students on a one-on-one basis and usually administered by the teaching assistant in the hallway just outside the classroom, were solely measuring speed. I observed the administration of these tests and noted that the teaching assistant would instruct the student to read straight through the paragraph. They were told that if they stumbled with a word they were to skip it and continue rather than attempt to decipher the word. They were also told that if they misread a word, they should not go back to attempt to read it correctly. On one occasion after these fluency tests were administered I heard the children in the classroom comparing their fluency scores. The interesting thing was that some of the students who had lower fluency scores were better readers in my opinion because they exhibited greater comprehension. Some students were good readers in Spanish but had little academic English vocabulary and this impacted their ability to comprehend the English texts. Because all of the instruction was in English in the classroom and all of the texts were in English, there was absolutely no opportunity for the students to display their language and literacy skills in Spanish. All but one of the focal students in my study showed signs of developing a sense of failure and feelings of shame regarding their English language and literacy needs. These students thought of themselves as poor readers who were regressing rather than improving. They described themselves as readers in the following ways:

Los otros niños leen mejor que yo. [Other kids read better than I.]

No tan bién como los otros estudiantes. [Not as good as other students.]

Last year I was one of the top, not the best but one of the better ones in reading and writing; but, now I think I am very low.

This last comment was made by a student who was previously in a bilingual transitional fourth grade class in which English was used for instruction and Spanish was used for scaffolding purposes.

Students developed numerous strategies to avoid displaying their English language and literacy needs. These "passing" strategies (see Monzó & Rueda, 2009) included reading very softly or mumbling so that even those sitting next to them could not hear, avoiding eye contact with the teacher, and putting down "anything" on assignments to look busy. These passing strategies were evident not only during language arts instruction but they seemed to occur much more often during this time. One child explained her need to pass during reading aloud practices this way:

> Es que aveces una palabra que viene siendo bién dura para mi, para otros no. Ellos lo leen rápido y en voz alta y yo no. Yo lo leo despacito y allí me quedo y la maestra me dice la palabra. Da vergüenza. Unos dicen, "¡No oigo! ¡No lee bien! ¡Apurate! ¿Qué dice?" Así. Por eso no me gusta leer. [It's that sometimes a word that is very difficult for me, for others it is not. They read it quickly and in a loud voice and I don't. I read it slowly and there I stop and the teacher tells me the word. Its embarrassing. Some say, "I can't hear! She doesn't read well! Hurry up! What did she say?" Like that. That's why I don't like to read.]

THEORETICAL APPLICATION: ACADEMIC IDENTITY

The findings in this section make clear that children learn more than just basic skills during reading instruction: They also develop a sense of what reading is and, critically, of their own identities as learners and readers. These academic identities powerfully influence children's motivation to engage in academic activities and persistence in school learning. Thus, teachers must examine their reading instruction in terms of how it enables children to acquire needed skills and how it contributes to children's identities as students and readers. As a teacher, how can you prevent students like those described here from developing a negative view of themselves as readers and learners while still maintaining high expectations and providing rigorous instruction?

Discussion

The findings above show that Latino parents engage in cultural practices embedded with values and beliefs that support the development of academic identities. Such practices include multiple opportunities to use Spanish and English language and literacy for multiple purposes, including language brokering practices, recreational reading, and common literacy practices related to daily family functioning. Although these forms of literacy were not academic, they may give children who are successful in these home literacy practices a sense that they can be successful in other types of literacy practices. This is especially true of language brokering practices that often place children in unfamiliar contexts where children have the opportunity to display leadership skills, quick decision-making, and problem-solving skills. Likewise, opportunities to manage and control activities for their families, some of which may be critical to family well-being are likely to support children's self-image as being capable of persisting in higher education even though the contexts may be unfamiliar.

In addition, parents sought to make their children feel a sense of responsibility toward academic success that went beyond showing them the importance of education for social and economic mobility. These data show that unlike popular misconceptions of Latino parents as deficient with respect to their ability to support their children in educational contexts or lacking the interest or understanding about our educational system to contribute to their children's academic development and identity construction, Latino parents foster a strong value for education and literacy. An important note, however, is that although parents may manage their home lives in ways that teach children the values for education and literacy, multiple sociocultural factors come into play in helping shape children's developing beliefs and values and ultimately, the identities they construct. The school literacy contexts seem to be of particular influence, especially since they tended to define literacy in purely academic terms, signaling the greater power and status allotted to school activities vis-à-vis home activities.

The broader discourses on race, class, and power in our society that relegate Latinos to second-class citizenry were not challenged in school contexts. Rather, they were legitimized by the use of remedial literacy programs aimed at English learners for the purpose of increasing standardized test scores, the demand for English-only, and the failure to access students' funds of knowledge. The consequences to children's sense of self included an increasing dislike of academic reading, narrow conceptions of literacy, and an increasing sense of failure with respect to English academic literacy at school.

Here we see children's beliefs and attitudes about academic literacy as a negotiation of the value for English literacy that children gain from daily family functioning (including the very real social and financial needs that parents face) and the experiences and understandings they construct from their participation in the literacy contexts of the school. This is not to say that the school is the only responsible agent in creating a narrow view of literacy nor the school's English-only policy the only socializing force pushing them to attempt to pass as English fluent. Culture is not handed down but rather negotiated and produced. We see this in the parents who opt to have their children read books at home when these are not practices they learned as youngsters. As parents have done creating home contexts that support education, children too make choices about whether to reproduce the cultural practices and associated values they are taught or whether to negotiate them with other sources of cultural experience. Indeed, children's cultural productions likely draw from multiple sources, including home, school, peers, and mass media.

Of serious concern is the very narrow focus on reading as decoding skills rather than broader notions of literacy to which the school socializes children. According to Lave and Wenger (1991), identities develop through communities of practice as one engages in said social practices. Academic identities require an understanding of text that goes beyond the mere words on the page. It is comprehension of text, analysis, evaluation, problem solving, and moving beyond text to imagine what has yet to be produced. Clearly in these highly structured programs that are scripted and fast paced, there is little opportunity for looking at texts in this way, and children need to not have just a few opportunities for this but rather to engage in this kind of academic literacy regularly. They need to learn to love to read for multiple and authentic purposes.

Disturbing is the sense of failure children in this study experienced as a result of a literacy program that failed to recognize the resources they bring to the classroom and thus failed to provide the scaffolding that would allow children to succeed academically and feel pride in what they do know and can do. This is crucial to developing academic identities, since children who feel shame in being English language learners are likely to hide their need for greater instructional support as these children did using a variety of passing strategies. A sense of shame for being an English learner is very much a proxy for feelings of shame in one's ethnicity and culture.

Teachers' Roles in Fostering Academic Identities

Children spend a lot of time at school and thus schools and teachers, especially, have opportunity, and in my view, the responsibility to work with parents to foster academic identities among Latino children. Teachers can and should foster academic identities among students through their everyday instruction and interaction with students. Teachers can also work with parents so that their approaches to fostering academic identities can be complementary. Below are three important ways in which teachers (and parents) can foster academic identities.

Help Students Develop Positive Academic Self-concepts by Countering Deficit Perspectives

An important path toward combating students' notions of self as deficient because they are not yet fluent in English language and literacy is to validate the home language and culture. This requires, first and foremost, that teachers take a very active role in getting to know students, their families, and their community. The best way to do this is through home visits and outings in the community such as those described in this study. Home visits show the children and families that you want to get to know them on their terms. It allows you to see what resources families have, if they have many books, if the children have a place to study, etc. When talking with parents, you may want to ask very open-ended questions about their history such as: Why did they immigrate to this country? What are their hopes for their children? What concerns do they have about their children's academic development? Visits to the community could include going to the market or to a restaurant. You may also do class activities that would give you information about your students' funds of knowledge, such as having your students write about the biggest problem they see in their community, the best places to visit and why. Or, you may design questionnaires for your students and/ or their parents to complete.

This knowledge should inform the ways in which you structure classroom assignments and homework, instructional units and themes, and classroom management practices. When students see themselves and their culture reflected in the curriculum, they are likely to feel confident about the material since it is familiar and they are able to contribute to discussions and have much to write about the topic in essays (Moll et al., 1992; Moll & Díaz, 1987). When they feel successful in academic activities, they are likely to develop positive academic self-concepts.

For English learners, allowing Spanish in the classroom is essential to offering students opportunities to see themselves in a positive academic light. The primary language has been shown to support English learners in literacy development, academic content, and English development (Cummins, 1996). In English immersion classes where teachers are not allowed to use Spanish and materials and assignments have been mandated to be in English only, teachers need to be creative about bringing Spanish back. In such classes, teachers need to first talk to students about why Spanish has been formally banned from the classroom so that they understand that it is not their own perspective but rather a political maneuver. Spanish can then be included through its use by students. Students should be encouraged to use Spanish for discussion of texts. Students can be grouped by varying levels of English fluency so that content can be deciphered and analyzed in both languages. Drafts of written assignments can be sent for homework and written in Spanish and these can then be translated to a final English product. Content area reading can be supplemented at home with additional materials in Spanish.

A clear understanding of the process of second language acquisition helps all parties recognize that difficulty with academic English is not an indicator of academic deficiency. Students and parents need to have information about second language acquisition with some expected benchmarks per year so that they may be able to see their growth and understand that it is a slow process to catch up to English-fluent peers.

Teach Literacy (not just Reading)

Literacy is more than just decoding and encoding (Rueda & McIntyre, 2002). Literacy is about having access to multiple perspectives (Bakhtin, 1981). At its core, this approach to literacy is about making meaning. It involves understanding the world by gaining access to multiple perspectives. The development of multiple languages and literacies involves asking critical questions about social relations of power as one attempts to make sense of others' perspectives. It involves engaging with texts critically, asking questions that go beyond the text, and imagining new worlds.

Of course, reading, or decoding, is important. However, it is a means to an end. Students should be aware that the purpose of reading is to understand text and make sense of the world through language. A focus on making sense and authoring texts makes the task of phonics and other types of decoding activities more authentic because students will understand that the purpose of these tasks is to facilitate literacy.

School literacy practices, especially those demanded through highly scripted programs, offer students little, if any, choice and are unlikely to be of particular interest to many students, as was evident in this study. These readings are chosen in an attempt to satisfy the academic needs and interests of a large and very diverse population of students rather than by teachers with specific knowledge of their students' needs, interests, and funds of knowledge. Furthermore, school literacy practices rarely serve authentic functional purposes. That is, these literacy practices, such as reading stories, writing essays, and completing worksheets are seemingly done only for evaluation purposes (grade). The teacher is often the only one privy to the results of such activities.

Project-based learning is an especially useful approach to engaging students in purposeful activity (Krajcik, Blumenfeld, Marx, Bass, & Fredricks, 1998). Generally, project-based learning is a multidisciplinary approach that engages students in developing multi-faced projects (often long-term) that involve multiple and varied uses of literacy as a means to understanding the world and particularly the questions one has about it. It is particularly useful as a way of integrating higher-level literacy in academic areas, including science, social studies, math, and art. It also lends itself well to drawing on diverse children's interests, concerns, and prior knowledge.

Integrating literacy in the content areas is one way of dealing with the mandates in many urban schools for exclusive and strict use of scripted programs such as those described in this study. However, it is my contention that as a teacher, you have to do what you feel is right for your students. This includes finding ways to enhance the scripted program by drawing whenever possible on students' funds of knowledge, adding or replacing assignments with ones that offer students' greater interest and opportunities for skill development, changing the forms of delivery, supplementing readings with Spanish readings, using and/ or allowing students to use Spanish for comprehension, discussion, and in their writing, even in English-only classes.

Help Students Dream Big

Students from middle-class families whose parents have college educations grow up listening to their parents talk about their careers. Generally people with careers enjoy their jobs and enjoy the identity that the career affords. College graduates may talk about their college experiences and watch or attend college sporting events, often with their children. If there are older siblings or cousins in college, children may visit them in the dorms and hear about the various college-related experiences they are having.

Many Latino immigrant students, like those I studied, have very little knowledge about colleges or universities in this country. In my study, the parents had only at most a grade school education in their countries of origin and so did not speak about college experiences. However, teachers can familiarize such students with college and university life by explaining what going to college was like for them, whether they lived on campus and what their day-to-day routine was while in college. They should talk about the academic demands but also about the experience of learning new things, developing new identities, or the experiences they felt were most positive and rewarding. They should talk about the sense of accomplishment that comes from getting a college education. In these ways and others, teachers must help students dream of the possibility of getting a college education.

Ideas for Discussion, Extension, and Application

1. In small groups, take turns interviewing each other on your parents' roles and efforts in fostering your academic identities. List examples and examine how these efforts aligned or did not align with mainstream school expectations.
2. Monzó's detailed examination illustrates ways in which the educational system can undermine students' identities as successful readers. Brainstorm questions that could help a teacher to examine how classroom activities and assessment practices might affect students' developing identities as readers and writers.
3. Imagine two diverse students and briefly make a list of behaviors signaling a sense of failure and feelings of shame regarding their English language and literacy skills. In small groups, discuss how you might intervene with students experiencing this sense of failure.

References

Auerbach, S. (2006). "If the student is good, let him fly": Moral support for college among Latino immigrant parents. *Journal of Latinos & Education, 5*(4), 275–92.

Bakhtin, M. M. (1981). *The dialogic imagination.* Austin, TX: University of Texas Press.

Crozier, G. (2001). Excluded parents: The deracialisation of parental involvement. *Race, Ethnicity and Education, 4*(4), 329–41.

Cummins, J. (1996). *Negotiating identities: Education for empowerment in a diverse society.* Ontario, CA: CABE.

Delgado-Gaitan, C. (1994). Consejos: The power of cultural narratives. *Anthropology and Education Quarterly, 25,* 298–316.

Delgado-Gaitan, C. (2001). *The power of community: Mobilizing for family and schooling.* Lanham, MD: Rowman & Littlefield Publishers.

Fillmore, L. W. (2000). Loss of family languages: Should educators be concerned? *Theory into Practice, 39*(4), 203–10.

Flores, B., Cousin, P. T., & Díaz, E. (1991). Critiquing and transforming the deficit myths about learning, language, and culture. *Language Arts, 68,* 369–379.

Gibson, M. (1998). Promoting academic success among immigrant students: Is acculturation the issue? *Educational Policy, 12,* 615–633.

Holland, D., Lachicotte, Jr., W., Skinner, D., & Cain, C. (1998). *Identity and agency in cultural worlds.* Cambridge, MA: Harvard University Press.

Krajcik, J., Blumenfeld, P. C., Marx, R. W., Bass, K. M., & Fredricks, J. (1998). Inquiry in project-based science classrooms: Initial attempts by middle school students. *Journal of the Learning Sciences, 7*, 313–350.

Lave, J., & Wenger, E. (1991). *Situated learning: Legitimate peripheral participation.* Cambridge, MA: Cambridge University Press.

Lopez, G. R. (2001). The value of hard work: Lessons on parent involvement from an (im)migrant household. *Harvard Educational Review, 71*(3), 416–37.

Moll, L. C., Amanti, C., Nett, D., & González, N. (1992). "Funds of knowledge for teaching." *Theory into Practice, 31*, 132–141.

Moll, L. C., & Díaz, R. (1987). Teaching writing as communication: The use of ethnographic findings in classroom practice. In D. Bloome (Ed.), *Literacy and schooling* (pp. 193–221). Norwood, NJ: Ablex Publishing Corporation.

Moll, L. C., & Greenberg, J. (1990). Creating zones of possibilities: Combining social contexts for instruction. In L. C. Moll (Ed.), *Vygotsky and education: Instructional implications and applications of sociohistorical psychology* (pp. 319–348). New York: Cambridge University Press.

Monzó, L. D. (2005). Latino parents' "choice" for bilingual education in an urban California school: Language politics in the aftermath of Proposition 227. *Bilingual Research Journal, 29*(2), 287–308.

Monzó, L. D. (2009). "They don't know anything": The consequences of deficit thinking in the home-school relations of a Latino immigrant community. Manuscript in preparation.

Monzó, L. D., & Rueda, R. (2006). A sociocultural perspective on acculturation: Latino immigrant families negotiating diverse discipline practices. *Education and Urban Society, 38*(2), 188–203.

Monzó, L. D., & Rueda, R. (2009). *Passing as English fluent: Latino immigrant children masking language proficiency.* Manuscript under review for *Anthropology and Education Quarterly, 40*(1), 20–40.

Ogbu, J. U., & Simmons, H.D. (1998). Voluntary and involuntary minorities: A cultural-ecological theory of school performance with some implications for education. *Anthropology and Education Quarterly, 29*(2), 155–188.

Olsen, L. (1997). *Made in America. Immigrant students in our public schools.* New York: The New Press.

Orellana, M.F. (2001). The work kids do: Mexican and Central American immigrant children's contributions to households and schools in California. *Harvard Educational Review, 71*(3): 366–389.

Rogoff, B. (1995). Observing sociocultural activity on three planes: Participatory appropriation, guided participation, and apprenticeship. In J. V. Wertsch, P. Del Rio, and A. Alvarez (Eds.), *Sociocultural studies of mind* (pp. 139–164). Cambridge, UK: Cambridge University Press.

Rueda, R., & McIntyre, E. (2002). Toward universal literacy. In S. Stringfield & D. Land (Eds.), *Educating at risk students: One hundred-first yearbook of the National Society for the study of education* (pp. 189–209). Chicago: The University of Chicago Press.

Stritikus, T., & García, E. (2000). Education of limited English proficient students in California schools: An assessment of the influence of Proposition 227 on selected teachers and classrooms. *Bilingual Research Journal* On-line. *24*(1/2). Available at: http://brj.asu.edu/v2412/articles/art6.html.

Villenas, S. (2001). Latina mothers and small-town racisms: Creating narratives of dignity and moral education in North Carolina. *Anthropology & Education Quarterly, 32*(1), 3–28.

Volk, D., & Long, S. (2005). Challenging myths of the deficit perspective: Honoring children's literacy resources. *Young Children, 60*(6), 12–19.

Vygotsky, L. S. (1987). *L. S. Vygotsky, Collected works*, Vol. I. (R. Rieber & A. Carton, Eds; N. Minick, Trans.). New York: Plenum. (Original work published 1934).

Vygotsky, L. S. (1978). *Mind in society: The development of higher psychological processes.* Cambridge, MA: Harvard University Press.

Wertsch, J. V. (1991). *Voices of the mind: A sociocultural approach to mediated action.* Cambridge, MA: Harvard University Press.

Wertsch, J. V. (1998). *Mind as action.* New York: Oxford University Press.

Teacher Commentary

Simeon Stumme

Cindy Martinez was a quiet first grade girl. Her hair was always perfectly braided in two long ponytails; she wore the optional blue and white uniform, and the black leather shoes. During circle time, she always sat in front; she completed all her assignments. At recess she played with her classmates; she came in red-faced and sweaty, but ready to tackle the next activity in class. Her homework was always complete. In class, Cindy was on task.

But by early January, I become concerned with what seemed like a lack of progress in her reading. Cindy could decode simple books in Spanish, the language we spoke in class, and could read a few high frequency words in English, the language I was mandated to teach in, but she was not developing reading fluency in either. I called her mother, and asked if we could meet to discuss Cindy's reading progress. She agreed. Cindy's family lived in a large apartment complex a few miles from school; the same one most of the Mexican immigrant students lived in. When we met, we spoke in Spanish, and I complimented her daughter's effort and dedication to her schoolwork. I reassured Mrs. Martinez that Cindy was behaving very well in class and that she got along well with her peers. And then I shared my concerns about her reading. I explained what I had noticed in class and proceeded to give her a packet full of flash cards with words in English and Spanish, simple decodable books, and a reading log I wanted them to fill out as a family. She thanked me, and walked out the door smiling with Cindy.

As they left, to my great surprise, Mrs. Martinez was not speaking Spanish or English to Cindy, but what I later found out was the language of their small village in Oaxaca, Mexico. How did I not know that Mixtec was Cindy's first language? If I didn't know this, what else did I not know about Cindy? What did I not know about the rest of the students in my class that might influence their academic progress?

The first six chapters of this book call on me, as a teacher, to critically explore my daily practice, my interactions with my students and my relationship with my students' parents. The authors challenge me to view parental involvement as a critical link in student success: a link that I have the power to influence. They do not offer lock-step solutions, programmatic interventions, or definitive answers. Instead, they insist on reflection and action. They challenge on me to explore how school Discourse shapes the way I think of the parents of immigrant and non-White students. They insist that I remain a learner, and that parents and children have the power to educate me. They remind me that parents of immigrant and non-White parents care deeply about the education of their children.

I have been an elementary school teacher for 11 years, in Southern California and in the Chicago, Illinois area. I have worked in bilingual programs and in post-Proposition 227 California, where English-Only became the law of the classroom. While most of my students have been of Mexican descent, they have not been a homogenous group. Some were born in Los Angeles; some were recent immigrants. Some students spoke only Spanish; some spoke English as their first language; a few spoke a third language. Almost all have been working-class. Currently, I am teaching in a Dual Language (DL) school in the suburban Chicago area. The students in my class are both native Spanish speakers (mostly working-class Mexican immigrants) and native English speakers (mostly middle-class White students).

Discourse

One of the points several of the chapters make is that the Discourse (Gee's term) of the school and the Discourse of the home do not match. As the chapters point out, "our way of doing schooling" is not always welcoming to the children and parents of non-middle-class White parents (see Chapter 6). This mismatch causes discomfort, a sense of them versus us, a belief of "otherness" held by both the teacher and the parent. Guofang Li defines Discourse as a "plural set of cultural practices or culturally appropriate ways of thinking, believing, valuing, acting, interacting, speaking, reading, writing, and listening." I do not believe that any of the authors promote the idea of changing the Discourse of the family so that it conforms to that of the school but rather promote a mutual understanding, and a melding of the family and school Discourses. But, something that I struggle with in my own practice is the way in which school Discourse is constructed and maintained. Is there room for change? How can I as a teacher change it? What is my role in changing it? Do I support non-welcoming Discourses without realizing it?

In my school, the most recent trend has been to provide individualized learning experiences to all students, especially those struggling with the core academic subjects. I am given time to reflect, plan and implement learning activities that meet the needs of my struggling students. I have an opportunity to attend weekly meetings during which I have time to brainstorm ideas and seek advice from other teachers. The experience provides an opportunity to improve my pedagogy, react to standardized assessments in constructive ways, and provide responsive instruction to my struggling students.

However, the Discourse of performance, test scores, review of basics, dominates the meetings. The meetings are a more concentrated version of the same "solutions" our school has always issued; now we are simply more efficiently doling out services to students. But the underlying Discourse of remediation and school-based solutions has not changed. The Discourse of my school simply does not have the vocabulary to allow me to find out about my students' home life, their family's immigration status, home literacy practices, and their definitions of academic success.

My challenge for the coming year is to shift the conversation of these meetings so that our team is learning from the families and about the families; I will propose that the meetings be equal measure academic and ethnographic. My job should not be confined to the walls of the school; I need to become a researcher of the community. My findings need to become part of the Discourse of the school.

Teacher as Learner

I do not think it is a coincidence that all the chapters in Part I rely on ethnographic data to draw their conclusions. Becoming an ethnographer requires becoming a learner. The authors of these chapters let the subjects, the parents and students, tell their stories. Just as the stories become the findings, the stories of our students and their parents should become part of the curriculum and pedagogy of the classroom.

I often find myself in a difficult position with parents of immigrant children. They see me as an expert on curriculum, pedagogy and classroom management; someone who can help them with the education of their children. And I do not shy away from talking about what my studies and experience have taught me about teaching and learning. But more recently, I have done so with more caution. These chapters have reinforced my desire to model for students a critical and thoughtful engagement with the world around me.

Much of my classroom time is spent organizing activities that I hope will create critical and thoughtful thinkers. Our classroom mantra is that we all need to become interested and interesting people. Interested people ask questions, listen, and work with a variety of others. Interesting people are able to share who they are and what they know; make connections between themselves and the world around them. I want my students to be interested in others, curious about the world and its people, willing intellectual risk-takers, and able to assimilate new information—critical learners. I expect my students to do it, why shouldn't I?

Something Perry suggests is that teachers use one of their individual assessment times to learn more about the family life of the students (I plan on trying this). I try to use parent–teacher conferences similarly, focusing on learning from the parents about their children. Instead of just reviewing grades and the behavior of students, I ask parents to tell me about their child. I ask, "What is your child like at home?," "What types of things does your child do at home?," "What interests do they have?," "How do you think your child is doing at school?," "What types of things do you think they do really well?," and "What do you think they could use some more help with?" By the end of our 20-minute conversation, I feel that I have a better sense of the child, the family, and their relationship to the school and schooling. This short conversation is my first attempt at learning from the family, of communicating to parents: I am interested in your child and you have valuable knowledge to share with me. It is an attempt to change the role of teacher from expert to that of an interested, curious, partner.

Families and Parents Care about the Education of Their Children

The research presented in the first half of the book, and my experience, tell me that immigrant parents care deeply about the education of their children. During my conversations with parents they repeatedly assert that they want a better life for their children, and education is the way to achieve it. My challenge has always been reflecting upon the ways in which my understanding of parental involvement is different than theirs and how we can reach a common practice.

It has been common at many of the schools I have worked at for language minority parents to "appear" at the classroom door. Usually, they stand by the door and look in, or peek their head around the corner to draw some attention. I hear teachers complain about these unscheduled interruptions; they guard their instructional time and feel reluctant to stop what they are doing and speak with parents. What most drives teachers crazy is that most of the questions the parents have could have been answered at the front desk or through the reading of the weekly notices the students take home.

These "interruptions" have never bothered me. To me, they represent parents taking control of their child's education; they demonstrate a willingness to take a risk; they show me that the parent is interested in what is happening at school. I guard my instructional time as much as the next teacher. But I see speaking with parents as a crucial element to my classroom success. I try to respond to the parents who come to my classroom as quickly as I possibly can. If I am doing a teacher-fronted lesson, I have the students do a "quick-write" on the topic we are addressing; if I am in a guided reading group, I have the students read quietly to themselves; if I am conferencing with a student, I ask them to come back as soon as I am done speaking with the parent. Usually our conversation lasts less than a minute or two; then I invite them to stay. If they want to discuss an issue that requires more time, I try to set up a meeting before or after school. I do not want parents from my class to feel like the father sitting in his car in the school parking lot waiting for his son to finish his performance.

Conclusion

The chapters in Part I are not a practical guide for including immigrant and non-White parents into the school community. They do not really even give examples of "promising practices." Still, they were written with teachers in mind, as statements of possibility and challenge. In diverse ways, they underscore an absolutely critical message: The more we know about the students we teach, the more likely we are to create opportunities for those students to succeed.

Part II

Curriculum Transformations

Learning with Families

8 Do You Hear What I Hear?

Using the Parent Story Approach to Listen to and Learn from African American Parents

Patricia A. Edwards and
Jennifer D. Turner

Mrs. Jackson:	No one here [at the school] gives us benefit of the doubt. They're ready to throw our kids out. They call us, but by the time they get to us, the deed has already been done. Like Mary said about her son: by the time she got to the principal to talk about the situation, her son was already kicked out. And that ain't right!!!
Ms. Williams:	Or when your child gets to school and does something wrong, the first thing teachers tell you is that you need to take your child to the doctor and get some pills.
Ms. Johnson:	And it's not always that the child needs medication. Sometimes the child is just going through a rough time, and teachers don't wanna take a little more time to see what the kids have gone through. My son has gone through a lot. He had his grandma pass away, so you know he is dealing with death a lot.
Ms. Anthony:	Yeah 'cause kids are going through all this and they can't focus in school. They are having a hard time learning when they've got these other situations to deal with. And when that happens, teachers need to know that they can call. Call us, we don't care what time it is. We're gonna come, it might not be right then, but we'll come that day. We care about our children, and we will do whatever is necessary to prevent our children from ending up in prison or in the grave.

The voices of these African American mothers are filled with passion and pain as they talk about their children's schooling experiences. Their stories demonstrate just how different the subjective experiences of African American parents and teachers can be, and that parents' and teachers' perceptions about home-school relationships, literacy, and schooling can indeed be "worlds apart" (Lightfoot, 1978, p. 170). Bridging the gap between the worlds of African American parents and the world of school is an essential goal, because this enables parents and teachers to work together as partners in the educational lives of African American children. Parent involvement is a cornerstone to literacy achievement and success in school, because "children who have more opportunities to engage in literacy-relevant activities at home have more positive views about reading, engaging in more leisure reading, and have better reading achievement" (Baker & Scher, 2002, p. 240), Parents who are involved in their children's schooling also garner positive benefits; they often become more aware of the influence that they have on their children's educational achievement, and they develop greater capacity to help their children practice school-based literacy skills at home (Epstein, 1995; Gadsden, Ray, Jacobs, & Gwak, 2006). In turn, teachers who communicate positively with African American parents learn to recognize the cultural and familial resources that African American children bring into classrooms, and are able to effectively build upon these resources to teach reading and writing in schools (Edwards, Pleasants, & Franklin, 1999).

While the benefits of strong home-school relationships are quite evident, it is much more difficult for teachers and administrators to establish and nurture these kinds of partnerships with African American parents and children (Edwards, Danridge, McMillon, & Pleasants, 2001). Otto (1969) contends "unless [parents and teachers] can communicate with mutual understanding [they] remain strangers or nodding acquaintances at best" (p. 1). Unfortunately, all too often the relationship between African American parents and schools may be affected by faulty perceptions schools hold related to their home lives, their culture, or their communities. Typically, school expectations of families reflect behaviors, value orientations, and capabilities of middle-class nuclear families. In this way, uniform standards for measuring familial competency exist that often ignore or negate the diversity among families as well as the contributions families bring to the educational settings (Tutwiler, 1998). The cultural differences reflected in African American families can result in a number of challenges for teachers and schools, including: (1) language differences that mitigate communication with teachers (e.g., using African American Vernacular English rather than "standard" English); (2) differences in cultural and community experiences orchestrated for children (e.g., not visiting museums); and (3) differences in perceptions about parent–teacher roles and schooling. These challenges can cause African American parents to be less visible in school, and as a result, some teachers and administrators may perceive these parents to be disinterested in their children's education (Edwards, 2004; Moles, 1993). Some teachers and administrators even question the quality of children's home lives, as well as parents' commitment to helping their children with school work, and project the stereotype of the "not interested" parent onto the children, which results in low expectations about these children's abilities and the abilities of their families to help them succeed in school (Auerbach, 1989; Lightfoot, 1978).

THEORETICAL APPLICATION: THE COMPETENCE OF DIVERSE FAMILIES

Teachers' perceptions and expectations of diverse families reflect their own personal experiences and may include fear of different cultural practices, values, and languages. These perceptions and expectations directly impact teachers' understandings and beliefs about students' educational potential. Deficit discourses about what diverse learners can or cannot do and their families' ability to participate impact teachers' ability to effectively support their learning and engagement in school. How can detailed ethnographic portraits of families challenge and change stereotypical images of diverse families and the potentially negative expectations that teachers have of children from these families?

Making matters worse, some teachers and schools inadvertently inhibit African American parent involvement by solely relying on traditional forms of home-school communication (e.g., report card conferences, back-to-school nights) to communicate with these parents. Some African American parents have had negative educational experiences, and do not feel comfortable coming into classrooms to talk about their children's literacy learning (Edwards et al., 1999). Still others want to be more involved but they cannot attend these school-related functions due to intense work schedules and/or family issues (e.g. lack of child care, caring for sickly relatives). Consequently, when teachers and schools act out of socio-cultural assumptions that devalue the contributions of poorer, less-educated families, use educational jargon that deepens the communication divide, or they ignore or disparage important economic, cultural, and language differences, they are sending a message to African American parents that they are not welcome or wanted in the school (Edwards & Danridge, 2001).

As African American literacy educators, we have listened to the voices of the African American parents countless times, and we know that they want to work with teachers and schools in positive and productive ways, but they may not know how. We also believe that teachers and schools *can* learn to work with and relate to African American families so that their children can become successful literacy learners. The aim of this chapter, then, is to describe "parent stories" as a useful approach that teachers and schools can draw upon when they seek to involve African American parents in their children's literacy education. We begin our chapter with a rationale for why parent stories can be used as a strategy for listening to and learning with African American parents. Next, we discuss how the parent story approach could be used for teachers and schools who want to listen and learn from African American parents. Specifically, we highlight four powerful messages contained within the stories told by six African American mothers of middle-school children. Finally, we conclude with a brief discussion of the implications that the parent story approach has for literacy teachers and schools who want to establish and nurture more productive relationships with African American students and their families.

Theoretical Framework

Our work with the parent story approach is situated within a social constructivist view of home-school relationships and literacy education. From this perspective, children learn literacy through sociocultural processes in a variety of communities and contexts, and eventually internalize this literacy knowledge and expertise (Au, 1998; Vygotsky, 1978). Thus, children are learning literacy in their homes long before they enter the classroom, and parents should be acknowledged as children's first and most important teachers (Edwards et al., 1999). It is important to note that while all families have their own literacy practices and events, these may not map onto the literacy skills and knowledge that are valued in schools and other mainstream institutions. In their qualitative study, Anderson and Stokes (1988) found that many African American families enacted numerous literacy practices in their daily lives, such as reading magazines, TV guides, and cook-books, and studying the Bible and other religious texts, as well as writing letters and recipes, and paying bills. However, not all African American families enacted the more traditional literacy practices, such as storybook reading and homework support, which are highly valued in school. This does not mean that African American families' literacy practices are less important than those found in main-stream schools and homes; rather, teachers and schools must find ways to gain access to the hidden literacies in the everyday lives of African American families and children if they are to work productively with them.

A social constructivist perspective also highlights the fact that teachers must learn to acknowledge that the literacy and cultural knowledge of African American children and families is essential to building strong home-school relationships and orchestrating effective literacy instruction in classrooms. As Taylor and Dorsey-Gaines (1988) argue:

> If we are to teach, we must first examine our own assumptions about families and children and we must be alert to the negative images in the literature . . . instead of responding to "pathologies" we must recognize that what we see may actually be healthy adaptations to an uncertain and stressful world. As teachers . . . we need to think about the children themselves and try to imagine the contextual worlds of their day-to-day lives.
>
> (p. 203)

These comments illustrate the need for practical tools and approaches which can alter teachers' dispositions and practices with African American students. Most teachers hold deficit views and/or negative assumptions about African American students and families, as well as others from diverse backgrounds, and have not had enough cross-cultural experiences and interactions to challenge those stereo-types (Nieto, 1996). Complicating matters further, most classroom teachers have not been adequately prepared to address cultural diversity by their teacher prep-aration programs, nor have these programs provided the necessary experiences in working with families from different backgrounds (Turner & Edwards, in press). Although professional organizations like the American Association of Colleges for Teacher Education, and the Association of Teacher Educators have defined the knowledge, skills, and dispositions needed to work with diverse children, few teacher preparation programs have incorporated meaningful coursework related to ethnically-diverse families and communities into their curriculum (Turner & Edwards, in press).

In addition, schools and teachers are increasingly separated from the com-munities where many African American children live, and as a result they are increasingly disconnected from these children's lives. Because teachers and schools need this vital information about children's home literacy environments and their lives outside of school, they need mechanisms and tools that enable them to learn from families by positioning parents as the "more knowledgeable others" (Vygotsky, 1978), and eliciting information about the "human side" of families and children (e.g., children's ways of learning and communicating, family routines, parenting styles and discipline). Accordingly, we see the parent story approach as an essential strategy for teachers and schools to establish and nurture meaningful, authentic, and affirming connections with diverse students, families, and communities.

Defining the Parent Story Approach

According to Vandergrift and Greene (1992), "every parent has his or her own story to tell" (p. 57). Thus, parent "stories" are the narratives gained from open-ended conversations and/or interviews between teachers and parents (Edwards et al., 1999). In these interviews, parents respond to questions designed to provide information about traditional and nontraditional early literacy activities and experiences that have happened in the home. By using stories as a way to describe the nature of the home environment, parents can select anecdotes and personal observations from their family lives to give teachers access to complicated social, emotional, and educational information that can help teachers unravel the mystery around their students' early literacy beginnings. Equally important, parent stories provide teachers with access to personal information about children's home experiences and family routines, literacy practices, which enables them to construct classroom environments that are more congruent with their cultural knowledge and background.

Collecting and Analyzing Parent Stories. Teachers collect parent stories through a series of interview questions (see Edwards et al., 1999 for specific questions). It is important to note that when teachers conduct the interviews, they will receive information from parents in small, decontextualized bits and pieces. Consequently, it is the teacher's task to put the information together in a way that offers coherent and compelling information about the home literacy environment that the parent(s) have orchestrated for their children. To accomplish this task, teachers must be willing to deeply listen to the parents and the stories that they tell. Metzger (1986) explains:

> Stories go in circles. They don't go in straight lines. So it helps if you listen in circles because there are stories inside stories and stories between stories and finding your way through them is as easy and hard as finding your way home. And part of the finding is the getting lost. If you're lost, you really start to look around and listen.
>
> (p. 104)

In this form of listening, teachers invite parents to tell their stories, shifting the power within the relationship between teachers and parents. Consequently, parents become the experts about their child especially when it comes to interpreting and describing their child's home environment and the role they play in preparing their child for school. Through the telling of these stories parents are recognized (whether they are literate or not) as the "authority" in describing their familial "funds of knowledge" (Moll, Armanti, Neff, & González, 1992) and interpreting the social methods and cultural codes used in their home literacy environment—all of which may be invisible to classroom teachers (Edwards et al., 1999). This is especially important given the perspective that parents and school teachers are a child's first and second most important teachers–parents must have the opportunity to give teachers personal information that may help teachers to understand how children can learn best in their classrooms. Although parents do not hold all the answers to their children's literacy problems, neither do teachers. Only by combining the knowledge of both of these groups of people will we have a more complete picture of children's home and school lives.

Using the Parent Story Approach to Learn about Individual and Multiple Families

Much of the research on parent stories describes how teachers can elicit information from individual parents (Edwards et al., 1999; Kidd, Sanchez, & Thorp, 2004). Oftentimes, teachers can collect parent stories when families come in for particular meetings, such as Back to School Night and/or parent–teacher conferences. Teachers may also opt to collect parent stories through visits to their homes as they participate in and observe their everyday lives (Edwards & Dandridge, 2001).

However, we also want to emphasize the fact that parent stories can be simultaneously gathered from multiple parents. This "group" perspective may be particularly useful for teachers who have several African American students (or students from other backgrounds) in their classroom, and they would like to learn more about general cultural characteristics, practices, and literacies from a larger group of diverse parents. Also, collecting stories from a group of culturally diverse parents may help teachers avoid making erroneous cultural assumptions based on information from one or two parents. In the next section, we highlight the possibilities of using the parent story approach to understand multiple stories and cultural experiences through our work with a group of African American parents.

"They Have to Understand That We Have a Story to Tell": Using the Parent Story Approach to Listen to a Group of African American Parents

School Context and Participants

Browyn Hill Middle School is located in a mid-sized Midwestern community. Most of the students are African American and Hispanic, with a few Caucasian students. While a small number of the students have managed to do well academically, most of the students are struggling with and/or failing in all their academic subjects. For several years, Browyn Hill's students have not met the annual yearly progress expectations and the superintendent recently threatened to close the school.

Over the past few years, tensions between teachers and African American parents had been mounting. Frustrated about the low test scores, Browyn Hill's teachers felt that they were doing all they could do to support the African American students. However, most of the African American parents felt that the teachers had labeled their children as "failures" and simply did not care whether they succeeded or not. Searching for answers, the principal read Edwards's book *A Path to Follow: Learning to Listen to Parents*, and invited her to the school to share this approach with his parents and teachers. During his initial meeting with Edwards, the principal explained, "We have communication problem between teachers and parents, and I believe inviting parents to share their stories might get my teachers' attention and move them to seriously listen to the voices of parents."

Our Work as Researchers

To begin the work on parent stories, the principal introduced Edwards to the parent consultant at Browyn Hill. The parent consultant served as a liaison between teachers and parents, and she was instrumental in contacting parents to ask them to volunteer to participate in the "parent story" interview. Edwards introduced her work by talking with a group of African American parents, explaining to them that she was interested in capturing their perceptions of how parents and children were treated at Browyn Hill Middle School. Specifically, she asked the parent group these questions: (a) What do you want teachers to know about you and your children?; and (b) What changes do you feel need to be made at Browyn Hill in order to address your concerns? By asking open-ended, non-judgmental questions, Edwards was opening up a "narrative space" where the African American parents could freely tell their stories about their children's schooling experiences, and stories about their own interactions with teachers and school administrators at Browyn Hill.

To analyze the messages within this group of African American parents' stories, we adopted a research-based approach (see Edwards et al. [1999] for teacher-friendly procedures for making sense of parent stories). We analyzed the transcripts from the focus group using qualitative content analyses (Patton, 1990). First, we watched the videotape of the focus group several times, with each of us taking notes and talking about issues that were interesting to us. After the transcript of the video was prepared, we independently coded the transcript, drawing upon the tentative themes that emerged during our collaborative viewing of the videotape. Finally, we came together to discuss our independent coding schemes, moving back and forth between our codes until we developed a new, integrated coding framework that was representative of the focus group data. We used this coding framework to re-examine the transcripts, and to generate common themes across the parent stories. According to Edwards and her colleagues (1999), these themes are representative of "important aspects of the parent stories [collected] through conversations with parents" (p. 42). In what follows, we discuss the four themes which emerged from our qualitative content analyses of the parent stories. We characterize them as "messages" to further emphasis the communicative nature of the parent stories, and to highlight the importance of listening to and learning from these parents' experiences and insights. Thus, the four "messages" are: (1) We care about our children and their education; (2) My children have been through so much; (3) We've got to trust each other; and (4) Please work with me.

Message 1: "We care about our children and their education"

Research indicates that some teachers believe that African American parents do not care about their children's education. In her teacher education study, Lazar (2004) found that while 90% of the student teachers believed that White parents provided books for their children at home, only 10% believed that black parents did this. These types of assumptions reflected "the general belief among the interns that [urban Philadelphian] children came from homes where caregivers did not, or could not, support children's academic achievement" (p. 56).

The parents' stories gathered in our study, however, painted a different portrait of African American parents. The mothers in the focus group spent substantial conversational time talking about their love for their children, and equally important, their desire to see their children succeed. As Yvonne shared:

> You know, I was told that my son was going to end up in prison or in grave. So imagine how I felt when I heard that from an educator! I would do everything possible to protect my child. I took him to counseling, I took him to anger management, I talked to him. I went out to find a mentor and you know, and I still heard "grave or prison." But I would do whatever I need, whatever is necessary to prevent my child from going there.

Clearly, this African American mother wanted her son to succeed, not only in school, but in life. Equally important, she was willing to try various strategies for helping her son (e.g., taking him to counseling, finding a mentor for him). This mother's story suggests that African American parents believe in the value of education, and they are willing to listen to educators who believe in their children's potential. Overwhelmingly, the African American parents in this study believed that teachers can make the difference in the lives of children, as Chenelle explained:

> When I was in school I looked up to my teachers cause my parents were not the best parents. I was a kid who was beaten at home. I acted out and a White counselor at school put me in a Big Brother Big Sister program, and got me a mentor. Because I had a mentor, I ended up being a better person. So instead of taking life in a negative way, I made it positive. But if children don't have that positive person or a positive adult like a counselor or a teacher who will show them the right path and showing them they do care about their decision, then they'll go on the wrong path.

In addition to believing that good teachers make a difference in the lives of individual children, the African American parents also discussed how schooling contributed to a better society. Shawna wanted her son to get a good education because

> At the end of the day if I die or something happens, he is gonna need to be able to support himself because if he doesn't, he'll end up in jail . . . Or the other issue is if he falls in love with somebody and they have kids, who is gonna support all those kids? Me? Society? No, he has to take care of his own responsibilities, and I want him to get a job to be able to support himself and be productive in the community.

Echoing this sentiment, Dolores responded:

> We need all children to learn and graduate because White, Black, Mexican, whatever you are, you need an education because we can't promise you anything. So we want to leave our kids with tools to make it. I don't want to leave my kids with no tools to make it. So I'm trying everything I know to get my kids those tools.

Message 2: "My children have been through so much"

The African American parents in the focus group not only wanted teachers to know that they cared deeply about their children, but also that their children had been through traumatic life experiences. This mother's comment was typical of the personal insights that the parents shared concerning the difficult circumstances in their children's lives:

> Sometimes the teachers don't want to take a little more time to see what the kids have gone through. We have a little black kid from Detroit, and he comes from homeless home. So here in this school they downgrade this black kid because he is in the first grade and he can't spell his name, and he can't count to 10. They downgrade him as a black child. He's a bright little boy and has been through so much.

At times, it was also evident that the mothers themselves were struggling to understand their children's lives and experiences. These parents reported being actively involved with their children, yet they still believed that there were some things about their children that teachers may learn about first. Dolores put it this way:

> Sometimes the teachers are the first ones to know if there is a problem. Like a young girl starting her [menstrual cycle] for the first time or a child being abused at home. It's a multitude of things, but to me, all I see is I have my child at night. I'm the mother at night, the teacher is the mother at day, or the male teacher is the father during the day because they are there with them all day.

Because the majority of African American mothers in this study had sons, the talk often turned to the difficulties of relating to boys, as this exchange illustrates:

Shawna: There are some things that males are not gonna talk to their mothers about. They can go to another male and talk about it. All male kids need to have a male figure in their life.

Trina: And it's hard for them to talk about a lot of things. Like a lot of things my son talks to me about sometimes I can't answer his questions. So I have to ask my husband who is not his daddy. [My son] won't talk to him, he wants [his stepfather] to come to him. He can't bring himself to go and talk to [his stepfather] about a lot of stuff he talks to me about.

It is important to note that the African American parents in this study did not expect the teachers to be miracle workers; they realized that the teachers were dealing with a range of issues and problems (e.g., large class sizes) in the classroom, and they understood that it was difficult for teachers to address all the students and their problems. Yet these African American parents wanted teachers to understand that their children might have had difficulty learning or behave negatively during class, not because they were "bad" children, but because they were trying to work through very challenging life circumstances. According to Yvonne, what was most frustrating to her was the fact that the teachers "don't try to find out the root of the problem. They don't talk to that child or the parents to find out what is going on . . . they are more prone to throw the Black kids off to the side." This idea that teachers were casting aside the African American children in their classrooms was so disturbing to these parents that it began to erode their trust in the teachers, the administrators, and the school system. Indeed, this issue of trust is at the core of the next message.

Message 3: "We've got to trust each other"

The African American mothers in this study identified several potential issues that mitigated the trust between the home and the school. Perhaps the most important issue, according to these parents, was the fact that many teachers seemed to perceive them in a negative light, based upon stereotypical images of African American people as loud, confrontational and aggressive (Noguera, 2003). Indeed, as this exchange illustrates, the African American mothers were fully aware of the negative images that some teachers held about them:

Shawna: They think we come here as parents to fight the teacher. No, just because my daughter says, "My mama's gonna come here and kick your tail" that does not mean that I am [laughing].

Chanelle: The teachers generalize about us as parents. Don't generalize!

Trina: They don't give us benefit of the doubt. They've already got us figured out. They think we are all bad parents, and then they're ready to throw our kids out of school.

All of the African American parents were also concerned that some teachers had negative impressions of their children because they had listened to negative information from the previous teacher. Dolores put it this way:

> Let's say your son is in sixth grade and before he gets to seventh grade, the seventh grade teachers already have an idea of him because they have already conversed about him. Like "You've got such and such in your class??! Oh my God!" So they've got some pre-formed notions about your kid before your kid goes into class. See, they already expect your kid to be bad before your kid walks through the door.

Based upon what the African American parents perceived as deficit views of their children, most reported that teachers or school administrators had requested that they have their children treated for various psychosocial conditions such as ADD or ADHD. According to Trina, "There is a lot of teachers that come to you, but you know, when they come to you, they don't say what your child is like or what your child is doing. They say 'You need to take your child to doctor and put him on medication.' Medication is not always a child's problem." For this group of African American parents, it was extremely difficult to work with their children's teachers because they felt that the school was not on their side, and would blame them for any problems that arose with their children. As Shawna observed, "If your child acts up, they think you're a bad parent. If your child acts automatically, it's automatically assumed that the child doesn't have home training."

In terms of instruction, the African American parents wanted to be able to trust the teachers to be able to handle classroom-related issues. For the majority of the African American parents in this focus group, this meant that they wanted the teachers to have the knowledge, competency, and skill to effectively manage the classroom and take a preventative approach to behavior issues. Consider the following exchange:

Chanelle:	A lot of young teachers that are coming from college into these schools. They come and don't have their own kids and they are not equipped to handle the children. They think Blacks don't wanna work, but they are not equipped, they are not experienced. My daughter says one teacher doesn't teach, she just sits there and cries.
Pat (researcher):	Well, what she is crying about?
Trina:	You know, she say kids talk about her and stuff and you know how kids are.
Shawna:	She says she can't get them under control. If one starts laughing, you gonna have everyone in the crowd laughing. If she can't quiet the one who started laughing, then she is not going to be able to stop the rest. And that's how she starts crying.

Several other African American parents were extremely concerned about the quality of literacy instruction that teachers were providing in the classroom. For example, Yvonne shared this story about her son:

> My experience has been a little bit different from most parents because my son has dyslexia, which is a disorder when it comes to reading. And so he has an IEP [Individualized Educational Plan] every year. So, OK, I come to the school district, we sit at a table to decide what services he needs, and the accommodation he needs in class. Then I find out the services aren't yet provided and the teachers don't have a copy of what accommodations he should have in the classroom. They are not sending any information about how he is doing in class, and that concerns me as a parent. If I repeatedly call a teacher, and you don't tell me that [her son's IEP is not being followed] . . . but you can call me about other things, that makes me upset. For me, [when I] deal with the teacher I can't see anything else . . . there is a trust issue there.

In light of their negative interactions and experiences with the teachers, it is not surprising that the African American parents' feelings of mistrust also extended to the school administration. For example, Joyce, who reported having frequent conversations with the principal, described several incidents which made her question the intentions of the educators in the middle school:

> I don't have a problem dealing with them [school administrators and teachers]. And when a group of parents go down to Dr. Thornton [principal] and say, "Your teachers are talking down to our students," and nothing is done, that's a problem. And he tells the kids, "I'm not gonna invest my time with you because you're not going to college anyway." And that upsets me because I'm thinking, "If you don't have any value of my child, then why are you working with him? You don't need to be in this profession."

Another mother affirmed these comments, adding that "If you come to the principal when you're Black, eight times of ten the teachers are going to win. You better have some clout because they are not going to listen."

Although the African American parents were generally disheartened by the school's responses to their children, they also recognized that a trusting relationship was a two-way street; in order to gain teachers' trust and respect, they realized that they had to keep trying to work with the school. When asked what they could do to support their children's literacy education, the African American mothers in the focus group generated numerous strategies including (1) working/reading with their children in the summer; (2) teaching children skills so that they would be "ready" for school; (3) involving children in mentoring programs and other supportive networks (e.g., Big Brother and Big Sister programs, the YWCA); and (4) helping to organize group sessions where parents and teachers could talk together. For these parents, however, the ultimate way to build trust between the teachers and African American parents was to work together and develop open lines of communication in the interest of the child. The importance of collaborative work between teachers and African American parents embodies the final message within their parent stories.

Message 4: "Please work with me"

The five African American mothers who participated in this focus group shared poignant stories about their children's schooling experiences, particularly those within the middle school that served as the site for this research. These stories greatly emphasized the parents' desire to have teachers communicate with them. More specifically, these parents wanted to be notified if there was a problem with their children in the classroom. As one mother explained,

> When you call me about something wrong that my child did, don't sit back and wait like four, five days later. Call me when it happens. Don't call me two weeks later and expect for me to reprimand my child for something that they did.

The parents reported that this was common practice at the middle school. Most parents did not realize that there was even a problem in the classroom until their child was suspended from school. Others stated that they did not know that their children were misbehaving in school until parent conferences, and they were frustrated by that point, because, as one mother put it, "they have a whole list of stuff by then!!"

Consequently, one of the critical themes in the parent stories told by the African American mothers at the focus group is that they were very open to working with the teachers and the school on disciplinary issues. As Trina explained, "I love all my kids. But if they're wrong, they're wrong. I'm not gonna stand behind them and let them be wrong. I tell them if you are wrong you're wrong, and if you're right, I then I'll back you up." Sometimes, teachers and school administrators do not communicate with African American parents because they do not believe that they will be able to be objective about their children's behavior and see the situation from the school's perspective. However, Joyce, and the other mothers, expressed a strong willingness to work with the school to address any behavioral issues that arose in the classroom:

> If you notify me that there is a problem, I will work out with you to be there. If I can't be there now because of time, I'll be there, bring your child, whatever we need to do, you as the teacher, me as a parent. Both parents, it might be me or grandma or me by myself, whatever your support group is. Be open to me about what you talk and I'll be open to what you talk to me about. Work your way around it as a teacher and I'll work around it as a parent.

What is striking about Joyce's comments is the way that she identified a broader range of caregivers, to include two-parent families, single-parent families, and grandparents. One of the perceptions that the African American parents held about the school was that teachers looked down on their children if they were not from two-parent households. According to Shawna, "Teachers think if there is no male in the household, then the kids are headed for trouble." Joyce's words, however, highlight the fact that teachers and schools need to be willing to work with any caregiver in a child's life. One of the mothers mentioned the famous African proverb "It takes a village to raise a child" to signify the group's belief that schools, parents, extended family members, and even community members needed to come together to educate their children.

In addition, the African American parents wanted the teachers to work with them to support their children's learning and progress in school. Several of the mothers described frustrations and anxieties about the homework that their children were expected to complete at home. Chenelle's comments exemplified the concerns of the group:

> I think that teachers at this school are not prepared. They need to know their subjects cause if they tell us to do algebra or history, you know, I have been out of school for 20 years and I don't get what they are doing in class [Group laughter]. Because some of the teachers don't even know their own subjects because the kids have to come home and ask their parents. My daughter asks me how to do something and I'll say, "But didn't your teacher show you how to do it?" So they need to go back to school and learn what they are supposed to be teaching.

Nearly all of the African American parents reported similar experiences, noting that they would have liked the teachers to provide directions or instructions for these assignments. For this group of parents, having greater clarification for their children's homework was an important step that demonstrated their willingness to work collaboratively with parents.

Envisioning New Possibilities for Home-School Relationships through the Parent Story Approach: Conclusion and Implications

In this chapter, we have discussed the parent story approach and its usefulness in helping teachers to listen to and learn from African American parents. The parent story approach allows "teachers to identify what it means, specifically, when we use the words 'home literacy environment' to talk about students' success or lack of success in school" (Edwards et al., 1999, p. xxvii). By eliciting detailed information about children's literacy experiences at home, and the multiple forms of literacy that these activities embody (e.g., cultural systems, language systems), schools can create a more comprehensive picture of students as literacy learners. The parent story approach, then, offers teachers and school administrators with a specific strategy to gain greater access to the hidden literacies in students' lives, especially those from culturally and/or linguistically diverse backgrounds, and enables educators to "purposefully and constructively . . . use [this information] to benefit students in the classroom" (Edwards et al., 1999, p. 76). In Table 8.1, we

Table 8.1 Questions that teachers can ask to elicit parent stories from groups of parents

1. How have you felt about your children's experiences in school?

2. What have you liked about your children's experiences in school, and what would you have wanted schools to do differently with you and your child(ren)?

3. How have teachers treated you and your child(ren) in the past? Do you think that being African American has shaped teachers' perceptions of you or treatment toward you and your child(ren)? Why or why not?

4. What kinds of relationships have you had with your child(ren)'s teachers? What has been positive about those relationships with teachers? What would you have wanted to happen differently in the relationship with teachers?

5. What would you like teachers to know about raising African American children? About teaching African American children?

6. What can teachers do to build stronger and more positive relationships with you? With your child(ren)?

provide a list of questions that can be used with a group of African American parents to promote the narrative process.

The parent story approach also empowers parents by giving them the chance to participate in their child's education in a personally meaningful way. By positioning parents as the authority, the parent story approach respects and values their expert knowledge of their children, their culture, and their home literacies. In the multiple parent stories collected in this study, for example, the African American mothers shared heart-wrenching narratives describing their frustrations, concerns, and painful experiences with the school and in their lives. We know that African American parents continuously wrestle with vast challenges—changing family demographics, time constraints, cultural divides, privacy issues, and, of course economics (Gadsden et al., 2006). When African American parents share their stories, it becomes an opportunity for teachers and school administrators to learn more about what is happening in the lives of their students. But we also want to emphasize the importance of sensitivity and empathy in listening to these stories, because this level of family information is highly-sensitive. Therefore, teachers and schools must be careful not to use the information gathered from African American parents' stories to reinforce their own negative assumptions or stereotypes about African American children, families, and communities; rather, they should use this important information to guide their literacy instruction and to develop stronger relationships with African American parents (Edwards et al., 1999).

THEORETICAL APPLICATION: PARENT STORIES

Parent/family stories reveal diverse families' hopes, dreams, fears, and struggles. This chapter provides complex snapshots of such stories and reveals the inherent delicacy of parent–teacher relationships, in which trust is the cornerstone to successful communication. Here, trust is actualized through listening and respect, keeping lines of communication open, and

giving each other the benefit of doubt. Moreover, the parent voices throughout this book confirm diverse parents' often invisible concern for and contributions to their children's education. What practical strategies can you, as a
teacher, use to establish trust with parents and hear their stories and
concerns about their own children? How can teachers open space for shifting
power relationships and parents' participation as experts on their own
children?

In contrast to much of the research on family stories that highlights how
teachers can gather stories from individual families (e.g., Kidd et al., 2004), this
chapter highlights the parent story approach as a mechanism for collecting and
understanding the narratives of a group of parents. We believe that this emphasis
is significant because it provides access to "insider" cultural information that
helps teachers make sense of community practices and literacies. Stories from
multiple parents can help teachers "examine people's usual ways of doing things,
trying to understand individuals' history of involvement in the practices of varied
communities, including ethnic or national communities" (Gutiérrez & Rogoff,
2003, pp. 21–22). In this study, the African American mothers' stories illustrated
how they drew upon a range of caretakers and other familial resources to work
with their children and nurture involvement with the school. As some researchers
(e.g., Clark, 1983; Heath, 1983) have argued, the expanded nuclear family is a
common cultural practice in many African American families, and should be
viewed as a cultural tradition rather than as an indication that something is
"wrong" with the nuclear African American family. Because teachers may need
additional insights about African American families and culture to engage in
the process of collecting and analyzing stories collected from African American
parents, we recommend that they read books presenting an in-depth perspective
on African American families and schooling written by scholars and by successful
African Americans (see Table 8.2).

Second, teachers and schools who use the parent story approach to listen to
groups of African American parents may be better able to use this information
to rethink educational policy and practices. For example, a teacher who listens to
one African American parent's story might perceive his/her issues with the school
as "one individual's problem." Listening to the voices of the six African American
mothers in our work, however, illuminates the pervasiveness and the severity
of several issues at this particular middle school (e.g., classroom management/
discipline, expectations related to schooling), because several African American
parents reported similar concerns and frustrations. Researchers like Noguera
(2003) recommend that teachers and schools empower African American and
other marginalized groups of parents to participate in reform efforts by organizing
sessions where these parents can share their views of the school, their concerns
about their children's education, and their thoughts about what the school could
do to improve home-school relations. Unfortunately, these researchers do not
offer schools a framework for organizing these discussions, or for interpreting
and implementing the information elicited from such discussions. Based on the

Table 8.2 Suggested book lists

Books on African American families and schooling by researchers

Clark, R. (1983). *Family life and school achievement. Why poor Black children succeed or fail.* Chicago: University of Chicago Press.

Foster, M. (1997). *Black teachers on teaching.* New York: The New Press.

Hacker, A. (1995). *Two nations: Black and white, separate, hostile, unequal.* New York: Ballantine Books.

Hale-Benson, J. (1982). *Black children: Their roots, culture, and learning styles* (Rev. Ed.). Baltimore, MD: Johns Hopkins University Press.

Hale-Benson, J. (2001). *Learning while Black: Creating educational excellence for African American children.* Baltimore, MD: Johns Hopkins University Press.

Heath, S. (1983). *Ways with words: Language, life, and work in communities and classrooms.* New York: Cambridge University Press.

Non-Fiction Books on African American families and schooling by African Americans

Bray, R.L. (1998). *Unafraid of the dark: A memoir.* New York: Anchor Books.

Bridges, R. (1999). *Through my eyes.* New York: Scholastic Press.

McCall, N. (1995). *Makes we wanna holler: A young Black man in America.* New York: Vintage Press.

McDonald, J. (1999). *Project girl.* New York: Ferris, Straus, & Giroux Publishers.

---

findings from this study, we believe that the parent story approach could serve as a guide for facilitating these important reform conversations between teachers and parents, and could potentially provide useful information to administrators as they rethink their school's policies and practices in an effort to promote educational equity for all students.

Finally, we recognize that the parent story approach may be a time-consuming process, and it can be painful for teachers and school administrators to uncover their own assumptions and biases. Yet this process is extremely critical, because the literacy lives of our African American children are at stake. Schools can complain about the changes in the family structure that fail to provide the support, continuity, and structure children need to function well in school. But that's not going to change the fact that it is the school's responsibility to figure out how to work within these constraints and still make connections with African American parents. By amplifying the voices of African American parents through the parent story approach, we hope that teachers and schools will think twice and stop rushing to judgment when they have an African American child in their classrooms. We also believe that the parent story approach can help build bridges between African American families and teachers in ways that enhance cross-cultural communication and understanding. For African American parents, this kind of empathic understanding can make the school feel more welcoming, and may initiate new forms of parental involvement and home-school connections that build African American children's knowledge of mainstream literacy practices. For teachers, listening to the powerful messages in African American parents' stories can help them generate new and exciting connections to home literacy practices that ultimately transform the nature of literacy instruction in classrooms and schools. Most importantly, we hope that through the parent story approach, teachers and administrators discover that African American parents—indeed, all families—must be actively included and involved in schools if our children are to succeed as literacy learners and as citizens in society.

Ideas for Discussion, Extension, and Application

1. Discuss what stands out or surprises you in each African American mother's statements of how the school viewed or responded to her sons. How would you, as a recently hired teacher, respond to the school's history and culture of marginalization?

2. In small groups, list common and subtle stereotypical images of African American families. For each stereotype, discuss the contradictory evidence provided by the mothers' stories.

3. Brainstorm and make a list of ways in which teachers can create opportunities to listen to diverse family stories. As a teacher, when and how often would you implement them? How would you use and protect the confidentiality of this information in your teaching and interactions with students and colleagues?

References

Anderson, A. B., & Stokes, S. J. (1984). Social and institutional influences on the development and practice of literacy. In H. Goelman, A. Oberg, & F. Smith (Eds.), *Awakening to literacy* (pp. 24–37). Exeter, NH: Heinemann.

Au, K. (1998). Social constructivism and the school literacy learning of students of diverse backgrounds. *Journal of Literacy Research, 30,* 297–319.

Auerbach, E. (1989). Toward a socio-cultural approach to family literacy. *Harvard Educational Review, 59* (2), 231–250.

Baker, L., & Scher, D. (2002). Beginning readers' motivation for reading in relation to parental beliefs and home-reading experiences. *Reading Psychology, 23,* 239–269.

Clark, R. (1983). *Family life and school achievement: Why poor Black children succeed or fail.* Chicago: University of Chicago Press.

Edwards, P. A. (2004). *Children's literacy development: Making it happen through school, family, and community involvement.* Boston: Allyn and Bacon, Inc.

Edwards, P. A., & Danridge, J. C. (2001). Developing collaborations with parents: Some examples. In V. J. Risko & K. Bromley (Eds.), *Collaboration for diverse learners: Viewpoints and practices* (pp. 251–272). Newark, DE: International Reading Association.

Edwards, P. A., Danridge, J. C., McMillon, G. T., & Pleasants, H. M. (2001). Taking ownership of literacy: Who has the power? In P. R. Schmidt & P. B. Mosenthal (Eds.), *Reconceptualizing literacy in the new age of pluralism and multiculturalism* (pp. 111–136). Greenwich, CT: Information Age Publishing.

Edwards, P. A., Pleasants, H. M., & Franklin, S. H. (1999). *A path to follow: Learning to listen to parents.* Portsmouth, NH: Heinemann.

Epstein, J. (1995). School/family/community partnerships: Caring for the children we share. *Phi Delta Kappan, 76,* 701–712.

Gadsden, V. L., Ray, A., Jacobs, C., & Gwak, S. (2006). Parents' expectations and children's early literacy: Reimagining parent engagement through parent inquiry. In R.T. Jimenez & V.O. Pang (Eds.), *Race, ethnicity, and education: Language and literacy in schools* (pp. 157–176). Westport, CT: Praeger Publishers.

Gutierrez, K., & Rogoff, B. (2003). Cultural ways of learning: Individual traits or repertoires of practice. *Educational Researcher, 32*, 19–25.

Heath, S. B. (1983). *Ways with words.* Cambridge: Cambridge University Press.

Kidd, J., Sanchez, S.Y., & Thorp, E. (2004). Gathering family stories: Facilitating preservice teachers' cultural awareness and responsiveness. *Action in Teacher Education, 53*, 153–167.

Lazar, A. (2004). *Learning to be literacy teachers in urban schools: Stories of growth and change.* Newark, DE: International Reading Association.

Lightfoot, S. (1978). *Worlds apart: Relationships between families and schools.* New York: Basic Books.

Metzger, D. (1986). Circles of stories. *Parabola IV* (4). Original work published in 1969.

Moles, O. (1993). Collaboration between schools and disadvantaged parents: Obstacles and openings. In N. F. Chavkin (Ed.), *Families and schools in a pluralistic society.* Albany, NY: SUNY Press.

Moll, L., Armanti, C., Neff, D., & González, N. (1992). Funds of knowledge for teaching using a qualitative approach to connect homes and classrooms. *Theory into Practice, 31*, 132–141.

Nieto, S. (1996). *Affirming diversity: The sociopolitical context of multicultural education.* (2nd ed.). New York: Longman.

Noguera, P. A. (2003). *City schools and the American dream: Reclaiming the promise of public education.* New York: Teachers College Press.

Otto, H. J. (1969). Communication is the key. In *Parents-children-teachers: communication* (pp. 1–4). Washington, DC: Association for Childhood Educational International.

Patton, M. Q. (1990). *Qualitative evaluation and research methods* (2nd ed.). Newbury Park, CA: Sage.

Taylor, D., & Dorsey-Gaines, C. (1988). *Growing up literate: Learning from inner-city families.* Portsmouth, NH: Heinemann.

Turner, J. D., & Edwards, P.A. (in press). Old tensions, new visions: Implications of home literacies for teacher education programs, K-12 schools, and family literacy programs. In G. Li (Ed.), *Multicultural families, home literacies, and mainstream schooling.* Albany, NY: SUNY Press.

Tutwiler, S. W. (1998). Diversity among families. In M. L. Fuller, & Olsen, G. (Eds.), *Home-school relations: Working successfully with parents and families* (pp. 40–66). Boston: Allyn and Bacon.

Vandergrift, J. A., & Greene, A. L. (1992). Rethinking parent involvement. *Educational Leadership 50,* 57–59.

Vygotsky, L. (1978). *Mind and society.* Cambridge, MA: Harvard University Press.

9 Home Visits

Learning from Students and Families

Maria Luiza Dantas and Michelle Coleman[1]

Miranda,[2] an eleventh grader, lives with her mother and aunt. They are all recent immigrants from Somalia. When I enter the home, Mrs. Moore (Miranda's mother) gives me a hug and makes room for me on the couch. Appreciating the welcoming gesture, I say "hello" and "how are you" in Swahili to both the mother and aunt. This exchange of words sparks a smile on Mrs. Moore's face. Meanwhile Miranda brings me pictures of her deceased father. While we are looking at the photographs, Mrs. Moore and Miranda's aunt begin to speak in Arabic as they glance at me. I can't help but think that they are talking about me. Miranda notices my distraction. Mrs. Moore asks Miranda a question in Arabic. I wonder if Mrs. Moore is speaking Arabic because she thinks I understand Swahili. Miranda first responds to her mother, and then explains to me that her mother thinks I am too young to be a teacher. She asks Miranda how long I have been teaching; when I reply six years, Mrs. Moore interrupts me in English—"Six years! Too young."

(Michelle Coleman)

Michelle's vignette provides a snapshot of her first visit to Miranda's house. Michelle had never conducted a home visit and expressed some fear and doubt about the usefulness of this experience. Miranda's mother was difficult to reach and it took two weeks to schedule the visit. Michelle was also not sure about Mrs. Moore's English proficiency and questioned her own ability to communicate effectively. However, despite these challenges, this encounter created new relationships and learning spaces for all three parties: the teacher, student and her mother. Many teachers are hesitant to plan home visits due to concerns about appearing intrusive, time limitations within already demanding family schedules, not speaking the families' language, and safety. Yet, most of the content of this book would not be available if it were not for the learning that took place inside families' homes. However, how these visits were conducted and the teachers and researchers' understanding of their purpose were intrinsic to building trust with and learning from families.

1 The authors would like to thank the School of Leadership and Education Sciences at the University of San Diego for its support in the development of this project.
2 Students and family names have been changed to pseudonyms.

Home visits in school settings can take different formats and purposes: initial contact with new families, information and orientation about school programs, relationship building, referral for special needs, assessment of home conditions, interventions, and teacher–parent conferences. The practice of home visits in the United States, which dates back to the 1880s, has also historically been linked to prevention, survey, assessment and/or intervention routines in professional fields such as social work, health care, special education, early childhood education services and psychology (Hancock & Pelton, 1989; Keilty, 2008; Sweet & Appelbaum, 2004). Thus, the term "home visit" carries multiple meanings and teachers' interactions with families at their homes (and outside school) will reflect their own understandings of it. McIntyre, Kyle, Moore, Sweazy and Greer (2001) use the term "family visits," given the history and multiple meanings attached to "home visits." Further, beyond the home environment, family visits can also take place at different locations – including community centers, parks, after-school activities – and involve interaction not only with parents but also other family members like siblings, grandparents, friends, aunts. This chapter uses "home visits" and "family visits" as mutually interchangeable.

Informed by sociocultural and ethnographic perspectives (Green, Dixon, & Zaharlick, 2003; Heath, 1983) and a funds of knowledge approach (González, Moll & Amanti, 2005; Moll, Amanti, Neff & González, 1992), we view home visits as rich contexts to learn from and connect with students and their families, as well as for teachers to explore prior expectations and the possibility of "frame clashes" (Mehan, 1979; Weade & Green, 1985). We focus on the role of family visits, guided by an ethnographic lens, as contexts for disrupting deficit views and making visible diverse students' and families' expectations, funds of knowledge and learning resources. In this chapter, we draw on two case studies of teachers' first home visits, discussing the challenges they faced and opportunities they experienced to gain more insight into their students' lives. In addition, we explore the practice of home visits as "culturally responsive pedagogy" (Ladson-Billings, 1994; Lee, 1997) and assessment. We address the following questions:

- What types of preconceived assumptions and expectations regarding families' ways of interacting and learning resources can home visits (and close observations of one student in different contexts outside school) make visible?
- What opportunities for teacher self-reflection and learning become possible through close analysis of frame clashes?
- How can home visits be resources for assessment of students' learning resources and relationship building with children and their families?

THEORETICAL APPLICATION: FRAME CLASHES

Frame clashes are a disruption of what one counts as the "normal" or taken-for-granted ways to participate in social interactions. In school contexts, they lead to misunderstanding, faulty assumptions, and negative stereotypes. An

example is a child who is often absent from school. The teacher is concerned and considers contacting child services. Fortunately, beforehand she
meets with the mother and learns about her overblown fears of her daughter
getting sick. The mother, who worked at an Emergency Care in her home
country, was traumatized by what she saw and experienced. The teacher
was then able to contextualize the student's situation and examine it from
two frames of reference. Go back to one of the prior chapters and identify a
frame clash. What was the nature of the misunderstanding? What were the
circumstances and expectations on each side? How could each side have
resolved it?

Lenses Guiding Our Work

A Sociocultural, Situated Perspective

Our work is grounded in a sociocultural and situated perspective that locates
learning and teaching processes within larger social, political and cultural contexts (Heath, 1983; Solsken, 1993; Weade, 1992). We view learning and teaching as
social practices that involve the acquisition of specific cultural and discursive
practices. Thus, learning (and teaching) need to be addressed within the socio-
cultural contexts in which they occur rather than viewed as an individual act and
accomplishment. Learning and teaching processes (including literacy practices)
reflect distinguishable discursive and interactional patterns and practices and
organization of time. Particular learning and literacy practices patterned by social
institutions and power relationships become dominant in school environments
(Barton & Hamilton, 2000). In this way, classrooms have their own culture, familiar to "mainstream" children from middle-class families who are often informally
exposed to school practices and routines, interactional patterns, speech genres
and literacies. On the other hand, children from ethnically, culturally, and
linguistically diverse families may find that this classroom culture conflicts with
practices in the communities in which they live (Daiute, 1993; Dyson, 1993).

Two pioneering ethnographic studies of home/community and school contexts
illustrate the impact of cultural discontinuities and potential sources of school
failure for ethnic minority children. Phillips' (1972) study of Warm Springs
Indian children's interactional styles at home and school demonstrate that children's participation patterns appear "normal" to their teachers when classrooms
present social conditions consistent with the children's prior experiences. Heath's
(1983) ten-year study of three communities in the Piedmont Carolinas also
illustrates how differences in communication patterns and social interactions
between children's communities and their school impacted how they performed
at school. One group of children interacted, explored materials, and responded to
time differently in comparison to mainstream children, and the teachers often
interpreted these behaviors as inappropriate. Both studies provide an analysis of
"cross-situational" conflicts and demands rather than focusing on surface features (Florio & Shultz, 1978). Heath's in-depth knowledge of the children's

experiences and communicative and social demands outside school helped the teachers' reframe their assessment of students' abilities and dispositions. However, in different circumstances, the cumulative effect of cultural (and linguistic) discontinuities can perpetuate a deficit view of diverse children and inadvertently promote their continued disengagement from school practices.

Learning is connected to children's social worlds and their construction of self and identity. By defining learning as a cultural and social phenomenon, a sociocultural and situated perspective illuminates the cost of disconnection between classroom curriculum and children's lives: a large and intrinsic part of diverse students' lives and learning resources become invisible in the school setting. Further, such students may learn to interpret their place in the social world and their families' and communities' accumulated bodies of knowledge from a deficit position.

Ethnographic Studies and Funds of Knowledge Approach

We believe that it is important to re-conceive the role of teachers (and students) as "ethnographers," especially in an era of globalization and increasing diversity (Egan-Robertson & Bloome, 1998; Frank & Uy, 2004). In this view, teachers must strive to take an insider's perspective to avoid decontextualized comparisons and ethnocentric bias and to gain a deeper understanding of the challenges that diverse children confront as they move between home and school environments. As teachers act as ethnographers, the focus is on what is significant within the children's cultural practices. Ethnographic studies represent a shift from traditional quantitative research in education as they provide detailed "descriptions of what actually happens to children as they learn to use language and form their values about its structures and functions . . . [and] what children do to become and remain acceptable members of their own communities" (Heath, 1983, p. 8). They contribute to a body of research focused on the ways that learning in the classroom is influenced by school, family and community ways of being and managing knowledge (among others, the chapters in this volume, Purcell-Gates, 2007; Taylor & Dorsey-Gaines, 1988).

González, Moll and their colleagues used the term "funds of knowledge" to address Latino families' and communities' accumulated bodies of knowledge and social and linguistic practices (González, Moll, & Amanti, 2005; Moll, 1994; Moll & Greenberg, 1990). Their extensive ethnographic research on funds of knowledge illuminated the complex functions of children's households within their social and historical contexts, and demonstrated how teachers' active involvement in ethnographic studies of households contributed to the development of instructional activities that mediated between children's and families' lives and classroom experiences. McIntyre's (McIntyre, et al., 2001) research on "family visits" built upon González, Moll and colleagues' study of household visits. Their research focused on the academic and social development of rural and urban children of Appalachian descent, and it also indicated the positive impact on students' academic achievement when teachers used information gathered in family visits to make adjustments to instruction.

Home Visits in Teacher Education: Taking an Ethnographic Perspective

The research we have just discussed suggests the significance of teachers acting as co-researchers and ethnographers and underscores the transformative shifts in their practices that can occur as a result. However, as previous chapters in this volume reveal, ethnography typically involves engagement in long-term relationships. We use the term "ethnographic perspective" for specific reasons. We argue for home visits guided by an "ethnographic state of mind" (González, Moll, Floyd-Tenery, Rivera, Rendon, González & Amanti, 1993) that informs teachers' views of families' culture and learning resources and their use of ethnographic tools such as observation methods, field notes, and interviews. Taking an ethnographic perspective involves investigating the nature of meaning within culture (Green et al., 2003). Culture plays a central role in determining what is important to learn and how learning takes place across contexts (Horowitz et al., 2005). By taking on the role of ethnographers, teachers can broaden their understanding and knowledge of their students' learning resources and expertise and provide a safe place for building relationships with families. González et al. (1993) speak of the "transformative nature of the household visits" guided by an ethnographic perspective:

> These are research visits for the express purpose of identifying and documenting knowledge that exists in students' homes. In contrast to other visits, these visits are part of a "systematic, intentional inquiry by teachers"—as Lytle and Cochran-Smith (1990, p. 84) define teacher research—about their students' household life. We are convinced that these research visits, in conjunction with collaborative ethnographic reflection, can engender pivotal and transformative shifts in teachers and in relations between households and schools and between parents and teachers (see González & Amanti, 1992; Moll, Amanti, Neff, & González, 1992).
>
> (pp. 3–4)

Similarly, McIntyre et al. (2001) demonstrate that family visits support the development of relationships on safe, "home" territory, and offer important insights about students' learning styles, emotional and social needs and behaviors, and current interests and concerns, and family discourse styles and routines.

Despite these benefits, we believe that home visits cannot be implemented without a clear framework and careful consideration of the purposes, difficulties, tensions, and potential consequences. Ethnic minority and high-poverty students already experience a number of social inequities and a differential access to quality education that contribute to achievement gaps (Akiba, LeTendre, & Scribner, 2007; Ladson-Billings, 2006). Home visits are delicate spaces in which such families expose themselves and may feel vulnerable. Teachers' presence carries symbolic power due to their professional role and responsibilities and can have lasting impact on families' perception of schools. Teachers, as most people do, can easily draw hasty interpretations based on limited experience and partial information.

Occasionally, teacher educators have used ethnographic methods with pre-service and in-service teachers for the purpose of creating teacher-researchers and providing observational tools (Cochran-Smith & Lytle, 1993; Florio-Ruane, 1990; Frank, 1999; Frank & Uy, 2004; González et al., 1993). For example, Frank and Uy found that "pre-service teachers who used an ethnographic lens during their [classroom] observation were able to delay critical evaluation of class-room practices and use field notes as evidence for their interpretations of what was happening during writing instruction" (p. 270). However, only a few studies address aspects of the process of implementing home visits (González et al., 1993) and recommendations for successful family visits (Kyle & McIntyre, 2000).

Context, Participants and Methods

An ethnographic perspective and tools guided the data collection and analysis of two teachers', Julie and Michelle, process of implementing home visits for the first time and its impact on their relationship with students and their families, and their own teaching. We used a cross-case analysis of two "theoretically diverse cases" (Yin, 2006): one elementary teacher and one secondary teacher. These case studies took place in the Midwest and Southern California.

Participants

This chapter focuses on Julie, a first grade teacher and her student, Bob, and on Michelle, an Advancement via Individual Determination (AVID) tutor and former middle school teacher, and her student, Miranda.

Julie, a 14-year veteran and Caucasian teacher, collaborated with Malu (first author) in a year-long ethnographic study of literacy learning and teaching practices in her first grade classroom which involved visits to the homes of four focal students. She was actively involved in the data collection process, took part in the home visits implemented in November, and viewed the research project as an opportunity for professional development and reflection on her teaching. She had strong knowledge of her school community, located in a small, culturally and socioeconomically diverse town (19,000 population) near to a mid-size Midwestern city (about 1,000,000). Julie always taught at the same school and lived in the same district area, which served a predominant lower to middle income, European-American community and included many students of Appalachian heritage.

Michelle implemented her first home visits as a graduate student, working on a master's degree in Curriculum and Teaching in Southern California. The home visits were a required assignment for a graduate course on Language, Literacy and Culture taught by Malu. Michelle had previously taught history for six years in Texas in a middle school with a predominantly Caucasian faculty and staff, and African-American and Hispanic student population. As part of her graduate studies program, she worked as an AVID tutor in a history high school class. She selected two of her Somalia tutees, Miranda and Sonia, to develop an in-depth case study guided by an ethnographic perspective and involving home visits and observations in the classroom and another context.

Methods and Data Sources

We used an ethnographic perspective and tools due to their "sociocultural substantiality" (Hymes, 1982). That is, an ethnographic logic of inquiry enabled us to understand meanings and patterns of behavior from an emic point of view—taking, as much as possible, the point of view of teachers, students and families—and to explore how cultural practices shaped what was available to be learned as well as what was learned. Our data sources involved participant observation, fieldwork journals, descriptive and interpretive field notes, audiotaping, collection of artifacts and documents, classroom maps, photographs, informal interviews with the teacher, students and families, and home visits. The data analysis process involved an iterative process of identification of patterns and underlying themes (Yin, 2006). We used the concept of culture as a system of frame clashes in order to identify and examine patterns guiding the teachers' arbitrary assumptions and expectations.

Taking on the Learner Role: First Experiences with Home Visits

Data from each case study illustrate commonalities with regard to the teachers' process of passing through initial roadblocks to opening space for dialogue and learning with the families and students. Both teachers experienced uncertainty and tension with the process, but their personal experiences and background helped them connect with the families and/or students in special ways. For example, parents were attracted to Julie's age, seniority and respect as a teacher in the community, and her own life experiences as a mother of three. These attributes made it easier in some ways for Julie to develop a rapport with parents. Julie experienced home visits as a parent but the thought of going into her students' home was still foreign and uncomfortable. In Michelle's case, her openness to different cultures and time in Africa as well as being a young and knowledgeable African-American teacher helped her connect with her Somalia female tutees. However, her difficulties in scheduling the home visit and not being Miranda's classroom teacher added to Michelle's uncertainty about the first visit. These cases suggest that first experiences with home visits can be stressful to any teacher. In the following sections, we examine data excerpts that illuminate the complexity of coming into students' homes and how these interactions, within an ethnographic frame, can support teacher's self-examination and relationship building with families, and assessment of students' learning resources and culturally responsive practices.

Initial Roadblocks: Examining Assumptions and Expectations

Example #1. First visit to Bob's home. Julie and Malu visited four families together in the month of November. Our first visit was to Bob's home. Julie sent a note on Monday to confirm the visit. She also tried to call Bob's family but their home phone number had been disconnected. On Wednesday, Julie asked Bob if he knew that we were going to his home tomorrow night. Bob said yes which confirmed that his family had received Julie's note.

> Julie and Malu left the school and arrived early at Bob's apartment. Julie had driven by in the morning in order to confirm it. She knocked at his door different times but no one responded. The small apartment building, divided into two apartments, was located close to the railroad tracks. No one answered the door and Julie started to think they were at Bob's old address. Julie suggested that we go back to the school to check out the year-updated student information. Bob had a new address and phone number. Julie called Bob's mom, Donna, who confirmed it was all right to still come and gave her directions to their house. Bob's new home was located on a relatively busy road in a different town in the same district. The small front yard area was covered with grass and weeds. Julie and Malu walked the narrow sidewalk towards the entrance door and connected garage. Donna opened the front door. As Julie walked into the living room, she first saw Bob and his 3-year old sister, Sue, standing behind Donna in the center of the living room. Donna invited them to take a seat at the couch next to a rocking chair. Then, she saw Bob's stepfather, Steve, sitting in the rocking chair with Bryce, Bob's eight-month old brother, on his lap.

Julie was skillful in navigating the initial roadblocks of (1) no direct parent confirmation of the home visit, and (2) going twice to the wrong home address and being late to their appointment. Despite her expectation of receiving a confirmation about our visit directly from the parents, she looked into another alternative by checking with Bob. His response also indicated that there was conversation on the topic of our visit at his home. Nevertheless, Julie was still not sure about the parents' openness to the home visit. She questioned if by not responding to her note they were indicating their lack of interest. The family's welcome came as a surprise. She did not expect to meet with all the family members including Bob's stepfather. This situation illustrates a "rich point" (Agar, 1994), when one's definition or assumptions about how things "should" take place is challenged and thus creates the opportunity for new understanding. Knowing first hand the difficulties of raising three children (and the fact that Bob's parents worked full time), Julie was touched by their warm reception. The matter of direct confirmation about the home visit lost its importance. Donna, Bob's mom, was pleased with the visit as well. She later shared that this was their first experience with a teacher's home visit and she appreciated the special interest in Bob's education.

The second roadblock, Julie's unsuccessful attempt at finding Bob's home, could have led into canceling the home visit appointment. Julie had planned ahead and driven by Bob's home before our visit. Though she was frustrated, her response was to find an alternative by going back to the school to check on another source for students' home addresses. Julie's own children's experiences with home visits led her to assume that Bob placed a special value on her visit to his home. She mentioned that her children enjoyed showing their bedrooms:

> *Julie:* He might want to show us his bedroom. I know when the kids' teachers used to do home visits that was one of the biggest things for them, to show their bedrooms.

Bob's family's reception and his own welcome and excitement to have Julie at his home confirmed her assumption. Bob was constantly showing something—children's books, a guitar, videos—or wanting to share a story with Julie during our visit. A few examples: he shared with Julie about his hiding in his grandma's furniture, and proudly showed his name on the yellow page book. He gave us a tour of his bedroom, which he shared with his baby brother, and toy room. He showed Julie his books and baseball trophies and T-shirt.

One surprising event and "rich point" took place after the home visit when Julie and Malu read a note from Donna to Julie with special information about Bob. Donna had sent the letter with Bob's classroom materials and Julie had not seen it yet. In the note, Donna provided a summary of Bob's life. Donna married Bob's father out of high school and divorced him after having serious problems. She then met another man, Bill, who became very close to Bob. They lived together, she became pregnant, and at the time she had Sue, Bill died of a head tumor. Bob missed him. Later Donna met her current husband, Steve, on a blind date and they just had a baby boy. Donna shared that she needed to reassure Bob through his adaptation to and authority problems with his stepfather. Julie was surprised with the content of Donna's letter. She was also relieved that she did not know about the letter before the visit. Bob's excitement and eagerness to share his experiences, and the closeness of his relationship with his mother, sharply contrasted with Julie's stereotypes of children from broken, low-income and limited education homes. She gained a deeper sense of respect for his ability to cope and actively participate in life.

Example #2. Arranging the home visit and concerns about Miranda's apartment location. Michelle's experience with the process of scheduling the home visit to Miranda's house turned out to be an initial obstacle. Her expectation to plan it via a phone call turned out to be a two-week back and forth communication process via Miranda as Mrs. Moore was difficult to reach due to her night work schedule. The home visit was also planned around the family's observance of Ramadan, a religious holiday.

> Having scheduled many parent–teacher conferences, I assumed arranging a home visit would work in a similar manner: call parent(s), explain nature of

visit and negotiate a time to meet within school hours. Experience taught me that there would be some problems with scheduling, but I did not expect most of the negotiating would be between myself and Miranda. Though the school had a parent liaison who was Somali and could help me with translating, due to Mrs. Moore's work schedule and not having an answering machine, I had to send letters and messages through Miranda. Another obstacle I faced was scheduling around the family's preparation and observance of Ramadan. Therefore, what I thought would take 30 minutes to negotiate and plan, turned out to be a two-week process. To say that I became frustrated would be an understatement. Not only was I on a timeline for conducting my home visit, but I just wanted to get it over with. There were times when I believed Mrs. Moore was making excuses to avoid meeting and/or talking with me. Wanting to give up, Miranda's persistence reminded me of the importance of the home visit and let me know how important my visit meant to her.

The disruption of Michelle's scheduling timeline made visible her expectations. It also made visible her assumptions of Mrs. Moore not being interested and available to meet with her. In Table 9.1, we summarize the disruptions that took place during the process of scheduling the home visit and during the home visit; in particular, Michelle's inability to contact Mrs. Moore directly, the appearance of

Table 9.1 Identifying disruptions and making visible expectations and assumptions

Disruptions	Expectations	Assumptions
Arranging the home visit Two-week process Contact with Mother via Miranda. Mother's work schedule and inability to use school translator. No answering machine Religious holiday	Home visit scheduling as a quick process Concern with project timeline.	Mother is not interested and not available. Communication difficulties.
Apartment appearance Clean and well-kept apartment and area surrounding it. Unkept adjacent apartment areas.	Apartment located in a poor area of town. Poor living conditions.	Unkept apartment complex. Miranda's apartment and area surrounding it would look the same.
Communication Mother's ability to speak Arabic, Swahili and limited English. Mother's hospitality and special arrangement of work hours.	Mother's limited ability to "communicate" (i.e., ask questions and understand and provide answers to school questions). Communication via Miranda.	Mother may not be able to understand and provide answers to school questions. Questioning the possible benefits of a home visit.

Miranda's apartment and complex, and Mrs. Moore's ability to communicate during the home visit.

These disruptions signaled frame clashes and helped identify expectations that fueled Michelle's implicit assumptions. Miranda's apartment was located in an unkept area of town, and Michelle expected Miranda's apartment and complex to mirror it. Michelle had concerns about the location of Miranda's apartment. She knew of the area as not being safe from the local newspaper and a local refugee agency. The large size of the apartment complex was intimidating and Michelle feared getting lost. Miranda assured Michelle that it was not that bad and it was safe.

In the field notes in Table 9.2, Michelle's first impression of the apartment complex confirmed her expectations (italics added to field notes). Michelle's repetitive use of the word "clean" indicates her surprise that is, the disruption of expectations of Miranda's apartment and surrounding area looking the same as

Table 9.2 First home visit field notes

Notetaking	Notemaking
Miranda's apartment complex is located in the Southern section of the city. Significant population of Somali and Ethiopians.	Familiar with this area, I was very apprehensive about my visit. This area is known for its low-income housing and high crime rate.
12 two-story apartment buildings. 4 buildings are connected to 1 courtyard. 3 courtyards in the middle. Total of 8 trash bins on either side of two apartment buildings. Long metal security gate enclosing each building.	Scared that I might not be able to find their particular apartment building. Decide to drive around the neighborhood. Notice how *unkept* the apartment complex was. I can see and smell *trash*.
3 boys entering apartments through gaps in the gate. 4 stores and 3 apartment buildings on Miranda's street. 4-way stop lights. 3 cars run red light. 2 police cars outside adjacent apartment building. 8 people sitting outside convenient store. . . .	Notice the gaps in between the bars and question the *security* of the apartment complex. Did not see Miranda's apartment building while driving, but if where they lived resembled what I had seen, I couldn't help but think how anyone could live under these conditions. Somewhat concerned about my *safety*, I reminded myself of the sacrifice Miranda's mother made in order to meet with me. . . .
I enter 3rd apartment building through a metal gate. I walk to the right of 4 trashcans and walk toward the courtyard. I see kids playing in the courtyard.	I get lost—a lot of buildings and they all look the same. The courtyard is big and green, *very clean*.
I walk towards Miranda's apartment door and push the doorbell. Miranda answers door. Her mother stands behind her and aunt sits on the couch.	Apartment is very small, *very clean* and sparse except for pictures on wall.

other parts of her apartment complex. Further, Michelle's assumption of what communication with Mrs. Moore would look like was disrupted.

This chapter's initial vignette shows Michelle's interaction with Mrs. Moore during her first home visit. Michelle expected that Mrs. Moore would speak Swahili, but she was surprised by her ability to switch between Arabic, Swahili and English without much translation from her daughter. Besides Mrs. Moore's ability to use three languages, their meeting spoke to Michelle about communication in a broader sense: Mrs. Moore's hospitality, openness to someone new, and commitment to her daughter's education by making special work arrangements and working extra hours.

Gaining Student Knowledge: Possibilities and Tensions

Example: Bob's conversations about school with mom. The main focus of our home visit was to learn more about Bob. In particular, among other things, his interests outside school and what he liked to do, his family routines, special toys, what his bedroom looked like, if drawing was an interest at home as it was in school, and the type of things Bob said about school at home. Julie was interested in learning about the kind of social interactions that Bob was exposed to in his neighborhood. She wondered if Bob's increased playfulness in the classroom was connected to not having friends in his new neighborhood and school being his social outlet. Bob recently had an incident in the classroom.

Donna: On our way home from the babysitter, what is a long drive now and I like that because before it was a short drive, I catch up on Bob's day and Sue's day. Bob tries to tell me all about his day.

Julie (surprised): Does he really?

Donna: That's how I found out, before you wrote a note about homework, that he had fallen out of the chair and made the girls laugh. I tried to explain to him that I know that's funny and that's important to him to make the girls laugh but it's also very important to Ms. Boyd that she teaches you.

(Julie and Malu smile)

Donna: And out of respect to Ms. Boyd, he has to listen. I said that he can play outside and fall off stuff outside and that he gotta listen to Ms. Boyd. I didn't want to be too hard because I know how important acceptance is and that was about that.

Julie (agreed with head movement)

Julie was surprised about Donna's knowledge and insight into what happened in the classroom. Her concerns in regard to Bob's increased socialization focus in class seemed somewhat separate to her focus on parents as literacy/learning partners. Donna's insight provided another angle of vision into and highlighted the complexity of Bob's many roles and goals as a first grader, young boy and peer. Julie gained a level of respect for the mother's knowledge and ability to connect with Bob as well as her understanding of young children's socialization process.

Julie did not expect that a young and full-time working mother would be so skillful at interacting with her child and maintaining ongoing dialogue and closeness between them. Her thinking matched a child-centered approached to learning in line with Julie's philosophy of education. This was a learning moment for both Julie and Malu.

Julie questioned her own ability to connect with Bob. His timid behavior led her to think that he did not like or connect with her. Therefore, it was a special surprise to Julie to hear differently.

Donna: Bob really likes you a lot.
Julie: I'm glad to hear it because I wondered sometimes.

Donna's angle of vision provided insight into Bob's ways of showing connectedness and pride for his school experiences. Her observation of Bob's fondness of Julie supported their relationship and bonding as Julie became more comfortable to take risks in their interactions. For example, to prepare for his student-led conference in late January, Bob met with Julie while his peers watched a funny movie. Though at times he would look wistfully at his peers, he was engaged and able to stay focused during their one-on-one meeting. Their interaction showed a stronger level of comfort and connectedness between them.

Bob: A lot of papers.
Julie: Hmmm?
Bob: A lot of papers.
Julie: A lot of papers, yes, I know.
Bob: We did this one this year.
Julie: Humm, humm. [pause] I like how you're looking at it really close to the side.
Bob: [stretches and makes a funny sound]
Julie: Why did you pick that one?
Bob: Ahmm, I like the stuff that rhymes.
Julie: What did you rhyme on that one?
Bob: Ring, sing, king, ding.
Julie: Nice job. You remember it really well.
. . .
Julie: Last one, kiddo. Good working through this with you. Get one out that shows that you really know how to work out a pattern. Oh, here are some more of your story problems. Do you wanna change [your selection] or add one?
Bob: This one.
Julie: Okay. Let's put this one too.
Bob: Because it's take away and they both go together like that in the take away.
Julie: You're right. They do.
Bob: I like this one.

Later on, at the day of the student-led conferences, Bob arrived with his mother, sister and baby brother. Donna mentioned to Julie that Bob was worried that he was late. He picked up his portfolio and seemed anxious to show his work to his mom. He was constantly interrupted by his siblings and Malu offered to stay with his baby brother. Bob read his penguin book first. Donna reinforced his reading and praised his pictures. At one point, he stopped and explained to his mom that penguins used to fly:

Bob: You know what? They used to fly, penguins did.
Donna: Did they?
Bob: Yeah. But wherever they got to the water they couldn't fly
Donna: Ahhh.

Bob continued to show and read each piece of work. His sister, Sue, became more interactive and participative in their conversation:

Sue: This is mouse, Mom. This is mouse.
Donna: Is that a mouse? You did a very good picture of a mouse.
Bob: A pattern. My ABC pattern. And the pattern is [pause] pickle, orange, blueberry, pickle, orange, blueberry, pickle, orange, blueberry, pickle, orange, blueberry, pickle, orange, blueberry
Sue: But this is
Donna: This is an ABC pattern. Cool.
Bob: A lot of papers.
Donna: [giggles]

Beyond the home visit, Julie created other classroom opportunities to interact with and learn about Bob and his family such as: a family survey in the beginning of the year, parent–teacher conference in November, student-led conference in mid-year, and ongoing written communication with Donna. Nevertheless, her interactions involved tension between a child-centered approach and meeting district proficiency standards. The home visit brought another layer of tension to Julie's teaching practice. Knowing more about Bob involved knowing more about sources of knowledge that did not match school parameters. His resiliency and effort could not be counted as part of final assessment measures. His risk taking and growth as a writer could actually count against him in the district's writing rubric criteria. Bob's writing showed his effort to use longer and difficult words to better express his thoughts. However, correct spelling was an important benchmark in the district's writing assessment. Bob's parents had concerns about his growth in reading and tried to work with him at home. Bob, who was placed in the school's early reading intervention in the beginning of the year, made slow progress. Julie did not resolve these tensions and concluded the year with a certain level of frustration. Yet, in the local space of the classroom, she opened opportunities for Bob to be and act as a learner beyond the label of being a "struggling reader."

THEORETICAL APPLICATION: CREATING HYBRID SPACES FOR LEARNING

Teachers' effectiveness requires constant negotiation of local and larger contexts: students' background, interests and academic proficiencies; families' expectations and funds of knowledge; the teachers' own philosophy of teaching; school routines; and institutional requirements and power structures. The lack of knowledge of students' lives, limited communication with diverse families, and misuse of assessments can restrict a teacher's ability to imagine hybrid contexts in which students can act and be viewed as successful learners. Imagine a successful teacher. What would s/he define as success? What types of practices and metaphors would guide her/his negotiation of tensions and roadblocks? What would the teacher's relationship with linguistically and culturally diverse students and their families look like?

Acting as Learners: Home Visits as Learning Spaces

Julie and Michelle's experiences put into perspective the complexity of diverse families' lives, their sacrifices and obligations. It illustrates how easily miscommunication can take place between school and diverse families, and how teachers' uninformed assumptions can become their reality. In addition, though the importance of parent involvement is often talked about, there is little discussion of what is the essence of trusting, safe relationships between teachers and families. Home/family visits are one space to build relationships. However, they require thoughtful preparation and clear understanding of purposes and roles. Teacher education programs, constrained by multiple credential certification requirements, often provide little or no information on how to conduct home visits.

Teachers are faced with the challenge of understanding and creating learning opportunities for linguistically, culturally and socio-economic diverse students and families who may be very different than them. Research on teachers' beliefs, stereotypes and cultural models indicate that they are resistant to change (Woolfolk Hoy & Murphy, 2001). These things are built over years of schooling and established by the time teacher candidates enter college. Home visits, as an example of multicultural teacher education pedagogy, offer the opportunity to immerse teachers in the process of acquiring knowledge and to reflect and examine beliefs and assumptions about themselves and others (Banks et al., 2005). Other examples of such a pedagogy include school and community visits and maps; service learning opportunities; studies of students, classrooms, schools and communities; and field experiences in diverse contexts with culturally responsive teachers.

By building a more complete picture of the student, family visits become a form of authentic assessment in which teachers become "cultural learners" (Freire, 1998) and families take back their position as experts. But, if conducted inappropriately, such home visits carry the risk of reinforcing teachers' and parents' stereotypes and distrust.

Teachers' power and impact on their students' lives cannot be ignored. Unquestioned deficit beliefs and expectations of ways of being can cause more damage to minority families' often fragile relationships with schools. On the other hand, as many chapters in this book demonstrate, when conducted with sensitivity and openness, home visits represent a valuable opportunity to learn from and with families. Guided by sociocultural and ethnographic lenses, family visits provide a window into students and their families' rich, complex and unique lives. In this way, they become tools to learn from families and document their children's successes, interests and sources of knowledge, and social, cultural and linguistic practices. Thus, they create opportunities: (1) to make visible deficit assumptions and develop a new level of appreciation of students and their families' experiences, resiliency and aspirations (e.g., Miranda's mother's ability to communicate with Michelle); (2) to broaden assessment practices and maximize diverse students' and families' access to the curriculum and participatory roles in school settings (e.g., Julie's broader picture of Bob as a learner and young boy); and (3) to juxtapose and situate different angles of vision—the teacher, student and family definitions of what counts as knowledge, appropriate performance and participation (e.g., Julie and Bob's mom's interpretation of his "falling off the chair" classroom event).

Walking Through the Process of Implementing Home Visits: Where Teachers Might Start

Home Visits: Key Questions to Consider

Here is a list of questions to guide teachers' thinking as they plan and conduct a home visit.

When Planning a Home Visit

- What is your purpose?
- How will the home visit support classroom learning and family involvement?
- What are your fears? Biases? Expectations? How will you keep an open mind to disrupt them and leave room for other ways of doing/living/being?
- What do you need to learn about the families before the home visit in order to prevent behaviors and questions that might be perceived as disrespectful?
- How will you contact parents/guardians? What options will you give them in terms of time and location? Will it be voluntary or part of the school procedures?
- When will you send a letter? Will you follow up with a phone call?

During the Home Visit

- What is your focus?
- What types of question will be important to ask?
- How will you be aware and handle a situation (behavior, question, non-verbal

language) that might be perceived as disrespectful or judgmental by the family/guardians?

- Will you talk about opportunities for the parents/guardians to participate in classroom/school activities? How and for what purposes?

After the Visit

- How will you sort out and follow up on the information collected during the home visit?
- What types of contact will you maintain with parents/guardians? How will you continue to build trust and relationship, and engage and empower minority families?

The Home Visit Process: Transformative Shifts

Successful family visits involve transformative shifts, especially shifts in perception of others and "what counts" as knowledge. They include a strong emotional component, and unexpected difficulties add tension to the process. The novelty and discomfort of going to someone's house, even a student's, adds a level of emotional stress to both the teacher and the family members. In addition, depending on the parents' school history and experiences, the family visit may be associated with an intervention, and not all families will be open to home visits. For example, one mother insistently asked Malu, on different occasions, about the purpose and what exactly the home visit would entail before it took place. This mother, the school's PTA president, was seriously concerned about being judged as a poor housekeeper. She set a clear boundary before the visit: "Derek's bedroom is off limits!"

Teachers often experience the home visit process with hesitation; however, some *common elements* can lead to successful family visits and transformative shifts in relationships with diverse families:

- *Dealing with hesitation and doubt* (suggested questions: How will the parents react to my invitation? Will they be available? Will we be able to communicate? If not, how can I find a translator? What will I see and observe? Will I be safe? How much time will the visit take and how will it impact my other responsibilities? How will it be helpful to my teaching?)
- *Moving through roadblocks* (suggested questions: What forms of communication—beyond a letter— will I need to use to access this family? Will I need a translator? What is their work schedule? How flexible are they to meet during the week and after school hours? Do they have other children? What types of accommodation do I need to make in order to adjust to the family situation?)
- *Taking the learner's role* (suggested questions: Am I following my guiding questions? Who is doing the talking? How much talking vs. listening am I doing? What have I learned new about my student's family?)
- *New insights into student's life* (suggested questions: What have I learned new about my student's life outside school? After-school and weekend routines,

sports and other activities, family traditions, family history, his/her views
about school?)

- *Gaining new levels of respect for families* (suggested questions: What are the
ways in which they support and care for the student, his/her learning and
growth? What are the family's strengths and learning resources?)

Other Things to Keep in Mind

Time constrains impact teachers' ability to implement home visits. One solution is to focus on selected students, and use this experience to ask questions
about other students. One important caution is the risk of generalizations. Each
student is an individual independently of being Hispanic, African-American,
Caucasian, and generalizations carry the risk of "boxing" students together.
Rather than looking for specific characteristics for particular groups of students,
home visits offer the opportunity to look into families' complex lives and
resources. It is also important to note that often teachers themselves do not
have the experience of raising children and family visits allow glimpses into
families' routines and multiple demands. Further, alternative forms of meeting
with families and gaining knowledge of students' learning resources need to
be considered beyond schools and homes. Community centers, public libraries,
local shops, public parks, etc. are some possibilities available for meeting with
families.

Ideas for Discussion, Extension, and Application

1. Discuss what surprised you about Michelle's first home visit. What
    would you do if you were faced with the same obstacles in a family
    visit?
2. Imagine yourself in Julie's position. How could you create opportun-
    ities to learn from other students' families?
3. In small groups, make a brief list of frame clashes that you as a student
    might experience when trying to enter a new school culture. Brain-
    storm practical ways in which teachers can use such clashes as learning
    opportunities and teachable moments.
4. In pairs, imagine a particular family situation and go through the steps
    of *planning* and *during* family visits as described in *Walking Through
    the Process of Implementing Home Visits*. Make a list of questions to
    ask during the visit. Next, role-play the family visit and discuss the
    experience.

References

Agar, M. (1994). *Language shock: Understanding the culture of conversation*. New York: HarperCollins.

Agar, M. H. (1996). *The professional stranger: An informal introduction to ethnography*. (2nd ed.). San Diego, CA: Academic Press.

Akiba, M., LeTendre, G. K., & Scribner, J. P. (2007). Teacher quality, opportunity gap, and national achievement in 46 countries. *Educational Researcher, 36*(7), 369–387.

Banks, J., Cochran-Smith, M., Moll, L., Richert, A., Zeichner, K., LePage, P., Darling-Hammond, L., & Duffy, H. with McDonald, M. (2005). Teaching diverse learners. In L. Darling-Hammond, & J. Bransford (Eds.), *Preparing teachers for a changing world* (pp. 232–274). San Francisco: Jossey-Bass.

Barton, D., & Hamilton, M. (2000). Literacy practices. In D. Barton, M. Hamilton, & R. Ivanič (Eds.), *Situated literacies: Reading and writing in context*. London: Routledge.

Cochran-Smith, M., & Lytle, S. L. (1993). *Inside/outside: Teacher research and knowledge*. New York: Teachers College Press.

Daiute, C. (1993). Youth genres and literacy: Links between sociocultural and developmental theories. *Language Arts, 70*, 402–416.

Dyson, A. (1993). *Social worlds of children learning to write in an urban primary school*. New York: Teachers College Press.

Egan-Robertson, A., & Bloome, D. (Eds.). (1998). *Students as researchers of culture and language in their own communities*. Cresskill, NJ: Hampton Press.

Florio, S., & Shultz, J. (1978). Social competence at home and at school. *Theory into Practice, 18*(4), 234–243.

Florio-Ruane, S. (1990). Creating your own case studies: A guide for early field experience. *Teacher Education Quarterly, 1*, 29–41.

Frank, C. R. (1999). *Ethnographic eyes: A teacher's guide to classroom observation*. Portsmouth, NH: Heinemann.

Frank, C. R., & Uy, F. L., (2004). Ethnography for teacher education. *Journal of Teacher Education, 55*(3), 269–283.

Freire, P. (1998). *Teachers as cultural workers: Letters to those who dare teach*. Boulder, CO: Westview Press.

González, N., Moll, L., & Amanti, C. (Eds.). (2005). *Funds of knowledge: Theorizing practices in households, communities, and classrooms*. Mahwah, NJ: Lawrence Erlbaum.

González, N., Moll, L. C., Floyd-Tenery, M., Rivera, A., Rendón, P., Gonzáles, R., & Amanti, C. (1993). *Teacher research on funds of knowledge: Learning from households* (Educational Practice Rep. No. 6). Washington, DC: National Center for Research on Cultural Diversity and Second Language Learning.

Green, J. L., Dixon, C. N., & Zaharlick, A. (2003). Ethnography as a logic of inquiry. In J. Flood, D. Lapp, J. R. Squire, & J. M. Jensen (Eds.), *Handbook of research on the teaching of English language arts* (2nd ed., pp. 201–224). Mahwah, NJ: Lawrence Erlbaum.

Hancock, B. L., & Pelton, L. H. (1989). Home visits: History and functions. *Social Casework, 70*(1), 21–27.

Heath, S. B. (1983). *Ways with words*. Cambridge: Cambridge University Press.

Horowitz, F. D., Darling-Hammond, L., & Bransford, J. with Comer, J., Rosebrock, K., Austin, K., & Rust, F. (2005). Educating teachers for developmentally appropriate practice. In L. Darling-Hammond and J. Bransford (Eds.), *Preparing teachers for a changing world: What teachers should learn and be able to do* (pp. 88–125). San Francisco, CA: Jossey-Bass.

Hymes, D. (1982). What is ethnography? In P. Gilmore, & A. Glatthorn (Eds.), *Children in and out of school: Ethnography and education* (pp. 21–32). Washington, DC: Center for Applied Linguistics.

Keilty, B. (2008). Early intervention home-visiting principles in practice: A reflective approach. *Young Exceptional Children, 11*(2): 29–40.

Kyle, D., & McIntyre, E. (2000). *Family visits benefit teachers and families—and students most of all* (Practitioner Brief No. 1). University of California, Berkeley: National Center for Research on Education, Diversity & Excellence.

Ladson-Billings, G. (1994). *The dream keepers: Successful teachers of African American children.* San Francisco, CA: Jossey-Bass Publishers.

Ladson-Billings, G. (2006). From the achievement gap to the education debt: Understanding achievement in U.S. schools. *Educational Researcher, 35*(7), 3–12.

Lee, C. D. (1997). Bridging home and school literacies: Models for culturally responsive teaching, a case for African-American English. In J. Flood, S. B. Heath, & D. Lapp (Eds.), *Handbook of research on teaching literacy through the communicative and visual arts* (pp. 334–345). New York: Macmillan.

Mehan, H. (1979). *Learning lessons.* Cambridge, MA: Harvard University Press.

McIntyre, E., Kyle, D., Moore, G., Sweazy, R. A., & Greer, S. (2001). Linking home and school through family visits. *Language Arts, 78*(3), 264–272.

McIntyre, E., Rosebery, A., & González, N. (Eds.). (2001). *Classroom diversity: Connecting curriculum to students' lives.* Portsmouth, NH: Heinemann.

Moll, L. C. (1994). Literacy research in Community and classrooms. In R. Rudell, M. Rudell, & H. Singer (Eds.). *Theoretical models and processes of reading* (4th ed.). (pp. 179–207). Newark, DE: IRA.

Moll, L., Amanti, C., Neff, D., & González, N. (1992). Funds of knowledge for teaching: Using a qualitative approach to connect homes and classrooms. *Theory into Practice, 31*(2), 132–141.

Moll, L. C., & González, N. (2004). Engaging life: A funds of knowledge approach to multicultural education. In J. A. Banks and C. A. M. Banks (Eds.), *Handbook of research on multicultural education* (2nd ed., pp. 699–715). San Francisco: Jossey-Bass.

Moll, L. C., & Greenberg, J. B. (1990). Creating zones of possibilities: Combining social contexts for instruction. In L. C. Moll (Ed.). *Vygotsky and education: Instructional implications and applications of sociohistorical psychology.* (pp. 319–348). Cambridge: Cambridge University Press.

Phillips, S. (1972). Participant strutures and communicative competence: Warm Springs children in community and classroom. In C. Cazden, V. John, & D. Hymes (Eds.), *Functions of language in the classroom* (pp. 370–394). New York: Teachers College Press.

Purcell-Gates, V. (Ed.). (2007). *Cultural practices of literacy: Case studies of language, literacy, social practice, and power.* Mahwah, NJ: Lawrence Erlbaum.

Solsken, J. (1993). *Literacy, gender, and work in families and in school.* Norwood, NJ: Ablex Publishing.

Sweet, M. A., & Appelbaum, M. I. (2004). Is home visiting an effective strategy? A meta-analytic review of home visiting programs for families with young children. *Child Development, 75,* 1435–1456.

Taylor, D., & Dorsey-Gaines, C. (1988). *Growing up literate: Learning from inner-city families.* Portsmouth, NH: Heinemann.

Weade, G. (1992). Locating learning in the times and spaces of teaching. In H. Marshall (Ed.), *Redefining student learning: Roots of educational change* (pp. 87–118). Norwood, NJ: Ablex.

Weade, R., & Green, J. (1985). Talking to learn: Social and academic requirements for classroom participation. *Peabody Journal of Education, 62*(3), 6–19.

Woolfolk Hoy, A., & Murphy, P. K. (2001). Teaching educational psychology to the implicit mind. In B. Torff, & R. Sternberg (Eds.), *Understanding and teaching the intuitive mind: Student and teacher learning* (pp. 145–185). Mahwah, NJ: Lawrence Erlbaum.

Yin, R. K. (2006). Case study methods. In J. L. Green, G. Camilli, & P. B. Elmore with A. Skukauskaite & E. Grace (Eds.). *Handbook of Complementary methods in education research* (pp. 111–122). Mahwah, NJ: Lawrence Erlbaum Associates and AERA.

10 Networks of Support

Learning from the Other Teachers in Children's Lives

Susi Long and Dinah Volk

Francisco (9 years old) sits on the couch with his mother who helps him with his spelling. They speak Spanish and spell the English words in English. At the same time, Julializ (5) and her cousins (7 and 3) are playing a Super Mario game on the TV. The older girls sit on either side of the younger one helping her, taking turns and arguing. They happily scream directions at each other and the screen—in Spanish with some code switching into English. When print in English comes on the screen, the older cousin points to it and reads out loud to the others. At the same time, Fernando (12) is sitting at the kitchen table working on some math homework with a young man from their church. They work for 40 minutes completing several worksheets in English. They speak Spanish and English.

Eight-year-old Kelli arrived in Iceland three days ago from the US. Elva and Birna (Icelandic neighbors, also 8) appear in roller skates at her front door. In carefully rehearsed English, Elva asks, "Do you want to play?" Kelli puts on skates and joins them. Soon the girls come into the kitchen for apple juice. As they drink, Kelli glances around the room and picks up a cooking timer. She twists the dial making the timer ring. Elva and Birna laugh. Kelli twists the dial again and laughs with the girls. They go upstairs where Kelli finds a puzzle. As the girls sit on the floor, Kelli examines a puzzle piece, shakes her head and says, "Mm mm" [no]. Birna points to the puzzle and says in Icelandic, "Nei, hér" [No, here]. Kelli follows Birna's direction by putting the piece in place and says, "Da" [inventing a word for "there"].

In these scenarios, the children interacted as both learners and teachers in multilingual and multicultural contexts. With the "other teachers" in their lives—their networks of support—they drew on familiar practices and invented new ones. In the process, they created new spaces for learning about language, literacy, and cultural roles and routines. The first vignette illustrates how Julializ, a bilingual kindergartner, was a part of a network of family and community members who supported each other. The children, using both Spanish and English, were teachers and learners: in the scenario above, the older cousins helped the younger one read the game text; on other occasions, Julializ took the lead reading Spanish while her cousin and brothers helped her read English. In the second vignette, Kelli interacted within a network of Icelandic peers. The children used gestures, laughter, and manipulation of objects as well as English, Icelandic, and their own language inventions to support communication, facilitate play, and learn about language.

All children and their families bring knowledge and skills about how to support their own and others' learning to classrooms every day. Homes and communities are rich in teaching strategies and resources from which teachers can learn as they expand their own instructional repertoires. This chapter focuses on ways that teachers might learn from these networks of support as well as from support networks among children in classrooms. Watching children interact with their peers, siblings, and adult family and community members, teachers can better understand and appreciate children in the complex contexts of their lives (Gutiérrez & Orellana, 2006). In the process, they begin to challenge deficit views of children and families (Long et al., 2008)—particularly children of color, those who speak English as a new language, and those who live in poverty—as they ask harder questions of themselves and consider new possibilities for education in schools. Taking a learner's stance, teachers ask: What can I learn from children and their networks of support to enrich my teaching? What can I learn from the other teachers in children's lives?

In the first half of this chapter, we provide examples from our own studies of children learning within support networks in multilingual and multicultural settings: Mexican American kindergartners and their friends at school (Long, Bell, & Brown, 2004); Latino first graders in a dual language classroom (Volk & Angelova, 2007); an American child and Icelandic peers at home and at school (Long, 1998, 2004); and a Puerto Rican kindergartner learning at home (Volk & de Acosta, 2004). We highlight teaching and learning strategies used by the children and the other teachers in their lives. The second half of the chapter builds from these examples to suggest specific curricular structures that teachers might use within and beyond classrooms to learn from the other teachers in their students' lives.

THEORETICAL APPLICATION: NETWORKS OF SUPPORT

This chapter offers in-depth portraits of learning partners, spaces and resources present in diverse students' homes and communities. It extends research on the ways of acting, interacting, knowing, and living used by members of cultural communities, growing out of their shared histories. It reinforces central themes across networks of support: reciprocity and trust as well as change and conflict. What types of inside knowledge can ethnographic vignettes provide to teachers? How can they be effectively used in teacher education contexts? What types of precautions would need to be put in place to avoid generalizations?

Ideas that Guide Our Work

We believe that children's learning is an inherently sociocultural process; children are cultural learners who reconstruct and appropriate, for their own use, patterns of thinking they experience through interactions with other members of their communities. Our perspective is guided by the work of scholars who extend this Vygotskian (1978) notion by describing intentional scaffolding in which participants, including children, move in and out of the roles of expert and novice as they engage others in the teaching/learning process (Chen & Gregory, 2004; Lindfors, 1999; Rogoff, 1990).

This theoretical base directs attention to varied strategies or *practices* used in particular contexts (González, Moll, & Amanti, 2005) representing "a shift from the assumption that regularities in groups are carried by the traits of a collection of individuals to a focus on people's history of engagement in practices of cultural communities" (Gutiérrez & Rogoff, 2003, p. 21). Consistent with this perspective, we understand literacy and language as social and cultural practices (Barton & Hamilton, 1998) that are co-constructed and rooted in the ongoing life of communities. Often these practices differ in some ways from those valued by schools and mainstream society (Heath, 1983; Street, 1999). Because there are rarely opportunities for teachers to examine these practices in the current school configurations, they are often ignored and even disparaged.

Studies compiled by Gregory, Long, and Volk (2004) counter this deficit perspective and add to a growing body of work identified as Syncretic Literacy Studies. Along with research by Dyson (2003), Solsken, Willet, and Wilson-Keenan (2000), and Gutiérrez, Baquedano-López, and Tejeda (1999), among others, these studies indicate that teaching/learning interactions—particularly in cross-cultural contexts—are often syncretic with children drawing on the multiple resources in their lives as they create new spaces and practices for teaching and learning.

Work in the fields of urban anthropology and sociology has long studied communities as networks of relationships. Wallman (1984), Pérez (2004), and Guerra (1998) look at the ways that members of marginalized communities create strong networks for obtaining and sharing resources. Moll and his colleagues have written extensively about the potential for these *funds of knowledge*—shared through networked relationships of reciprocity and trust—to inform transformation in classroom teaching practices (González, Moll, & Amanti, 2005). This research suggests the fruitfulness of continuing to study young children as members of multiple interconnected communities where they learn from and contribute to complex networks of support.

Stories from Our Studies: Learning from Children's Networks of Support

In this section, we share examples from our studies of children's interactions with peers, siblings, and family members conducted with an ethnographic commitment to long-term, in-depth observations in real-world settings (Agar, 1996;

Denzin, 1997). Positioned as learners and viewing participants as experts, we focused on the many competencies of children and families as they interacted in homes, communities, and classrooms. Data were collected by audio- and video-taping interactions, interviewing participants and other cultural insiders, drawing network maps, and compiling literacy artifacts. Considering the immediate contexts of our studies as well as the broader social contexts in which they were situated, we constructed patterns in participants' use of varied teaching/learning strategies as well as anomalies to those patterns. Using data from our findings, we share examples that demonstrate the expertise of children as members of important support networks.[1] We encourage teachers to read with an eye for how they might similarly position themselves as learners in the lives of students by focusing on ways children and the other teachers in their lives do the following:

- use a range of sophisticated strategies to facilitate participation in language and literacy communities;
- skillfully syncretize experiences from multiple contexts to create new spaces and strategies for teaching and learning; and
- demonstrate sensitivity to learners' needs as they move in and out of the roles of expert and novice.

Children and members of their support networks use a range of sophisticated strategies to facilitate participation in language and literacy communities

Example #1: After moving to Iceland from the United States, 8-year-old Kelli learned to get along in new school and community contexts with the support of a large network of teachers. Of those teachers, three Icelandic peers, Elva, Birna, and Guðbjörg, were the most important. With Kelli, they developed and used a range of strategies as they played together to facilitate her participation in language communities. One of many examples of this strategy development and use occurred one day at play as Guðbjörg initiated an interaction by inventing new lyrics to a mutually-familiar song, *Old MacDonald*. As Guðbjörg sang in Icelandic, Kelli—who was in the early days of learning the language—listened, recognized the tune, and joined in by singing the part of the song most familiar to her, "Ee I Ee I O." As she built confidence, Kelli eventually contributed her own lyrics, using the Icelandic she knew. At one point, Guðbjörg corrected Kelli's use of a word and, in the last lines, drew from her knowledge of America (from Kelli) and of Portugal (from family holidays) to complete the song (Figure 10.1).

---

1 Data excerpts are presented in the original languages (Icelandic and Spanish) with English translations. Double slashes are used to indicate overlapping speech, single parentheses indicate observer's comments, and double parentheses indicate unclear speech.

	Icelandic	English translation
Guðbjörg:	Frændi keyrir kassabil.	Cousin drives a go-kart.
	Ee I Ee I O	Ee I Ee I O
	Hún Guðbjörg situr aftan í	Guðbjörg sits in the back
K & G:	Ee I Ee I O	Ee I Ee I O (Kelli joins in)
Guðbjörg:	Hún keyrir út að Hotel Borg	She drives to the Hotel Borg
K & G:	Ee I Ee I O	Ee I Ee I O
Guðbjörg:	Þau verða það í alla nótt.	They stay there all night
K & G:	Ee I Ee I O	Ee I Ee I O
Guðbjörg:	Þau dansa Þar í alla nótt.	They dance there all night
Kelli:	Já! Þau dansa Þar í alla nótt.	Yes! They dance there all night
K & G:	Ee I Ee I O	Ee I Ee I O
Kelli:	Þegar þau, uh, nei, voru búín í dansi þá foru þeir -	When they, uh, no, were finished dancing, they went -
Guðbjörg:	Þau	They (correcting Kelli's use of þeir)
Kelli:	Þau - út.	They - out. (picking up on the correction)
Guðbjörg:	Í Ameriku. Nei, út í Portugal	To America. No, to Portugal
K & G:	Ee I Ee I O	Ee I Ee I O

Using specific teaching/learning strategies and comfortable enough to risk approximation and experimentation, Kelli and Guðbjörg created these lyrics together. In the process, Kelli learned about Icelandic vocabulary and grammatical usage, gained confidence in risking engagement in a new language, and had the opportunity to participate as both contributor *and* learner.

Example #2: The second example took place in Julializ's home and was part of an almost daily ritual of Bible reading in this Pentecostal family. Following her mother's direction, Julializ located a psalm and her mother used teacher-like language to ask questions and remind her about appropriate literacy behaviors. She then prompted Julializ to recite a prayer required before reading that mentioned every family member and invoked the assistance of God and His angels for this religious literacy task.

Throughout this interaction (see next page), Julializ and her mother co-constructed several strategies for scaffolding Julializ's developing literacy, gradually giving her a more active role. These strategies included joint oral reading, with the mother reading just a beat ahead of Julializ in overlapping turns; echo reading; and independent reading with prompts. Sra. Torres expected that, with this support, Julializ would be able to read this sacred text and referred frequently to her promise as a reader and a member of their church community.

In examples #1 and #2 and in this chapter's opening vignettes, children and members of their networks of support facilitated learning (Table 10.1). Crafting sensitively-timed feedback, they supplied and rehearsed words and phrases,

	Spanish	English tTranslation
Sra. Torres:	Ok vamos a leer.	Ok let's read.
Julializ:	Vamos a leer. // //...	Let's read.
Sra. Torres:	Y ala//baré.//	And I will praise.
Julializ:	//Alabaré.//	I will praise.
(Sra. Torres & Julializ read, Julializ a beat behind her)		
Sra. T. & J:	//Con todo mi corazón. Delante de los dioses, Te cantaré salmos.//	With all my heart. Before the gods, I will sing psalms to You.
Sra. Torres:	//Me pos//traré	I will bow down.
Julializ:	//Me pos.// ¿Aquí ma?	I wi. Here ma?
Sra. Torres:	Sí en la dos, allí mismo.	Yes in the two, right there.
Sra. T. & J:	//Me postraré hacia Tu santo templo.//	I will bow down toward Your holy temple.
Sra. T. & J:	//Y alabaré.//	And I will praise.
Sra. T. & J:	//Tu nombre// por Tu misericordia y Tu fidelidad. Porque has engrandecido Tu nombre y Tu palabra sobre todas las cosas. El día que clamé, me respondiste. Me fortaleciste con vigor en mi alma.//	Your name for Your compassion and Your faithfulness. For You have exalted Your name and Your word over all things. The day I called You answered me. You made me strong and bold in my soul.
Sra. Torres:	Te alabarán.	They praise You.
Julializ:	No hagas rápido mami	Don't go fast mommy.
Sra. Torres:	Oh ok. I'm sorry. Mami por la cuatro. Aquí. Te.	Dear on the fourth. Here. You
Julializ:	Te.	You
(Sra. Torres provides text, Julializ echoes)		
Sra. T then J:	Alabarán.	They will praise.
Sra. T then J:	O Jehová.	Oh Jehovah.
Julializ:	¿Dónde?//	Where?
Sra. Torres:	Aquí. Porque han oído.	Here. Because they have heard.
Julializ:	Porque han oído.	Because they have heard.
((echo reading continues, later Julializ reads independently with prompts from Sra. Torres))		
Julializ:	Allaabaa-. Alabad. A Jehová. Porrr-. Porrr-	Prraai-. Praise. To Jehovah. Beee-. Beee-.
Sra. Torres:	Cuando dices "¡por....!"	When you say "be....!"
Julializ:	Por. Que. El. Es.	Be. Cause. He. Is.
Sra. Torres:	Divídelo en sílabas mami.	Divide it in syllables dear.
Julializ:	Bus. Errr. Bue. No.	Gos. Orrr. Goo. D. (Good.)
Sra. Torres:	Eso.	That's it.

rephrased ideas, and responded to incorrect forms with correct ones. Their interactions took place in contexts characterized by specific conditions: engagement in activities of interest to them; comfort in risking experimentation; and time to experiment with a range of supportive strategies.

Table 10.1 Strategies and conditions that supported learning in children's home and community interactions in the opening vignettes and in Examples 1 and 2

Networks of support	Strategies and conditions supporting learning	Learning that took place within supportive networks at home
Opening vignette and Example #1 Elva, Birna, and Guðbjörg	Strategies: • Laughter and intonated sounds • Gesture and facial expressions • Invented words • Using objects and artifacts • Using English as well as Icelandic. • Supplying words • Rephrasing ideas for one another • Responding to incorrect forms with correct ones • Asking for and providing sensitively-timed assistance • Repeating and practicing words and phrases through song and play Conditions: • Mutual interest • High comfort level that encouraged risk-taking • Extended periods of time	Kelli learned: • Familiarity with the new language sounds • Specific Icelandic vocabulary • Some aspects of grammatical usage • That she could successfully participate even when she didn't speak Icelandic fluently All of the children learned: • They could create learning and teaching strategies that would support interaction • How to manipulate existing knowledge and material resources to support interactions (using the cooking timer and the puzzle, changing words in a commonly-known song)
Opening Vignette and Example #2 Julializ, her mother, brothers, church brother	Scaffolding strategies: • Joint oral reading, with the mother reading just a beat ahead of Julializ in overlapping turns • Echo reading • Independent reading with prompts • Spanish and English as resources Conditions: • Expectations of success • Mutual engagement with important texts • Family context • All participants were interested • High comfort level that encouraged risk-taking • Extended periods of time	Julializ learned: • Readers can use their fingers to underline words • Readers break words into manageable chunks • Meaning and memory are useful tools when reading • She could control other's instruction as needed • She could read a significant text All of the children learned: • They were teachers as well as learners • Spanish and English are resources for learning • Family and community support school success • Literacy is useful in school and play settings • They belonged to multiple literate communities

Children and members of their support networks skillfully syncretize experiences from multiple contexts to create new spaces and strategies for teaching and learning

Example #3: Learning to get along in Iceland, Kelli constantly drew from both her English-speaking and Icelandic worlds to create new arenas for learning and teaching. Evidence of this syncretism occurred in almost every interaction. For example, in the fourth month of Kelli's first year in Iceland, as she and Guðbjörg played with a set of multi-colored dominoes, Kelli drew on a diverse range of cultural resources as she pointed to the dominoes and began singing the color names in Icelandic:

	Icelandic	*English translation*
Kelli:	Gulur, rauður, grænn og blár. Svartur, nei svartur.	Yellow, red, green and blue. Black, no black (pointing to Guðbjörg's black shoes to communicate that there are no dominoes that color).
Guðbjörg:	Nei.	No.
Kelli:	Hvítur, fjólublár.	White, purple (pointing to Guðbjörg's purple collar, meaning there are no white and purple dominoes).

Kelli & Guðbjörg singing together:

	Fjólublár. Gulur, rauður, grænn og blár, svartur, hvítur, fjólublár.	Purple. Yellow, red, green and blue, black, white, purple (pointing to dominoes, Guðjörg's shoes and collar).

As they sang and pointed, Kelli utilized a range of prior experiences to support the girls in creating a new space for play and language practice. She drew on a history of inventing songs with her mother and with Guðbjörg, and past experiences playing with dominoes. She used a tune both girls knew from the local children's choir and she experimented with Icelandic words learned in previous play episodes.

Example #4: With her brothers and cousins, Julializ often engaged in sociodramatic play. In a long interaction playing "church" they syncretized languages and literacies from their experiences in school, in religious literacy events at home and in their Pentecostal church and Sunday school, and from popular culture. As can be seen below, the children made frequent use of oral recitation and memorization, literacy practices that contrasted with those used in their classrooms that emphasized the construction of individual meaning. Within Julializ's network of support, oral recitation and memorization were valued practices that provided children with an induction into literacy and an opportunity to participate actively in a personally significant community.

In the following excerpt, Julializ began the church service by appropriating the

words of her kindergarten teacher ("Ok. Hoy voy a . . . ." [Ok. Today I'm going to
. . .]) and then reviewing the proper practices for a religious literacy event for
Hilary, her 3-year-old cousin. She went on to recite a prayer, read a psalm from a
Bible by reciting it from memory, and sing a song that she sang in church with a
song sheet.

	Spanish	*English translation*
Julializ:	Ok. Hoy voy a predicar primero. Ok. (( )) orar.	Ok. Today I'm going to preach first. Ok. (( )) to pray.
Zoila:	Ok! I'm waiting.	
Julializ:	(to Hilary) ¿Y tus ojos? Tienen que estar cerrados. Tienen que estar cerrados, ¡he-lo-o!	And your eyes? They have to be shut. They have to be shut. He-lo-o!
Zoila:	(laughs) . . .	
Julializ:	This little girl (( )). ¡Hilary! ¡Cierre los ojos! Ok. Alaba . . . Gracias Señor. . . .	This little girl (( )). Hilary! Shut your eyes! Okay prai . . . Thank you Lord . . . .
Julializ:	Ok. Señor, gracias Señor por todo esto que tú nos has dado. Cuida toda la gente Señor amen gracias Señor.	Ok. Lord, thank you Lord for all this that you have given us. Take care of all the people Lord amen thank you Lord.
Zoila:	That's all?	
Julializ:	Ok el salmo. (looks through Bible) Diecisiete. No. Uno uno siete, ¿ok? Ya usted lo cogio ¿ok? . . . Cuan- cuando terminen digan amen . . .	Ok, the psalm. Seventeen. No. One one seven, ok? You already have it ok? . . . Whe- when you finish say amen . . . .
Julializ:	Ok (holds Bible) alabar a Jehová naciones todas pueblos todos alabarle. Porque ha engrandecido sobre nosotros Su semiricordia (*sic*) y la felidad (*sic*) de Jehová es para siempre aleluya amen. (brother explains that Julializ has memorized the prayer)	Ok praise Jehovah all nations all people praise You. Because You have exalted over us Your empassion (*sic*) and the faifulness (*sic*) of Jehovah is for always halleluyah amen
Julializ:	Ok, vamos a cantar "Este corito es." (sings) Este corito es. Para alabar a Dios.	Ok, let's sing "This little choir is." This little choir is. Here to give praise to God.

After this opening, Julializ and Zoila sang another song based on a Bible story,
discussed the offering, and sang again. They inserted the song "Amor prohibido"
[Forbidden Love] from the movie *Selena* starring Jennifer Lopez into the church
service and, when Julializ's mother objected to this worldly song, switched to a
religious one. The mother's indirect comment, "De la iglesia se pasaron a una

mujer del mundo" [From the church they've gone on to a woman of the world] appears to have been understood by the girls as an objection to the juxtaposition of the texts since they had listened to the song repeatedly. Thus, the girls' syncretic literacy became an opportunity for Sra. Torres to explain appropriate literacy practices in their community.

In the Icelandic and Latino examples above, children and members of their support networks drew on multiple worlds and diverse resources as they taught and learned from each other about valued literacies. In the process, they expertly and syncretically created new spaces for teaching and learning about specific aspects of culture, language, and literacy (Table 10.2).

Table 10.2 Children's syncretic interactions—drawing from multiple worlds and diverse resources to create new spaces for learning

Networks of support	Syncretic interactions: children learning and teaching by drawing on diverse resources	Teaching and learning that took place through children's syncretic interactions
Example #3 Kelli and Guðbjörg	Kelli drew on: • Prior experience building with dominoes and inventing songs • A song learned in Icelandic church choir • Knowledge of a few Icelandic color words Guðbjörg drew on: • Prior experience inventing songs • A song learned through Icelandic church choir • Knowledge of Icelandic color words	Kelli: • Reinforced knowledge of and ability to use Icelandic color words • Reinforced knowledge of Icelandic church song • Affirmed that, in this company, she could risk participation and experiment with language • Affirmed that, in this company, she could use objects and prior experiences to create a place for communication Guðbjörg: • Provided a knowledgeable partner for Kelli's reinforcement of color word knowledge • Affirmed that she and Kelli could interact with one another even when they had limited knowledge of each other's home languages
Example #4 Julializ, Zoila, and Hilary	Julializ and Zoila drew on: • The school teacher's words • Oral recitation and memorization practices from church • Preaching practices from church • Bible reading practices at home and in Sunday school • Popular culture: song from a familiar movie	Julializ and Zoila: • Received instruction about appropriate language for church • Practiced valued literacies needed for participation in a literate community • Learned more about appropriating resources from a variety of experiences to support learning Hilary: • Received instruction and demonstration about appropriate practices for religious literacy

***Children and members of their support networks are sensitive to
learners' needs; they act as teachers as well as learners, moving in and
out of the roles of expert and novice***

Example #5: In the study of Mexican American kindergartners, English-
and Spanish-speaking children took on roles as teachers as well as learners
revealing insight and sensitivity to each other's needs. One example occurred in
September when the teaching assistant, a native-Spanish speaker, was reading
an English picture book to Marcial, who spoke a few English words, and Maya,
a developing bilingual. The teaching assistant asked Marcial to describe an
illustration:

Assistant:	Tell me what you see here (pointing to the illustration).
Marcial:	(looks closely at the illustration)
Assistant:	What do you see here?
Marcial:	(looks at the illustration, but says nothing)
Maya:	¿Qué ve usted aquí? What do you see? (translating the teaching assist-ant's question into Spanish for Marcial)
Assistant:	Tell me about the picture. (prompting Marcial in English)
Maya:	He is looking. (explaining Marcial's behavior to the assistant)
Assistant:	Marcial, what do you see here?
Marcial:	Hay un chico y un perro. [*There's a boy and a dog*]
Maya:	He sees a boy and a dog. (translating for the assistant)

Throughout this lesson, Maya played a critical role as expert mediator. Sensitive
to the needs of Marcial *and* the teaching assistant, Maya provided support by
translating the teaching assistant's question into Spanish, explaining Marcial's
behavior, and translating Marcial's words into English. Maya seemed aware of
Marcial's need to study the illustration and think before answering. The teaching
strategies she chose allowed Marcial to listen to the sounds of both English and
Spanish in a small group context where he also learned about a school-styled
question–answer format and picture-reading as a literacy strategy.

Example #6: In almost every interaction involving Kelli and her Icelandic peers,
each child moved in and out of the roles of expert and novice. For example, in
Kelli's first month in Iceland, she and Elva were playing when Elva, in the novice
role, picked up a toy spider and asked Kelli, "Konguló. Konguló. What this á
Ensk?" (Spider. Spider. What's this in English?). Kelli replied, "Spider." Then
Elva, moving into the role of expert, asked if Kelli wanted to hear the word in
Icelandic, "Me say á Íslensku, spider?" (Me say in Icelandic, spider?). Kelli
nodded and Elva said, "Konguló." The girls were sensitive not only to each
other's desire to learn language but to have opportunities to participate in the
role of expert.

Example #7: Within the support network among peers in the dual language first
grade classroom it was common for children to facilitate each other's learning of

Spanish and English. On several occasions, however, the English speakers complained about having to speak Spanish and the Spanish speakers argued about how to respond.

	Spanish	English translation
Karla:	¿Porqué ella no está hablando español?	Why isn't she speaking Spanish?
Beatríz:	Porque está aprendiendo.	Because she's learning.
Karla:	No habla. Si no habla no aprende.	She's doesn't talk. If she doesn't talk, she doesn't learn.
Beatríz:	Nosotros no te tratamos [sic] así.	We don't try [treat] you like that.

In this interchange, both Karla and Beatríz took on the teacher role, debating the best way for the English speakers to improve their Spanish. Karla, who was just learning English, spoke from her own experience. Beatríz, a skillful bilingual who had more experience with English speakers, urged patient accommodation. Their sensitivity to the emotional and academic needs of language learners allowed them to demonstrate their expertise and reflect on teaching and learning.

Example #8: Julializ and her cousin Zoila were also often sensitive teachers in each other's lives, exchanging the roles of teacher and learner, depending on the task and the expertise required. When they worked together to read a list of English words, Zoila took the lead because she was in an English-only first grade and was a more competent reader in English. However, in the church play cited in Example #4, their roles were reversed when Zoila declared that Julializ should be the pastor, since the Bibles they were reading were in Spanish and Julializ, who was learning to read in Spanish in her bilingual kindergarten, was the better Spanish reader.

In each of these scenarios, peers supported each other. Repeatedly, data excerpts from our studies revealed children's awareness of each other's needs across cultural and linguistic contexts. Their sensitivity to and expertise in the roles of teacher and learner, and the learning that resulted provide powerful examples of the kind of expertise that can inform classroom teaching (Table 10.3).

We Learned That . . .

The children in our studies participated in multiple networks in and out of school that supported their learning and in which they used a range of strategies, some similar to and some different from those used in schools. They were active participants as teachers and learners in these co-constructed networks where they felt comfortable enough to risk participation and in which they appropriated and syncretized literacy practices from other contexts in their lives. These findings led us to consider how we might engage teachers in learning, for themselves, about children's networks of support.

Table 10.3 Children as teachers, aware of and sensitive to learners' needs

Networks of support	Children as sensitive teachers and learners	Learning that took place when children were teachers
Example #5 Marcial and Maya	Maya: • Recognized the need to mediate between the teaching assistant and learner. • Translated the teaching assistant's English into Spanish for Marcial • Translated Marcial's Spanish into English for the teaching assistant • Noticed that Marcial needed thinking time, honored that need, and alerted the teaching assistant to it	Maya: • Affirmed her own abilities as a mediator • Reinforced strategies for supporting learners. • Rehearsed her own bilingual abilities Marcial: • Was exposed to the sounds of both English and Spanish in a focused, small group context • Learned more about interactions within a question–answer/school format • Learned more about picture-reading as a literacy strategy
Example #6 Kelli and Elva	Elva: • Looked to Kelli for English expertise • Gave Kelli some control of the learning by asking if she wanted to know the Icelandic word for spider	Kelli: • Affirmed that she could be a teacher as well as a learner • Learned the Icelandic word for "spider" Elva: • Learned the English word for "spider" • Saw Kelli as a teacher as well as a learner
Example #7 Karla and Beatríz	Karla: • Affirmed that to learn language, you must use language Beatríz: • Recognized the need to adapt to the learning process of other language learners • Recognized the importance of reflecting on your own experience	Karla and Beatríz: • Learned that people learn in different ways • Learned that patient accommodation is an important part of supporting learners • Reflected on their language learning experiences • Affirmed their roles as peer teachers
Example #8 Julializ and Zoila	Zoila: Recognized Julializ's superior strengths in Spanish (despite her own strengths as an English speaker) and her ability to take on the pastor role	Zoila and Julializ: • Affirmed their own abilities as teachers of peers • Affirmed important strategies for supporting learners • Rehearsed their bilingual abilities

THEORETICAL APPLICATION: SYNCRETIZED PRACTICES

Syncretism is a process through which children and adults draw on their experiences in multiple worlds to create new practices. The examples in the above sections illustrate two central themes: (1) The nature of expertise within syncretic practices is reciprocal and fluid. This adds complexity to Vygotsky's discussion of teaching within the zone of proximal development. Participants often switch roles, with teachers becoming learners and learners becoming teachers. (2) Teaching within networks of support often involves a range of informal, supportive strategies (e.g., sensitively-timed feedback, supportive contexts for risk-taking and experimentation, meaningful activities, use of language to mediate thinking). Syncretized languages and literacies are co-created regularly in classrooms, whether officially or non-officially. How can teachers recognize and validate syncretic practices observed in the classroom? How can they become an opportunity to explain academic literacy practices?

Where Might Teachers Start?
Ideas for Learning about Children's Networks of Support

Insightful, skillful, and sensitive teaching happens all the time in and out of school among children and their family and community members. While much has been written about the value of these resources (Haight, 2002; Heath, 1983; Hull & Schultz, 2002; Taylor & Dorsey-Gaines, 1988; Valdés, 1996; Zentella, 2005 to name a few), with a few exceptions (Allen, 2007; Irvine, 2003; Nieto, 2004; Schultz, 2003), there is little written about how teachers might draw on these insights to learn about students in their own classrooms. In the following pages, we provide suggestions for teachers (summarized in Table 10.4) so that they might consider ways to broaden their repertoire of practices as they learn from students' networks of support.

Learning About Home and Community Networks of Support:
Classroom-Based Engagements

Me Box.   Many teachers use a "Me Box" as an introductory activity at the beginning of the year. Students share stories using collections of personally-significant artifacts from their home and community lives. While this is often considered a getting-to-know-you engagement, Me Boxes can also be used as windows into the other teachers in students' lives. In one sixth grade class, for example, a student used a necklace from her Me Box to create a poem which provided insights about her grandmother—a wise teacher in her life—and about conditions that supported their teaching-learning relationship:

Before my wonderful grandmother died
She gave me an eye-sparkling
Necklace. From then on, I
treasured it and I knew it was
special because when she gave it to me,
she had a twinkle in her eyes. I knew.
I, I can feel
that golden crisp snake
that wraps about that neck of mine.
I, I can see it now.
When the sun twirls and turns
out of the darkness,
I can see my grandma's necklace
all gusty and dusty and all.
I can see it round hers,
now round mine.

Teachers focused on understanding students' home and community support networks can use writing such as this as an opportunity to learn about the other teachers in students' lives. In this case, the classroom teacher might use the poem as a basis for asking questions such as: Tell me more about the kinds of things you like to do and learn with your grandmother. What did she teach you? What did you do together as you learned? Why did you like learning from your grandmother? Then asking him/herself: How might I use knowledge of those conditions and strategies to broaden my own instructional repertoire?

Songs, Family Traditions, Recipes. Learning about songs, family traditions, and favorite foods can provide further windows into children's networks of support. As children and family members share these important aspects of their worlds and explain why they are meaningful, teachers can pay attention to the teaching and learning that takes place. In the following example, a student explains why a particular family recipe is important to her:

> My grandmother says that when I was a little girl, I would always cry because I wanted to help her cook. She said that I wanted to stir everything even if I wasn't supposed to. My granny is a warm-hearted person so she let me stir until I got tired. She would tell me to go wash my hands and come help her cook. Being four years old, I really thought I was doing something. One particular day, she made macaroni and cheese and she let me stir. My cousins thought it was good and decided that they wanted me to start cooking the macaroni and cheese from then on.

At first glance, such stories may seem simplistic, but by attending to them teachers can understand more about what supports individual children as learners and can use that knowledge to inform their own teaching. In this instance, we see a child learning to make macaroni and cheese by *cooking alongside her grandmother/teacher* who was *warm-hearted* and let the child take an *active and responsible role* in the process. The grandmother-as-teacher created a context in which the child could *develop as expert* eventually *taking on complete responsibility for a valued task.* Each of these strategies and conditions can be thoughtfully transposed to classroom settings: children reading alongside experts who demonstrate their own joy in reading, building warm-hearted relationships between teachers and students, and creating contexts in which children, as active and responsible participants, develop expertise and are viewed as experts.

Literacy Walks, Community Interviews, and Mapping. Students can also bring information about the other teachers in their lives into the classroom through engagements such as literacy walks in their communities (Taylor et al., 2000). They can interview shopkeepers, gas station attendants, beauticians, pastors, and family members, documenting their stories and the ways they use literacies. Students uncover teaching/learning strategies for teachers by asking how these community members are supported as they learn their professions. Using disposable cameras, children create community maps or records of these important people and the texts in their communities and bring documentation into the classroom. The variety and richness of communities' literacies and learning strategies can then be celebrated and utilized to support classroom instruction. In one example, Boutte and Hill (2006), write about class of third graders conducting an inquiry into ten African American barbershops. Learning sophisticated research techniques, the students uncovered funds of knowledge and networks of support providing a springboard for further literacy events at school. Similarly, Botelho (2006) writes about CD documentaries created by students as they interviewed Latino family and community members and shared from the wisdom of the other teachers in their lives.

Observing in Classrooms to Uncover Children's Expertise and Teaching Strategies. Teachers can also broaden their instructional repertoires by observing and learning from children's interactions in the classroom (Paley, 2005). In order to do so, it is essential to create multiple daily opportunities for meaningful peer interactions. In the dual language first grade described earlier, teachers often organized cooperative learning activities, putting together Beatríz, who was bilingual, with Karla who was just learning English, and two girls who were learning Spanish. Depending on the language of the activity and the content to be mastered, the children negotiated expert and novice roles as they interacted purposefully. Observing them, the teacher was able to see every child as knowledgeable and she could learn from the teaching strategies the children used to support each other. It is important to note that children will create their own supportive relationships if collaborative peer activity is nurtured through classroom structures such as sociodramatic play and other invitational centers, literature discussion groups, author's circles, and purposeful inquiries.

Table 10.4 Learning about networks of support: Engagements within the school walls

Engagements for uncovering home and community networks of support	Questions to prompt further reflection

• Me Box Conversations
• Sharing:
  o Favorite family songs
  o Family traditions
  o Favorite family recipes
  o Photos
• Literacy walks, interviews, and community mapping
• Classroom observations: Noticing how children support one another through sociodramatic play and other invitational centers, literature discussion groups, authors' circles, inquiry/research groups.
	• What are the stories behind Me Box artifacts, songs, traditions, recipes, and the professions of community members?
	• What do the stories reveal about home and community knowledge and expertise?
	• Who are the other teachers in children's lives who help them develop this knowledge and expertise?
	• How are literacies used?
	• What strategies do children's other teachers use to support learning?
	• What conditions support the learning?
	• How might we learn from these strategies and conditions as we plan for teaching in schools?

How one engagement can broaden a teacher's repertoire of instructional strategies

- Ella pulls a garden trowel from her *Me Box* and explains that her grandmother taught her the secret of growing tomatoes
- The class identifies Ella as a tomato-growing expert
- Probing further, the class discovers that Ella's grandmother used specific strategies to teach:
  - She worked with Ella as a gardening partner,
  - She explained how to garden in the context of real gardening
  - She demonstrated gardening skills and strategies, then asked Ella to give it a try
  - She allowed Ella to experiment as a gardener given rich gardening materials and resources
- Ella wanted to learn because:
  - She adored her grandmother and wanted to do something her grandmother loved and did well
  - Her grandmother made her feel competent by providing authentic praise
  - Ella felt safe enough to take risks (when she made mistakes, her grandmother patiently demonstrated)
- Learning from Ella's grandmother-as-teacher, Ella's classroom teacher can broaden her repertoire of strategies for teaching reading by:
  - Developing a caring relationship with Ella by getting to know her well and letting her know that she is loved and valued
  - Providing a rich collection of literacy materials that build on Ella's expertise and providing opportunities for Ella to experiment meaningfully with them
  - Working with Ella as her reading partner, the teacher sharing her/his own joy as a reader
  - Demonstrating reading skills and strategies in the context of reading Ella enjoys, then asking Ella to give them a try, celebrating her attempts
  - Providing authentic praise for Ella's efforts by pointing out all that she knows about reading

Learning about Home and Community Networks of Support:
Teachers Venturing Beyond the School Walls

Our work convinces us that to truly understand and learn from students' networks of support, it is essential that teachers interact with children, and family and community members on their turf—beyond the school walls. To get to know families and community members in new ways, teachers can attend events such as community fairs, dinners, athletic events, and services at local religious institutions and spend time in children's homes. The impact of these experiences can lead to important shifts in perspectives about children and their families (Long et al., 2008) that are fundamental to being able to learn from the other teachers in students' lives. The following comments from teachers reflect this transformation in attitude:

> I found myself falling into the typical stereotype of judging the children, their homes and families before seeing them for myself. I went into it with a slightly negative attitude [but] I found myself truly interested in the life that he lived. I learned that [among other things] family is greatly valued in his home.

> After I visited my child's home [as a learner], I felt like I had been through a life-changing experience. My child had the warmest, most welcoming family. They could not wait to share their life with me and were only to happy to teach me about their lives. I would never have known what a loving family my student came from if I did not take time to get over my negativity to go and visit him.

Once deficit views of children and families are challenged, it is easier to recognize the richness of teaching/learning interactions in home and community settings and to consider changes in classroom practice. In one of many examples, a teacher, inspired by Haight's (2002) study of African American children in Sunday School, spent time in a student's home, church, and Sunday School observing how family and community members supported the child who was struggling with literacy in school, but succeeding in Sunday School:

> I attended church and Sunday School [and] found . . . an environment rich in literacy. The lessons the students studied and the choral reading they took part in had a high level of vocabulary and all children were expected to join in the reading. The newsletter that was sent home with [church] members included upcoming events, but the 14-page publication was largely devoted to celebrating the accomplishments of the children in the congregation . . . I wondered if Jonathon ever feels as celebrated in the school setting as he does in his church.

Through her experiences beyond the school walls, this teacher countered her own deficit views of the student and his family. She identified multiple literacies used proficiently by the child outside of school. She found a community dedicated to high and positive expectations in the upbringing of children, witnessed children's inclusion as participants in important events, and experienced celebrations of children's accomplishments large and small—all strategies and conditions that supported the child as a learner. As a result, she was able to ask hard questions of herself about whether or not the child felt similarly supported in school.

Redefining "Home Visit". For these kinds of experiences to be transformative, a redefinition of what is commonly considered the "home visit" is required. Rather than looking at home visits as vehicles for telling parents how to support their children, the teachers in these examples saw them as opportunities to *learn from family and community members as experts in their children's lives*. With this stance, teachers were able to uncover for themselves—as we did in our studies—rich funds of knowledge, networks of support, and strategies used by the other teachers in students' home and community contexts.

Make a Place for Regular, Focused Conversations. Key to the success of experiences beyond the school walls are opportunities for teachers to regularly share their own questions, concerns, conflicts, and epiphanies about home and community networks of support. Through these conversations, teachers build a commitment to venturing beyond the school walls and new possibilities emerge. Including family and community members as key participants in these conversations is essential to the depth of insight possible. This means working together to ensure that: all voices are heard, issues explored are those proposed by community members as well as teachers, all group members have opportunities to lead discussions, time and space for meetings are convenient for all group members, and sessions alternate between school and community venues. Table 10.5 suggests some films and books that might be used as reflective tools when teachers and families meet together to learn about the wise teachers in children's lives.

Addressing Challenges. There are, of course, challenges to this idea of regular interactions in homes and communities and making time for reflective conversations. Given already overcrowded school days and personal lives, time is often in short supply for teachers and families. Addressing this challenge requires careful thought, planning, and commitment to making bold decisions. Teachers and administrators can take this step by creating: (1) schedules that allow administrators to take over classes so that teachers and children can spend time in homes and communities; (2) regular opportunities for children to work in combined classes freeing teacher time; and/or (3) schedules in which, monthly (in some school systems, this is done weekly), children attend school for a portion of the school day with child care provided. Since day-time visits are not possible for many working families, teachers might bank this time using weekdays to address personal needs, freeing them to spend some time during evenings or weekends in homes and communities. Although conversations about such out-of-the-box

Table 10.5 Resources to support reflective conversations

Films such as:
- *Family Across the Sea* (about the St. Helena's Island, SC delegation to Sierra Leone)
- *The Language You Cry In* (the Sierra Leone connection to Gullah in GA)
- *The Rabbit Proof Fence* (the systematic attempt to erase Aboriginal culture)
- *A Class Divided* (Jane Elliott's Blue Eyes, Brown Eyes experiment about racism)
- *Sweet Honey in the Rock 30th Anniversary Tour* (a look at African heritage in the US)
- *"Yo soy boricua, pa'que tu lo sepas"* (exploration of what it means to be Puerto Rican)

Children's books:
- *The Bracelet*, Uchida
- *The Jacket*, Clements
- *My Name is María Isabel*, Ada
- *Mama, Where Are You From?* Bradby
- *Quinnie Blue*, Johnson
- *My Mama Had a Dancing Heart*, Gray & Colon
- *I Love Saturdays y domingos*, Ada

Reading and discussing professional literature:
- Allen's (2007) *Creating Welcoming Schools*
- Delpit's (1995) *Other People's Children: Cultural Conflict in the Classroom*
- Delpit and Dowdy's (2002) *The Skin That We Speak*
- Gonzalez, Moll, & Amanti's (2005) *Funds of Knowledge: Theorizing Practices in Households, Communities, and Classrooms*
- Greenfield and Cocking's (1994) *Cross-Cultural Roots of Minority Child Development*
- Gregory's (2008) *Learning to Read in a New Language*
- Haight's (2002) *African American Children at Church*
- Nieto's (1999) *The Light in Their Eyes: Creating Multicultural Learning Communities*
- Purcell-Gates' (1995) *Other People's Words: The Cycle of Low Literacy*
- Zentella's (2004) *Building on Strengths: Language and Literacy in Latino Families and Communities*
- Tatum's (2007) *Can We Talk About Race?*
- Taylor and Dorsey-Gaines' (1988) *Growing Up Literate*
- Taylor's (1997) *Many Families, Many Literacies*
- Valdés' (1996) *Con Respeto*

Questions for Reflection and Conversation

- What kinds of knowledge do people in this text/film possess that might not be typically valued in schools—historically and currently?
- What can happen to people as learners when home and community knowledge is not valued or is marginalized or negated?
- Who are the wise teachers in this text/film? What strategies do they use to teach? What conditions support the learning?
- What might we learn from these teaching and learning situations to broaden our teaching attitudes and repertoires? What might we do differently in our classrooms?

possibilities can be easily closed down when visions are limited to the status quo, discussions that include school *and* community members have the potential to generate possibilities far beyond those presented here. Table 10.6 presents some suggestions about making a place for venturing beyond the school walls.

Table 10.6 Learning about networks of support: Venturing beyond the school walls

When teachers venture beyond the school walls, they open possibilities for. . .	How can schools make time for seeking understanding beyond the school walls?
<ul><li>Breaking down stereotypes and overturning misconceptions about children, families, and communities</li><li>Uncovering funds of knowledge in home and community settings previously viewed as lacking or limited</li><li>Identifying and learning from the other teachers in children's lives and the strategies those teachers use to teach</li><li>Uncovering conditions that support learning in homes and communities; making comparisons to conditions that support or hinder learning in schools</li></ul>	<ul><li>Begin by making a place for regular faculty conversations about home and community networks of support thereby building a commitment to understanding home knowledge as foundational to teaching in schools</li><li>Use adults in the building creatively:<ul><li>Provide a block of time each week when classrooms are covered by other personnel</li><li>Compensate evening or weekend time spent in homes and communities by providing compensatory time so that teachers can address personal or professional needs</li><li>Shorten the school day once a month/ week</li></ul></li></ul>

Conclusions

Learning from children's networks of support means taking time to build relationships between home and school and reflecting on the stance we take toward worlds that are different from our own. We cannot build on what children and their family and community members know or create mutually generative relationships, if we do not first value each other's knowledge as legitimate. Too often we give lip service to honoring multiple ways of interacting in the world and then default to our own cultural perspectives to define what is "right" and "useful." In contrast, teacher-as-learner moves beyond a focus on *individuals* and comes to understand, value, and learn from the *networks of support* in children's home and community worlds, making that knowledge integral to teaching and learning in classrooms. Just as we learned from Kelli, Elva, and Guðbjörg; Maya and Marcial; Julializ and Zoila; and Karla and Beatríz, we can learn from children in our own classrooms and their families as we seek to build more effective repertoires of teaching and learning practices.

Ideas for Discussion, Extension, and Application

1. In which ways do the stories of Kelli, Elva, and Guðbjörg; Maya and Marcial; Julializ and Zoila; and Karla and Beatríz add to your current understanding of diversity? How does each story add to your working knowledge of learning resources available in families and communities?

2. Imagine a student who recently immigrated to the United States. How would you, as a teacher, access information about his/her funds of knowledge and networks of support? How would you incorporate this network to facilitate his/her adaptation and success in school?
3. Put together a Me Box. In small groups, take turns sharing Me Box stories. What did you notice about group members' expertise or funds of knowledge? What did you learn about their networks of support and the practices or strategies that family and community members in those networks use to teach and learn? Select one Me Box for further discussion. How could you use this knowledge to inform your teaching? How could this knowledge be misused?
4. Long and Volk argue for the practice of regular conversations among teachers and between teachers and family and community members. How can teachers fulfill this recommendation? Brainstorm and make a list of possible challenges and solutions.

References

Agar, M. (1996). *The professional stranger: An informal introduction to ethnography*. San Diego: Academic Press.

Allen, J. (2007). *Creating welcoming schools: A practical guide to home-school partnerships with diverse families*. New York: Teachers College Press.

Barton, D., & Hamilton, M. (1998). *Local literacies: Reading and writing in one community*. London: Routledge.

Botelho, M. J. (2006). We have stories to tell: Gathering and publishing stories in a Puerto Rican community. *School Talk, 11*(4), 2–3.

Boutte, G. S., & Hill, E. L. (2006). African American barbershops: If schools were barbershops. *School Talk, 11*(4), 5.

Chen, Y., & Gregory, E. (2004) "How do I read these words?": Bilingual exchange teaching between Cantonese-speaking peers. In E. Gregory, S. Long, & D. Volk (Eds.), *Many pathways to literacy: Young children learning with siblings, grandparents, peers, and communities* (pp. 117–128). London: RoutledgeFalmer.

Delpit, L. (1995). *Other people's children: Cultural conflict in the classroom*. New York: New Press.

Delpit, L., & Dowdy, J. K. (2002). *The skin that we speak: Thoughts on language and culture in the classroom*. New York: The New Press.

Denzin, N. K. (1997). *Interpretive ethnography: Ethnographic practices for the 21st century*. Thousand Oaks, CA: Sage.

Dyson, A. H. (2003). *The brothers and sisters learn to write: Popular literacies in childhood and school cultures*. New York: Teachers College Press.

González, N. E., Moll, L. C., & Amanti, C. (Eds.). (2005). *Funds of knowledge: Theorizing practices in households and classrooms*. Mahwah, NJ: Lawrence Erlbaum.

Greenfield, P. M., & Cocking, R. R. (Eds.). (1994). *Cross-cultural roots of minority child development*. Hillsdale, NJ: Lawrence Erlbaum.

Gregory, E. (2008). *Learning to read in a new language: Making sense of words and worlds*. Los Angeles: Sage.

Gregory, E., Long, S., & Volk, D. (2004). *Many pathways to literacy: Children learning with siblings, grandparents, peers, and communities.* New York: RoutledgeFalmer.

Guerra, J. C. (1998). *Close to home: Oral and literate traditions in a transnational Mexicano community.* New York: Teachers College Press.

Gutiérrez, K. D., Baquedano-López, P., & Tejeda, C. (1999). Rethinking diversity: Hybridity and hybrid language practices in the Third Space. *Mind, Culture, and Activity, 6*(4), 286–303.

Gutiérrez, K. D., & Orellana, M. F. (2006). The "problem" of English learners: Constructing genres of difference. *Research in the Teaching of English, 40*(4), 502–507.

Gutiérrez, K. D., & Rogoff, B. (2003). Cultural ways of learning: Individual traits or repertoires of practice. *Educational Researcher, 32,* 19–25.

Haight, W. (2002). *African-American children at church: A sociocultural perspective.* Cambridge: Cambridge University Press.

Heath, S. B. (1983). *Ways with words: Language, life, and work in communities and classrooms.* Cambridge: Cambridge University Press.

Hull, G., & Schultz, K. (2002). *School's out!: Bridging out-of-school literacies with classroom practice.* New York: Teachers College Press.

Irvine, J. J. (2003). *Educating teachers for diversity: Seeing with a cultural eye.* New York: Teachers College Press.

Lindfors, J. (1999). *Children's inquiry.* New York: Teachers College Press.

Long, S. (1998). Learning to get along: Language and literacy development in a new cultural setting. *Research in the Teaching of English, 33*(1), 8–47.

Long, S. (2004). Passionless text and phonics first: Through a child's eyes. *Language Arts, 81*(5), 61–70.

Long, S., Anderson, C., Clark, M., & McCraw, B. (2008). Going beyond our own worlds: A first step in envisioning equitable practice. In C. Genishi, & A. L. Goodwin (Eds.), *Diversities in early childhood education: Rethinking and doing.* New York: Routledge.

Long, S., Bell, D., & Brown, J. (2004). Making a place for peer interactions: Mexican American kindergartners learning language and literacy. In E. Gregory, S. Long, & D. Volk (Eds.), *Many pathways to literacy* (pp. 93–104). London: RoutledgeFalmer.

Nieto, S. (1999) *The light in their eyes: Creating multicultural learning communities.* New York: Teachers College Press.

Nieto, S. (2004). *Affirming diversity: The sociopolitical context of multicultural education* (4th ed.). Boston: Pearson.

Paley, V. G. (2005). *A child's work: The importance of fantasy play.* Chicago: University of Chicago Press.

Pérez, G. M. (2004). *The Near Northwest Side Story: Migration, displacement, and Puerto Rican families.* Berkeley: University of California Press.

Purcell-Gates, V. (1995). *Other people's words: The cycle of low literacy.* Cambridge, MA: Harvard University Press.

Rogoff, B. (1990). *Apprenticeship in thinking: Cognitive development in social contexts.* New York: Oxford University Press.

Schultz, K. (2003). *Listening: A framework for teaching across differences.* New York: Teachers College Press.

Solsken, J., Willet, J., & Wilson-Keenan, J. (2000). Cultivating hybrid texts in multicultural classrooms: Promise and challenge. *Research in the Teaching of English, 35*(2), 179–212.

Street, B. V. (1999). *Multiple literacies and multi-lingual society.* London: NALDIC Literacy Papers: National Association for Language Development in the Curriculum.

Tatum, B. D. (2007). *Can we talk about race?* Boston: Beacon Press.

Taylor, D. (1997). *Many families, many literacies.* Portsmouth, NH: Heinemann.

Taylor, D., Altiere, M., Sultana, S., & St. Jean, P. (2000). Making literacy webs in schools, families, and communities. *School Talk, 6*(1), 1–3.

Taylor, D., & Dorsey-Gaines, K. (1988). *Growing up literate: Learning from inner-city families*. Portsmouth, NH: Heinemann.

Valdés, G. (1996). *Con respeto: Bridging the distances between culturally diverse families and schools: An ethnographic portrait*. New York: Teachers College Press.

Volk, D., & de Acosta, M. (2004). Mediating networks for literacy learning: The role of Puerto Rican siblings. In E. Gregory, S. Long, & D. Volk (Eds.), *Many pathways to literacy: Young children learning with siblings, grandparents, peers, and communities* (pp. 25–39). London: RoutledgeFalmer.

Volk, D., & Angelova, M. (2007). Language ideology and the mediation of language choice in peer interactions in a dual language first grade. *Journal of Language, Identity, and Education, 6*(3), 177–199.

Vygotsky, L. (1978). *Mind in society: Development of higher psychological processes.* Cambridge, MA: Harvard University Press.

Wallman, S. (1984). *Eight London households.* London: Tavistock.

Zentella, A. C. (2005). *Building on strengths: Language and literacy in Latino families and communities.* New York: Teachers College Press.

11 Issues in Funds of Knowledge Teaching and Research

Key Concepts from a Study of Appalachian Families and Schooling

Ellen McIntyre

One Sunday morning, a rural Kentucky classroom teacher and I, her collaborating researcher, attended a ribbon-cutting ceremony at the brand new African American church in the county. One of Louise Ann's students, Shontay, age 6, did the actual cutting of the ribbon because she was the youngest child in the church. The mood was celebratory and we were welcomed as featured guests. The next week at school, Louise Ann told all the children in the class about the event. She explained that Shontay received special attention because she was the youngest.

Shontay offered, "My cousin is 6 too, but I am younger."

Louise Ann asked, "Oh? How do you know?"

Shontay shrugged. Louise Ann said "When is your birthday, Shontay?"

Shontay replied, "December 24th."

"When is your cousin's birthday?"

Shontay shrugged. Louise Ann went to the calendar on the wall. "Let's figure out your exact age, OK?" She proceeded to show the primary grade children how to calculate ages to the month and day, and she did this for Shontay, who was then 6 years old, 9 months, and 6 days old. Then, she asked the class, "When was her cousin born?" Students made guesses until Louise Ann illustrated through counting on the calendar that mathematically, the child must have been born after December 24th and before September 18th of the year after Shontay was born in order to be 6 and still be younger than Shontay.

This simple lesson illustrates one aspect of the kind of teaching that Louise Ann was attempting to do in the late 1990s. Within the context of a large, longitudinal, multi-site study project, teachers and researchers worked to enact "funds of knowledge" (Vélez-Ibáñez & Greenberg, 1992) teaching. That is, we made efforts to understand and value families' skills, knowledge, and experiences and we attempted to make curricular connections to the family understandings for purposes of better student engagement and achievement. Louise Ann acknowledged Shontay's out-of-school experiences and spontaneously turned it into a short math lesson. In addition to spontaneous lessons the teachers also developed highly planned units of study based on family knowledge and experiences.

In this chapter, I will focus on three teachers who had made remarkable changes to their instruction. In doing so, I will highlight some of the issues that arose for us as we attempted to implement this instructional philosophy. Then, I will reflect on issues that arose when researching in this way *with* and *on* teachers, students, and their families.

The Study: Purposes and Theoretical Perspectives

This was a longitudinal, ethnographic study designed to track children's academic development in and out of school. We invited teachers we knew who were reaching out to families in positive and unique ways, to participate in the study. Together we visited the homes of several target children approximately every eight weeks for two years. We referred to these visits as "family visits" rather than "home visits" in efforts to reduce the associated fear some families may have with that term. The focus of the visits was on how we could reach out to parents in ways that enabled us to see school from the students' and families' perspectives. As with all the authors of the chapters of this book, our collaborative team was committed to recognizing the knowledge, skills, and values families hold as resources that could be used to enhance learning. We wanted a reciprocal sharing of information that would improve instruction at school through the building of lasting, trusting relationships between homes and schools. To do this, we not only visited homes, but we also spent time in the communities of the families. We attended festivals, ball games, church ceremonies, picnics, and gatherings at campsites. We conducted extensive interviews of the families based on the family history and culture interview protocol developed by scholars at the University of Arizona (Moll & González, 2003). In this effort, we collected data on families' "funds of knowledge" (Moll & González, 2003; Moll & Greenburg, 1990) and their interests. Funds of knowledge are defined as the various social and linguistic practices and historically accumulated bodies of knowledge that are essential to the functioning of a given family (Vélez-Ibáñez & Greenberg, 1992). Funds of knowledge are derived from families' work; for example, in the families we studied, common funds of knowledge involved mechanics, bookkeeping, farming, and cooking. Funds of knowledge can also include knowledge families have about leisure activities such as sports, television, or hobbies and knowledge families acquire in their places of worship or from community organizations.

As part of the collaborative study, the teachers and researchers spent time focused on improving teaching by creating meaningful, dialogic, rigorous, joint productive activities that extended from family and student understandings. To extend the curriculum from family knowledge, we "contextualized" instruction (Tharp, Estrada, Dalton, & Yamauchi, 2002) whenever it seemed appropriate. We did this in two ways. We used families' funds of knowledge as a starting point to develop curriculum. For instance, in one classroom, the teachers taught lessons in literacy, mathematics, and science in an integrated unit on how we get food, basing the instruction on what students in this rural community knew of farming. The second way the teachers contextualized instruction was to begin with curriculum from their state guide and, where possible, make conscious efforts to link the curriculum to something in the students' lives. The researchers documented these instructional practices, with special attention to contextualization practices, and the teachers collected documents of home-school communication, homework practices, and family involvement in school functions. Together, we examined these data in an effort to describe strategies for reaching out to parents in effective ways. Aspects of this study have been published previously. To read more about the research method see McIntyre, Kyle, & Rightmyer (2005). For more on findings and instructional implications, see Kyle, McIntyre, Miller, & Moore (2002); McIntyre, Kyle, Hovda, & Stone (1999).

Background: The Setting

The communities in which the study took place were rural areas each surrounding a small town, and each community about an hour's drive or a bit more from an urban area. Only a few of the families studied referred to themselves as "Appalachian," instead self-identifying mostly as "country," "small town," "rural" and even "hillbilly" (said in a positive way). Indeed, a few of the families talked of "down home" as a place further into the more mountainous part of the state. However, most families have Appalachian roots (Drake, 2001; Heath, 1983; Lewis & Billings, 1997; Lohman, 1990; Purcell-Gates, 1995). In this chapter, I introduce two communities from the larger study.

Fisher County

Fisher County resides 50–75 minutes southeast of an urban area, and the small town of 800 lies within the county one hour from the city. At the time of the study, only 74% of the adults in the county were high school graduates, and only 11% had a Bachelor's degree or higher, as compared to the nation's percentage at 24%. And while the median income in this county was slightly above the state's average of $33,000 in the year 2000, many failed to fulfill their dream of farming. In 1990, 58,000 Kentucky's residents earned a living through farming, forestry, or fishing. By 2000, that number had dramatically dropped to 16,000 (http://factfinder.census.gov).

There was only one elementary school in Fisher County at the time of the study. Carla and Louise Ann team-taught a group of primary grade students in the large, run-down building in town. Their two classrooms were joined by a half wall. While Louise Ann was responsible for the 5–7 year-olds, and Carla was responsible for the 7–9 year olds, nearly all the teachers' planning and much of their teaching was conducted jointly. Both women were in their early thirties at the start of the study and had been teaching fewer than 10 years. While both held Masters degrees in education, neither teacher regularly participated in professional organizations, research, or professional development outside of school-sanctioned activity. Geography made such participation inconvenient, and both women had outside-of-school responsibilities. For example, Louise Ann was active in her church and the care of her parents. Carla seasonally assisted with harvesting tobacco on her family's farm after school and on weekends.

Both teachers were community-oriented and participated in annual festivals, parades, ceremonies, dedications, and so on. They knew many of the residents in town. Both had made "home visits" prior to the start of the study and were not uncomfortable in the families' homes. It was not a stretch for them to re-think "home visits" as "family visits" and to see them as a way to collect information that they could use to improve their own instruction. Both teachers enthusiastically joined the study team.

Beardon

South of the city, within another rural county, lies a small community called Beardon, which is also the county seat. Beardon looks less like a town than a block of buildings set on a country road with the courthouse, a furniture store, beauty salon, bank, florist, paint store, funeral home, and three churches (Baptist, Methodist, Pentecostal). The mixed economics is evident on the drive through the county: There are scores of tiny box houses, some neatly decorated with flowers hanging from the porch in summer and others more shack-like with peeling paint, an unsteady appearance, and a yard full of "stuff" from cars to toys. Next door to one of these might be a large mansion-like old house with a beautifully landscaped yard. And next to that might sit a trailer alone on a lot. Winding through the county roads, one finds a quilt outlet, fishing club, gun club, and golf club. This county is, like Fisher County, 98% white with a similar occupational and economic make-up as in Fisher Creek, but this was the poorest county we studied, and only 9% of the adults in this county have a Bachelor's degree.

At Beardon Elementary, one of many schools in this large, rural county, Karen taught a group of primary grade children. At the time of the study, Karen had several years' teaching experience, most of them before she left teaching to raise her two children. She returned to teaching in her early forties, wise, mature, and ready for a career. She came back just as the state was undergoing a dramatic educational reform initiative, and Karen was "forced" to learn anew how to teach. She was lucky. The constructivist, child-centered philosophy of the reform matched Karen's understandings about children's development, emotional and academic needs, and best practices. Unlike Louise Ann and Carla, Karen was an outsider to the community in which she taught. She admitted to being wary of conducting family visits as part of the study. This didn't continue, however, as we quickly learned that the community was safe and comfortable, with friendly, helpful people.

Funds of Knowledge of Appalachian Families

There were many similarities across the two communities: the White majority, the rural county, the distance from the city, low education levels of adults, and poverty (some of it extreme). Through interviews and observations, we delineated a list of understandings, skills, and values many of the families held. These included knowledge of farming procedures (particularly tobacco and dairy); equipment, safety, and responsibility around the farm; basket-making, crocheting, and other crafts; cooking; car mechanics; television; church rules, procedures, and beliefs; the Bible; construction; lawn work; sports; workings of organizations such as the

Veterans Administration and the Department for Human Resources. Common funds of knowledge across all families included food, religion, and television. Common funds of knowledge across all the children included animals, television, and other popular cultural media.

Additionally, many of the families held similar values. Many had a strong sense of identity about being a country person. Many viewed family as a priority, and were respectful and dedicated to all members. Some families lived with extended families, either out of necessity or by choice. Others lived very near extended family. Many also had a sense of community and responsibility to their town or church. There seemed to be a commitment to the geographic area, not uncommon for people of Appalachian descent (Hillis & Ralston, 2001; Wallace & Diekroger, 2000). All the families valued hard work and education, although reading and writing in the traditional sense were not common activities for most families.

These funds of knowledge and values affected how the families operated on a weekly basis, and ultimately, how teachers interacted with and taught the children. This information enabled us to gain a deeper understanding of the relationship between home and school from the families' perspectives. We learned very specific information about individual families. For instance, we learned that Amber at Fisher County loved nature and art and knew much about both, and that Amber's mother was distressed about Amber not getting instruction in art and she was afraid Amber would lose interest and fail to develop her talent. With this kind of information, the teachers had opportunities to change instruction to better meet the needs of the children. Indeed, the most immediate action with Amber was to institute lessons about artists within reading groups using the famous "Getting to Know the World's Greatest Artist" series of books. Amber, with a small group of other interested students, had the opportunity to learn about the lives and work of Renoir, Picasso, Matisse, Degas, Warhol, Rothko, and others.

We learned also what interests and values the families had. For example, Christianity played a major role in many of the families' lives. Most were Southern Baptist, but a few were "just Christian" and fewer still, Pentecostal. Church activities abounded for many, both during the week and on Sundays. Some of the children sang in the choir, and many other church-related events occurred year-round. Church provided a social network for many and even a support group for some. Religious paintings hung in some of the homes, and many of the families talked about church as one of the most positive parts of their lives. Through knowledge like this, we were able to better communicate with the students and families in ways that ultimately affected their schooling. For example, merely acknowledging having seen a student at church or Sunday school and a reference to what was read there seemed to awaken children's interest in what was read at school. Or, activities such as creating a mini math lesson from a conversation about a church activity, such as in the opening example of this chapter, were simple ways of acknowledging the out-of-school lives of students and their families. The teachers made explicit connections between the two places without ever bringing religion into the public school. In the next section, I explicate this instructional approach more vividly to illustrate how what the teachers learned from the family and how the community visits became powerful tools for engaging the children more deeply in academics.

The Teaching Approach

The teachers in these two schools worked on this study as collaborators, providing data, reflecting on their instruction, and meeting together monthly to talk about how to best meet the needs of the children. In particular, the teachers worked toward implementing a constructivist (Richardson, 2003) approach to teaching, In order to do this, the teachers attended to the five standards for instruction outlined by the Center for Research on Education, Diversity, and Excellence (CREDE): (1) joint productive activity (teachers and students work together on joint products); (2) language across the curriculum (teachers help students apply literacy strategies and language competence in all areas of the curriculum); (3) rigorous curriculum (teachers design instruction to advance understanding at complex levels); (4) instructional conversation (teachers instruction in small group using academic dialogue as tool for learning); and (5) contextualization (teachers contextualize instruction in students' experiences). This last standard is the focus of this chapter, as it is derived from the research on funds of knowledge teaching. Yet, as I hope to make clear, these instructional standards work in concert. For more on these standards, see Tharp, Estrada, Dalton, & Yamauchi (2002).

At times during the study, the teachers planned highly contextualized lessons based on what they knew about students' and families' funds of knowledge. These lessons were often interdisciplinary as a part of a unit of study on a particular topic. Louise Ann and Carla planned lessons around agriculture, and they culminated it in "Agricultural Field Day," a community event that showcased uses of the land. Karen developed a unit on "Experts" in which all students worked with family members to become expert at something and prepare to share their expertise with the whole class. All the teachers varied activities to include students' preferences and provided a variety of grouping opportunities such as time for individual and cooperative work.

Family Knowledge and Mathematics

Some of the finest examples of how teachers contextualized instruction with students' family knowledge occurred in their mathematics teaching. However, math was the area in which sustained contextualization seemed to elude all the teachers. Indeed, sustaining this kind of teaching is an issue I address in a later section of this chapter. Still, these examples illustrate the possibilities of contextualized instruction based on families' funds of knowledge.

At Beardon, Karen knew that many of her students' families were interested and adept at cooking. Some were homestyle cooks who worked without recipes, but most relied on cookbooks. Karen wanted to see her students assisting the adults at cooking (in efforts to get them to avoid so much prepared food so many people live on today), and so she decided to explicitly teach the children how to read recipes. With recipes on the overhead projector, Karen conducted "think aloud" lessons in which she modeled her own thinking on the parts of a recipe and how to organize the cooking. She also brought in measuring cups and spoons and turned the lesson into a measurement activity. Her second and third graders learned not only a reading skill, but they learned more about fractions and the mental and physical preparation it takes to cook from a recipe. Karen planned a subsequent "Family Night" (Kyle, McIntyre, Miller, & Moore, 2005) in which children and guardians cooked together.

At Cane Creek, Louise Ann and Carla prepared for "Agricultural Field Day," a community-wide event in which farmers presented and celebrated their work, by initiating lessons prior to the big day. They wanted to capitalize on children's knowledge of farming to learn more complex concepts about agriculture and to improve their mathematics and literacy skills. In one lesson, the teachers led the class of primary grade students in creating a graph of foods they preferred that came from the farm. One child offered, "rhubarb!" and it received a chorus of "Yea, me too!" Children mentioned tomatoes, corn, milk, and "salad." One child said, "Hamburger!" and it started an argument about whether hamburger came from the farm. Louise Ann explained how the beef came from the cow and was processed and put in stores, but that originally it came from the farm. Louise Ann added it to the list, but this got the children (and Louise Ann) thinking, and after some discussion, the class decided they had better list only foods that they could eat directly from the farm without going elsewhere, or they would have to list nearly everything. After listing and tallying the foods, Louise Ann showed the children how to create a bar graph from the information. Thus, while the children learned how to create and read a graph, they were also learning a bit about the economics of farming and what happens to some foods before they are eaten.

A second lesson in preparation for Field Day focused on economics, estimation, and problem solving. The teachers filled a plastic swimming pool with 29 gallons of water, filled a box with 20 pounds of grain, and brought in 75 pounds of hay (about two bales). After observing and discussing this scene, the teachers told the children that this was what one cow ate in a day! Then, they asked the children estimation questions such as, "What would the room look like if we had to feed two cows? Three cows? Four? How many rooms of feed would we need to store enough food and water for twenty cows?" These conceptual economics and mathematics problems were discussed and children had the opportunities to draw or write about their thinking (McIntyre, Sweazy, & Greer, 2001).

These lessons were some of the more ideally planned and implemented mathematics lessons that connected closely to students' family knowledge. They illustrate the promise of this kind of instructional and curricular approach. However, they did not occur often for a variety of reasons discussed later in this chapter.

Contextualized Reading Instruction

Literature was an easier curricular area for contextualizing instruction in the experiences of the children. All teachers had a wide array of books, both fiction and nonfiction, for reading. They took the time to select books they knew their individual students would enjoy. They selected books with the same ethnicity, family structure, housing arrangements, geographic location, and interests (baseball, pets) that they knew the children were experiencing. One teacher from the larger study often emphasized these connections, for example by saying, "Oh! Jeremiah, I found this great book about Michael Jordan. I know you are interested in him and I thought you might want to read this." Another teacher gathered multiple picture books about grandparents because many of her students had close ties to grandparents. Louise Ann and Carla found many books about famous African Americans for their one black student. They also personally selected a "just right" book or two for each child to read at home with family members every day. Karen too provided books on students' interests. One of her students in particular was interested in cooking because his mother worked in food preparation. Karen invited him to take one of her cookbooks home (cookbooks were part of the library collection). She said, "I encouraged him to take home a children's cooking book over the weekend. There was a lemonade recipe in there that he tried. He said he tried it and it wasn't too good. After discussing it, he tried it again and it was fine."

Contextualization can also occur in less obvious, but equally important ways by simply connecting to students' prior understandings from previous lessons, making learning explicit, and scaffolding students' understandings (Tharp et al., 2002; Tharp & Gallimore, 1993). The following examples illustrates the more subtle ways that contextualization occurs.

> It is February of 2000, and Karen's second and third graders are busy reading and writing by 9:15 a.m. Pairs of children are sitting on the couch, floor, or reading center with pillows and stuffed animals reading books of their choice. A few are at the tables writing from their writing folders. Upon entry Karen cannot immediately be found. She is in the back of the room, on the floor with three children. She is directly teaching them a comprehension strategy using nonfiction text on bears. It is a complicated text for this age group, but Karen pursues the lesson, showing her expectations that the children can read this. She reads a part of the text aloud: "Before North America was settled by Europeans, grizzlies enjoyed a much larger range that extended across the plains, the western states and into Mexico. Now, because of habitat loss and human threat, the grizzlies' homeland is more isolated and restricted to higher treeless areas, valley bottoms and tundra." She points to the map on the wall and indicates the western states, plains, and where Mexico is in relation to Kentucky. She says, "That's what they mean by 'range'. It means they had much more room to roam than they do now. Why? Why don't they have as much room?"
>
> A child responds (which wasn't captured.)
>
> Karen says something else, then says, "Sometimes when I read something that happened a long time ago, I have to close my eyes and imagine what it was like then, and what it is like now. Now, we have lots of houses and buildings and cities, but back then we didn't. Now, this land is our habitat [a word the children are already familiar with], but then it was the bears'

habitat. You try it. Close your eyes and imagine what it was like back when grizzlies roamed this area and what it is like now. I will read the next part to you." She reads to the next sentence to them, and asks, "so, what does this [the grizzlies' homeland is more isolated and restricted] mean?"

A child says, "It is more dangerous."

"It could be more dangerous, but why?"

"Because there are more people now."

"Yes, the area is *restricted*; it means they don't have as much room as they did before." (She indicates again on the map.) The dialogue goes on a bit, and then Karen asks the children to read the next page on their own, and then to close their eyes and imagine what the author might want us to "picture in our minds." The children read, but all seem to struggle. Karen senses this, and first reads the page fluently to the children and then again talks them through the page by closing her eyes and telling the children "the pictures she is making in her mind" as she thinks about what the author is communicating about bears. After more guidance through the book, she dismisses the group saying, "We will read some other books on bears" tomorrow.

In this vignette, Karen taught in small groups, based on students' needs. She incorporated science and social studies content (bears and habitat) within her literacy lesson, attempting to get children to construct understandings of history at the same time as learn an explicitly-taught and demonstrated comprehension strategy (imaging or visualizing). Her expectations were high for this second and third grade group, indicated by the vocabulary, complex thinking and reading she expected them to do. She contextualized instruction through building on previously learned concepts such as habitat and the different housing structures of today. She also contextualized instruction through the use of maps, by referencing previous instructional strategies, and through her expert scaffolding in helping readers learn new words and visualize what they are reading. Importantly, contextualization is about building on students' understandings, those acquired at home (i.e. "spontaneous" concepts, as described by Vygotsky, 1978) as well as those learned in school (i.e. "scientific" concepts, as described by Vygotsky, 1978).

This lesson illustrates an important point within this chapter: Contextualized teaching, or funds of knowledge teaching, is not merely a cute thing to do once in a while. It is a philosophy of teaching based on a sociocultural theory of teaching and learning (Cazden, 1988; Rogoff, 2003; Tharp & Gallimore, 1993; Vygotsky, 1978), and the standard of contextualization must work in concert with the other standards described earlier in this chapter (joint productive activity, rigorous curriculum, language and literacy across the curriculum, and dialogic teaching). In the following example, a very enthusiastic Louise Ann contextualizes instruction, but the lesson lacks rigor or productivity.

It is August in the second year of the study. It is a little after 10:00, the usual time for reading instruction. The children are sitting on the rug area and Louise Ann, the teacher, is sitting on a chair with two books in her hands. She says to the children, "This morning when I was looking through the bookshelves, trying to decide what I would read today, I found one book and thought, 'This one is perfect.' It's called, *Stop Those Painters*. Now, why would Miss _____ choose this book today? Does anybody have any ideas?"

One child says, "It's about painting the walls."

"What happened this summer?" Louise Ann explains that the entire building has been painted. She continues, "I know it feels neat to run your hands across the wall, 'cause it feels really neat. But, we need for you not to touch it for a long time because the paint is not hard enough. We need to be real careful so that the paint can completely dry so it lasts a long time. When I found this book, I thought it would be a good one to choose."

Louise Ann begins to read the book with lots of expression. She stops at one point to ask, "Why do you think they wanted them to stop painting?" A child responds (can't hear).

"What were they painting?"

The kids chorus, "The windows!"

Louise Ann asks, "What would happen if we painted the windows?"

A child says, "We couldn't see outside."

The teacher reads, "Painters painting ham and cheese, stop those painters, stop them please!" and many of the children yell, "Yuck!" (This is a rhyming book.) Louise Ann stops at one point, and tells the kids to close their eyes (in anticipation of the picture). She shows the book of a person painting the tree. All the kids laugh. The kids laugh and laugh as the teacher continues to read and show the pages of painted cows, teachers, toys, girls, and boys. A child says, "Miss _____, what if they painted you!?" Louise Ann tells a story about this summer when she was at the school and she touched wet paint and nearly ruined her favorite, hot-pink shirt. She finishes the book. All children appear engaged.

Louise Ann regularly used literature to teach reading and spent much time motivating children about the content of the books she would read to her primary grade students. This lesson is similar to Karen's but with subtle, yet significant differences. Louise Ann contextualized the lesson by connecting to students' experiences with the paint. She teaches the children to make pictures in their minds (although not explicitly) as she reads to them. The key difference is the lack of rigor. While the children and teacher clearly enjoyed the lessons, the students were not pushed beyond what they could already do. The children didn't do the reading or much of the thinking. She attempted dialogue with the children but often did not succeed in getting the children beyond recitation. While attempting to implement the concept of contextualization and dialogic teaching, Louise Ann recognized that this lesson was not quite as developed as she had hoped.

THEORETICAL APPLICATION: CONTEXTUALIZED TEACHING

While contextualization, drawing on and making connections to children's out of school experiences, can enhance student engagement and the meaningfulness of academic activities, the examples in this section illustrate a critical point: Contextualized teaching does not necessarily, in and of itself, produce robust learning. In addition to contextualization, teachers must attend to a number of key pedagogical elements—clear and challenging objectives, carefully sequenced instruction, rich dialogue, differentiation that accounts for differences in children's skill levels, and thoughtful assessment—in order to optimize children's learning. Think of a lesson or unit that you might have experienced, observed, or taught that connected with children's experiences and fostered engagement. Did the lesson or unit result in optimal learning for the students? Why or why not? If not, what other key pedagogical elements were missing? In planning contextualized instruction, how can you make sure to account for the variety of elements that result in robust learning? What elements may be particularly challenging for you to incorporate?

Writing Instruction as Key to Connecting Home and School Lives

All three teachers implemented what they viewed as a "writing workshop" in their classrooms, based on models developed by Graves (1983) and others. However, Karen had participated in the National Writing Project soon after returning to teaching, and her workshop was distinctly different from Louise Ann's and Carla's.

In Karen's classroom children self-selected topics and worked on pieces from "writing folders" over a period of several drafts. Karen was highly cognizant of the importance of writing about what you know, and so she made special efforts to invite her students to write about their families and family knowledge. The children created family scrapbooks and histories. They wrote about their animals, siblings, television programs, and other important events and activities in their lives. They "published" their texts in a variety of ways on a regular basis (about once a month) through "fact books" (chapter books on topics they had studied), persuasive essays, stories, personal narratives, poetry, letters, messages to friends on "message boards" and reports on topics they studied. For example, Karen was recorded saying to one child during the writing workshop period, "You had a birthday this summer. Can you write about your birthday? Your grandmother that [whom] I know? Did she come to your birthday?" (The child nods.) "I want you to take some time to think about that day. You might even look at photographs at home if you have any because they can help you remember a lot. Then you can decide if you want to write about it." During each workshop period, Karen taught mini-lessons on skills, and was *expert* at modeling her own thinking while writing as a demonstration for the children. She also explicitly connected reading with writing, such as when she said, "Did you hear that simile, 'as quiet as a rabbit in danger'? I know some of you use similes in your stories."

Louise Ann and Carla also purposefully helped students write about what they knew. They both knew so much about each of their student's families and the children's out-of-school lives, and then brought this knowledge into the classroom to invite their students to write. Louise Ann helped one student make a "goat book" that illustrated the care of goats, and Shontay wrote about the ribbon-cutting ceremony. Carla regularly encouraged her students to write about their families—who they are, their work, the excursions they take, and so on, similar to topics in Karen's room. Yet, these teachers rarely took the students beyond the draft and oral sharing of their texts. Only twice during the school year, did the teachers assist the students through the entire writing *process* culminating in a completed product that others could read. Neither teacher demonstrated how to write nor connected techniques of published writers to their students' texts. This is not surprising or uncommon. While the state reform emphasized more writing, not all teachers were provided with good professional development on how to teach writing. The contextualization the teachers practiced in their instruction was critical for engaging the students, but it was not sufficient. This brings me to reflect on some of the issues that arise when doing funds-of-knowledge teaching and research.

Issues in Funds of Knowledge Teaching

It is critical to address the issues that arose during the implementation of the funds-of-knowledge approach if this model of instruction will be valued. First, some teachers were more successful than others at contextualizing instruction within students' knowledge, skills, and experiences. Teachers must have a deep understanding of the content they are teaching in order to make thoughtful connections with students' experiences. We provided professional development for the teachers and assisted them in making well-planned curricular lessons or units based on family knowledge. For Karen, one demonstration and a few group discussions were enough for her to take off with funds of knowledge teaching. It wasn't as easy for Louise Ann and Carla. At times, their expectations seemed lower than they should be, and some activities were less than rigorous.

Mathematics seemed to be the curricular area that was left decontextualized from students' experiences more often than the others. The teachers worried about not following the scope and sequence provided by math textbooks, and so an explicit connection between family knowledge and math teaching was an "extra" and often done when researchers were scheduled to observe. While other researchers have shown how mathematics can be intricately woven into this philosophy of teaching with elementary children (Kahn & Civil, 2001), many examples are with older students (González, Andrade, & Carson, 2001) where teachers may have had more mathematics training and thus could have a better sense of where curricular connections can occur.

One reason that the model is not easy to implement is that contextualizing instruction within family knowledge isn't enough to lead children's development. Too often, teachers created lessons on concepts or skills students already knew, rather than teaching just beyond what they knew or could do alone. As Vygotsky explained, instruction should be within students' zones of proximal development, defined as "the distance between the actual developmental level as determined by independent problem solving and the level of potential development as determined through problem solving under adult guidance or in collaboration with more capable peers" (Vygotsky, 1978, p. 86). It takes knowing students well (which all teachers did) and knowing what the next concept or skill should be to help students move in their development. This was somewhat more difficult. The CREDE standard of "rigorous curriculum" does not simply mean tough standards or prep school level work; actually, it is meant to signify instruction that is one step beyond what students can do on their own. Thus, if Louise Ann had the students read the book about painting by echoing her reading demonstration or by chorally reading some lines with her, the students' literacy learning may have been pushed just far enough for an opportunity to learn. Since learning leads to development (Vygotsky, 1978), it is imperative that lessons occur within students' zones of proximal development in order for development to happen.

Thus, contextualized lessons must occur in concert with all the other CREDE standards. Not only should the curriculum be rigorous, it should also include opportunities for oral language or literacy development, be dialogic, and have some sort of joint product as an end goal. In the above example, while some children offered answers to questions by the teacher, a more inclusive lesson may have had students talk in small groups about the topic before the all-class sharing time. It could have included an opportunity for joint productive activity. For example, the lesson may have included homework in which students and families were to read two books and compare them in a Venn diagram or other graphic organizer. The math lesson opening this chapter could have included joint productive activity by getting students in pairs to compare ages by years, months, and days. Clearly, funds of knowledge teaching takes immense planning in order to integrate family knowledge in ways that help students acquire "scientific" understandings that systematically improve literacy and mathematics skills. If this kind of teaching is done only spontaneously, the potential is there for this approach to be viewed as "funzy-wunzy" (Cambourne, 1988) or "anything goes."

Finally, implementing a funds of knowledge approach to teaching through attention to the five CREDE standards requires an examination of the existing school curriculum and pedagogical standards. It requires looking carefully at district and state mandates to see how the curriculum can be better contextualized on a broad, systematic basis. The teachers in our study had to deal with district mandates, and only some of the teachers were able to balance the mandates with their student-oriented curriculum. In our study, we talked a bit about how the funds of knowledge approach and CREDE pedagogy in general can be applied to any curriculum, but not all the teachers managed to view the approach as a philosophical stance toward teaching and learning. After the study period ended, I visited Louise Ann and Carla's classrooms and informally asked how they were attempting to build curriculum around students' understandings. Louise Ann hesitated and explained that the school received a new grant for a reading program and they were focused on that now. The program was not theoretically opposed to the sociocultural approach to teaching that they had been working on. Yet, they saw it as something different and gave themselves permission to ignore the specifics of the standards they had been working on.

We learned that it is necessary for teachers to take time to reflect on the relationship between what they are attempting to do and what others are expecting them to do.

THEORETICAL APPLICATION: CONTEXUALIZED TEACHING

Two of the three teachers described here appeared to give little attention to contextualized teaching after the conclusion of the research study. This raises a serious concern about the sustainability of such teaching. Why might teachers' commitment to the important principle of contextualization wane? Given the many demands on teachers, how can they sustain this commitment? Where can they find the motivation, support, and resources to continue to develop their ability to connect to and build on children's out-of-school experiences and learning resources?

Issues in Doing Funds of Knowledge Research

Our goal in this study was to learn information from the families that could improve teaching. Sometimes, not surprisingly, we learned information that took us on emotional roller coasters. We learned painful information that caused us to question our next moves—what to do when we see there is no food in the house, whether to intervene when we believe parents may benefit from a parenting class, how to help children cope with previous abuse or the death of a sibling. We learned to be prepared for dealing with uncomfortable or disagreeable situations. We have come away from some visits depressed and unable to help or unsure how. To do this kind of work, we must be prepared to be a little depressed at times. Of course, just as often, we came away exhilarated at the love and humor we found in the homes.

As in many schools serving poor children, the teachers in these classrooms still struggle with daily challenges. These challenges can manifest themselves in episodes such as hitting, throwing objects, swearing, and tantrums. We know that these children, in their young lives, have faced such experiences as: the death of a father and subsequent remarriage of the mother; the death of an older brother due to "huffing" (breathing in fumes from a household item such as paint, glue, or air conditioner coolant for the purposes of intoxication); parents' divorce; changes in custody arrangements; an alcoholic parent; sexual abuse, and other such emotionally charged events (McIntyre, Kyle, Hovda, & Stone, 1998). Understanding these events in the lives of our students is immeasurably important. We have often wondered how much we must have missed about our students' lives before we began the visits.

Our research team discussed "deficit" and "difference" views of children, and we worked to learn to appreciate differences in our students and build on them. But we also learned information during the family visits that has challenged our own views of the differences. There are simple differences such as how much the families read books or watch television, but we have also been met with racism and homophobia. We have been confronted with religious views different from our own and different approaches to child discipline. Learning to respect differences can be conflicting at times, and we found we needed time to "process" data by talking with each other about our feelings. This processing time with another who shares respectful views of children and families is critical for this kind of work and should be built into teaching time.

We had begun our study with respectful views of the many poor and working-class Appalachian and "Affrilachian" (Walker, 1996) families we were to encounter. Yet, to some extent, some of us held "text-book" beliefs about these groups of people, expecting cultural patterns that have been written about from an anthropological perspective in efforts to elicit respect toward and interest in the many varied subgroups of Americans. Yet, as helpful as the literature was, we also learned how different the children and their families were from one another. Our concepts of "culture" began to disintegrate as we became part of these families' lives and discovered what seemed like an infinite number of home routines, literacy acts, educational practices, and funds of knowledge. In addition, practices and knowledge were not static; they changed for the families over the course of the many years we worked together. We soon learned that we cannot study participation in a culture without studying change; people's performance depends in large part on the circumstances that are routine in their community. As Rogoff (2003) explains, "Humans develop through their changing participation in the sociocultural activities of their communities, which also change" (p. 11). Thus it is critical when doing this work to remain open-minded.

From this study, several instructional implications can be derived:

- Get to know students' and their families' out-of-school lives—their work, interests, relationships, family routines and practices, and behavior.
- As often as possible, see your students outside the school—in their homes, playgrounds, ball fields, grocery stores, houses of worship, and civic centers.
- Talk with families about students in positive ways as often as possible. Let them know you care about their children.
- Invite families into the classroom—to observe, share something about themselves, perform clerical work, or assist in teaching.
- Plan an instructional unit around topics of family interest, and be sure to teach far beyond what the students already know.
- Be sure to talk with another educator about this work. Talk with someone about what you see, think, and feel when learning more about your students and their families. Talk with someone about how to communicate respectfully with families. Talk with someone about planning instructional lessons around student and family knowledge and interest.

In conclusion, our efforts to embark on a funds-of-knowledge or contextualized approach to teaching had immense rewards. Most obviously for all teachers and families were the positive relationships that formed and the deep interest in education. Additionally, most of the teachers were forced to examine their practices and work toward change. It was not easy, however, and some were more successful than others. Thus, a funds of knowledge or contextualization approach to teaching requires courage, flexibility, and openness to change.

Ideas for Discussion, Extension, and Application

1. This chapter moves toward practical applications of a funds of knowledge or contextualization approach. What surprises or stands out to you about Karen, Louise Ann and Carla's experiences?
2. This chapter problematizes the practice of family visits, identifying real tensions and conflicts that can occur when gaining entry into diverse family homes. Issues include trust and confidentiality, ethical responsibilities, teacher versus researcher roles, respect for what counts as difference, etc. In small groups discuss these issues and ways to process and respond to them.
3. Sustainability can become a critical issue in teachers' attempts to implement a contextualization approach. What are the implications of excluding contextualized instruction for diverse learners' engagement in academics and success in schools?

References

Cambourne, B. (1988). *The whole story: Natural learning and the acquisition of literacy in the classroom.* New York: Ashton Scholastic.

Cazden, C. (1988). *Classroom discourse: The language of teaching and learning.* Portsmouth, NH: Heinemann.

Drake, R. B. (2001). *A history of Appalachia.* Lexington, KY: The University Press of Kentucky.

González, N., Andrade, R., & Carson, C. (2001). Creating links between home and school mathematics practices. In E. McIntyre, A. Rosebery, & N. González (Eds.), *Classroom diversity: Connecting curriculum to students' lives.* (pp. 100–114). Portsmouth, NH: Heinemann.

Graves, D. (1983). *Writing: teachers and children at work.* Portsmouth, NH: Heinemann.

Heath, S. B. (1983). *Ways with words.* Cambridge: Cambridge University Press.

Hillis, M., & Ralston, E. (2001). Developing a rationale for multicultural education in rural Appalachia. *Rural Educator, 23,* 7–12.

Kahn, L. H., & Civil, M. (2001). Unearthing the mathematics of a classroom garden. In E. McIntyre, A. Rosebery, & N. González (Eds.), *Classroom diversity: Connecting curriculum to students' lives* (pp. 37–50). Portsmouth, NH: Heinemann.

Kyle, D. W., McIntyre, E., Miller, K., & Moore, G. (2002). *Reaching out: A K-8 resource for connecting with families.* Thousand Oaks, CA: Corwin Press.

Kyle, D. W., McIntyre, E., Miller, K., & Moore, G. (2005). *Bridging school and home through family nights.* Thousand Oaks, CA: Corwin Press.

Lewis, R., & Billings, D. D. (1997). Appalachian culture and economic development: A retrospective view on the theory and literature. *Journal of Appalachian Studies, 3,* 3–42.

Lohman, R. A. (1990). Four perspectives on Appalachian culture and poverty. *Journal of Appalachian Studies*, 2, 76–88.

McIntyre, E., Kyle, D. W., Hovda, R. A., & Stone, N. (1999). Nongraded primary programs: Reform for Kentucky's children. *Journal for Education for Students Placed at Risk*, 4(1), 47–64.

McIntyre, E., Kyle, D. W., & Rightmyer, E. C. (2005). Families' funds of knowledge to mediate teaching in rural schools. *Culture and Education*, 17(2), 175–195.

McIntyre, E., Sweazy, R.A., & Greer, S. (2001). Agricultural field day: Linking rural cultures to school lessons. In E. McIntyre, A. Rosebery, & N. González (Eds.), *Classroom diversity: Connecting curricula to students' lives*. (pp. 76–84). Portsmouth, NH: Heinemann.

Moll, L. C., & González, N. (2003). Engaging life: A funds of knowledge approach to multicultural education. In J. A. Banks & C. A. M. Banks (Eds.), *Handbook of research on multicultural education* (pp. 699–715). San Francisco: Jossey-Bass.

Moll, L. C., & Greenberg, J. B. (1990). Creating zones of possibilities: combining social contexts for instruction. In L. C. Moll (Ed.). *Vygotsky and education: Instructional implications and applications of sociohistorical psychology* (pp. 319–348). Cambridge: Cambridge University Press.

Purcell-Gates, V. (1995). *Other people's words: The cycle of low literacy*. Cambridge, MA: Harvard University Press.

Richardson, V. (2003). Constructivist pedagogy. *Teachers College Record*, 105(9), 1623–1640.

Rogoff, B. (2003). *The cultural nature of human development*. Oxford: Oxford University Press.

Tharp, R. G., Estrada, P., Dalton, S., & Yamauchi, Y. (2002). *Teaching transformed: Achieving excellence, fairness, inclusion, and harmony*. Boulder, CO: Westview Press.

Tharp, R. C., & Gallimore, R. (1993). *Rousing minds of life: Teaching, learning, and schooling in social context*. Cambridge: Cambridge University Press.

Vélez-Ibáñez, C., & Greenberg, J. (1992). Formation and transformation of funds of knowledge among U.S. Mexican households. *Anthropology and Education Quarterly*, 23(4): 313–335.

Vygotsky, L. S. (1978). *Mind in society: The development of higher psychological processes*. Cambridge, MA: Harvard University Press.

Walker, F. X. (1996). *Affrilachia*. Lexington, KY: University Press of Kentucky.

Wallace, L. A., & Diekroger, D.K. (2000). *The ABCs in Appalachia: A descriptive view of perceptions of higher education in Appalachian culture*. ERIC document, October. Clearinghouse RC023531.

12 How Knowledge Counts

Talking Family Knowledge and Lived Experience into Being as Resource for Academic Action

Elizabeth Yeager and
Ralph A. Córdova, Jr.

It was early in the year in our fourth grade classroom, the day we were beginning to think about our work in science. We were building a list together of the 'actions of scientists,' trying to construct a beginning idea of work *we* would be doing as scientists that year. I explained what we were going to do and then I asked the question for the first time.

Mr. C.: So, what do scientists do?

Vanessa was the first to raise her hand, slowly followed by several other students.

Vanessa: They ask questions.

Mr. C.: Like what?

Vanessa: They learn about plants . . . I interviewed my grandma about spider webs and how she stops cuts with them. I made an oral history . . .

I immediately recognized that Vanessa was referring to experiences she and several other classmates had had in their third grade year, because I was their third grade teacher. What's more, the other 16 students who had been in that class recognized and accepted what Vanessa said as well. What Vanessa shared with our class—that she drew on her work with and interview of her grandmother as a resource for describing the work of scientists and saw her grandmother's knowledge as a form of scientific knowledge—did not surprise me. I also knew that she had asked to use her work with her grandmother as the basis for her science fair project in third grade—and had done so. In fact, what Vanessa said seemed 'ordinary', so ordinary that we (the other students and I) accepted, without further comment, the action that Vanessa proposed—"They ask questions"—and her rationale. I wrote the action on the chart we were constructing together and we continued this beginning of the work of science in our class in fourth grade.

(Ralph Córdova, teacher)

In this vignette, Vanessa and her teacher, along with other students in this fourth grade classroom, accepted as 'ordinary' an interaction in which Vanessa linked work with and knowledge from a family member's lived experience with the academic work of science. Through this interaction, Vanessa, a student from a linguistically diverse family and school-defined as having a 'learning disability,' proposed to the group a potential action, an inquiry practice, in which scientists might engage—asking questions. She also drew on family knowledge and her own academic and literate work in acquiring that knowledge—interviewing and writing an oral history—as evidence to support her proposal, thereby linking her own actions with the actions of scientists.

It was this perceived 'ordinariness' of talking about and drawing on family knowledge and experience in the context of academic work that raised questions for us, initially as teacher researchers of life in our own classrooms, and then as researchers more distanced from the classroom. How did talking about and drawing on family knowledge and lived experience as resource for work in academic disciplines become 'ordinary' for Vanessa and her teacher, as well as other students who accepted what Vanessa proposed to the class? Where did Vanessa's statement come from—what were the roots of and routes to this moment in time in the early weeks of this fourth grade class?

In this chapter, we examine questions raised by Vanessa's and her teacher's interactions. Since Vanessa linked what she said in fourth grade to what she had done the year before, with the same teacher, we travel back in time by engaging in what we call backward mapping across time and events to examine the first days of Vanessa's (and her peers') third grade experience. We do so in order to unfold the ways in which Ralph, one of the authors of this chapter, and Judy,[1] his teaching partner (job share) in third grade, created opportunities for learning (Tuyay, Jennings, & Dixon, 1995) that honored and included family members and their potential funds of knowledge, while constructing, with their students, a *common language, or discourse, for learning of the classroom* (Lin, 1993). In and through this process, family members and their knowledge/lived experience were shaped as resources for accessing and engaging in/with complex disciplinary knowledge and practice, a resource on which Vanessa and others drew as they began (re)constructing what would count as the work of science in fourth grade.

THEORETICAL APPLICATION: LANGUAGE OR DISCOURSE *OF* THE CLASSROOM

The local discourse *of* the classroom is jointly constructed over time by members of a particular social group through what they say and do together. Ways of talking and enacting disciplinary knowledge become commonplace to insiders, though outsiders can only understand it by taking a close look into the history of the classroom community. The language or discourse *of* the classroom creates opportunities for learning; that is, what is constructed and *available* to be learned at the group level. Teachers' discursive decisions to include family knowledge as an academic resource has direct implications to how students view their own and their family members' lived experiences. Imagine being a student in a particular classroom and grade level and being asked by

1 The authors would like to express their appreciation and thanks to Judy Hug, third grade teacher, for helping to write this chapter into being through her teaching with Ralph Córdova in the year studied and for her job-sharing work for eight years with Ralph.

your teacher to guide a new student into the classroom routines and learning events, roles and expectations, and ways of interacting. What would the new student need to know in order to appropriately participate in classroom routines? What would become apparent about the classroom culture, social practices and academic resources?

Addressing questions of how family knowledge comes to count, or not count, in classrooms as academic resource, is important for teachers and researchers, given the complexity teachers and their students face as, every day, students enter diverse classrooms bringing with them, as Moll and his colleagues argue, "funds of knowledge" that are constructed in and through their family, neighborhood, and community experiences (González, Moll, & Amanti, 2005); that is, funds of potential knowledge(s) resources on which they do or could draw for understanding, acting, talking, and being in the world. Often, however, these "funds of knowledge" and experience can be lost as potential resources in the face of increased reliance on standardized measures of achievement, time constraints, and the potential narrowing of what is available to be learned, particularly in disciplinary areas such as social science, science, mathematics, the arts, and others. Rather than seen as resource, home, neighborhood or community knowledge and lived experience may be viewed from a deficit perspective, as barriers to learning, and as irrelevant to the academic work of school (e.g., Comber, 2000).

One challenge presented to teachers, then, is not only to understand how to learn from family funds of knowledge themselves (González et al., 2005), and how to afford students opportunities to work with and learn from family members in a variety of ways (e.g., Botelho, Turner & Wright, 2006; Córdova, 2008; Dyson, 1999; Olmedo, 2004). It is also how to discursively shape with students a *view of* family members, and their funds of knowledge and lived experience, as *relevant* to, and potential resource for, accessing and engaging in and with academic disciplines—how to 'talk,' as well as 'act,' family members, as well as their funds of knowledge, into being (Dixon & Green, 2005; Green & Dixon, 1993) as academic resources and part of the everyday life of classrooms.

To make visible how this occurred in Ralph and Judy's third grade class, we first examine how teachers oriented students to life in what they named their classroom "community" and initiated academic work on the first day of class, as well as how practices initiated or foreshadowed on the first day were also identified across the first week of school. Finally, we briefly focus on how academic work with family members in social science and science was initiated and included inquiry and literate practices initiated during the first week of class. In doing so, we hope to make visible *how* teacher/student discourse matters in (re)shaping family members and family knowledge and experience as resource for academic action.

Additionally, we provide ways of understanding how Ralph's role of teacher as ethnographer became an important resource for his work in developing a discourse of the classroom, as he, and Judy, constructed *opportunities for learning* (Tuyay et al., 1995) what it meant to be a student, mathematician, historian, ethnographer, scientist, interviewer, and more in this classroom (Reveles,

Córdova & Kelly, 2004; Yeager, 2003). We draw on what was learned by taking an ethnographic perspective on everyday classroom life to uncover what occurred in Ralph and Judy's classroom. We do so in the hope that what we make visible might serve as resource others may draw on who seek to create opportunities for students to access and engage with rich disciplinary knowledge and practice while drawing on funds of knowledge from multiple sources.

An Ethnographic Perspective as Resource

To frame how an ethnographic approach became a resource for both Ralph and his students, we first present his voice as a teacher researcher in order to uncover the ways in which teachers can connect research and practice and begin to *theorize that practice* as they work with students (and their families or family knowledge) in the small moments of classroom life (Yeager & Green, 2008).

> Classrooms ought to be places where culture(s) is created, not reproduced. In other words, we become aware of the ways in which teachers and students co-construct and create a space for learning that has never existed before. And if we create culture, what sort of culture is it that we envision for ourselves as teachers and for our students? I need, then, to engage my students, from the very first day of school, in developing conversations where the subject of learning is not just the "official" curricular content, but how we shape it. And through our learning and developing understandings, how we are then shaped by the very cultural setting we've been in the process of co-constructing. This leads me, as a teacher researcher, to develop ears and eyes that notice on two levels: the moment-to-moment events of everyday classroom life and how it is shaped by my students and me, and the over-time constitutive constructing of classroom life. From these two angles of vision, then, I see the need to pay attention not only to how I purposefully introduce ethnographic language and theoretical approaches to my students in the moment, but what consequence it has for student learning, in and across moments.
>
> My students learn that we are always in the process of becoming. For example, becoming scientists is a dynamic process in which we're always engaged; not something you arrive at once you are an adult and in college. If it's something we create together, what sort of scientists do we wish to become? What do scientists do? Where in our everyday lives can we find examples of scientific inquiry, whether explicit or tacit? My students also learn that we must stop frequently to examine what it is that we have been learning about science, but also about ourselves, the doers of science—young scientists.
>
> This requires an orienting lens and for me, an ethnographic perspective enables me to always ask, "what's happening here?," as I attune myself to learn to see learning.
>
> (Ralph, Santa Barbara Classroom Discourse Group, 1992)

Ralph's perspective on teacher as ethnographer provided him (and later his students) with a lens for understanding life in his classroom and constructing opportunities for learning for his students. We begin our exploration of how theory guided our ethnographic perspective by presenting excerpts from an essay on his classroom community by a student, Arturo, who became a student ethnographer in Beth's, another author of this chapter, fifth grade class.

> In our Tower [name of classroom, located in school tower] community, we have our own language as well as the languages we bring from outside (like Spanish and English) which helped us make our own language. So, for example, someone that is not from our classroom community would not understand what insider, outsider, think twice, notetaking/notemaking, literature log and learning log mean. If Ms. Yeager says we are going to "make a sandwich", the people from another class or room would think that we were going to make a sandwich to eat. Of course we aren't, but that is part of our common language . . .
>
> . . . These words are all part of the common Tower community language and if someone new were to come in, we would have to explain how we got them and what they mean. We also would tell them that we got this language by reports, information, investigations, and what we do and learn in our Tower community.
>
> (Arturo, 1994–95)

In his essay, written at the end of the school year on what it meant to be a member of his particular classroom community, Arturo makes claims about the ways in which life in classrooms shapes and is shaped by the discursive and social interactions. He argues that outsiders to his class need to understand how ways of knowing, being and doing are talked-into-being over time in relationship to particular events and activity at the group as well as individual level. The argument that Arturo makes about the interdependent nature of learning and development echoes conceptual arguments in sociocultural theory. For example, Lima (1995) argues:

> We have two dimensions of development [and by implication, learning]: one that resides in the individual and the other in the collectivity. Both are interdependent and create each other. Historically created possibilities of cultural development are themselves transformed by the processes through which individuals acquire the cultural tools that are or become available in their context.
>
> (pp. 447–448)

In other words, Arturo, at age 10, like Ralph, understands the constructed, local and situated nature of the developing text(s) of the classroom. He also understands how he, as a member of the class, is afforded particular opportunities for learning, which in turn, shape personal or individual knowledge of content, practices, and processes required within the group (Yeager & Green, 2008). In our research community (Santa Barbara Classroom Discourse Group), we call these consequential progressions (Putney, Green, Dixon, Durán, & Yeager, 2000).

In the sections that follow, we will continue to tie the understandings that Arturo and Ralph inscribe, and that Vanessa makes visible in her interaction with her teacher and her peers, with current theories about classrooms as cultures-in-the-making and learning as a collective and individual, interdependent process. In this way, we make visible how everyday knowledge and practices of students and the professional knowledge of this teacher constitutes sociocultural theory that is consistent with perspectives on the study of language, discourse in use, and knowledge construction. Drawing on this view of theory-practice relationships, we construct a theoretical perspective on the *language of the classroom* that teachers can draw on to construct their own principles of practice for exploring and discursively shaping multiple knowledges and lived experiences as academic, social, and cultural resources, not barriers, in their classroom (e.g., Dixon, Frank & Green, 1999; Green, Dixon & Zaharlick, 2002).

Initiating Family as 'Ordinary': Toward a Language *of* the Classroom

In order to trace the roots of and routes to Vanessa's and Ralph's interaction during the first weeks of fourth grade, we chose to examine, given the space and scope of this chapter, the beginning of the year during which the actions Vanessa referenced occurred—the first day of class in third grade. As Arturo argued above, life in classrooms, including what is 'talked-into-being' as a common discourse of the classroom, is constituted in the discursive work that members of the group do together, and requires teachers and students alike to continually shift how they are reading and interpreting the developing texts being constructed. What is constructed as "class" and ways of being, knowing and doing in that class, occurs over time in and through small moments of actions and interactions that are both explicit and implicit. How students know where to sit as they first enter the classroom, or how they are greeted as they enter, are examples of small moments that are both visible and often invisible, that students must learn to read and interpret in order to know what to do, how to position themselves within the group, who they can be, what can be talked about, how, with whom, in particular contexts, what to do, what to display and what to know (Yeager & Green, 2008). Thus what occurs on first day(s) is important to understanding how particular ways of being, knowing and doing in a classroom are initiated.

The small moments that occur over time and events, particularly when taken cumulatively, have potential important consequences for the kinds of opportunities for learning what it means to be a student (or mathematician, reader, writer, historian, scientist, member of a group, and so forth) that are available and to whom they are available. Moments of discourse and action can be seen as texts that become observable and available to be read by members, if members learn how to read them. This reflects arguments made by Erickson and Shultz (1981), who view people as contexts for each other and people's actions as texts to be read and interpreted.

In unfolding the events of the first day in this third grade classroom, we make visible the discursive work of teachers and students across those events. Through this process, we identify ways Ralph and Judy initiated, through constructing a series of *public texts* with students, in and through discourse and actions, a range of practices for talking and acting a discourse of the classroom into being, in and through which students were afforded opportunities to orient to drawing on family members and family knowledge and lived experience as potential resource for engaging in the everyday life of the classroom.

Figure 12.1 represents a map of the unfolding sequence of activity, constructed

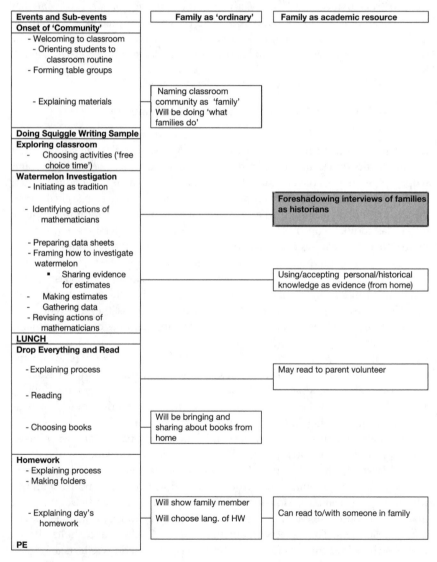

Figure 12.1 Day 1: formulating family as 'ordinary' classroom resource.

from video records of the first day. In this figure, the work of students and teachers is represented as actions. In column one of Figure 12.1, we identify the major events on which time was spent across the first day. In columns 2 and 3, we identify moments within those events in which the notion of 'family' was initiated or *foreshadowed* as what would be an 'ordinary' part of everyday life, as well as moments in which teachers began to orient students toward a view of family members and family knowledge as resource for academic action.

As can be seen in Figure 12.1, column one, we have termed the first event, the "onset of community", although, based on teacher knowledge, 'class' might be said to have begun prior to the official start of school that day. That is, students visited the classroom before class to talk with teachers. Many came with family members, some of whom the teachers knew from having had siblings in previous years. When the bell rang, students gathered outside the classroom, were greeted and teachers introduced themselves, especially important since these teachers shared one job and Ralph would be teaching one day per week (participating fully in the first and last weeks of school, at family events, and during parent–teacher–child conferences, among other things). In addition, students were instructed how to come first to the floor as a group after entering and putting materials on desks.

It was in the floor space that students were oriented to 'group,' as teachers welcomed students, asked them to share what they already knew about third grade, and introduced students to 'routines' of the class, such as how they would independently indicate whether they were eating lunch in the cafeteria on a particular day. Judy introduced students to the routines in English while Ralph, a bilingual teacher, explained these routines in Spanish (even though this was not 'officially' a bilingual class). *Drawing on two languages as resource* enabled all students, including those few who were more proficient in their heritage language (Spanish), to access what was being made available at the collective level. In and through these opening sequences, the teachers initiated ways of being, doing and knowing that included *making choices, sharing personal/historical experiences* with the group, and *asking questions*, thus affording students opportunities to *contribute to the construction of public texts* available to be 'read' by the group.

It was in the second phase of the first event—Explaining materials—that class as a "community" was formulated and named. As seen in column two, it was also during this phase that the notion of "family" was initiated. Students were seated at their table groups with a box of supplies, such as crayons, placed in the center. As seen in the following transcript segment, Judy began this phase by providing students with a *rationale* for taking responsibility for caring for the materials, both individually—as members of a larger group—and as a table group.

> You are a member/ of a community of learners./ When you walk/through that door/ you become part of a big/ family/ that works/ together./ ... And we/ become/ like a family together./ We have/ to learn/ to be good/ to one another/and respect each other/ and respect/ the classroom/ that we all/ share/ together./ So that's what/ families do,/ right?/ They take care of each other,/ they help/ each other,/ k?/ They're there/ for each other./ Well, this is a bigger family ...

In this segment, Judy is creating what we call a *meta-discourse about key organizing practices* (Yeager & Green, in press), and a referential system for how to name these practices. Through this *meta-discourse* (Yeager, 2003), Judy afforded students opportunities for ways of being and acting with each other and with the classroom that were linked to being members of a community, which, in turn, was linked to being in a family. At the same time, she defined what families do (*naming the practice*), in this moment, in particular ways—taking care of each other, helping each other. In this small moment, which had potential consequences for future events, Judy (and later Ralph, in Spanish) afforded students opportunities for drawing on what they might already know about families as resource for knowing how to take particular kinds of responsibility in relation to other members of their classroom community or "family."

THEORETICAL APPLICATION: META-DISCOURSE

Meta-discourse is language used to talk *about* practice (i.e., talk about actions and language use). It is reflexive and responsive. Building on discourse-in-use perspectives, this perspective on meta-discourse supports a view of teacher *discourse*, rather than instances of teacher 'talk', as central to both historically linking texts and practices across time and (re)formulating classroom life for students, making what is constructed and what students need to bring and use in order to make sense of the evolving text of the classroom available. This chapter shows the use of teacher meta-discourse to (re)formulate family knowledge as academic resource. Teachers, *with* students, made discursive choices that served to contextualize practices, while making connections necessary for students to draw on family knowledge as resource for learning disciplinary knowledge. What kinds of discursive choices and connections might you make to make visible for students what resources they would need to bring and use in a particular new context, such as reading this chapter?

As seen in Figure 12.1, similar small moments occurred across the day in which particular practices were initiated or *foreshadowed* ("you *will* be doing this") that signaled to students the potential role of family members in the everyday work of this classroom. For example, as seen in column two and three of this event map, when the academic work of D.E.A.R. (Drop Everything and Read), a period for daily reading books of choice, was initiated, the teachers foreshadowed ways in which this event would occur on subsequent days. Not only would students choose and read books in the classroom, they would also have the opportunity to bring and share about books from home, and to read to a parent volunteer. Significantly, teachers did not formulate these practices as special, but as ways of doing that would be regular parts of the school day across the year.

Finally, homework was formulated (begun to be talked into being) as something that would be shared with parents on a nightly basis. Students were to *talk with family members about their work.* Students could *choose the version of the homework* that was in the language (Spanish or English) most accessible for family members. Again, what was foreshadowed on this day had potential consequences for the ways in which students would access family knowledge and experience across the year. Family members were initiated as important participants in the students' academic experiences.

As Figure 12.1 makes clear, Ralph and Judy initiated a series of public texts on this first day in ways that served to formulate or foreshadow practices that were to be ordinary, routine parts of everyday life and that began to orient students toward family members as active participants in the academic, cultural and social life of the classroom community—and to construct a discourse of the classroom that linked being a member of this community with ways of being, talking, and acting with and about family. In asking students to share personal/historical/family knowledge, including what they knew about third grade, for example, Judy invited students to create intertextual ties (Bloome & Egan-Robertson, 1993) between background knowledge (including family knowledge) and current actions needed to participate in the group in order to create a developing text that was available to all students and to create the discourse practices and referential system that initiated, what Arturo called, "our own language of the classroom." In order to understand how family members and family knowledge and lived experience were initiated—or foreshadowed—as potential resource for accessing and engaging in disciplinary work, however, we shift our ethnographic eyes (Frank, 1999) or lens to take a more focused look at one event—the initiation of academic work in mathematics.

Initiating Academic Work: Formulating Family Knowledge in Context of Inquiry Practices

The event called the "Watermelon Investigation" occurred both prior to and following recess on the first day of class in third grade, and continued until lunch. Ethnographic data indicate that this event was actually part of what we call a *cycle of activity* that occurred over the first five days of school, culminating on Day 5 in a process of thinking back on and individually and collectively evaluating the work of the investigation.

As seen in Figure 12.1, the investigation on Day 1 unfolded across six phases, in which students would orient to the work as mathematicians, would investigate watermelons (investigating weight on this first day), using a variety of inquiry and literate practices to do so. The investigation occurred in shifting interactional spaces (Herás, 1993). In other words, students moved from whole group spaces to table group to working alone, back to table group, and to whole group in order to do the work of the investigation. Thus students were afforded opportunities to access the mathematical investigation and its content in multiple spaces, both public and private.

Ralph initiated the Watermelon Investigation by situating it within a "tradition" in his classrooms. During this phase, he *invited students to contribute to the public text* by sharing any historical knowledge they might have about the investigation tradition, including what they might know from siblings who had been in Ralph's previous classes.

During this time, he also told students that they would be "thinking like" mathematicians and "doing the work" of mathematicians. Ralph afforded students the opportunity to draw on personal/historical knowledge of mathematics, while at the same time *reformulating* that knowledge in particular ways in the context of making a list of the actions of mathematicians. Ralph invited students to contribute to this list by asking them, "What do mathematicians do?" During this process, he made a reference to what he knew to be second grade curriculum by invoking what students might know about verbs and "action words" and what they represented. He also asked students to "Think about your own experience. What do *you* do?" In other words, the teacher reformulated (talked into being) sharing personal/historical knowledge and experience as an academic practice in this context.

Table 12.1 presents a transcript segment in which Ralph makes visible, using a *meta-discourse* about the actions and practices, what it is he is asking students to do and why. This table represents a way of closely looking at the discursive work that is potentially being accomplished in and through the talk (Bloome, Carter, Christian, Otto, & Shuart-Faris, 2005). In this case, the teacher is speaking to the whole group as they construct the collective text, a list of "actions of mathematicians." The teacher first situates what it is he is asking students to do and then provides a rationale for this that is linked to doing the work themselves as members of the discipline. In other words, he affords students opportunities for *positioning themselves as mathematicians* in their

Table 12.1 Day 1: orienting students to family in context of academic work

Teacher discourse	Potential work being accomplished
so/I want us to think about what it is that mathematicians/do because/I want you	Providing rationale for engaging in particular practice (generating list of actions of mathematicians)
to be/thinking/like mathematicians	Orienting students to actions *as* members of discipline—will be thinking *as* mathematicians
we're going/to start another project next week/some time in social studies	Foreshadowing future work in new academic discipline
where you're going/to do interviews	Foreshadowing new practice—interviews
with your families	Will be gathering information from families
I'm going to ask/you to think like historians	Foreshadows work with families in context of work students will be doing as members of discipline (thinking like historians)
people/who do and/write histories	Families as potential resource for "people who do or write histories"

future work by situating what they will do in this context of *thinking like mathematicians.*

He then reformulates what it means to do the work of members of a discipline in this class, by foreshadowing work in another discipline, social science, where students will be asked to "think like historians", "people who do and write histories". In doing so, the teacher also foreshadows what students will do in the context of a particular inquiry and literate practice—interviewing. Critically, by *linking the work that students will do with family members to the work of members of an academic discipline,* the teacher, in and through his discursive choices, orients students to a locally situated view of family members and knowledge as potential resource for doing that work as historians, as resource for learning what it means to be "people who do and write histories."

In the next phase, the teacher and the students jointly framed what it would look and sound like to investigate watermelons. In doing so, Ralph initiated and engaged students in a range of inquiry practices that they would later use when they worked with their own watermelons in table groups, always discursively linking these practices to both the list of actions of mathematicians and to the work students were doing by "thinking like mathematicians." The inquiry practices included, for example, generating and asking questions about the watermelon (a practice also critical to interviewing), making estimates and supporting estimates with evidence (as opposed to "guesses"), gathering data (observing, holding watermelons to estimate weight, using a scale to weigh watermelons), as well as literate and social practices such as writing to record data, sharing ideas, estimates and evidence with others, listening to others.

As students each made personal estimates about a watermelon in the whole group, Ralph asked, "What is your estimate? What evidence are you basing that on?" As students shared, personal/historical/family experience and knowledge, such as holding a baby brother who seemed to weigh much the same as the watermelon, going to the store with a family member and holding a watermelon, holding a toy that seemed comparable, were accepted as legitimate forms of supportive evidence for the estimates made. Later, students would have the opportunity to revise their estimates based on new data/evidence, such as weighing the watermelon using a scale. In this initial framing of the investigation, then, personal/historical/family experience was reformulated as one potential resource on which to draw for engaging in the academic inquiry practice of supporting with evidence.

Throughout this investigation, as students worked with their table group to investigate their own watermelon, Ralph continually made visible multiple ways in which members were taking up actions of and thinking like mathematicians, as well as the *value of multiple sources and kinds of data (including family experience),* some stronger as supportive evidence than others, depending on how they were used. In this way, he made visible the interdependence of collective development and the development of individuals-in-the-collective, such as Vanessa, as well as the importance of the common language and practices being formulated to what would constitute that interdependent relationship over time.

(Re)Formulating Patterns of Practice Across Days

By unfolding much of the first day of class, we made visible ways in which Ralph and Judy initiated and formulated, to talk into being, practices that would potentially become part of students' repertoire of action for knowing, being and doing in this classroom, including those that would link family, family members, and family knowledge and experience to what would count as everyday life, including disciplinary knowledge and practice. In using a meta-discourse about practices, teachers not only named those practices, and then made visible what engaging in those practices would look and sound like in this classroom, they also provided an explicit rationale for engaging in and using the practice (Yeager, 2003; Yeager & Green, 2008) (e.g., this is what mathematicians do; this is what members of the class do; this is what families do). In this way, they helped students initiate a set of norms and expectations, as well as roles and relationships, for different events within the class, which were important for constructing a common community, or what we call, a culture-in-the-making, of which drawing on family members and family knowledge as resource for academic action would be an integral part.

To become part of a repertoire of actions, to become *patterns* of practice or *principles* of practice, however, processes and practices must be repeated, constantly (re)formulated over time, both proposed to and recognized by the collective and, potentially, by individuals-in-the-collective. In the following brief analysis, we make visible patterns of practice that were (re)formulated across the first week of school in this classroom.

As Table 12.2 shows, a range of practices in at least five major areas were formulated or foreshadowed on the first day of class. Practices formulated on the first day were sometimes repeated everyday across the first four days of school as part of an ongoing process (ethnographic evidence shows that these same practices continued across the first three weeks of school). But sometimes new things were introduced and/or Ralph or Judy reformulated with students how a practice would be used in new ways in new contexts. For example, practices involving family members, such as talking with parents about home and school work, in a general way, were reformulated on subsequent days during the first week.

Table 12.2 Range of patterns of practice initiated and (re)formulated—first week of third grade

Major areas of practice

- Inquiry practices (e.g., observing; asking questions; gathering data from multiple sources; supporting with evidence; interviewing to gather data)
- Literate practices for engaging in academic work (e.g., writing to learn; sharing ideas, personal/historical experience; note taking; reading)
- Social practices (e.g., working in multiple interactional spaces; caring for materials)
- Practices involving doing the work of and "thinking like" members of academic disciplines
- Practices for orienting to and engaging with family members/knowledge as resource

On Day 2, for example, students were given a photo of themselves engaging in the work of mathematicians with watermelons; then asked, for homework, to describe, in writing, what was happening in the picture (foreshadowing their future work as ethnographers) and to tell a family member about the investigation. On the following day, the practice was again reformulated as sharing in the public space what was learned with and/or from family members. In this case, as a student shared what she had described and how she was asked questions by a family member, Ralph asked, "Who asked you and what did you say?" After the student responded, the teacher continued, "So you told her about the watermelon investigation. Did you tell her something specific about the watermelon investigation? What did you tell her?" Ralph made visible to the students that what was being shared was important information and potentially helpful to all as they moved further into the investigation. In this way, the teacher discursively reformulated talking with family members (and what they asked and shared with the student) in explicit ways, including asking others to listen carefully, as resource not only for the particular student, but also as potential academic resource for the group as a whole.

Finally, each practice that was foreshadowed on Day 1 was (re)formulated across subsequent days. For example, interviewing, foreshadowed by the teacher on the first day as an important discipline-based inquiry and literate practice that students would engage in (and referenced by Vanessa in fourth grade), was initiated on Day 3 as a way of learning about other students, and reformulated as interviewing family members to gather data in the second and third weeks of school.

In each case, as Ralph or Judy discursively formulated the practice, he or she named it as part of the common language of the classroom and then reformulated it with students in each of the new contexts. Building a repertoire for actions in the first moments, then, is not just a tool but an ongoing way to reformulate practice as resource for future academic study.

Reformulating Family Knowledge as Disciplinary Resource

In this section, we present a brief analysis of the ways in which patterns of practice (re)formulated during the first week of school were again reformulated in the context of initiating the study of "everyday life" and disciplinary work as ethnographers and scientists. We focus on how the teacher made meta-discursive choices that served to frame for students the work they would be doing as integrally linked to the work of engaging in and with family members and their "funds of knowledge" as resource for academic action within and across disciplines. Since practices that were referenced by Vanessa in her interaction in fourth grade (e.g., interviewing) were among those (re)formulated in particular ways during the first weeks of school in third grade, we focused on Ralph's teaching Mondays when what we will make visible occurred.

Day 5 of the school year consisted of a series of linked events that, together, served to (re)formulate the inquiry practice of *observing carefully to gather data*, initiated during the Watermelon Investigation, as the work of ethnographers who seek to understand and learn from "everyday life" in different groups or "communities" and spaces. In the initiating event, Ralph and his participant-ethnographer partner, John, framed for students what it meant to be an ethnographer who "notices" what is happening in everyday life and engaged them in observing as ethnographers and taking notes on video segments from the first week of school.

In discussing what students "noticed" in the video, the teacher situated the work of noticing everyday life in the context of understanding what counted, where, when, as academic disciplines: "Just like we began noticing what we do as mathematicians in our Watermelon Investigation, we will be noticing what scientists do when we learn science." In doing so, Ralph made what we call an *intercontextual link* (Floriani, 1993) between what students had done in a previous disciplinary context and what they would be doing in another, science—in the context of a third discipline, ethnography. Finally, as Arturo theorized in his essay, Ralph and John discussed how everyday life, whether in classrooms or at the grocery store, is made up of what people do and say together and how people who "notice" that life in particular ways can learn from people by studying what they do: "This year we're going to learn to become noticers, or ethnographers . . ."

At the end of the day, students were introduced to a homework assignment that built on their work in the morning, in which they would "practice" being ethnographers by observing and taking notes on an everyday family event at home, and bringing the notes *to share with others* in their next class session with Ralph. The following transcript segment is from Ralph's framing of this particular assignment and makes visible the ways in which he meta-discursively provided students with a rationale for observing everyday life at home as resource for doing current and future disciplinary work:

> Tonight we're going to practice/being an ethnographer . . . /The reason that we're going/to be/doing this/ . . . /Next Monday/when we're here/we're going to be able to see/what all of our families do./We're being ethnographers right now/and you need to know how to do this,/so when we start social studies,/ you know how to be able to use/these skills of observation/to help you/

Another way of thinking about the work Ralph accomplished in and through his meta-discursive choices, is that, in affording students at the collective level a rationale for what studying an everyday family event would later enable them to do, he created a discursive pivot (Córdova, 2004; Larson, 1995) in the space of explaining the homework around which and to which individuals-in-the-collective could orient in order to make sense of their past, present, and future linked actions.

Finally, the teacher linked what was discursively formulated as "everyday life" in the morning event to what students would be doing as homework, by making visible that home is a space where everyday life occurs and therefore a place for engaging in academic work as ethnographers, as well as a place where families engage in actions that can be studied and brought into the classroom as data for future disciplinary learning in the group. In doing so, he linked home with classroom, signaling the permeability (Córdova, 2008) of both places as potential spaces for learning.

Ethnographic evidence indicates that what was (re)formulated on Day 5 was consequential for what was initiated as 'preparing the mind' to do science and "think like scientists", in and through work with family members, (as well as in other disciplines), on subsequent teaching days for Ralph. For example, on Day 10, Ralph invited students to share with the class what they learned from observing everyday life at home. In placing their family observations in the public space as potential resource for the collective, the students, with their teacher, were able to contribute to the public text being constructed and in so doing shaped a collective view of everydayness as potential material resource for engaging in disciplinary work and building disciplinary knowledge. In and through this process, Ralph was able to subsequently frame the day's homework as drawing on *family* knowledge in order to begin constructing *disciplinary* knowledge and practice in science. He did so by (re)formulating interviewing as an ethnographic practice that included inquiry practices in which students had already engaged. In and through this homework, an interview with a family elder about "a favorite science memory," students would be able to access one kind of scientific knowledge—applied knowledge and/or experience in everyday life.

Across the first three weeks of school, practices both initiated and foreshadowed on Day 1 were discursively reformulated as patterns of practice, available to students as potential resource. Practices such as collecting data based on family interactions, and sharing and discussing the data in the public space of the classroom as a way to (re)formulate what could count as learning mathematics, social studies and science, were becoming "ordinary" parts of everyday classroom life.

Conclusion and Implications for Teaching and Research: What We Are Learning?

In this chapter, we have made visible a set of principles of practice that guided teachers in discursively creating, with their students, a common language or *discourse of the classroom* in which family members and family knowledge were (re)formulated as academic resource for accessing new and varied knowledge(s), as well as engaging in discipline-based inquiry practices such as gathering data from multiple sources, generating and asking questions (as interviewers), observing, and supporting with evidence, among others. In turn, what was (re)formulated across time served to shape shared family knowledge and what was learned from disciplinary-based work with family members as resource for the collective as well as for the individual student member of the classroom community.

Drawing on our ethnographic perspective enabled us to make visible how family knowledge as academic resource was formulated as part of the discourse *of* the classroom in third grade and how Vanessa drew on the opportunities afforded her in the previous year to position herself as a scientist in fourth grade, contributing to what was available to be known and understood by the collective. In doing so, we were able to look again at how what we took for granted in our classrooms—drawing on family knowledge as resource for academic/disciplinary action—had been constructed as such, in hopes that this might serve as resource for others or for starting new conversations about how multiple funds of knowledge come to count in particular ways in classrooms.

In other words, engaging in multiple layers of analysis, from an interactional ethnographic perspective (e.g., Castanheira, Crawford, Dixon, & Green, 2001) as both teacher researchers and researchers more distanced from the classroom, became an important way for us to make visible not only *that* family members' knowledge and lived experience were valued as academic resource by both teachers and students, but *how* that knowledge and lived experience was discursively shaped as a powerful, disciplinary resource for both the collective and individuals-in-the-collective.

From this perspective, 'talking funds of knowledge into being' requires more than a shift in curriculum or pedagogical stance in order for interacting with and drawing on family knowledge and lived experience to move beyond activity and beyond the moment for an individual student. Teacher talk, or rather teachers' discursive choices—what they say, when, how, for what purposes—*with* students, matters. Teacher meta-discursive choices can afford students opportunities for linking particular actions to new perspectives about whose knowledge counts, when, where, how, under what conditions, and for what purposes—and for understanding that different knowledges and knowledge practices count in different ways for different purposes. As Arturo describes, we create the everyday, common language (discourse) of the classroom in and through what we do and say. When teachers, with students, draw on multiple resources to shape a particular kind of common discourse of the classroom, then it is possible for both teachers and students, as well as family members, to view family, home, and community funds of knowledge as relevant to, and resource for, accessing and engaging with rich, complex disciplinary knowledge and practice.

Ideas for Discussion, Extension, and Application

1. If, as a teacher, I view family members and family knowledge as resources for school learning, then what do I need to know, ask, and do in order to "talk this view into being" with my students? What do I hope our evolving classroom texts and practices would look and sound like from the first moments of the first day of class?
2. How can teachers continually construct with their students, across the year, a view that connecting to and inquiring into what has been accomplished can be a foundation for subsequent learning?
3. How could teachers engage with their principal, teacher colleagues, parents and community members in conversations focused on bringing into focus the overlapping nature of school and family social worlds so that all can learn from each other?

References

Bloome, D., Carter, S., Christian, B., & Otto, S., & Shuart-Faris, N. (2005). *Discourse analysis and the study of classroom language and literacy events: A microethnographic perspective.* Mahwah, NJ: Lawrence Erlbaum Associates.

Bloome, D., & Egan-Robertson, A. (1993). The social construction of intertextuality in classroom reading and writing lessons. *Reading Research Quarterly, 28*(4), 305–333.

Botelho, M. J., Turner, V., & Wright, M. (2006). We have stories to tell: Gathering and publishing stories in a Puerto Rican community. *School Talk, 11*(4), 2–3.

Castanheira, M., Crawford, T., Dixon, C., & Green, J. (2001). Interactional ethnography: An approach to studying the social construction of literate practices. In J. J. Cumming & C. M. Wyatt-Smith, special issue of *Linguistics and Education: Analyzing the Discourse Demands of the Curriculum.*

Comber, B. (2000). What *really* counts in early literacy lessons. *Language Arts, 78*(1), 39–49.

Córdova, R. (2004). Disjuncture in teacher preparation as rich points for developing professionally: An ethnographic investigation of the inter-relationships of supervisors' and teachers'-in-preparation discursive construction of principles of practice. Dissertation. University of California, Santa Barbara.

Córdova, R. (2008). Writing and painting our lives into being: Learning to see learning in the transformative spaces between school and home. *Language Arts, 86*(1), 18–27.

Dixon, C., & Green, J. (2005). Studying the discursive construction of texts in classrooms through interactional ethnography. In R. Beach, J. Green, M. Kamil, & T. Shanahan (Eds.), *Multidisciplinary perspectives on literacy research* (pp. 349–390). Cresskill, NJ: Hampton Press.

Dixon, C., Frank, C., & Green, J. (1999). Classrooms as cultures: Understanding the constructed nature of life in classrooms. *Primary Voices K-6, 7*(3), 4–8.

Dyson, A. H. (1999). Coach Bombay's kids learn to write: Children's appropriation of media material for school literacy. *Research in the Teaching of English, 33*(4), 367–402.

Erickson, F., & Shultz, J. (1981). When is a context? Some issues and methods in the analysis of social competence. In J. Green & C. Wallat (Eds.), *Ethnography and language in educational settings* (pp. 147–150). Norwood, NJ: Ablex.

Floriani, A. (1993). Negotiating what counts: Roles and relationships, content and meaning, texts and context. *Linguistics and Education, 5*(3 & 4), 241–274.

Frank, C. (1999). *Ethnographic eyes: A teacher's guide to classroom observations.* Portsmouth, NH: Heinemann.

González, N. E., Moll, L. C., & Amanti, C. (Eds.) (2005). *Funds of knowledge: Theorizing practices in households and classrooms.* Mahwah, NJ: Erlbaum.

Green, J., & Dixon, C. (1993). Talking knowledge into being: Discursive and social practices in classrooms. *Linguistics and Education, 5*(3 & 4), 231–239.

Green, J., Dixon, C., & Zaharlick, A. (2002). Ethnography as a logic of inquiry. In J. Flood, J. Jensen, D. Lapp, & R. J. Squire (Eds.), *Handbook for methods of research on English language arts teaching* (pp. 201–224). Hillsdale, NJ: Lawrence Erlbaum.

Heras, A. (1993). The construction of understanding in a sixth-grade bilingual classroom. *Linguistics and Education, 5*(3 & 4), 275–300.

Larson, J. (1995). Talk matters: The role of pivot in the distribution of literacy knowledge among novice writers. *Linguistics and Education, 7*(4), 277–302.

Lima, E. (1995). Culture revisited: Vygotsky's ideas in Brazil. *Anthropology & Education Quarterly, 26*(4), 443–457.

Lin, L. (1993). Language of and in the classroom: Constructing the patterns of social life. *Linguistics and Education, 5*(3 & 4), 367–409.

Olmedo, I. (2004). Storytelling and Latino elders: What can children learn? In E. Gregory, S. Long, & D. Volk (Eds.), *Many pathways to literacy: Young children learning with siblings, grandparents, peers, and communities* (pp. 77–88). London: RoutledgeFalmer.

Putney, L., Green, J., Dixon, C., Durán, R., & Yeager, B. (2000). Consequential progressions: Exploring collective-individual development in a bilingual classroom. In P. Smagorinsky, & C. Lee (Eds.), *Constructing meaning through collaborative inquiry: Vygotskian perspectives on literacy research* (pp. 86–126). Cambridge: Cambridge University Press.

Reveles, J. M., Córdova, R., & Kelly, G. J. (2004). Science literacy and academic identity formulation. *Journal for Research in Science Teaching, 41*(1), 1111–1144.

Tuyay, S., Jennings, L., & Dixon, C. (1995). Classroom discourse and opportunities to learn: An ethnographic study of knowledge construction in a bilingual third grade classroom. *Discourse Processes, 19*(1), 75–110.

Santa Barbara Classroom Discourse Group (1992). Do you see what we see? The referential and intertextual nature of classroom life. *Journal of Classroom Interaction, 27*(2), 29–36.

Yeager, E. (2003). "I am a historian": Examining the discursive construction of locally situated academic identities in linguistically diverse settings. Dissertation. University of California, Santa Barbara.

Yeager, B., & Green, J. (2008). "We have our own languages as well as the languages we bring": Constructing opportunities for learning through a language *of* the classroom. In J. Scott, D. Straker, & L. Katz (Eds.), *Affirming students' right to their own language: Bridging educational policies and literacy/language arts teaching practices.* New York: Routledge.

13   Respecting Children's Cultural and Linguistic Knowledge

The Pedagogical Possibilities and Challenges of Multiliteracies in Schools

Maria José Botelho, Sarah L. Cohen, Lisa Leoni, Patricia Chow, and Padma Sastri

Vignette 1. Lisa introduces a new writing project to her eight-grade class. She asked the children to reflect on their own lives in order to develop a topic.

Lisa: Class, if you were to write a children's storybook about an event in your life, your personal interests, and curiosities, what would you write about?

One student, Kanta made an immediate connection to her life:

Kanta: Ms. Leoni, can I write about leaving Pakistan and moving to Canada?

Lisa: Of course, Kanta! That's a wonderful idea and I can't wait to read your story.

Kanta continued brainstorming possibilities:

Kanta: Ms. Leoni, can we write the book with other students in the class because some of us live close to each other and that way we could work on this at home?

Lisa: Yes, Kanta! Who are you thinking of working with?

Kanta: Well, Sulmana and I are best friends and we always like working together and Madiha is new to Canada and new in our school. I want her to be in our group so I can help her because she only speaks Urdu and doesn't speak English yet.

Seated nearby, Sulmana and Madiha looked on with excitement.

Lisa: I'm sure Madiha and Sulmana would love to work with you (smiling at the other two girls). You know girls, some of the students are writing their books in two languages, perhaps your group would like to do the same.

Kanta piped up: I love speaking Urdu, but can't write it that well, but Sulmana, she is amazing at it and Madiha can help too.

The next time Lisa met with this group to hear about their narrative plan she learned that Sulmana had gone home that night to tell her mother that she needed to practice reading and writing in Urdu so she would do it well for this book. The three girls told Lisa that they had already met after school to figure out the story line.

Kanta: Ms. Leoni, we finished our narrative plan last night at Sulmana's house and we decided that our main character would be called Sonia, but she would really be me, Sulmana and Madiha. Is that okay?
Lisa: Oh, I see. Sonia in your book will represent all of your experiences moving to a new country—is that right?
Sulmana: Yeah, and Madiha thought of that name.
Lisa: I like the ideas you've set out in your narrative plan. You're ready to begin the writing.
Sulmana: But, where do we start?
Lisa: Why don't you start by talking about your ideas in Urdu so that Madiha can fully understand and be included in the process? In order to develop Sonia's character, you will all need to think back to your personal memories and feelings and remember the time you left Pakistan and moved to a brand new country. What do you remember feeling and thinking?[1]

Vignette 2. A handful of grade 5 children have accepted the invitation to add to Thornwood Public School's[2] multilingual "Welcome" bulletin board, mounted every September, in time for the school's Open House/BBQ evening. Patricia has just finished responding to an especially artistic and informative poster when another child seizes the opportunity to talk to her about something that has been on her mind. Months earlier, she and her family had attended Thornwood's cross-generational workshop series, "Parent Involvement as Educator" (PIE).[3]

Meghana: Why don't you have any Telugu/English books?
Patricia: I'm sorry. I couldn't find any to buy for our dual language collection. Why don't you write one for the library?

With that, Meghana sets off with a mission. She recruits her grandmother in publishing a cultural story about uprooting bad habits and cultivating good ones. With her dual language book, she leaves a legacy of pride in her linguistic and cultural heritage and ensures that Telugu-speaking newcomers to Thornwood will feel welcomed, respected for their cultural experiences, and inspired to use their

1 Lisa was a teacher collaborator on the Canada-wide SSHRC funded research project, "From Literacy to Multiliteracies: Designing Learning Environments for Knowledge Generation in the New Economy (Early, Cummins, & Willinsky, 2002; www.multiliteracies.ca).
2 Thornwood, through its many initiatives and the "Dual Language Showcase," has been embracing its linguistic and cultural diversity and encouraging children to use their first language to foster their acquisition of a second language since 1998.
3 This project was initiated by Dr. Sandra R. Schecter of York University and partially supported by grants from the Social Sciences and Humanities Research Council of Canada. Visit http://thornwood.peelschools.org/esl_website/text/pie_project.htm for more information.

accomplishment of another language to raise their voices.[4] Patricia's spirit soars as her vision of a compassionate, multiliterate community of learners flourishes at Thornwood.

Introduction

Many children in Canada and the United States are kept from their most powerful cognitive and social tool, their first language (L1). By the year 2030 the U.S. Census Bureau projects that an estimated 40 percent of school-age children will need English language teaching. Presently in Canada's Greater Toronto Area (GTA), an estimated 40 percent of the current school population are English language learners (ELLs). Cultural and language diversity has always been a reality in Canada. At the time of this writing, we are three Canadian elementary school teachers (Lisa, Padma, and Patricia), a doctoral candidate (Sarah), and a university professor (Maria José). Our chapter builds upon the conceptual framework guiding this volume in light of the growing cultural and linguistic diversity found in schools and classrooms similar to Lisa's. Specifically, we will consider the pedagogical possibilities of respecting children's cultural and linguistic knowledge and drawing on it as resources for learning multiliteracies. Inviting children and families to create dual language texts to augment school library book collections, as Patricia recommends to Meghana, is one literacy practice that honors children's lived experiences and reconciles the roles of teacher and learner.

In constructing this chapter, we were engaged with multiliteracies, that is, speaking, listening, writing, critical reading, and using digital technologies (e.g., voice recording, emailing, and word processing) to facilitate this collaboration. We reconsider school literacies by examining and reconceptualizing literacy, learning, culture/identity, the role of the teacher, and family and community engagement, when and where school happens, and the assessment of student learning. We argue that all children benefit from multiliteracies practices. Even within a mandated curriculum teachers *can* draw on children's cultural and linguistic knowledge; the example above illustrates how Lisa invited her students to co-publish a dual language book on their collective experiences of moving to Canada. Providing her students with opportunities to think critically about their lived experiences helped them make connections to the grade 8 curriculum unit on immigration.

Multiliteracies Framework: Ideas that Guide Our Work

Home languages other than English or French are often viewed in Canadian schools as largely irrelevant to children's educational progress. The assumption is that if teachers do not speak the multiple languages represented in their classrooms, there are no teaching opportunities other than the use of English (or French) as the official language of teaching. We challenge this normalized

---

4 See http://thornwood.peelschools.org/dual/books/telugu/meghana.htm for more information.

assumption and document ways in which children's L1 and literacies can be incorporated into classroom teaching. These teaching practices affirm children's sense of self, nurture academic confidence, and validate their prior knowledge, which is encoded in their L1, as a foundation for learning English and academic content (Chow & Cummins, 2003; Cohen, 2008; Cummins, 2006; Cummins, Bismilla, Cohen, Giampapa & Leoni, 2005; Schecter & Cummins, 2003). We argue on the basis of these findings that teaching for transfer from L1 to English represents an important teaching practice for promoting academic and social engagement and success.

We build on multiliteracies pedagogies and theories (Cazden et al., 1996; Cope & Kalantzsis, 1999; Pahl & Rowsell, 2005; Schecter & Cummins, 2003), which recognize literacy practices as a dynamic and complex repertoire of social practices that help us participate in our daily lives (e.g., text messaging, email, shopping lists, voice messages, listening to the radio, viewing television programs, etc.). Botelho (2007) suggests that multiliteracies theories promote the development of teaching practices that do the following:

- invite children to use their L1 and literacies as resources for learning;
- demonstrate that speaking, listening, writing, reading, representing, and viewing are processes;
- create learning experiences that connect these language modes;
- help *all* children to access the language of power (i.e., standard Canadian English);
- consider literacy practices as tools for understanding ourselves and actively participating in the world;
- enable children to construct knowledge and create multiple texts through dialogue and critical inquiry;
- use digital technologies and other modalities (e.g., visual representations, movement, drama, etc.) as tools to support children's construction of knowledge and make visible their meaning making.

THEORETICAL APPLICATION: MULTILITERACIES FRAMEWORK

The concept of multiliteracies recognizes the multitude of communication and meaning-making systems that people utilize in their everyday lives. Multilingualism, new communication technologies, hypertext and other multimedia texts have become central in many children's out-of-school experiences and to many future career paths. Consequently, in order to connect to students' lived experiences and learning resources and to prepare them for viable work in an information-and-technology economy, schools must consider how to transform traditional literacy curricula into multiliteracies curricula. Have you observed students involved in powerful use of the Internet, production of hypertext, media study, or multilingual communication and literacy? What would a curriculum that, while not neglecting traditional print literacy, incorporates these kinds of sophisticated multiliteracies look like? How might such a curriculum build on diverse students' learning resources and foster their engagement in literate inquiry, meaning making, and communication?

By weaving in our critical reflections connected to the multiliteracies framework, we articulate possibilities and challenges of these theories. We are committed to teaching practices that affirm and foster children's cognitive, linguistic, sociocultural, and sociopolitical processes with oral, written, and visual texts, which promote English language learning and academic engagement. In the following section we contextualize our work in the sociopolitical context in which we teach.

The Sociopolitical Context of Our Work

The demographic context in which Lisa, Padma, Patricia, and Maria José teach and Sarah conducts research is similar to what is found in most of the GTA and increasingly across Canada. In fact, rising levels of immigration are becoming the norm throughout Canada. Currently, the GTA is home to the second highest number of internationally born residents in the world (Canadian Heritage, www.canadianheritage.gc.ca/progs/multi/spmc-scmp/conference/15_e.cfm). These statistics are projected to increase by the year 2017, with half the population of Toronto and Vancouver predicted to be visible minorities (Canada at a Glance, 2006). We are privileged to work in the GTA and greatly benefit from its culturally diverse population.

While some immigrant families are materially better off in Canada, many live within isolated circumstances. Immigrant communities often are or become insular whether for survival, support and/or a heightened group identity. This isolation can lead to social problems (e.g., mental illness, gang participation, alienation). The new context can undermine how families care for their children. Because parents' educational and professional experiences are not always recognized in Canada and the families' socio-economic standing can be reduced by immigration, the children witness the devaluing of their parents' cultural and educational background.

Language and power are bound: In Canada, we ideologically value bilingualism, when it is a combination of the standard French and English varieties. These are the languages that afford people with social privilege and power. Schools recognize linguistic diversity within a hierarchy of languages. Furthermore, some parents come to us with an internalized colonized belief that their L1 will get in the way of their children succeeding in school, relegating its use within the boundaries of their home and cultural community. Consequently, these children's knowledge is devalued and excluded from the school curriculum. We assert that as the world becomes smaller as a result of globalization and digital technologies, schools need to make room for the language practices of the children they serve. The immigration process expands the language community beyond the school community. And yet, languages are not just for the children who are here; children need to be able to communicate with family members in their L1 and often there is continued travel between the homeland and the new country. Keeping children's languages alive is imperative.

Methodology

This chapter represents our collective work: our social commitments, words and practices together. The following sociopolitical themes emerged from our dialogue over a six-month period in 2007. We recorded our meetings and transcribed relevant passages. We then critically read the transcripts, locating recurring themes. These themes are not inherent to the practices of multiliteracies, but reflect our critical engagement with these pedagogies within the sociopolitical context of our teaching. While these themes intersect in many ways, we showcase the questioning of each definition or role, and propose new ways of thinking about and collaborating with school communities. We examine the implicit definitions of literacy, learning, culture, identity, the role of the teacher, family and community participation, where and when school happens, and the assessment of student learning, as well as speculate on new territories for multiliteracies pedagogies.

Literacy

We argue that school literacies need to be reconceptualized to include the dynamism in the lives of our students. Multiliteracies need to become a vital part of the classroom, and for that to occur, teachers need to learn about the literacies that children already know. Active participation in their communities and cultural centers (e.g., dance, music, drama, martial arts) provide children with important knowledge and skills. Our work leads us to consider how we can value and use the "funds of knowledge" that children and their families bring with them, to enrich the school curriculum. Under the theme of family and community engagement, we further explore these possibilities.

Multiliteracies pedagogies recognize the role of digital technologies in people's lives. They too have created a situation in which the boundaries between countries, people, media, and languages are dissolving. The ease with which children can access multilingual and multimodal information on the Internet (e.g., current events about their homeland, and music from anywhere in the world) has the potential to change their membership to any fixed community. Digital technologies enable a child to share her work with her father in Jordan via a web cam, or families to access newspapers in their L1. Schools must recognize that families are living transnational lives, participating in communities across countries. When teachers understand that these connections are vital to children's lives and learning, they can utilize these resources to construct and expand opportunities for literacy in the classroom. Digital technologies can facilitate the sharing of languages and stories across different regions to promote analysis and understanding of different uses of languages such as colloquialisms and cultural stories (Cummins, Brown, & Sayers, 2007; www.multiliteracies.ca).

Multiliteracies also require the development of teaching practices wherein children are made aware of different registers and discourse communities as well as different genres of literacy (Cazden et al., 1996). It is critical that classrooms are places where children and teachers can explore together how webs of power are reflected through and created by language, in the texts, and by the images that permeate their daily experiences (Botelho, 2007; Cummins, 2001). In addition to enabling children to read between the lines of everyday texts, when the classroom context is one of collaboration and critical inquiry, this can create a sense of community among children across cultural and linguistic lines.

When literacy teaching is inclusive of different genres of story as well as different manners of telling a story, the privileging of a single definition of literacy (e.g., print-based, linear) becomes disrupted. We become aware that not all cultures share the Western orientation to linear- or text-based representations. For example, cultural stories from India are told through dance, movement and expression to recount historical events that include places, people and conflict. In our practice we question what is deemed standard or nonstandard, what the required conventions are, who establishes them, and who benefits from the rules inherent in the conventions, and who loses (Christensen, 2000).

Teachers sometimes impose an ethic of "correctness" and "appropriateness" when it comes to the way that the English language ought to sound and be spoken. In many ways, this imposition gets in the way of opportunities for children to maintain the language(s) of their identities. More dangerously, it strips away the child's sense of self. Once this happens, chances are the child might be silent in class, resist classroom learning, and/or experience decreased confidence when working with peers. Ironically, the "corrections" from the teacher might stem from good intentions, thinking that they will increase children's access to academic discourse and social power.

The teaching and learning of standard English is a pedagogical and sociopolitical imposition. When we think of the English language, there are many dialects that come to mind. Language is an expression of people's history, culture, art, philosophy, and/or religion. Language also reflects, maintains, and creates people's socio-economic location. It is unrealistic to think that all English speakers use language the same way. Therefore, teachers must capitalize on this language diversity to ensure that children become masterful at negotiating language use across contexts.

Learning

In this section, we consider how traditional school settings define learning and propose ways to broaden the ways in which teachers think about learning in our classrooms. The knowledge and skills that are encouraged are often school-based and are most likely defined by the ministry of education, school district, school, and teachers. Children come to internalize the "language" of the school and the school's learning expectations.

Critical inquiry encourages children to take control over their learning by defining their own learning goals, posing their own questions, mapping out how they are going to answer questions, locating resources, and reflecting on their experiences. Children use the language modes of speaking, listening, writing, reading, representing, and viewing for real purposes, challenging the teaching of language arts as a subject. Multiliteracies become the processes and modalities by which children explore their questions.

Teachers have an important role in this process because they can either validate or devalue it. For instance, when teachers build on children's background knowledge and prior lived experiences, it forms the basis for new learning. An affirming reaction from the teacher regarding children's discoveries and new understandings sends messages that their learning is valued and important. Purposeful learning does not mean receiving oral lessons from the teacher or studying textbooks; it means children having opportunities to direct and design how they will represent their learning; and collaborate with their peers, their families, and other classes and schools. Creating a caring community of learners where each child is not only a learner, but a teacher and a leader opens up many possibilities.

An affirming learning environment keeps children motivated to come to school, reflects children's identities, and encourages free thinking, experimentation, curiosity, and critical investigation about the world. It allows teachers to establish a respectful learning environment where children feel comfortable to explore issues and define their own learning goals. This kind of classroom allows children to feel comfortable and safe; it is like *home*. Teachers come to learn *with* and *from* children.

We are calling for a *community-centered* approach to teaching that places the child and their families and communities at the center of classroom life. This approach embraces the children's lived experience. It is difficult for students to "engage" with the curriculum and school when they cannot draw a parallel with that experience and their personal lived experience (Cummins, Chow, & Schecter, 2006). Although we cannot change the curriculum, we can definitely change the resources we use in our classrooms and move away from textbooks because they standardize our learning and experience. Multiliteracies are *part of* not an add-on to curriculum. Children and families can produce "identity texts" (Cummins, 2004), that is, lived experiences as texts, as products of their multidisciplinary individual or collaborative work. Identity texts talk back to publishing practices that underrepresent or render invisible certain communities (Botelho, 2004; Botelho & Rudman, 2009). (Visit www.multiliteracies.ca for inspiration. See Ada and Compoy (2003) and Botelho, Turner, & Wright (2006) for guidance.)

Culture and Identity

Culture is often defined as "the complex whole" of values, customs, beliefs and practices, which makes up the cultural experience of a particular group (Tyler, [1871] 1958). This definition has guided teaching practices for quite some time, translated into food and festival, and heroes and holidays approaches to classroom teaching. However, we argue that this definition is a contradiction with our diverse world of transnational social networks, hybrid identities, and local, national, and global power relationships. The definition of culture with which teachers align themselves shapes their teaching practice and work with communities.

We align ourselves with a more complex view of culture, defining it as the historical, sociopolitical, and creative product of social practices that reflect people responding to, making sense of, re/organizing, and acting upon the world (Botelho, 2004). Our definition sees culture as not static, isolated, permanent, or bounded, but dynamic, permeable and influenced by multiple social factors. Culture is thus learned, and not biologically determined; it is a complex web of power relations enacted at interpersonal, group, and institutional levels.

There is cultural diversity between as well as within cultural groups. In addition, many families themselves are made up of more than one religious or cultural group. Similarly, there are families who have Canadian-born children who are ELLs, and internationally born children who arrive in Canada with great knowledge of English. Therefore, it is necessary to be cautious of terms that simplify and reduce difference and to reflect on questions such as:

- Who defines our cultural difference and how are we defined?
- In what ways are we grouped by how we look and/or by the languages that we speak?
- How do we perceive cultural difference in our classrooms?
- How do our social memberships and other social factors shape our perceptions?

Similar questions are important to ask in relation to identity and we suggest that teachers engage in reflecting on these in order to critically examine how they view identity in relation to their own lives and those of their students:

- What is identity?
- What social factors shape how we identify ourselves?

Identity is often defined as fixed and unified, unfolding over time with a stable core in place. However, we draw on the work of Hall (1996) who defines cultural identity as "superficial or artificially imposed 'selves', which a people with a shared history and ancestry hold in common" (pp. 3–4); it is an unchanged "cultural belongingness." Identity is a process that is never complete. Hall (1996) argues that

> identities are about questions of using the resources of history, language and culture in the process of becoming rather than being: not "who we are" or "where we came from" so much as what we might become, how we have been represented and how that bears on how we might represent ourselves.
>
> (p. 4)

Identities are constructed within language use (discourse), as such they are social constructions, not biologically determined. Identities play a role in how we perceive ourselves sociopolitically. Children embody many historical and social experiences, all interacting in different ways and constructing multiple identities.

Schools figure largely in identity construction; they are construction sites. If we closely consider this metaphor, we realize that construction sites can be safe and unsafe zones. They have a supervisor on the premises who has the building plans in hand; she possesses the "big picture" of the project. In the school classroom, the construction site is created by school policies and teaching practices. Depending on what the institution and practitioner deem suitable for the child, the construction of identities is dictated and developed from these complex interactions.

The Role of the Teacher

A discussion of the role of the teacher by its very nature requires an articulation of what it is that constitutes how we define teachers' roles and responsibilities. Cummins (2001) explains role definition as that which "refers to the mindset of expectations, assumptions and goals that educators bring to the task of educating culturally diverse students" (p. 19). He recognizes that teachers often are forced to define their role in opposition to the prescribed role definitions constructed by school policies and teaching practices.

We define the teacher's roles as advocates, facilitators, and collaborators. Bound up with a definition of teacher role is the responsibility that we share to learn about our children and to go beyond a fixed notion of the "average student." Rather than lowering expectations for student learning, an inclusive stance fosters children's engagement with the curriculum by making it relevant to their lives. We argue that by reflecting on our assumptions about children, teachers *can* make choices that reflect an appreciation for children's realities while fostering high academic engagement (Commins & Miramontes, 2006). When we challenge ourselves to shift from what they do not know (deficit) to what they do know (funds of knowledge) perspective, recognize the diversity of our children as an asset and possess high expectations for all children (Cummins, 2001). It is essential that this framework of inclusion and concurrent high expectations be communicated to all families regardless of their cultural background, proficiency in English, residency status or level of formal education. By communicating an appreciation for the learning opportunities that are inherent in a diverse classroom, we can help families realize that English language learners' experiences and knowledge contribute in many ways to creating a classroom environment where all children can develop to their full potential as global citizens.

We include the issue of *space* as a feature of the teacher role in the sense that space refers to not just physical place but also the context of the work happening in the classroom. Erickson and Schultz (1992) explain that: "contexts are constituted by what people are doing and where and when they are doing it" (p. 148). The role of the teacher includes the responsibility for *creating or constraining the space(s)* for learning. The ways that interactions are orchestrated and what features of learning are given prominence over others, will contribute to the types of opportunities for imagining, engaging with and participating in literacies in schools.

Creating space in the classroom requires us to know our children. During "Meet the Teachers" night in Patricia's grade 1 classroom, she spoke to Sara's father to explore what quiet Sara could do on her assigned "Show and Tell" day. Patricia was thrilled to learn that Sara could read in her L1 and suggested to her father that Sara might like to read a Korean book to the class. Sara amazed her classmates, most of whom were just learning to read in English, with her well-developed reading skills. Although her oral language development did not allow her to retell the Korean folktale in English, her receptive language allowed her to turn the pages of the book as a junior Korean student retold the story in English. Patricia immediately had a better idea of her English listening comprehension and her literacy skills. It was a stress-free, quick, and informative assessment that would guide her teaching. With Sara's enhanced status, she became more confident: speaking more loudly, participating more vocally, and interacting with her classmates more actively.

Underlying this entire discussion related to the teacher role is the theme of social power relations that are encountered at a micro-level in our classrooms (Cummins, 2001). How we position ourselves in relation to the children we teach can either challenge or perpetuate the injustices that are found in our society. The ways in which we organize our classrooms are reflective of what we value. These practices in turn send messages to children regarding our selection of particular texts, images, literacies, and technologies and convey ideas about what is essential for school success and what are considered markers of academic discourse and knowledge. For example, which books are included in the classroom and school library, how they are made accessible to families, and how they are used send messages of inclusion or exclusion. When teachers work to define their role around the lives of the children, children and families become foregrounded in the curriculum. This is a critical element to enabling children to see themselves in their schoolwork and contributes to their ability to invest in it.

Family and Community Participation

We believe that involving families in school activities and literacies represents a great challenge and opportunity for educators, that is, even more salient for the families of children from diverse linguistic and cultural backgrounds. In this section we examine some of the underlying themes involved in bringing children's families into the classroom. We ask:

- How can we facilitate meaningful family and community involvement?
- What kind of structures can we help put in place to embrace parents' willingness to work with the school in enhancing their children's academic experience?
- How can we build on families' capacity to provide their children with enriching learning experiences?

The preservation of cultural heritage is of great significance to all communities. Families hope schools will respond culturally and respectfully to them and that the school environment and curricula will reflect the rich diversity in the community. Families have high expectations for their children. Therefore, we need to analyse the opportunities for family involvement beyond attending school functions and meetings. By expanding the opportunities to include activities outside the school, we can address some barriers to participation (e.g., discomfort with speaking English, lack of familiarity with the education system, different cultural expectations for teacher–parent interactions). The dual language initiatives at our schools rely on families to translate and audio-record dual language text and families appreciate the opportunities to make meaningful contributions.

A re-orientation toward family participation also means asking ourselves how can we do the following?:

- invite and facilitate family participation in their children's education whether in the home or in the school;
- support, reinforce, and expand parents' knowledge and skills by emphasizing what families can do to support their children's learning within the context of the family;
- provide families with opportunities to share their values, practices, educational experiences, and expectations, as well as to support one another with insights to personal challenges and issues.

Fostering family participation is a whole school responsibility, requiring the commitment of administrators, teachers, support staff, and other members of the school community. In our vision of respectful schools, transformative practices and intentions encompass a range of actions (Table 13.1).

Table 13.1 Practices/intentions

Practices/intentions	What it looks and sounds like
Reception process • Create an inviting and supportive environment	• Multilingual signs; friendly office staff who reflects cultural and linguistic diversity; use of multilingual settlement workers • Purposeful dialogue allows teachers to familiarize families with the Ontario school system so that they can better support their children. • Ask children and families how they identify culturally and what languages they speak.
Communication within the learning community • Support and strengthen home/community/school relationships	• Newsletters, school/class website, e-mail, students' agendas, multilingual documents, web links, telephone trees, etc. • The Internet can help absent students, ill or on extended vacations, keep up as files can be exchanged and work can be submitted online.

Use of home languages

- Enhance communication between home and school and among family members
- Make visible the knowledge of children and their families

- Foster a school community where all participants are respectful and curious about each other's cultural and linguistic experiences. Children are often curious about the unfamiliar but are inexperienced in finding out more information. Teachers can foster a genuine curiosity.
- Teachers, parents, children, etc. act as translators, use of multilingual web links (e.g., PDSB, www.peelschools.org, and "Newcomer's Guide websites, www.settlement.org/edguide)
- Commercially produced dual language book collection (www.thornwood.peelschools.org/dual/index.htm) and dual language identity texts (www.multiliteracies.ca), multilingual announcements, language ambassadors, explicit encouragement for additive bilingualism
- Invite families to visit the classroom and tell/draw/write stories with their children in their own languages. These visits can also be voice or video recorded for later use.
- Languages possess social histories: Look at patterns of language dispersal across the world. For example, ask why is English so widely spoken? Why is Portuguese the sixth most spoken language in the world? Cultural contact and conquest are prominent factors in the spread of these languages.

Clarify school expectations

- Make school culture and practices accessible to families, inviting them to participate and advocate fully for their children

- Explicitly highlight provincial expectations (e.g., Ontario's learning skills on provincial report card) (www.thornwood.peelschools.org/esl_website/text/learning_skills.htm)
- Invite families to observe and participate in school learning experiences

Community resource centre & lending library

- Connect parents to community services
- Use community as a resource
- Explore diverse childrearing practices
- Facilitate family fun

- Bulletin board displays newsletters and Community Information Fairs in school during Open House help keep families informed of resources in the community
- Teacher-sponsored/guided family excursions
- Library includes board games, puzzles, CDs, DVDs, parenting books, etc.

Portfolios and student-led conferences

- Encourage students to be reflective learners

- With peers
- Sharing provide opportunities for assessment as learning with teacher
- Meet on an ongoing basis to discuss learning and set goals with families and teacher
- Meet to support the learning process and assist student to set and carry out their goals

(Continued overleaf)

Table 13.1 Continued

Practices/intentions	What it looks and sounds like
Parent Involvement as Educator (P.I.E.) • Communicate to families that their involvement with the school is a critical aspect of their children's success and enriches the school community • Foster meaningful relationships within families, among families, as well as between home and school.	• 6–8 week sessions for grades 1 to 3 family workshop on topics selected by parents and teachers and facilitated by staff, guest presenters, and parents • Kindergarten PIE during noon hour to accommodate families of morning and afternoon students. Focus is on play-based activities to support early learning and development. • Community agencies commit to provide programs once a month as part of their outreach program. • Alumni lead sessions and answer questions re: transition to middle school for Grade Five PIE • http://thornwood.peelschools.org/esl_website/text/pie_project.htm
Volunteer program • Invite parents, older students, and educators interested in gaining experience in Canadian school to enhance student learning	• Support programs and services (e.g., Breakfast Club, library, school office, field trips)
Home reading program • Promote reading and discussion at home using a variety of text, including dual language books	• Teacher share multimodal opportunities that accompany borrowed text from the classroom library (e.g., library pocket with one follow-up family activity per book) (www.ed.gov/pubs/CompactforReading/content.html)
Multicultural events • Develop awareness and pride in the contributions of different cultural groups to the world	• Supplement to existing curriculum and practices (e.g., daily announcements, displays, presentations) and announcements based on Peel's monthly "Celebrating Faith and Culture Backgrounder" and student and parental input • http://www.gobeyondwords.org/main.html • Showcase a variety of literacies, literatures, and art (i.e., musical, visual, dance) from diverse cultural backgrounds. Invite artists to facilitate workshops and purchase culturally specific media so children experiment with different art forms.

Where/When School Happens

To fully embrace multiliteracies pedagogies, we have found that it is necessary to redefine where and when school happens. This means making sure that we as well as families are crossing the bridge between home/community and school. School learning can be extended outside the school building. For example, Lisa has led a "Summer Institute" program with her school board for the past eight years where literacy programs are held inside the *Ahmadiyya* mosque and Peace

Village[5] community offices where the majority of the school's student population lives. These literacy programs are an extension of the school program and provide literacy enrichment opportunities for students, especially those who benefit from extended learning during the summer months. The programs offered in Peace Village mimic a dual language program where students and teachers are speaking, reading and writing in Urdu and English. This has been a unique aspect of the program since successful literacy learning relies heavily on students being able to make personal connections and build on their prior knowledge. Teachers from the Ahmadiyya community are employed to teach and many mothers volunteer in the program. Having mothers gather in the program fosters bonds of friendships, partnerships between families, and further understanding of school teaching practices. Most importantly, having the school staff go into the community sends a loud and clear message to the families that says "we care!"

We can also expand our notion of where learning happens by considering the city and surrounding communities as an extension of our classroom. Children should be given the opportunity to get to know the community they live in through field trips, neighborhood explorations, and engagements with community members as part of the school curriculum. We invite community members into our schools to share practical arts and other life skills (e.g., conduct workshops with students on cultural dance, art, and games; use the abacus). We see these experiences not as an extra or an add-on, but as an essential part of school learning and community building.

Assessing Student Learning

In rethinking how we teach multiliteracies and interact with children and families, we think it is essential to consider what constitutes student success. Who defines it? How is it measured? How do the assessment tools we use showcase or obscure children's learning? How do we allow for a diversity of developmental timelines?

Assessment and evaluation can set the stage for important conversations. The problem comes with what is done with the information gathered about children. Is it to label children, or is it to inform our teaching? In what ways and for what purposes do we assess children's literacies?

During one class observation in Lisa's classroom, she was reading a story with Zerrin and Avi called "The Crowded House" from a reader she was using with the class. She began by looking at each page with them. Although Avi had been in Canada just three months at that point, his excitement at seeing a story with elements that were familiar to him was evident by his animated participation. While not always silent, Avi this day was more than typically engaged and vocal.

Avi: Oh I know this. One family. It's no good this house.
Lisa: Yes, a small house, and lots of people.

5 Peace Village is a 50-acre residential community surrounded by mosque. It is located north of Toronto and predominately inhabited by Ahmadi Muslims. See www.peacevillage.ca

Avi (with much excitement in his voice and gesturing heavily):   After, after this
    the man is waking the Rabbi. This too Hebrew Rabbi said very not good
    this house. Now to go outside the sheep.
        (Lisa starts to say something but Avi continues excitedly.)
Lisa: How about. . . .
Avi: Now there's no room to move now no animals it's good it's happy no
    animal.
Lisa: So we're going to read the story together.
        (She begins to read the story, when she gets to the name of the main character
        "Yitzak," Avi corrects her pronunciation.)
Lisa: What does it mean to be a farmer?
Avi: Outside work—with cows outside
Lisa writes on board: *Yitzak*—[name of] farmer
                    7 people—small house
                    1 bed for everybody

Zerrin does not know what rabbi means. Lisa tries to explain by saying he is a
religious leader. Avi gets up to get a book from the class called "What I Believe" to
look for a picture to help Zerrin understand. When Zerrin indicates that she
understands, Lisa asks what this person is called in Turkish. Zerrin says: *Hoja.*
They return to the story.
Lisa: Okay, so Yitzak goes to the Rabbi and says I have a problem. What's the
    problem?
Avi: (with much excitement, loudly and quickly): Big family, small house. Goes
    to Rabbi, still a problem.

At the end of this lesson, Lisa wrote a cloze passage (sentences with key vocabulary left blank for students to fill in, using the context of the sentence to guide
their choices) on the board based on the story for Zerrin and Avi to copy and
complete. She explained that for homework she wanted them to pretend that they
are telling the story to a friend who does not know what happens and that they
should write this retelling in their first language.

    This lesson provides an example of the kind of cultural and linguistic inter-
change that Sarah observed as part of the class work on countless occasions in
Lisa's classroom. The story she read this day provided several opportunities for
Avi to share his expertise. Having grown up on a Moshav, a type of cooperative
agricultural community made up of individual farms in Israel, he was intimately
familiar with farm animals and farm work; being Jewish, he could relate to the
religious model being represented in the book and share this understanding with
his classmate, Zerrin, and he could also instruct his teacher on the correct pronunciation of a name from his language. Lisa made use of the context of this story
to help Zerrin understand the connection between a Rabbi in the Hebrew faith
with the Turkish name of the religious leader in her Muslim faith and Avi broadened this relationship to ask Lisa about the comparable person in the Catholic
faith that she had grown up with. This vignette demonstrates Lisa's acceptance
and encouragement of her students taking on the role of teacher and her that of

learner as well as her inclusion of her students' cultural and linguistic lives and experiences in her assessment and teaching practices.

In many cases, literacy teaching relies on a set of assessment tools that do not reflect the complexities of multiliteracies (Peterson, Botelho, Jang, & Kerekes, 2007). There is a mismatch between literacy practices and assessment tools. Street (2005) argues that the current forms of assessment "reduce literacy to a few simple and mechanistic skills that fail to do justice to the richness and complexity of actual literacy practices in people's lives" (p. 38). Assessment tools should consider a diversity of literacies, languages, modalities, and texts: Assessment constructs literacy practices and literacy practices construct assessment. We should assess code breaker, text participant, text user, and text critic practices (Luke & Freebody, 1999; Botelho, 2007), analyzing children's interaction with and construction of multiple texts. Focused observation is still one of the strongest tools available to help teachers get to know children intimately, take stock of their learning, and plan for teaching.

Pahl and Rowsell (2005) recommend some possibilities for portfolio assessment. One suggestion is to invite children to divide their portfolios into compartments that showcase their experiences with speaking, listening, writing, reading, representing, and viewing. Children can gather artifacts that represent their home-school literacy practices, and/or artifacts that reflect their identities. Another recommendation for organizing the portfolio, they claim, might be based on print or digital text genres such as fiction, nonfiction, poetry, websites, video, videogames, to name a few. The portfolio organizational tabs can reflect the children's personal learning journeys. Portfolios offer children spaces for affirming their literacy practices, reflecting, taking ownership, and planning for future learning.

Another powerful assessment tool is to ask children to lead a discussion with parents and educators, using these portfolios to showcase their multiliteracies learning. The teacher can help children prepare for student-led conferences and help them to articulate their strengths and next steps for learning, when meeting with other classmates, parents, and teachers. Student-led conferences can facilitate dynamic discussions between children and their families as well as honor children's learning and life experiences. Furthermore, they can be conducted in children's home languages and thereby facilitate greater family understanding and participation.

Conclusion: Redefining School Culture

Access to one's home/community language for learning and living is a human right. Children's understanding of the world is encoded in their cultural and linguistic knowledge and experiences (Cummins, 2001). Therefore, they become valuable resources for children and schools to utilize. We argue that as such literacy learning needs to be constructed as the development of all the languages and literacies children bring to school. This is the social and pedagogical responsibility of all teachers and schools. The paradigm shifts we are proposing in this chapter require that we redefine "how we do school" and enlist teachers to participate in these reconceptualizations.

Teachers are members of school cultures. Everything we do and do not do contributes to the making of these communities. Values shape how we perceive the world and how we interact with each other. How we organize our classrooms, the materials that we choose, and how we interact with children and their families and communities construct a value system, implicitly and explicitly. In one of our meetings, Padma invited us to consider the future that children represent: "These are the children who are going to take care of us. How will the children take care of us, whether we stay in Canada or whether some of us return to our homeland? We're all connected. What kind of people are we bringing up?" These questions brought tears to our eyes and a sense of urgency to our teaching. Our work confirms that: research partnerships greatly contribute to professional learning; literacy teaching is a community responsibility; and community life is curriculum. What values are we teaching our children? What kind of society are we creating with our teaching? Critical engagement with multiliteracies pedagogies brings us closer as people, to who we are, where we have been, and where we might want to go, *together.* The social interactions among children, families, teachers, and the community can create new sociopolitical relationships and possibilities, constructing and reconstructing the worlds in which we live and teach, thus recreating culture.

Ideas for Discussion, Extension, and Application

1. This chapter highlights the fact that the increasing diversification of schools has occurred simultaneously with the increasing diversification of 21st century literacies and stresses that teachers can better serve culturally and linguistically diverse students by incorporating multiliteracies in the classroom. While this is an emerging perspective, the World Wide Web offers a number of examples of diverse students engaged in sophisticated multiliteracies. Browse these two relevant websites: www.sp.uconn.edu/~djleu/fourth/ten.html and www. multiliteracies.ca and share an important discovery with your peers.

2. The authors make clear that creating classrooms that support culturally and linguistically diverse students may involve values and commitments that conflict with prevalent societal views on immigrant communities and language diversity. Think about your own views on and values related to cultural and linguistic diversity and schooling. How might they conflict or correspond with current societal beliefs and values?

3. The transnational nature of many students' lives, participating in communities across countries and states, creates a multitude of learning spaces often invisible to teachers. What are the pedagogical possibilities and related practices?

4. Botelho and collaborators question the ethic of "correctness" and "appropriateness" in the teaching of English language. This is a controversial topic embracing not only the teaching of English Language

Learners but also minority students who speak a different dialect other than standard English. In pairs or small groups, make a list of arguments from both sides of the debate (e.g., Botelho et al.'s position versus emphasis on standard English-only instruction). Examine and identify the values and commitments of each position.

References

Ada, A. F., & Compoy, F. I. (2003). *Authors in the classroom: A transformative education process*. Boston: Allyn and Bacon.

Botelho, M. J. (2004). Reading class: Disrupting power in children's literature. Unpublished dissertation, University of Massachusetts, Amherst.

Botelho, M. J. (2007). Naming practices: Defining critical multicultural literacies. *Orbit, 36*(3), 27–30.

Botelho, M. J., & Rudman, M. K. (2009). Critical multicultural analysis of children's lierature: Mirrors, windows, and doors. New York: Routledge.

Botelho, M. J., Turner, V., & Wright, M. (2006). We have stories to tell: Gathering and publishing stories in a Puerto Rican community. *School Talk, 11*(4), 2–3.

Canada at a Glance (2006). Diversity. Online. www.dfait-maeci.gc.ca/canada-europa/united_kingdom/pdf/CAG-Diversity.pdf. (Accessed 15 May 2006).

Cazden, C., Cope, B., Fairclough, N., Gee, J. P., Kalantzis, M., Kress, G., Luke, A., Luke, C., Michaels, S., & Nakata, M. (New London Group). (1996). A pedagogy of multiliteracies: Designing social futures. *Harvard Educational Review, 66*(1), 60–92.

Chow, P., & Cummins, J. (2003). Valuing multilingual and multicultural approaches to learning. In S. R. Schecter, & J. Cummins (Eds.), *Multilingual education in practice: Using diversity as a resource* (pp. 32–60). Portsmouth, NH: Heinemann.

Christensen, L. (2000). *Reading, writing, and rising up: Teaching about social justice and the power of the written word*. Milwaukee, WI: Rethinking Schools Ltd.

Cohen, S. (2008). Making visible the invisible: Dual language teaching practices in a monolingual instructional setting. Unpublished dissertation, Ontario Institute for Studies in Education/University of Toronto.

Commins, N. L., & Miramontes, O. B. (2006). Addressing linguistic diversity from the outset. *Journal of Teacher Education, 57*(3), 240–246.

Cope, B., & Kalantzis, M. (Eds.). (1999). *Multiliteracies: Literacy learning and the design of social futures*. New York: Routledge.

Cummins, J. (2001). *Negotiating identities: Education for empowerment in a diverse society* (2nd. ed.). Los Angeles: California Association for Bilingual Education.

Cummins, J. (2004). Multiliteracies pedagogy and the role of identity texts. In K. Leithwood, P. McAdie, N. Bascia, & A. Rodigue (Eds.), *Teaching for deep understanding: Towards the Ontario curriculum that we need* (pp. 68–74). Toronto: Ontario Institute for Studies in Education of the University of Toronto and the Elementary Federation of Teachers of Ontario.

Cummins, J. (2006). Multiliteracies and equity: How do Canadian schools measure up? *Education Canada, 46*(2), 4–7.

Cummins, J., Bismilla, V., Cohen, S., Giampapa, F., & Leoni, L. (2005). Timelines and lifelines: Rethinking literacy instruction in multilingual classrooms. *Orbit, 36*(1), 22–26.

Cummins, J., Brown, K., & Sayers, D. (2007). *Literacy, technology, and diversity: Teaching for success in changing times*. Boston: Pearson, Allen and Beacon.

Cummins, J., Chow, P., & Schecter, S. R. (2006). Community as curriculum. *Language Arts,* *83*(4), 297–307.

Erickson, F., & Schultz, J. (1992). Students' experiences of the curriculum. In P. W. Jackson (Ed.), *Handbook of research on curriculum* (pp. 465–485). New York: Macmillan.

Hall, S. (1996). Who needs "identity"? In S. Hall, & Paul du Gay (Eds.), *Questions of cultural identity* (pp. 1–17). Thousand Oaks, CA: Sage.

Luke, A., & Freebody, P. (1999). A map of possible practices: Further notes on the four resources model. *Practically Primary, 4*(2), 5–8.

Pahl, K., & Rowsell, J. (2005). *Literacy and education: Understanding the new literacy studies in the classroom.* Thousand Oaks, CA: Sage.

Peterson, S. S., Botelho, M. J., Jang, E., & Kerekes, J. (2007). Writing assessment: What would multiliteracies teachers do? *Literacy Learning in the Middle Years, 15*(1), 29–35.

Schecter, S., & Cummins, J. (Eds.). (2003). *Multilingual education in practice: Using diversity as a resource.* Portsmouth, NH: Heinemann.

Street, B. (2005). New literacies studies: Next stages. *Orbit, 36*(1), 37–39.

Tyler, E. ([1871] 1958). *Primitive culture.* New York: Harper & Row.

Teacher Commentary

Christine Kane and Kim Douillard

Not long ago I pointed out to my students that not all children have a comfortable home and enough food to eat. They had a hard time grasping this idea and when pressed to consider why some people might not have comfortable homes or adequate food immediately drew the conclusions that the parents of these poor children must be drinking alcohol or taking drugs. As I continued to think about this reaction and why their immediate conclusion were related to substance abuse, I realized that most of the information that they (and their parents) receive about populations different from them come through news stories, television shows, and other media representations. Without a means to consider alternative explanations, stereotypes prevail.

(Kim Douillard)

Engaging All Educators as Resources Towards Social Change

The second six chapters of this book call on us, as teachers to understand that education is the common socializing activity organized, funded and regulated by authorities for all students in our society. Educators are the critical link for students to develop academic self-efficacy and empowerment, to become global citizens and active participants in the meaning-making process of their lives. As educators we must provide our students opportunities to recognize and reshape literacy practices that are most intimately connected to their economic, social, cultural, educational and intellectual welfare. We must also recognize the inequities that exist in our society and educational system in order to provide experiences that allow the students we teach to better understand the world they live in so they can fully participate as an informed citizenry.

Our Teaching Perspective

Our understanding of the social, economic and cultural power that education perpetuates has been clarified by our experiences in the classroom. We are Christine Kane, an urban educator serving a population of working class African-American and Latino families and Kim Douillard, a suburban educator serving a population of primarily middle-class Caucasian families and a smaller percentage of English language learners. We believe that in order to tackle the enormous responsibility of shaping future generations for a more equitable society it will take the joint efforts of all teachers—not only those working with students who currently experience poverty or those whose backgrounds are ethnically, linguistically, and/or culturally diverse, but also those teachers who teach students whose parents currently have social positions of power and will likely grow up to hold social positions of power themselves. We have found that discussion of and interaction with issues of "reform," social justice, and equity in schooling do not typically take place with teachers who teach in more affluent neighborhoods, and that urban and suburban educators seldom come together around issues of teaching pedagogy or curriculum in meaningful, mutually informing ways.

We believe that critical dialogue in our classrooms, regardless of location and economic status, has been a vital component to combat media generalizations and stereotypes concerning diverse population of learners. Suburban teachers often do not see themselves as part of the equation or responsible for the educational experience of diverse students in urban or less affluent neighborhoods—not because they don't care or because they want diverse students to fail—but because they lack the information from an insider's perspective to combat media representations of cultural or linguistic stereotypes. Our collaborative work and critical dialogue from both perspectives—a suburban teacher of an affluent student population and an urban teacher of diverse urban student population—regarding issues of equity (educational, economic, linguistic, etc.), have helped to shape our understanding that, as educators, we are all part of the solution in moving every student onto pathways of self-empowerment and educational success.

The pedagogy of those educators who work in affluent schools directly impacts students who will eventually inherit economic and cultural positions of power in our society. The pedagogical practices and core set of beliefs that educators working with students in a position of power impart can positively impact the opportunities afforded students without positions of social power to aid them in economic autonomy. Mariam Wright Edelman (Riley, 2008) reminds us that the future we hold in trust for our own children will be shaped by our fairness to other people's children.

Examining Our Pedagogy

One key point that several of the authors in the second section of this book, *School-Home Connections in a Multicultural Society: Learning from and with Culturally and Linguistically Diverse Families*, make is that much of what is accepted as school curriculum and testing mandates are based upon the funds of knowledge implicit in the social structure and lifestyles of middle-class students, the majority of whom are Caucasian. Assumptions about the conditions for homework completion, parent involvement in school, what counts as literacy, and even about housing, finances, work schedules, and typical gender roles privilege students whose lives are in sync with the assumptions, and can work to disenfranchise and "other" students whose lives are not represented or seen as "normal" by school practices. These assumptions make it urgent that educators recognize and find ways to incorporate the funds of knowledge that students bring with them—to help students make sense of the information presented at school so they can see themselves and the learning as relevant and connected to the other parts of their lived experiences. It is also essential for teachers to highlight and celebrate not only student differences, but also diverse ways of knowing and operating in the world and in school.

In synthesizing the educational research presented in Part II both as an urban and suburban educator, we have gained a deeper understanding of funds of knowledge and how they are utilized in culturally responsive classrooms in a wide variety of ways. Pioneered by Dr. Luis Moll and colleagues at the University of Arizona, pedagogy derived from funds of knowledge attempts to improve participation and heighten students' interest by using an inquiry-based method that draws upon their home and community resources. Although we wholeheartedly agree with the premise of using funds of knowledge to guide pedagogical practices, we have great concerns about how educational researchers interpret these and how educators may enact this type of pedagogy in their own classrooms with diverse learners. We propose applying Sonia Nieto's (1994) model of moving towards a culture of critique, where as educators we go beyond tolerating, accepting or respecting the funds of knowledge that students bring with them to the classroom but push ourselves to embrace the ways our students' funds of knowledge will inherently invite complexity, critical dialogue and even conflict into the classroom.

Funds of knowledge are intellectual, social and emotional resources that enable modest income families to survive with dignity and respect. It is dismissive to focus on their deficits instead of their inherent potential to learn, their diverse linguistic and cultural backgrounds, or their hard-earned resiliency. However, drawing on students' funds of knowledge is such an important and complex process that educators can be overwhelmed when considering the wide array of resources that students and families can draw from to enhance and support learning. We are continuously pushing our own teaching practices beyond trivializing funds of knowledge into a one-hit-wonder model or an "activitized" event where a teacher can make the easy mistake of assuming that a classroom activity that includes elements of a students' culture is enough to make the lesson relevant and rigorous. There is great danger in assuming that students who share common racial, ethnic or language characteristics bring the same funds of knowledge to the classroom. As the authors included in Part II of the book remind us, building classroom activities around topics such as hip hop music or cultural holidays (Day of the Dead, Cinco de Mayo, Martin Luther King, Jr. Day) are not enough to capitalize and build rigorous curriculum that honor the strengths and ways of knowing that students bring to school. We know that taking a narrow approach reduces the complexity of students' lives and ignores the rich funds of knowledge that students bring to the classroom every day that the teacher and/or school system may not be prepared to develop—and therefore, creates a deficit perspective of focusing on what students' lack—instead of what they have to offer. This is even more problematic when information about diverse populations is represented only through the stories of cultural heroes. Martin Luther King, Jr. and Rosa Park both made a huge impact on the history of the United States and are important not only to African Americans but to all Americans for their contributions. Those individuals and their stories, however, are not enough to help either diverse students or middle-class white students recognize the mismatches that many students face in school or understand the lives and experiences of students from various ethnic, racial or linguistics groups.

The chapters in this book illustrate potential sources for information about students' lived experiences: home visits, parent interviews and focus groups, observations of students at work or play, and opportunities for students to mine their families' and their own experiences for academic connections. These sources can be a place for teachers to rethink their curriculum—and more importantly, their pedagogy.

Funds of Knowledge as Classroom Practice

In order to invite diverse voices, ways of knowing, and lived experiences into the classroom, we have learned to be open to ambiguity and have a flexible approach to learning. Teachers who know all the answers and expect students to learn in particular ways will struggle to incorporate this diversity and complexity into the classroom. There are specific conditions in our classrooms that support both rigorous academic expectations and a welcoming approach to multiple ways of knowing and learning. Here are few that we feel are essential:

1. We believe that diverse students are capable of rigorous academic work and acknowledge that success does not have to mean assimilation into or embracing of mainstream American culture. All students need opportunities to understand the various uses and expectations for learning in our society without feeling the need to abandon their own beliefs and experiences to be successful.
2. We strive to maintain a classroom community where students and teachers can take risks, explore, make mistakes, and learn from each other. We participate in collectively generating the most productive solutions to social problems, with the understanding that we will disagree, and that the disagreement can extend us to possibilities we could not have imagined.
3. We are aware of and continuously monitoring our own language use and the way our words influence what counts as learning in the classroom. Peter Johnston (2004) reminds us that a teacher's choice of words, phrases, metaphors, and interaction sequences influence the ways students see each other and work in a classroom. As urban and suburban educators we must remember that the way we choose to talk about who is and who is not present in the classroom will have a direct impact upon student's perceptions and understandings.
4. We take an inquiry stance to learning—shifting the role of teacher from imparting information to integrating students' experiences and prior knowledge into the curriculum. Framing instruction through an inquiry stance repositions curriculum as the outcome of instruction rather than as the starting point. This social construction of knowledge allows students and teachers to co-construct meaning collaboratively.

5. We intentionally use multicultural literature that emanates from and is focused on the experiences of diverse learners whose cultures, histories and stories have long been marginalized in dominant American society and does not perpetuate tokenism or stereotyping (Bishop, 2008). To illustrate this approach, derived from Mary Cowhey (2006), we ask our students open-ended questions. Questions allow students to consider a variety of perspectives. Critical questions include: (1) Who has the most power in the story? (2) What words/images make you think that? (3) Who doesn't have much or any power? Whose voice is silenced? Why do you think they don't have a voice? (Brennan, 2008).

6. We explicitly invite parent/guardian voices into the classroom even if they are unable to be physically present or if they do not have the same linguistic knowledge as the dominant school culture. Yeager and Córdova (Chapter 12 in this volume) begin with the premise that the funds of knowledge that students bring with them are connected to rigorous academic content. Students conducted interviews with family members to gather a broader understanding of the ways science and math are operationalized outside of school. The underlying assumption is that families have expertise and knowledge in these curricular areas that benefit classroom instruction. The teacher's role then departs from that of dispenser of information and assumes the role of facilitator that interconnects the students' lived experiences and the school curriculum.

We began this critical dialogue in order to enact social change. Our belief as educators is that we are responsible for creating cultures of critique where students learn to situate themselves as agents of social change in society. We know that social change towards equity requires the effort and resources of educators in both suburban and urban neighborhoods working collaboratively. As James Baldwin wrote, if you can change the way people look at reality, then you can change that reality (Watkins, 1979).

References

Bishop, R. (2008). Multicultural literature: Story and social action. *School Talk, 13*(4).

Brennan, M. (2008). Multicultural literature: A multiliteracies perspective. *School Talk, 13*(4).

Cowhey, M. (2006). *Black ants and Buddhists: Thinking critically and teaching differently in the primary grades*. Portland, ME: Stenhouse.

Johnston, P. (2004). *Choice words: How our language affects children's learning*. Portland, ME: Stenhouse.

Nieto, S. (1994). Affirmation, solidarity, and critique: Moving beyond tolerance in multicultural education. *Multicultural Education, 1*(4), 9–12, 35–38.

Riley, K. (2008). *The lights of El Milagro: How one charter school's revolt could transform public education*. BookSurge Publishing.

Watkins, M. (1979). James Baldwin writing and talking. *New York Times Book Review, 3*, 36–37.

Part III
Conclusion

14 Home–School–Community Collaborations in Uncertain Times

Francisco Ríos

Soon after arriving at the University of Wyoming, I was invited to meet with Latino parents at one of the elementary schools in the state. I was told that there would be several teachers there, including one who was identified as a strong advocate for the local Latino community. As we sat in this teacher's first grade classroom, we began to discuss how parents were interacting with the school: what seemed to be working and what were some challenges to those collaborative relations. The teacher-advocate quickly chimed in, leading much of the discussion, as if speaking for the parents who sat in the room. She spoke of the difficulty of getting parents to come to "pajama night" where parents would come to school dressed in their pajamas and would read to their children as they would if this were an every night bedtime routine. She mentioned that despite having cookies and punch, the parents of the White children attended but the parents of the Latino children rarely attended. The teacher then went on to say that when these Latino children come to school, "They just don't have any language."

The parents in the room sat quietly, embarrassed, I imagined, as I was, at having heard what this teacher "advocate" was sharing. If she was the best school advocate, I thought to myself, what must the other teachers be thinking and doing?

It was for me clear evidence that this teacher was bringing a White, middle-class orientation to her work in the school. She assumed (among other things) that all parents had pajamas (could afford them or wore them), that they all engaged in reading books to their children before bedtime, and that the parents would be able to come to the school that evening with their child (and not be working, for example, or taking care of other relatives; presumably, the cookies and juice should have been enough enticement). The evidence of a deficit perspective about these Latino children and their families was clear in the assertion that these children "don't have any language." What I assumed she really meant was that these children arrived at the school not speaking much English. Had she considered that these children came to school speaking a language, Spanish, that is deep and rich, the language of Miguel de Cervantes, Gabriela Mistral, and Gabriel Garcia Marquez? By her statement, it seemed that this teacher had not.

I begin this concluding chapter with a teacher narrative that captures the kind of deficit thinking and middle-class assumptions that I have experienced as a scholar/advocate for culturally and linguistically diverse populations. This narrative is typical of the kind of thinking and the assumptive world which mark orthodox interactions between school professionals and caregivers as well as local community members who are working, with the best intentions on all sides, to construct productive settings for the children in their care. This is not to suggest that teachers are maliciously motivated. Just like this teacher who was "respected" by the community, they can be well meaning with good intentions. But they are often lulled to acting and believing that their implicit theories are natural, correct, and universally understood and accepted.

I describe this thinking and these assumptions as orthodox because there are, as important, counter-stories of teachers who have challenged that thinking and those assumptions, and who act as learners of their children and the contexts that they live in outside of the schoolhouse door. Many of these teachers' stories are detailed in this book. But these positive counter-portraits are new conceptions of teachers engaged in socio-cultural work that, unless they are evidenced on a far broader scale, will fail to drown out the more orthodox conceptions, as described above.

This chapter is an endnote to this volume, highlighting important lessons that we learn from these scholars. It will advance a conceptual framework for making sense of the many factors potentially impacting school-home-community collaborations. The chapter will discuss the broader socio-political context in which these attempts at collaboration are nested. It will end with a call for further research that builds on this strong socio-cultural foundation of scholarship to move forward in our understandings and professional practices aimed at school-home-community collaborations.

A note about this use of school-home-community collaborations. These three social structures are most important in the lives of children. For children to be as successful as they possibly can, all three need to be healthy and functioning, interacting in positive and productive ways. Thus schools, as a central social structure with an interest in children's welfare, should have a commitment to assure that homes and communities are healthy and thriving. They also need to learn about these two social structures as they search for ways to connect what happens within them to the day-to-day workings of the school (that is, to make connections to these social structures as seamless as possible). This extends the work of the school to think more broadly about what it means to educate its nation's young.

Lessons Learned

Diversity continues to both inform and inspire new ways of thinking about home-school-community collaborations. In each of these chapters, the authors acknowledge both the increase in diversity and the general low performance of children from these communities. But not all diversity is equally understood (*Sarroub*) and, as important, some differences are met with a more favorable response than others. For example, consider the kinds of community-based social services and governmental support the Somali refugees received as described by *Perry*. Alternately, we know that immigrants, especially those who may be in the country without proper documentation, are left without access to government services (*Botelho et al.*) and are often afraid to avail themselves of other social services for fear of leaving a record of presence which might be used for deportation—even when those services would be of substantial assistance to those from immigrant communities.

A second lesson, evidenced in the previous chapters, is the unstated belief that all caregivers hold the well-being and future growth/development of their children in high regard. I argue this is a productive belief to maintain and to act upon. Given this belief, then, the authors seek to help us learn to meet caregivers where they are, wherever they are, in an effort to make meaningful collaboration work. What the authors help us to see is that this positive regard for children plays out differently across home-community settings. A corollary to this unstated belief is that caregivers also differ in whether they see schools as fostering or inhibiting their child's development (*Edwards & Turner*). Like the former belief, perhaps it helps us to understand that all families value *education* but not all may value *schooling* (Valenzuela, 1999). The chapters, for example, evidence caregivers who not only want their children to become academically proficient (including, becoming highly literate) but hold aspirations of higher education for their children (even for those undocumented immigrants for whom immigration status may present a formidable barrier to higher education participation) (*Monzó*). While caregivers may not bring some of the specific experience and knowledge of how to help them achieve these specific goals (e.g., taking the right courses in high school to assure they meet university requirements), the authors point out the caregivers assist their children in other important ways, both tangibly (great financial sacrifice, for example) and intangibly (expressing high aspirations, for example). To be sure, as education professionals engage with caregivers, they must be prepared that all they find will be not pleasant. That is, listening and learning may be difficult because caregivers may want to identify the weaknesses of the school, the class, and the teacher. Are we ready for that (*Edwards & Turner*)?

A third lesson learned is the need to rethink orthodox terminology, evidenced by alternative conceptions of words within different social-cultural contexts. For example, *Perry* points to different conceptions of family (who it includes, how it shifts and changes). *Volk and Long,* as well as *Li,* point out that it is often siblings and other community members who play the role of school liaison between caregivers and the school. Words like "involvement," or "educated"—what they mean, how they are understood, and how they play out—all need to be rediscovered in light of differing social-cultural communities. These different conceptions of words recognize the varied ways in which parents come to understand schooling based on individual experiences, social group values and norms.

The next lesson is that a "funds of knowledge" approach is a productive stance within a broader socio-cultural framework (*McIntyre*). One of the strengths of such a conception is that it has great practical value with respect to professional application. The funds of knowledge approach is constructive in moving from deficit-oriented thinking and interacting to a strengths-based approach when working with caregivers from diverse communities. Thus educators must become "learners" (*Schulz*) in their search to uncover the "learning resources" (experiences, relationships and networks, knowledge, etc.) that caregivers can and do provide for children which can assist them in their academic, social, and individual pursuits. The question several of these authors seek to answer, within this funds of knowledge conception, is how do parents/caregivers support children in their schooling in ways not usually understood by white, middle-class educators?

The fifth lesson is, perhaps, commonsense. We need to always recall that the schoolhouse door swings both ways (*Dantas & Coleman*). That is, we most typically think about the myriad of ways teachers can invite parents into the school. Indeed, caregivers can play a critical role within the school both as cultural mediators/educators, as advocates for their children's education, as informants of their children's background experiences, and as mediators/educators of their cultural and linguistic heritages (among a host of other roles). However, several chapters also demonstrate the importance of teachers moving out into the local community where the children live and play and, when appropriate, into the homes of those children. This requires a new set of expectations on teachers, a new skill set, a new way of thinking about one's work—which will take many teachers out of their comfort zones. Schools can be (indeed, must be) structured, to support teachers who engage in these activities outside of the school (as described by *Volk & Long*). The knowledge gained, the skills developed, and the goodwill created with caregivers and community members are all worth the efforts in this regard.

The sixth lesson is about the importance of story and narrative in advancing the work of educational reform and improvement. The stories shared here at the beginning (and sometimes throughout) of chapters are significant. These stories of teachers, children, caregivers, and families provide a glimpse into the real-life social and cultural worlds people inhabit. They also provide impetus for the gathering of stories by teachers of the children and caregivers in their charge. In doing so, we also need to strengthen our understanding of how teachers interpret these stories and help them do so through a lens of empathy, understanding, and care—and not simply to reinforce existing stereotypes (*Compton-Lilly*).

The last lesson learned is, perhaps, the most important. Teachers are neither bound by the culture of the school, their home culture, or the culture children bring with them to the school. Rather each class is a new opportunity for teachers and children to be co-constructors and active agents in the construction of a unique classroom culture. An especially strong example of how this kind of agency plays out is evidenced in the work by *Yeager and Córdova*. Recall their work to create a sense of family or community within the classroom. This, in and of itself, is a worthy goal for any classroom but most especially those classrooms with students from marginalized communities. In their work, this sense of family and community prefigures the kinds of family and community connections with caregivers that they hope can develop concomitantly throughout the school year.

An important caveat about these lessons learned needs to be clearly stated. We need to always recall that schools, and teachers as the primary professionals there, also have a major responsibility to assure that quality educational experiences are part and parcel of the everyday work of education. It is often the case, as my opening narrative suggested, that education professionals see families as THE answer to all that ails public education. This near exclusive attention to caregivers and communities lets schools abdicate the responsibilities they have to always interrogate their own practices, policies, and procedures, as well as the assumptions by which they are informed (see, for example, Villenas & Deyhle, 1999, for a larger discussion of this caveat). Schools must always be mindful of their role as primary agents in the education and socialization of any nation's children—and constantly engage in reflective practices aimed at improving upon those aspects of schooling that they can control.

Conceptual Framework

As I read the previous chapters, I was struck by the description of the many factors that might conceivably impact school-home-community collaborations. Anyone reading these, I assume, would need to rethink simplistic notions of why caregivers may or may not participate in ways they are expected to by schools. It would move teachers away from saying that caregivers "just don't care about the education of their children."

In an attempt to understand that for myself, I offer a beginning conceptual framework for understanding the myriad of factors that might impact the collaboration of schools with homes and communities. My hope is that it makes more visible the complexity of factors operating for and against school collaborations. I also hope it serves as a rubric that educational professionals can employ as they think about those facilitative and debilitative factors operating in their particular context. In doing so, I do not want to suggest that this is an all-inclusive list and I invite readers, based upon their own reading of the previous chapters and their own experiences, to add to this conceptual framework. Understand that the specific variables operating, as described in Figure 14.1, differ from community to community, school to school, and home to home. The factors supporting and/or preventing involvement for refugee students in the Midwest may be far different from those factors at work for Latino immigrant students in the southwest which will differ, no doubt, from those factors at operation for lower class Whites in the Appalachian valleys of the US. And these are all different from those experiences as described for the poly-diverse communities in urban areas in Canada.

As you think about this, also recognize that these factors can be either facilitative or debilitative, or can depend on other factors to determine whether they are facilitative or debilitative. For example, holding White middle-class expectations about caregivers (especially those who are neither White nor middle class) is debilitative. Recognizing and affirming multiliteracies is facilitative. Stressing strong competence in English may be facilitative if parents also feel that primary languages other than English and bilingualism are also affirmed. Thus you will note that the home and school clusters are nested within the broader social-political context (which impacts the meaning of these variables) and that these variables interact with each other.

Broad Social-Political Context of School-Home-Community Collaborations

- *Political Factors* – such as immigration reform, refugee policies, globalization, national language(s) debates (especially English-only), etc.
- *Economic Factors* – such as meaningful work opportunities, poverty prevention programs, welfare support, workforce development opportunities, wage minimums, etc.
- *Community Factors* – such as community-based organizations, access to public services (e.g., libraries, parks, youth recreation services), informal community services such as mentoring program or religious services, healthy/safe community settings, etc.
- *Cultural Factors* – such as assimilation pressures, transnational identity development opportunities, etc.
- *Education Factors* – such as re/segregation, school funding, educational reforms (including standards and standardized assessments, scripted curricula, bilingual education provisions, etc.)

School Factors

- Teacher Beliefs/Ideologies
- Teacher Professionalism
- Classroom-Based Activities
- Classroom Environment
- Curriculum Connections
- Curriculum Priorities
- Epistemological Assumptions
- Teacher-Children Relations
- School-Home Practices
- Quality of School Experiences
- School Culture
- School Structure
- School Partnerships
- School Language Policies, Programs, Practices

Home Factors

- Prior School Experience
- Conceptions of "School"
- Perceptions of the Specific School
- Family Structure
- External Factors (above) Preventing Engagement
- Social Networks in Homes
- Caregiver Expectations
- Role of Primary Languages
- Role of English
- Settlement Adjustments and Supports
- Response to Assimilation Pressures
- Family Circumstances
- Access to Technology
- Funds of Knowledge

Figure 14.1 A conceptual framework for understanding home-school-community collaborations.

School Variables

I wish to provide more explanation about the school and family factors evidenced in Figure 14.1 before turning my attention, in the next section of this chapter, to the broader social and political context of school-home-community connections. Some of the school factors include the following:

- *Teacher beliefs/ideologies*—includes assumptions teachers may have about families, caregivers' and caregivers' role vis-à-vis schools; expectations for caregiver involvement; knowledge of students' cultures; knowledge and experience in the local community.

- *Teacher professionalism*—includes teacher identity, critical reflection and sense of agency about their work; teacher knowledge and education (preservice and inservice); professional development (formal and informal).
- *Classroom-based activities*—includes "developing" a framework and resulting expectations for caregiver involvement; incorporation of culturally responsive practices; student identity development as learners/academics.
- *Classroom environment*—includes the social organization of the classroom; degree to which students feel a sense of "community" and "family" within.
- *Curriculum connections*—includes the explicit attempts to connect home and community knowledge/resources to meaningful content-specific knowledge.
- *Curriculum priorities*—includes incorporation of multiple literacies; inserting specific content into the curriculum because it is valued by caregivers and the community even if it's not valued in the school (e.g., art, music, dance).
- *Epistemological assumptions*—includes which languages and knowledge are privileged and have power in the classroom (and how these privileges are communicated); knowledge goals such as transmission and recitation versus social construction and critical reflection; what constitutes demonstration and assessment of knowledge.
- *Teacher–children relations*—includes the degree to which children feel valued and believe they can trust the teacher; includes feeling a sense of empowerment in the classroom as children and as learners.
- *School home practices*—includes degree to which these practices value and use the languages of the home, including the use of cultural liaisons/mediators, and translators; the non-school "places" where caregivers are asked to meet with professionals; encouraging community activities and organizations into the school.
- *Quality of school experiences*—includes academic achievement gains; teacher expertise; support programs.
- *School culture*—includes the values, mission and organizational culture of the school that explicitly and implicitly state the school's beliefs about collaborations.
- *School structure*—includes the ways in which educational professionals are provided time (and rewarded) to foster such collaborations; includes whether home-community liaisons are full-time professionals who work on behalf of the caregivers, community, and the school.
- *School partnerships*—includes those partnerships with local community-based organizations and community groups; partnerships with local colleges and universities.
- *School language policies, programs, practices*—includes how literacy, English, primary languages other than English, and cultural diversity are understood and promoted in the school, in the home and in the community.

Family Variables

As with the school variables, several family variables operate to either support the kinds of collaboration that schools want or to thwart that collaboration. In this sense, it's important to again recall that caregivers, due to a variety of factors and while still striving to provide the best for their children within the home and community context, may not think collaborating with schools is a good thing. Some of these home variables include the following:

- *Prior school experiences*—includes whether caregivers' own experiences with schools were positive or negative.
- *Conceptions of "school"*—includes the understandings and expectations caregivers have of the role of schools; caregivers' conceptions of what constitutes a "successful" education; the shape and meaning of caregiver "involvement."
- *Perceptions of the specific school*—includes how caregivers think about the school their children attend; the specific class, the peers, and the teacher(s) working with their children during any particular time frame.
- *Family structure*—includes who is and who is not part of the family; expansive or restricted definitions of "family."
- *External factors preventing engagement*—includes job(s) restrictions, child care opportunities, and after-school programs; community conditions (e.g. safety, economic growth and development, gentrification).
- *Social networks in homes*—includes who is actually active in the child's life and with what kind of role commitments; encompasses both adults and other children/youth.
- *Caregiver expectations*—includes those expectations they have for themselves, for others, and for the children themselves.
- *Role of primary languages*—includes whether there is a strong push to maintain and develop primary languages other than English; the impact on home communication that is a result.
- *Role of English*—includes the perception of the importance of learning English and the degree to which this is an obligation of caregivers to promote this (especially when this is positioned in opposition to primary languages).
- *Settlement adjustments and supports*—includes any settlement challenges (finding work, culture shock/stress, new languages and customs) as well as the supports available to them to adjust to these new cultural and linguistic contexts in constructive ways.
- *Response to assimilation pressures*—includes whether families willingly accept and pursue assimilation strategies, accept and pursue cultural insulation to preserve traditional cultures/languages, or seek some kind of bicultural/multilingual response; oftentimes, this is influenced by the degree to which a transnational identity is developed and fostered.
- *Family circumstances*—includes the need to move in search of other employment or social system supports; immigration status and the fear of deportation and family dispersal (when adults are undocumented but children are US citizens).

- *Access to technology*—includes access to a variety of technologies (from phones to internet via computers) as a source for developing/strengthening a variety of literacies.
- *Funds of knowledge.*

Because much has been made in several chapters about the funds of knowledge caregivers bring which can positively assist children in meeting academic and social goals within the school, I wish to highlight the importance of these as they play out in the everyday practices of specific families. Families oftentimes don't explicitly realize that they possess funds of knowledge that could be of value to the teaching-learning enterprise. The practices of offering advice, helping children be resilient in the face of life challenges, and expressing to others the hopes they have for their children in their presence (as but three examples) may be just part and parcel of how families act. Alternately, sometimes they recognize that these are important assets in support of their children's education but are frustrated by education professionals who do not recognize them as such or who highlight what the caregivers are NOT doing for their children (i.e., helping them with their homework, speaking English-only to them). Finally, it would be helpful if caregivers can be made aware of the kinds of funds of knowledge evidenced in their community and in other communities. This knowledge would help to develop and increase the kinds of assets which caregivers can provide and which serve a constructive role in the education of children.

The Broader Socio-Political Context

Schools, as public spaces, are never politically neutral. In serving a socialization purpose, they advance a particular political ideology. Consider how this has operated historically where schools were more explicit sites of cultural and linguistic oppression (Spring, 2007). Children who spoke a primary language other than English, in many schools, were punished for speaking that language even outside the classroom. Many Native American children were removed from their families and sent to boarding schools in the blatant attempt at cultural assimilation made manifest by the saying: "Save the child, kill the Indian." It was common for immigrant children to receive "American" names; their cultures were largely absent in the curriculum or were negatively portrayed. Many poor children attended schools that were structured to replicate their existing social and economic standing, being prepared as they were for low wage labor opportunities while their more affluent counterparts were attending schools structured to prepare them for management occupations (Anyon, 1980; see also Boaler, 1998, for an example of how traditional, reform-minded approaches actually decrease academic achievement for women and students from lower socio-economic classes). Given the not too recent past of these schooling policies, and the memory people have of them, we should not be surprised by any caregiver's reluctance to collaborate with schools in the education of their children. To relate this more directly to school-home collaborations, in my work on the Wind River Reservation, I have learned that visits to people's homes by teachers can sometimes be unwelcomed. This is due to a long history of teachers, acting as agents for the state, using such visits to gather evidence for removing children from their homes.

Contemporarily consider recent Supreme Court rulings against attempts to foster school integration in Louisville and Seattle, coming as they are on the heels of several other court rulings that seem downright hostile to integration efforts. Consider statewide political propositions, successful in highly diverse states such as Arizona and California. They legalize the language of instruction (English-only), who can be there to learn (anti-immigrant access to public services in education, such as Proposition 187 in California), and whether efforts to achieve greater diversity in the teaching staff can be advanced (anti-affirmative action). Consider political legislation such as No Child Left Behind (NCLB), the most sweeping federal mandate for American public education. It seeks to standardize the state curriculum, to standardize how it must be taught (scripted, phonics-based curricula), to standardize how it must be measured, and to standardize teacher qualifications. It highlights the potential of the Open Court literacy series that focuses on skills-based, low-level recitation activities and not on the kinds of comprehension activities that would make literacy more exciting for the students.

All this is taking place in the context of both internal colonialism (that is, colonization of people within a nation's own borders) as well as external colonization (evidenced, most explicitly, by the US presence in Iraq). Colonizing activities (for example, the US government's sponsorship of a terrorist organization in Nicaragua whose aim was the overthrow of a democratically elected but socialist government) created conditions for many people to be displaced from their homelands (displacement serves as a precursor to increased immigration for many). It is taking place within a neoliberal political ideology within the US (what Edelsky, 2006, calls "capitalism with the gloves off"); that is, capitalism is to be unrestrained and unrestricted. It means, globally, the unrestrained export of American business, American products, and American culture. Within the US, it means opening doors to businesses to privatize what have been, historically, public sector responsibilities—including the schooling of this nation's children (see Ladson-Billings & Tate, 2006, for an extended discussion of neoliberalism's impact on American education).

As one example, consider the widespread, and often contentious, debates around immigration. Children who hear these debates are sent messages about whether or not they are welcomed in the country. Since communities and schools are a reflection of the country of which they are a part, communities and schools also send these welcome and not welcome messages out as well. Children and their caregivers hear these messages and they must negotiate the tension that they enflame. Children and their caregivers hear everyday about how they are a problem (Chávez, 2005). In addition, consider how cultural and linguistic assimilationist policies work against the kind of academic support many parents want and are able to enact (around bilingualism, as one example, as it bumps up against English only). Clearly schools are not politically neutral. But schools can be and have been sites of efforts at liberation and the struggle for educational equality (Spring, 2007). This happens when educational professionals and community activists are willing to engage in their work by way of a sociopolitical consciousness (Ladson-Billings, 2006). This sociopolitical consciousness includes the explicit and deliberate advocacy for children and their caregivers, especially those who come from marginalized communities. It includes both an awareness of the larger context of this work (as described above) and efforts to mitigate their negative impact at the local level. Finally, it includes an awareness that these oppressive ideologies and resulting structures do not "just happen" to schools and communities; we allow them to happen (Apple, 2006). That is, people create these ideologies and structures. As education professionals who want the very best for our children, their caregivers, their communities, and their schools, we have an obligation to interrogate and resist them.

A socio-political orientation would also ask us to be willing to engage in discussions of really hard-core issues: racism, sexism, and homophobia. It asks us to raise difficult questions about who is privileged by advancing the kind of educational reform envisioned by the NCLB. It asks us to consider questions of capitalism and classicism and their role in the maintenance of a subordinated working class for labor exploitation with schools acting as a primary agent. It asks us to wonder what this nation really believes about healthy children, healthy families and healthy communities given how difficult it is to gain funds for these while simultaneously providing a near limitless amount of money to finance unpopular (both here and abroad) military actions. And finally, it asks us to always be mindful of the role of "power" in all these discussions and actions.

A socio-cultural perspective, as described in this volume, is an important ally in this work. As evidenced here, it requires that teachers and schools create space for children and their caregivers to share their understandings of phenomena and then to build on those within the classroom. It provides impetus for our resistance to more standardized and prescribed approaches to teaching, since we learn about the uniqueness of children, caregivers, families, and communities. A socio-cultural framework helps us to uncover the ways that school policies and practices can serve as barriers to children's success but also provides us a vision of schools as resources which can be used in the affirmation of language and culture—that which makes us truly human. A socio-cultural perspective asks us to rethink our taken-for-granted (implicit) theories, to envision schools as they might be, and to forge the kind of collaborative relations with caregivers and their communities which might result in their children's academic and social success.

Given the broader social-political context, there are many pressures preventing the implementation of socio-cultural approaches to schooling: lack of time, lack of institutional structure, near exclusive emphasis on academic content and its (standardized) assessment. As Compton-Lilly describes, a socio-cultural perspective, in the end, depends upon the educational professionals who work in schools to assert more productive approaches to teaching, learning and collaborating with homes and communities.

Call for Future Research

Given my reading of these chapters, important next questions might include some of the following:

- To what degree are the funds of knowledge employed by communities linked to the "culture-specific" repertoires of practice? How generalizable, if at all, can these be for that specific cultural group?
- What is the role of ethnic-minority teachers vis-à-vis the work involved with employing a socio-cultural perspective to literacy activities? In what way might they be able to help White, middle-class teachers uncover and understand these different conceptions and practices?
- How are teachers prevented from engaging in a socio-cultural perspective at schools by external constraints? If space is provided, how do teachers make sense of these in ways that do not reinforce the tangled web of ideologies (Weiner, 2000) that often guide their thinking and reinforce existing power relations and social patterns?
- How would taking a socio-cultural perspective impact children's academic achievement, measured broadly?
- Finally, how are children making sense of school-home-community collaboration efforts?

We would do well to be mindful that any research we engage in must employ both a micro level analysis (how children and caregivers see the world, for example) as well as a macro level analysis (including people's understanding of status and power differentials, as well as the colonizing ideologies that are used to justify them).

The authors of this volume build on and extend a strong tradition of socio-cultural thinking and scholarly work that has emerged in the recent past. It now rests with you, dear readers, to understand collaborations between schools and communities in all its clarity and complexity—and to explore (as learners) new conceptions in the spaces where you find yourself. It also rests with you to take these understandings into classrooms and homes/communities in efforts to better serve the children who are in your charge.

References

Anyon, J. (1980). Social class and the hidden curriculum of work. *Journal of Education*, *162*(1), 67–92.

Apple, M. W. (2006). Interrupting the Right: On doing critical educational work in conservative times. In G. Ladson-Billings, & W. Tate (Eds.). *Education research in the public interest* (pp. 27–45). New York: Teachers College Press.

Boaler, J. (1998). *Experiencing school mathematics*. Philadelphia, PA: Open University Press.

Chávez, S. (2005). Community, ethnicity and class in a changing rural California town. *Rural Sociology*, *70*(3), 314–335.

Edelsky, C. (2006). *With literacy and justice for all*. Mahwah, NJ: Lawrence Erlbaum.

Ladson-Billings, G., & Tate, W. F. (2006). *Education research in the public interest: Social justice, action and policy.* New York: Teachers College Press.

Spring, J. (2007). *Deculturalization and the struggle for equality.* New York: McGraw-Hill.

Valenzuela, A. (1999). *Subtractive schooling.* Albany, NY: SUNY Press.

Villenas, S., & Deyhle, D. (1999). Critical race theory and ethnographies challenging the stereotypes. *Curriculum Inquiry, 29*(4), 413–445.

Weiner, L. (2000). Research in the 90s: Implications for teacher preparation. *Review of Educational Research, 70*(3), 369–406.

List of Contributors

Maria José Botelho, OISE/University of Toronto and University of Massachusetts Amherst

Patricia Chow, Peel District School Board

Sarah L. Cohen, Northern Illinois University

Michelle Coleman, Richardson Independent School District, Dallas, Texas

Catherine Compton-Lilly, University of Madison-Wisconsin

Ralph A. Córdova, Jr., Southern Illinois University, Edwardsville

Maria Luiza Dantas, Educational Consultant and Visiting Scholar, University of California, Santa Barbara

Kim Douillard, Cardiff School District

Patricia A. Edwards, Michigan State University

Christine Kane, San Diego Unified School District

Lisa Leoni, York Region District School Board and OISE/University of Toronto

Guofang Li, Michigan State University

Susi Long, University of North Carolina

Ellen McIntyre, University of South Carolina

Patrick C. Manyak, University of Wyoming

Lilia D. Monzó, Chapman University

Kristen H. Perry, University of Kentucky

Francisco Ríos, University of Wyoming

Loukia K. Sarroub, University of Nebraska-Lincoln

Padma Sastri, Peel District School Board

Melissa M. Schulz, Miami University of Ohio

Simeon Stumme, Concordia University, Chicago

Jennifer D. Turner, University of Maryland

Dinah Volk, University of Cleveland

Elizabeth Yeager, University of California, Santa Barbara

Index

abacus 251

absences 60, 68, 158

abstractions 6

abuse 145, 214

academic identity 116–20; definitions 114–15; reading 124–25; teacher roles 125–28; theory 123

academic skills 2–3, 6, 37–38, 46–47, 50; change 260–61; children's knowledge 240, 243, 246–47; collaborations 267–68, 271, 273–76; connections 95, 98, 102, 104–6; discontinuities 80, 89; dynamics 54; family knowledge 218–20, 226–34; funds of knowledge 202, 204, 206, 211, 216; home visits 159; identity 112–28; individualized learning 132; meetings 133; motivation 123; parent story approach 143–44; parental roles 112–13; resources 218–34; support networks 188, 190; vocabulary 122

Accelerated Reader Program 65–67, 72

accents 121

accommodations 91, 148, 172, 188–89

accomplishment 128

accomplishments 64–67, 195

accountants 49

acculturation 42, 44–46, 56, 80, 113

achievement 80–81, 89–91, 98, 113, 160, 201, 220, 271, 273, 276

adaptation 140, 198

addresses 163–64

administrators 38, 69, 96, 99, 108, 122, 138, 147–54, 196, 248

adult learning centers 65, 68, 70–71

Advancement via Individual Determination (AVID) 161

affiliations 37, 82–83

affluence 49, 258, 273

Affrilachian families 215

Africa 21–22, 24, 27–28, 31, 162

African American families 1–2, 91, 137–54, 161–62, 173, 192, 196, 201, 208, 257, 259

African families 23, 29, 32, 37, 82, 150

after-school activities 48, 157, 172

Agricultural Field Day 206–7

agriculture 206–7, 252

Ahmadiyya study 250–51

alcohol 214, 257

algebra 150

alienation 241

alphabet 4

Amanti, C. 8

ambiguity 260

American Association of Colleges for Teacher Education 140

American Dream 72, 82

American families 19, 22, 24, 29–33, 46; change 259–60; collaborations 274; connections 100; discontinuities 79–80, 82–84, 88, 90; funds of knowledge 215

analysis 141–44, 152, 157–58, 161–62, 230–31, 242, 248, 276

Anderson, A.B. 140

anecdotes 141

anger management 144

Anglo-American families 49

anomalies 180

answering machine 165

anthropology 78, 90, 179, 215

Appalachian families 161, 201–16, 269

application 38, 56, 74, 86, 91, 109; children's knowledge 254; family knowledge 234; funds of knowledge 216; home visits 173; identity 128; parent story approach 154; support networks 197–98

appropriateness 243, 254

appropriation 114, 184, 188

Arab American families 76–91

Arab families 23, 29

Arabic language 22, 25–27, 31, 82–83, 85–87, 156, 167

Miller, K. 203
Minnesota 23
misbehavior 68, 84, 149
misplacements 121
Missouri 23
Mistral, G. 265
misunderstandings 157–58
Mixtec language 131
mobility 2, 77, 124
modeling 211, 226
modesty 84–85
Moll, L. 5–6, 8, 10, 78, 159, 179, 220, 259
money 29, 48, 66, 71–72, 79
Monzó, L.D. 112–28, 267
Moore, G. 157, 203
morals 3, 82, 85–86
mosques 36–37, 85, 88, 250
mothers 20, 144–46, 148, 152, 154;
children's knowledge 251; funds of
knowledge 214; home visits 156, 162,
164, 166, 169; support networks
181–83, 185–86
motivation 123, 210, 214
movies 45, 48, 55, 185, 194, 196
Muhammad, Prophet 84
muhathara 85
multi-sited analyses 43–44
multilingualism 25–26, 177–78, 238, 240,
242, 248–49, 272
multiliteracies 237–548
multiplication 3
music 31, 55, 84, 242, 259, 271
Muslim families 23, 76–91, 252

naming practices 226
narratives 5, 103, 106, 141, 143, 151–52,
211, 238, 265, 268–69
National Writing Project 211
Native American Indian families *see* North
American Indian families
nativism 113
navigation 86, 100, 163
Nebraska 24, 90
negotiation 43, 88–89, 97, 113–15, 124,
165, 193
neoliberalism 274
Neufeld, B. 76
New York 23, 43
news 23
newsletters 31, 107–8, 195, 248–49
newspapers 6, 45, 62, 242
Nicaragua 274
Nieto, S. 259
No Child Left Behind (NCLB) 274–75
Noguera, P.A. 152
North Africa 82
North African families 89
North America 31, 41, 83, 208

North American Indian families 79, 91,
158, 273
North Carolina 23
notices 118, 134
novels 55
Nuba Mountains 31–32
nuclear families 20–21, 31, 38, 138,
152
numbers 4, 11

Oaxaca 131
observation 22, 44, 62–64, 108, 116;
change 260; children's knowledge 251,
253; family knowledge 232–33; funds of
knowledge 204, 207, 212, 215; home
visits 160–62, 168, 172; identity 122;
parent story approach 141; support
networks 179, 191, 193
officials 34
Ogbu, J. 78–81, 83, 86–87, 89, 91
Ohio 32
Omaha 24
one-way transmission model 20–21,
32–33
onset of community 224–25
Ontario 248
Open Court 119–21, 274
open houses 107–8, 118
opportunities 134, 137, 157, 163, 170–73;
change 258, 260; children's knowledge
238–39, 242–44, 246–49, 251;
collaborations 268, 273; family
knowledge 219–20, 222–23, 226–29,
234; funds of knowledge 205, 213;
support networks 179, 181, 187, 191,
193, 196
opposition 79, 81, 86, 91
Oprah's book club 62
ordinary 218–19, 223–31
orienting concepts 6–13
orphans 21–25, 27–31
other teachers 177–98
otherness 132
Otto, H.J. 138
outings 33
outreach 250
outsiders 114, 219, 222
overarching themes 1–6
overcrowding 196

Pacific region 41
Pahl, K. 253
pajama nights 265
Pakistan 237–38
Palestine 88
Palestinian families 76, 81–82, 86–89
Parent Involvement as Educator (PIE) 238,
250